The Economic Theory of a

SOCIALIST
ECONOMY

By Burnham P. Beckwith, (Ph. D.)

GREENWOOD PRESS, PUBLISHERS

NEW YORK   1968

PREFACE

The first draft of this book was written in the years 1932 to 1934, but the author was unable to find a publisher at that time. Thereafter, other interests occupied the author's attention until 1944, when a comprehensive revision of the manuscript was begun in anticipation of the present publication.

Since the year 1932, when the author began writing this work, a number of other writers have made important contributions to the economic theory of a Socialist economy. H. D. Dickinson, the earliest and ablest of these authors, had an article on "Price Formation in a Socialist Community" in the June 1933 issue of the *Economic Journal,* and in 1939 he published a more complete treatment of the subject, *The Economics of Socialism.* Between 1934 and 1938 a series of articles on economic calculus under Socialism, by E. F. M. Durbin, Oskar Lange, Maurice Dobb, and A. P. Lerner, did much to develop the theory of production control and pricing under Socialism. In this discussion A. P. Lerner stressed the importance of using marginal rather than average costs of production in controlling prices and production. In 1937 R. L. Hall published his brief but lucid and competent study, *The Economic System in a Socialist State.* Hall and Dickinson are the only English economists who have attempted to cover in some detail the economic theory of a Socialist economy. Oskar Lange's article "On the Economic Theory of Socialism," originally published in the *Review of Economic Studies,* was republished, with an excellent introduction by Benjamin E. Lippincott, by the University of Minnesota Press in 1938.

The fact that a dozen able articles and three brilliant pioneer monographs on the economics of Socialism have appeared does not, of course, make additional studies of this subject unnecessary. There will be more articles and books written on Socialist economics than have ever been written on Capitalist economics, and in that long series the present work will still rank as a pioneer study.

BURNHAM P. BECKWITH

BERLIN, GERMANY
September 1948

v

CONTENTS

Preface to the Reprint Edition

As noted in the original preface, several non-Marxist authors contributed to the economics of socialism before this book was published in 1949. So far as I am aware, there have been no significant contributions since then. Certainly no more recent treatise on the economic theory of a liberal or market socialist economy has been published in English. And the older contributions are nearly all out-of-print.

Of course, Soviet literature on socialist economic theory is extensive, but Soviet economists are unable or unwilling to abandon Marxist, pre-marginal-value theory and apply marginal analysis to economic problems. Consequently, their writings seem naïve and confused to Western economists. There has been steady improvement in Soviet economic theory since 1949, but Soviet economists have not yet accepted, let alone improved, pre-war marginal-utility welfare economics.

While no new treatise on the principles of liberal socialist economics has appeared since 1949, many articles and books on welfare economics have been published. The chief thesis of so-called "new welfare economics" is that rational economic calculation is impossible or impractical, a thesis flatly rejected in this book. It was long customary to criticize socialists for rejecting rational economic calculation. Now it is the capitalist new welfare economists who reject rational economic calculation and, at least implicitly, defend arbitrary, irrational economic decisions and plans. I have criticized them in detail in my *Marginal-Cost Price-Output* (Columbia University Press, 1955).

Since 1949, I have modified and elaborated my own theory of socialist price-output control. I now believe that marginal cost should be defined as current direct cost at the internal margin, and I distinguish sharply between marginal analysis, useful only in the control of current output and of variable factors, and total (cost-benefit) analysis, useful only in the control of investment and other lumpy factor shifts. This new theory is stated in detail in my *Marginal-Cost Price-Output Control*.

I have also revised and elaborated my controversial thesis that welfare economics should be entirely scientific, i.e., that prescription of economic policies requires no prior ethical value judgements, all of which are literally senseless. This revised thesis is stated in detail in my *Religion, Philosophy, and Science* (Philosophical Library, 1957).

I wish to remind the reader that this reprinted treatise is the only book on socialist economics which urges the use of refined profits and losses to control the output of all goods sold for a price, and which therefore explicitly rejects and condemns the planning of future outputs and prices (including rents, interest rates, and wage rates). Liebermanism is a small but significant step towards the application of these principles. I am confident that the Soviets will take many more steps towards the application of the economic policies advocated in this treatise.

A Spanish-language edition of this book was published in Mexico City by Aguilar, .A. de Ediciones in 1953.

Burnham P. Beckwith
Menlo Park, California
February, 1968.

THE ECONOMIC THEORY OF
A SOCIALIST ECONOMY

CHAPTER I.   INTRODUCTION

A.   SUBJECT AND PURPOSE

The purpose underlying this treatise has been to state the economic theory which should govern the administration of a Socialist economy and the various economic units within it. To criticize Capitalism or justify Socialism is no part of this purpose,[1] the existence of a Socialist economy being assumed without debate.

The very great need for such a work is indicated by the fact that although one-sixth of the earth's surface is already organized as a Socialist economy, no comprehensive and scientific treatise on the economic theory of such an economy has ever been published in any language.

The rapid rise of Socialism is the most remarkable historical event of our time. Karl Marx died unheralded and virtually unknown barely fifty years ago. Today his devoted followers are numbered by the millions in every nation of the earth, and in the course of the present century the world Socialist movement is certain to achieve power in many, if not all, advanced industrial nations. Christianity took four hundred years to conquer the Roman Empire and caused no important immediate change in the organization of society or the daily life of the people. Socialism promises to spread over the entire globe in less than two centuries from the death of its greatest teacher, and gives every indication that it will revolutionize the form of society and transform all social relationships.

Not only is there need for a comprehensive and acceptable statement of economic theory which may serve as a basis for the management of the U.S.S.R. and the other states apt to come under the control of the Socialist movement in the course of this century, but there is also a need for an outline of the new society to aid propaganda for Socialism. This need has been stated by Professor Colsten E. Warne of Amherst College.

The American Socialist movement has lost in vigor and effectiveness in part through its failure to prepare specific blueprints of the social system which it proposes to substitute for the present chaos. The movement, like others, has had its orators who have paraded the land, shouting promises of the new day which will be at hand when systematic socialization has reached its zenith. These promises have to date been unconvincing. They have, despite their sincerity, been classed

[1] For a defense of Socialism by this author, see John Putnam (pseudonym), *The Modern Case for Socialism*, rev. ed. (Boston, Meador Publishing Company, 1946).

3

by a suspicious public with the "new era" pronouncements of industrialists—talk which has brought apathy and disillusionment to the American electorate. For the most part, the attitude now taken by voters is one of hopelessness. Promises seem meaningless. Talk is cheap.

It is my purpose to suggest briefly the broad outlines of a new policy which would, if developed, gain support from many who have hitherto been apathetic toward socialization. This policy is specifically:

1. That Socialists should draw more exact blueprints of the new order which they propose to establish—these blueprints being definite as to:

    a) How production is to be planned.

    b) How unemployment is to be avoided.

    c) How and where control is to be placed.

    d) How income is to be distributed.

    e) How prices are to be fixed.

2. That these blueprints should be based in considerable measure upon the planning experience of other countries—especially Soviet Russia—so that many of the pitfalls of central planning may be avoided.

3. That the Socialist movement should in its propaganda draw attention more to a concrete and well-rounded program—a goal—rather than casting all of its shafts at the breakdown of the present system.

Surely there now exists an awareness of the mal-functioning of Capitalism. Fewer bombastic speeches are needed to shatter the defenses of the old order. What is now needed is the undertaking of the difficult and time-consuming task of preparing a manual of the new order—a guide to twentieth century socialism.[2]

The foregoing quotation states quite clearly the general subject and major purpose of the present treatise.

Marx and Engels and their closest followers were not interested in developing the economic theory of a Socialist economy. Not only did they confine their theoretical work to an analysis of Capitalism as the title *Das Kapital* plainly suggests; they explicitly condemned the writing of utopias and the development of detailed plans for the new social order. Karl Kautsky, in his book on the Erfurt program, wrote:

The useless and the harmful thing is the making of positive propositions for bringing in and organizing the socialist society. Propositions for the shaping of social conditions can be made only where the field is fully under control and well understood.[3]

[2] C. E. Warne, "A Proposed Socialist Blueprint," in *Socialist Planning and a Socialist Program*, Harry W. Laidler, editor (Falcon Press, New York, 1932), pp. 105–6.

[3] Heinrich Ströbel, *Socialisation in Theory and Practice* (P. S. King & Son, Ltd., London, 1922), p. 12. Ströbel discusses the Marxian attitude toward detailed planning at some length, pp. 7–16. For a similar discussion see Skelton, *Socialism, A Critical Analysis*, pp. 177–82.

This characteristic attitude of Marxian thinkers toward the economic theory of a Socialist economy seems to have been due in part to an over-reaction against the imaginative excesses of earlier Utopian Socialists. It is a waste of time for an able man to devote his life to "writing the kitchen recipes of the future," as Marx put it, in recording his own scornful refusal. Yet personal choice and financial necessity do actually cause most able men to devote their lives to writing the kitchen recipes of the present—witness the enormous ability and energy devoted to solving the trivial and transitory business problems of Capitalism. Moreover, it is possible to develop a theory of Socialist administration which will not be concerned with kitchen recipes but with problems of outstanding importance only. And this work, being purely theoretical, may be done even before "the field is fully under control." As for Kautsky's other point, that such a theory cannot be developed until the field is fully understood, this is a truism, sound but irrelevant. Any writer who attempts to solve the major problems of a Socialist economy must obviously have some understanding of what is involved; the more understanding the better. But any implication that such understanding is unattainable in advance of the actual establishment of the system is wholly unwarranted.

A better justified—though unavowed—reason for not preparing Socialist blueprints has been the more urgent need for the development of a thorough criticism of Capitalism. Socialism is a reaction to the gross inefficiency and injustice of the prevailing system. Every prospective convert must sense this inefficiency before he will take any interest in Socialism, and every theorist must understand the nature of this inefficiency before he can go on to develop the theory of a society in which these evils will be eliminated. It is very easy to remain in this first stage of Socialist thought without ever attaining the second. The evils of Capitalism are tangible and ever present before our eyes. They attract and hold the attention much more easily than the problems of the new society. Hence, as long as the primary task of Socialists is that of active propaganda, it is inevitable that they will neglect the problems of the new society.

Moreover, once a Socialist has passed beyond the stage of understanding the defects of Capitalism, he is faced, not by the problem of developing the economic theory of a Socialist economy, but by the more immediate problem of discovering the proper method of transforming Capitalism into Socialism. This question, therefore, has received the bulk of the attention of those theorists who have passed beyond the criticism stage.

From one point of view, it may seem quite illogical that Socialists have undertaken a careful criticism of Capitalism and urged the transition to Socialism without any clear and detailed conception of the new order. Capitalist critics have made the most of this point. However, while Socialist theorists have urged a radical transformation of society without picturing in detail the structure that is to rise, they have repeatedly stated the basis upon which the new society is to rest: *co-operative social ownership and utilization of the means of production.* They have, to be sure, been unduly optimistic. The economic problems of such a society are not as simple as some have supposed, and a revolutionary proletariat cannot be expected to solve them quickly. But it is an enormously valuable contribution to have designed a form of economic organization which eliminates the major contradictions inherent in the Capitalist order. This alone is sufficient to justify the Socialist movement in its criticism of Capitalism and in its propaganda for the new order.

B. DEFINITION OF TERMS

The subject of this treatise has already been indicated in a general way. However, a more detailed statement of the precise field to be covered, and of the relationship of this field to other divisions of Socialist economic theory and to other social sciences, is desirable. It is appropriate, therefore, to define and discuss the two terms contained in the title. What, precisely, is meant by "economic theory" and "Socialist economy"?

1. A Definition of Economic Theory

In this work it is assumed that the three terms "economic theory," "political economy," and "economics" are synonymous. Political economy is the older and more accurate title for the science which is today commonly called economics. The latter term has become conventional only within the last fifty years. Its triumph is, in part, a logical result of laissez faire or liberal economic theory. If that government is best which interferes least in business and economic affairs, clearly the adjective "political" has little place in the title applied to the science of economic phenomena. Even under Capitalism, however, the great majority of economic problems are at the same time political problems. Taxation, tariffs, money and banking, business cycles, public utilities, railroad transportation, social legislation, etc., all provide economic problems which are already being settled by purely political means. Under Capitalism, economic problems which are not at the same time political problems really belong to the entirely distinct field of business administration. Socialism, of course, will make them political also.

The term "political economy" is also preferable to the term "economics" in that the former stresses the political or social viewpoint of the true economist. Even when dealing with economic problems not yet the subject of political action, the economist is interested solely in the welfare of the political or social body as a whole, rather than in the welfare of any specific individuals.

The term "economics" possesses a very real advantage in its brevity, however. Because of this advantage we shall use it as a synonym for the longer expression, "political economy," wherever convenient. Euphonic rather than logical considerations are responsible for the use of the term "economic theory" rather than the term "political economy" in the title of this treatise.

The most common orthodox definition of political economy is some form or other of John Stuart Mill's statement that political economy professes "to investigate the nature of wealth and the laws of its production and distribution."[4] This definition has many defects. In the first place, it neglects personal and impersonal service, a very important form of economic income which is not covered by the term "wealth." In the second place, political economy is little concerned with the "nature" of wealth. This is either a mere problem of definition or a subject of research for the physical sciences. The chief objection to Mill's definition, however, is that it includes the fields of innumerable other sciences. The geologist is primarily interested in the nature and discovery of certain forms of wealth. The electrical engineer devotes his time to problems of the production of an economic good—electrical energy. Indeed, most scientists are merely specialists in some form of production.

According to the definition formulated by Alfred Marshall, political economy is "a study of mankind in the ordinary business of life; it examines that part of individual and social action which is most closely connected with the attainment and with the use of the material requisites of well-being."[5] This definition likewise is of little value as a description of political economy because it is all-inclusive. Every type of activity is merely the "ordinary business of life" to some person or other. All sciences are concerned with the attainment and use of the material requisites of well-being. Moreover, all the requisites of well-being are material— that is, they are all physical or natural objects or events—and no type of individual or social activity is more closely connected with these natural requisites of well-being than any other. Certainly music, art, literature, and play are as physical[6] and as closely related to well-being as the digging

---

[4] Mill, John Stuart, *Principles of Political Economy*, I, 1.

[5] Marshall, Alfred, *Principles of Political Economy*, p. 1.

[6] In popular thought the term "physical" is confused with the term "tangible." Actually, processes or events are as physical as tangible objects.

of ditches. Marshall's definition of political economy betrays the influence of religious or metaphysical reasoning because it attempts to divide reality into the material and the non-material or spiritual.

Other bourgeois economists have defined economics as the science which deals primarily with value and prices, or with problems or phenomena expressed in terms of price.[7] This definition, too, is unsatisfactory, for it is quite easy to imagine an entire economy which makes no use whatsoever of money, prices, and values. Prices may be an effective tool or means of economic control, but economics is primarily concerned with the problems of control themselves, not with a certain solution of them. Economic problems may be described in terms of price; but it is the former, not the latter, which constitute the elemental material or subject matter of economics.

The fact that these orthodox definitions of political economy tend to be all-inclusive is due to the fact that all human activity is economic, or may become economic under certain conditions, and all of it produces, or may under certain conditions produce, economic welfare.[8] The econ-

[7] Thus J. D. Black defines economics as "the science and art of the utilizing of human and natural resources to best advantage, *in so far as considerations of value or price are involved*" (*Introduction to Production Economics*, p. 6, copyright by Henry Holt and Company, Inc., New York, 1926). In attempting to differentiate between the subject matter of economics and the subject matter of the physical sciences, Black asserts that "the science of economics has to do with the *value properties* of things, as distinguished from the physical and chemical properties" (*ibid*). If economics and the natural sciences were purely descriptive, this might be true. But, when the economist and the natural scientist attempt to solve problems, they are both concerned with the cost of the process and the utility of the product. A chemist who experiments with different fertilizers is just as much concerned with *value properties* as an economist who discusses different degrees of the division of labor. The only difference between them is that one specializes in the chemical problems connected with production while the other specializes in the economic problems of production.

[8] Certain economists have attempted to distinguish between economic and noneconomic utility. Thus Arthur Cecil Pigou writes: "Human beings are both 'ends in themselves' and instruments of good. On the one hand, a man who is attuned to the beautiful in nature or in art, whose character is simple and sincere, whose passions are controlled and sympathies developed, is in himself an important element in the ethical value of the world: the way in which he feels and thinks actually constitutes a part of welfare. On the other hand, a man who can perform complicated industrial operations, sift difficult evidence, or advance some branch of practical activity, is an instrument well fitted to produce things whose use yields welfare. The welfare to which the former of these men contributes directly is noneconomic: that to which the latter contributes directly is economic." *Economics of Welfare*, 4th ed., 1932 (Macmillan & Co., Ltd., London), pp. 12–13. This is pure metaphysics. "The ethical value of the world" is a typically meaningless metaphysical concept. The

omist is, or should be, as much interested in the services of musicians and philosophers as in the services of barbers and domestic servants. The production of fine pictures and statues presents as many problems to political economy as the production of bread and butter, if not more. It is perfectly true that up to the present time economic theorists have devoted more attention to the economic problems involved in the production of bread and butter than to the economic problems involved in the production of oil paintings and fine statuary; but this is due to the greater value of the annual output of bread and butter, and will change when the value of the annual output of paintings and statues becomes greater than the value of the annual production of bread and butter.

The field of political economy should be defined, not by limiting it to certain types of human activity or to the production of certain utilities. Rather, it should be limited (*a*) to activities, of any kind whatever, performed for a certain purpose, and (*b*) to certain types of problems connected with such activity. In the first place, then, human activity is not economic activity unless it is carried on in order to obtain a compensation in the form of other goods and services. If a man plays baseball for the pleasure of the game only, he is not engaging in economic activity. In the second place, economics does not include problems of the technique of individual trades and industries, except in so far as these problems are common to many or all forms of economic activity.[9] This is the fundamental distinction between political economy and all other sciences which investigate economic activity.

In summary, political economy may be defined as the science which deals with the problems common to many or all forms of human activity carried on in order to secure scarce goods and services. In civilized communities, such human activity is organized on a group basis. Hence political economy is a social science.

a) THE RELATIONSHIP OF POLITICAL ECONOMY TO
OTHER SOCIAL SCIENCES

An understanding of the nature of economics requires some attention to its relationship to other sciences.

All sciences may be classified into three fundamental groups: (1) sci-

good, the true, and the beautiful are likewise metaphysical concepts, as ordinarily defined, that is, when defined as ends in themselves. Utility is the sole end in itself. Only when the good, the true, and the beautiful contribute to it can they have any value.

[9] "Production is always some special branch of production . . . . but political economy is not technology" (Karl Marx, *A Contribution to the Critique of Political Economy*, 1904, American edition, p. 270).

ences which deal with inanimate nature, the true natural sciences; (2) sciences which deal with animate nature, the biological sciences; and (3) sciences which deal with man in society, the social sciences.

As a social science, economics makes use of all pertinent knowledge accumulated by the natural and biological sciences. From these it is readily distinguished. But difficulty arises when an attempt is made to distinguish between economics and certain of the other social sciences with which the subject matter is closely connected. For that reason, the next few pages will be devoted to a discussion of these relationships. First let us note the relationship between political economy and philosophy.

Philosophy.—Philosophy is frequently classified by bourgeois thinkers as a social science. Actually, however, it is not a science at all. Over a century ago Auguste Comte, in his brilliant exposition of the law of the three stages, explained that human thinking in every field of knowledge has passed through three distinct logical phases. These three stages are: (*a*) the religious; (*b*) the metaphysical; (*c*) the scientific. The first two stages were completely sterile; they resulted in the development of no valid or useful knowledge whatever.[10] Modern philosophy is still largely in the second or metaphysical stage; hence it has developed no valid or useful knowledge. While philosophy, due to its metaphysical method, has yielded no valid or useful knowledge, certain fields of philosophy, such as logic, aesthetics, and ethics, are now being cultivated in a scientific way by specialists in psychology and other sciences, and important discoveries have already been made. These problems and discoveries, however, belong to the special sciences which have handled them, or ought to handle them, and not to the field of philosophy.

Ethics has been considered as one of the major divisions of philosophy from its very beginning. In the last century, however, certain scientific students of ethical problems have attempted to establish an independent and valid science of ethics. This indicates a serious lack of comprehension of the nature of scientific ethics. Ethics cannot be changed into an independent science by the application of the scientific method to its problems. This does not mean that ethical problems are not subject to an application of the scientific method, but that when so treated they become a part of some new or old science.

All problems of human conduct are ethical problems. The sole purpose of any and every science is to solve problems of human conduct. Whatever the scientist or technical expert determines is the right way to

---

[10] This generalization applies to the logical stages, not to a historical stage. Even when religion and philosophy were most widely accepted, many men solved practical problems by crude scientific methods.

act is the ethical way to act. Every field of human conduct, every possible human act, is, or ought to be, the object of scientific study and research. The scientist may make mistakes, but he always knows more than anyone else about the problems of human conduct which fall within his field. The effect of adultery, or theft, or idleness, or lending at interest, or charity is something that can be determined by scientists of one kind or another far more accurately than by any layman, priest, or philosopher.

Since political economy is solely concerned with problems of individual and social conduct, it covers many of the questions once assigned to ethics. This does not mean that ethical principles affect its conclusions. Rather it means that its conclusions constitute ethical generalizations. Scientific ethics can never be more than a collection of conclusions arrived at in the special sciences.

It is sometimes said that science can provide only more effective means for realizing moral ends. This is partly true. However, the assumption that a metaphysical ethics can discover proper human ends is quite unsound. Most sciences are concerned solely with devising means to achieve given ends, but psychology is concerned, among other things, with the discovery of final ends. These are supplied by nature or heredity in the form of instincts or drives. All life is a struggle to satisfy hereditary purposes, modified in innumerable ways by environment. The great fallacy of metaphysical ethics is the belief that these final ends can be discovered by processes of logical deduction. Only an inductive science can discover them and, since they are hereditary, they cannot be consciously altered except when a stronger instinct conflicts with a weaker one and results in eugenic measures to breed out the latter.

Political Science.—The relationship of political economy to political science under Socialism requires little explanation. In a Socialist society the problem of the organization of the state will become but a part of the problem of the organization of the national economy. The same organization will perform the services which have in the past been distinguished as the separate functions of political and economic organizations. Political science will disappear as a distinct social science, to become an indistinguishable part of the special field of economic organization, a major division of economics.

In Marxian terminology, the state will "wither away" and, for this reason, there will be no need for a theory of the organization of the state.

Sociology.—Sociology is ordinarily defined as "the science of society" or in closely similar words having about the same meaning. This definition is so broad that it includes all the social sciences, political economy among them. Perhaps for this reason many of the subjects covered in the conventional course, Principles of Sociology, such as population and community organization, are taken from the older and better developed sciences of political economy and political science. The term "sociology" should either be defined in such a way as to avoid this duplication of effort by limiting it more narrowly, or else it should be replaced by a new name or names accurately describing that part of contemporary sociology which is really distinct from other social sciences.

In addition to dealing with a large number of economic and political problems, the conventional Principles of Sociology devotes considerable attention to the family, the church, and social relationships of the kind popularly referred to as "social life." It is difficult to form any general definition which would include these topics and at the same time exclude the subject matter of economics and political science. Moreover, these topics probably do not have enough in common to justify grouping them together as a single science. Modern sociology, like ancient philosophy, is a sort of dumping ground for subject matter not treated in other divisions of knowledge. For these reasons we believe that the term "sociology" should be abandoned as the title of a specific social science. Its subject matter should be divided up among the older social sciences and such new social sciences as social anthropology, social psychology, and criminology.

Business Administration.—Political economy and the new science or sciences of business administration are so closely related that few theorists attempt to distinguish between them. In American universities, business courses were originally given by the older departments of economics, but today many departments and schools of business administration have virtually swallowed the economics department.

Under Capitalism it is possible to distinguish very clearly between the problems of political economy and the problems of business administration. The former science is concerned with the economic problems of political bodies and the economic welfare of the group, while the latter deals with the business problems of individuals and corporations. Thus, a treatise on political economy may include chapters on taxation, money and banking, the regulation of public utilities, immigration, population, Socialism, etc. Business administration, on the other hand, is divided into such fields as scientific management, marketing, accounting, statistics, corporation finance, personnel management, and the like.

In addition to the theory relating to these economic problems of political bodies, Capitalist political economy also includes the general theory of production, distribution, and exchange—often termed "pure" economic theory to distinguish it from the "applied" theory noted above. The sole value of this pure theory to the economist, however, is to provide a useful foundation for an approach to the practical problems of his science.

In so far as this pure economic theory is of value to the student of business administration it belongs also to that field. However, American businessmen and professors of business administration make little use of pure economic theory. A knowledge of marginal utility theory does not seem to increase private profits, and the sole concern of the science of business administration is private profit.

In a Socialist economy it will no longer be possible to say that political economy is concerned with the business problems of society while business administration is concerned with the business problems of the individual capitalist. Society, acting through political bodies, will operate industry as well as fix taxes, control foreign trade, etc. How, then, can we distinguish between the field of economics and the field of business administration in such a society? It is only possible to assert, rather vaguely, that the more universal and general problems, those common to all industry, belong in the field of economics, while those sciences which are concerned with the technique of some particular trade or profession—such as advertising, accounting, or statistics—or with the managerial problems of a single industry, belong within the field of business administration.

It is worthy of note that economic principles often conflict with the principles of business administration in a Capitalist state. Thus, private advertising may be costly and wasteful from the point of view of the economist, and at the same time highly profitable from the point of view of the student of business administration. Under Socialism, of course, there will be no possibility of conflict between the principles of economics and the principles of business administration.

The theory of many branches of business administration, such as accounting and statistics, can be taken over relatively intact by the new Socialist science of business administration. The theory of other branches, such as retail store management, banking, and insurance, will have to undergo a radical revision; while that of still others, such as investment banking, advertising, and speculation, will be virtually discarded as a whole. The development of a comprehensive Socialist science of business administration will require the efforts of many able students. It is a task which cannot be undertaken too soon, but it lies outside the scope of this treatise.

2. A Definition of a Socialist Economy

Having defined economic theory, or political economy, we may turn our attention to a definition of the second term in the title of this work, "a Socialist economy."

"Socialism" may refer to a body of economic theory, to a movement supporting Socialist theory, or to the economic order which will result from the victory of the Socialist movement. "Socialist economy" is a more specific term, referring to the last-mentioned concept only.

Although Socialists disagree on many fundamental points of economic theory, they do agree on certain basic and distinctive principles. They advocate: (1) social ownership and operation of the means of production; (2) a much more equal distribution of the national income; and (3) democratic control of industry. In this book the adjective "Socialist" is applied only to a person, movement, body of theory, or economy which advocates or embodies these three basic principles.

It should be emphasized that the foregoing definition of Socialism is broad enough to include Co-operation, Anarchism, Syndicalism, Guild Socialism, State Socialism, and Democratic Communism. In general, the economic principles developed in the present study are applicable to the organization and control of each of the various kinds of Socialist economic order advocated by these movements although, obviously, each of these movements differs from all the others on certain vital points to which it owes its name and individuality. The chief point on which these various schools of Socialism disagree is that of organization, particularly as to whether it should be centralized or decentralized. The present treatise solves this problem in a certain way, one which cannot please all, or perhaps any, of the existing schools. However, the problem of organization is but one of a large number of questions discussed in this work. Disagreement on this point need not prevent anyone from accepting the major economic principles set forth.[11]

3. CLASSIFICATION OF SOCIALIST ECONOMIC THEORY

There are three major divisions of Socialist economic theory. The first of these, both in point of origin and in degree of contemporary development, is the analysis and criticism of Capitalism and Capitalist economy. *Das Kapital* and the majority of the writings of Marxian theorists belong in this classification. To the second division of the economic theory of Socialism belong the studies which deal with the problem of transforming a Capitalist economy or industry into a Socialist one. This division includes such questions as whether revolutionary tactics are more effective than parliamentary tactics, whether capitalists should be expropriated or remunerated, which industries to socialize first, how rapidly to carry on the process of socialization, etc. Both of these divisions of

[11] To a certain extent, the same thing may be said of Fascism and Monopoly Capitalism. Any state which has eliminated competition should, for instance, adopt and apply the theory of production control here advocated.

Socialist economic theory are entirely distinct from the third, the economic theory of an established Socialist economy, which is the subject of this volume. The author assumes without discussion both the desirability and the existence of a Socialist economy, restricting his discussion to the economic problems of such an economy.

Each of the three major divisions of Socialist economic theory may be further subdivided into three distinct parts: doctrine, history of doctrine, and methodology. Only the first of these, doctrine, is treated in this study. It is treated, moreover, not by analyzing and comparing the theories of other contemporary writers, but by formulating a new and comprehensive body of doctrine. In other words, the present work is a contribution to or synthesis of current theory, not a critical analysis and classification of contemporary theory. Finally, economic theory may be divided into static and dynamic theory. This study deals primarily with static theory.

The following brief outline may make clearer the foregoing analysis of Socialist economic theory. That portion of it covered in this treatise is underlined.

I. The economic theory of Socialism
   A. Critical analysis of Capitalism
      1. Methodology
      2. History of theory
      3. Theory
   B. Theory of transition
      1. Methodology
      2. History of theory
      3. Theory
   C. Theory of a Socialist economy
      1. Methodology
      2. History of theory
      3. <u>Theory</u>
         a) <u>Static</u>
         b) Dynamic

C. THE THEORY OF THIS TREATISE

Now that both of the two terms in the title of our treatise have been defined, a few introductory remarks concerning the theory set forth in this treatise are in order. First let us note the relationship of the theory of this work to the theory of orthodox Capitalist political economy. Then we shall consider its relationship to existing Socialist theory.

1. Relationship to Bourgeois Economic Theory

The majority of both orthodox and radical economists have been convinced that the economic theory of a Socialist economy would be quite different from that of a Capitalist economy.[12] The doctrine of the present treatise, however, is essentially an application of orthodox Capitalist economic theory to the problems of a Socialist economy.

[12] "Thus, if one were to ask how much of current economics would be valid for a systematic Socialism it must be admitted that the salient features of our competitive price economics would disappear. What might be the theoretical economics of Socialism it is difficult to formulate. Money and prices would seemingly have no place—at least no necessary and central place.

"Exchanges, if any remained, would be merely incidental and sporadic, or occasional, and in any case, non-essential. On the one side, economics would shade off into administrative theory, a sort of political science. Seemingly, however, its central and unifying problem would be that of utility rather than of market value or price."—H. J. Davenport, *Economics of Enterprise* (The Macmillan Company, 1913), p. 31.

Many orthodox economists have naïvely assumed that economics is a science which deals only with the problems of Capitalism. For instance, Frank H. Knight states, "Economics is the study of a particular form of organization of human want-satisfying activity which has become prevalent in Western nations and spread over the greater part of the field of conduct. It is called free enterprise or the competition system." *Risk, Uncertainty and Profit* (1921 ed.), p. 9. This attitude not only implies that the basic principles of Capitalist economics have no validity under Socialism, but that whatever principles do apply under Socialism cannot be called economics.

Maurice H. Dobb, however, disagrees with our conclusion. In "Economic Theory and the Problems of a Socialist Economy" (*Economic Journal*, December 1933), he wrote (p. 588):

"As a rule, it has been assumed that in a socialist society the main propositions of economic theory would apply with undiminished force. . . . .

"For instance, H. D. Henderson speaks of 'the existence in the economic world of an order more profound and more permanent than any of our social schemes, and equally applicable to them all' and of economic laws and relationships which 'seem altogether more fundamental than our present industrial system' (*Supply and Demand*, pp. 11 and 141); while Wieser similarly declares that 'the communistic state must retain the same laws in force, or its economy will become chaos' (*Natural Value*, p. 164). Wieser even goes so far as to identify natural value with 'value as it would exist in the communist state.' Pareto asserts that under Socialism 'commodities will be distributed according to the rules which we have discovered in our study of a regime of competition' (*Cours*, Vol. II, p. 364), and Cassel assures us that 'new lines of economic policy, adopted by Socialist reformers, which promise anything for the future, tend, so far as prices are concerned, merely to work out the classical ideal of a system of prices' (*Theory of Social Economy*, I, 76)."

In answer to Dobb, we would say that the silence of the great majority of orthodox economists on this point indicates dissent. If they believed that their

In their efforts to justify the prevailing economic order, orthodox classical and neoclassical economists have developed a rather complex theory of what ought to happen in a well-regulated economic system. According to orthodox theory, for instance, labor ought to be employed where it has the maximum marginal utility. Whenever changing economic conditions reduce the marginal utility of labor in one industry and increase it in another, a portion of the labor force previously employed in the former industry ought to be transferred to the latter. This transfer should be continued just up to the point where the marginal utility of labor in these two industries is again equal. Precisely the same rules ought to govern the distribution of land, capital, and executives. Orthodox theorists have fully explained the utility of such movements of the factors in production. They have developed equally sound theories concerning other economic problems. Instead of urging the adoption and application of these principles of economic behavior and control, however, they have committed the great error of asserting that under the existing system uncontrolled economic forces bring about relatively complete obedience to or observance of these rules. In spite of the gigantic losses of individual investors, they have continued to affirm that under Capitalism, capital automatically flows into the most productive fields of investment. In spite of the gross inequality in wages and salaries which prevails even in the same trades[13] and professions, orthodox economists have claimed that under Capitalism, labor automatically flows into the most productive and best-paid work. This entire viewpoint of orthodox political economy is essentially unsound. It is largely wishful thinking. While there are significant tendencies in the direction of automatic observance of the above economic principles, these tendencies have been greatly overemphasized by orthodox theorists.[14] Moreover, even these theo-

theories would apply under Socialism as under Capitalism, they would say so, for theorists are always inclined to claim the maximum scope for their theories. Moreover, there can be no question concerning the fact that the overwhelming majority of Socialist theorists, the men most interested in this question, have long believed that the economic theory of a Socialist state would be fundamentally different from the economic theory of Capitalism. Only since 1929 have there been a few protests by Socialist theorists against this dominant Socialist view.

[13] Witness the wide divergence between textile wages in our Northern and Southern states.

[14] Maurice Dobb has written: "To draw one's assumptions as did the classical economists, from a state of classless individualism and then to apply them to a system of capitalist undertaking, is to commit a grave fault; for in the former system the extent of monopoly and advantage will be so small as to be virtually negligible, while in the latter system it will constitute the principal feature. It is in this confusion, indeed, that the chief fallacy of *laissez faire* consists: it is a

rists admit that "friction" and various other factors prevent the immediate and complete fulfillment of these ideal principles of economic behavior.[15]

While these orthodox economic theories are not accurate descriptions of what happens under Capitalism, they may easily be converted into ideal principles of administration to be followed by the rulers of a Socialist economy. Because of the ignorance of private investors and the guile of bond salesmen, capital rarely flows into the most productive and remunerative field of investment under Capitalism. Nevertheless, the erroneous statement or implication found in the conventional Capitalist economic treatise, affirming that capital does, for the most part, flow into the most productive fields of investment, may easily be converted into a sound rule of conduct for those in charge of capital investment in a Socialist economy. More important yet, the same method of measuring the productivity of capital may be used.

In other words, a Socialist government does not need a new system of economic theory to justify or guide its conduct. In large part, it merely needs to adopt orthodox economic theory and take positive steps to change this grossly inaccurate description of Capitalism into a living Socialist reality. This involves changing facts to fit a theory, not changing theories to fit facts. Socialism is inevitable because only a Socialist state can change economic facts as it will, because it alone can assume full control over all economic activity and make it conform with the ideal pictured by the great neoclassical economists.[16]

---

doctrine which, like much of the democratic theory accompanying it, would be very fair wisdom in a classless society."—*Capitalistic Enterprise and Social Progress* (George Routledge & Sons, Ltd., 1925), pp. 143–44. This work contains a very excellent study of the role of friction and monopoly in a Capitalist society.

[15] The most important recent development in bourgeois economic theory has been the increasing recognition of the existence of monopoly, duopoly, oligopoly, and other forms of imperfect competition, and the resulting efforts to develop a theory of imperfect competition.

[16] "Only in a Socialist community, where production can be carried on in the full light of statistical measurement and publicity, is it possible to realize the true principles of economic valuation. Capitalist society, with its deviations from equilibrium due to inequalities in individual income, to competition, to monopoly, and to the material ignorance of entrepreneurs concerning other entrepreneurs' activities, is a very imperfect approximation to the economic ideal. The beautiful systems of economic equilibrium described by Boehm-Bawerk, Wieser, Marshall, and Cassel are not descriptions of society as it is, but prophetic visions of a Socialist economy of the future."—H. D. Dickinson, "Price Formation in a Socialist Community," *Economic Journal*, June 1933, pp. 246–47.

It is undeniable that orthodox Capitalist economic theory has many
minor defects, particularly when used as a guide to Socialist control. In
the course of this treatise, attention will be directed to some of these
defects in orthodox theory, but the author's principal purpose is to stress
the fact that orthodox Capitalist economic theory can be applied to a
Socialist economy. This point may seem obvious to some, and consequently unworthy of the stress laid upon it here. An examination of
Socialist literature, however, will convince the reader of the almost complete absence of this point of view in the existing theory of the movement.
The apologetic nature of orthodox Capitalist theory, together with the
fact that few Socialists are thoroughly conversant with it, has caused
radical theorists to react rather violently against it. They have been led
by the apparently successful use of this theory as an apology for Capitalism into concluding that an entirely new and distinctively Socialist body
of economic doctrine is required to provide a theoretical basis for the
movement. That is why Marx tried to formulate new theories of value,
distribution, and exchange. That is why the Socialist movement has clung
so tenaciously to Marxian value theory. Once Socialists grasp the point of
view set forth above, Marx will be replaced by Marshall as the chief
guide to the solution of the economic problems of a Socialist economy.
Karl Marx was a far greater thinker than Alfred Marshall, but his
enduring contributions were not in the field of static economic theory
dealt with in this treatise, but in the field of dynamic economic theory.
The theory of economic evolution, not the labor theory of value, is
Marx's masterpiece, and the errors of the latter in no way weaken the
logic of the former.

2. Relationship to Marxian Value Theory

There is no need to repeat in this work the orthodox bourgeois criticism of the labor theory of value, although this criticism is essentially
sound. Rather, the author desires to turn the flank of the Marxian value
theorists by asserting: (1) that the labor theory of value is not a necessary or integral part of the case for Socialism, and (2) that Marxian
value theory is of little if any help in the solution of the practical problems of a Socialist economy.

The principal arguments in favor of Socialism are: (1) that it will
eliminate the huge wastes due to competition, (2) that it will eliminate
private inheritance and the unearned income resulting from inheritance,
(3) that it will give work to all who ought to work and relief to all
who require it, and (4) that it will result in democratic control of industry. None of these convincing and fundamental arguments for So-

cialism rests upon the labor theory of value. None of these will be weakened by the rejection of this theory.

The labor theory of value and the corollaries based upon it have been used to persuade the worker that he is underpaid and unjustly exploited by the capitalist. Since few workers understand the labor theory of value, however, their widespread assent to the conclusions drawn from this theory must be ascribed to other causes. Most workers always have considered themselves underpaid and always will. No elaborate theory of value and profits is necessary to persuade them of this fact. If any explanation of low wages is needed, it is enough to point out to them that this is a result of private ownership and control of the means of production.

As a matter of fact, workers receive almost the full value of their labor under Capitalism. Capitalist wages are low because of: (1) the gross inefficiency of Capitalism—four gas stations on a corner where one would more than suffice; (2) almost universal overpopulation; and (3) the fact that rent and interest go to private owners of land and capital. Socialism may fail to eliminate overpopulation, but it will certainly eliminate both the gross inefficiency of production and the private ownership of capital characteristic of competitive Capitalism. The resulting increase in national income will increase all shares in income—rent, interest, and wages—at least twofold. In addition, all rent and interest will accrue to the working class. The sharp rise in workers' income brought about by these changes will not be due to the elimination of exploitation, but to the other factors noted. Socialism does not propose merely to give to the worker the full value of his labor. It proposes to increase greatly the value of his labor and to give him his proper share of rent and interest in addition. In other words, Socialism proposes to increase the productivity of labor and to give to the worker the full value of the product, which is always much more than the full value of his labor since it includes rent and interest.

The second point against the labor theory of value is that it cannot be used to solve the problems of a Socialist economy. If anyone believes that it can be used for this purpose, let him attempt to do so. How can the labor theory of value be used to fix wages, determine prices, control the volume of production? No Marxian theorist has been able to answer these questions.

While the labor theory of value is useless in this connection, orthodox bourgeois value theory provides an invaluable tool for such work. There is no need to enlarge upon this point here, since the entire treatise is devoted to a demonstration of this point.

3. The Major Contributions of the Treatise[17]

In the opinion of the author, this treatise has four fundamental contributions to make to the theory of a Socialist economy. To state them briefly at this point may help the reader to grasp the significance and purpose of much of the subsequent discussion.

In the first place, this is one of the first books in English to apply marginal theory to the problems of Socialist administration. Marx developed his economic doctrines before the rise of the Austrian school. Subsequent Socialist theorists have adhered so closely to Marxian doctrine that they have been unwilling to accept the marginal analysis of value and distribution—this in spite of its well-nigh universal acceptance by Capitalist economists, who did not hesitate to scrap the older cost-of-production value theory accepted by both Socialist and Capitalist theorists up to 1870. In other words, Socialists have refused to accept and make use of the most important advance in the content and method of value theory since the foundation of the science by Adam Smith. This has greatly handicapped their static economic theory and exposed them to innumerable attacks by orthodox economists. The present work undertakes to remove the foundation for these attacks without yielding any important point of Socialist doctrine on the inefficiency of Capitalism and the nature and necessity of Socialism. Marginal utility analysis can be used for Socialist purposes far more effectively than the older Marxian value theory.

The second major contribution of this treatise to the economic theory of a Socialist economy is its suggestion of the use of a profit-loss mechanism for the control of production. This solves the basic problems of what and how much to produce, and at the same time decentralizes the control of production by giving to the manager of each unit in production an independent test of the wisdom of his decisions. It is hoped that the mere conventional association of the terms "profit" and "loss" with Capitalism will not prevent the impartial consideration of this proposal. The use of a profit-loss mechanism for the control of production is the opposite of economic planning. This fundamental point, ignored by Dickinson and Hall, is stressed throughout the present work.

The third principal contribution of this treatise is its marked emphasis upon the desirability of individual freedom in a Socialist state. The principles here set forth permit the consumer to have complete freedom in his

---

[17] This section states the original (1932) purposes of the author. Several able economists have published articles and books since 1932 which develop essentially the same idea.

choice of goods; they permit the worker entering the labor market to exercise a previously unknown freedom in his choice of a job; and finally, they permit the worker to determine his own hours of labor. The net result should be that workers will have far more freedom in a Socialist state than they now have under Capitalism.

The fourth major contribution is the application of the old but largely ignored theory that prices should equal marginal costs to all the pricing problems of a Socialist economy. The few economists who accept this theory have failed to realize its significance because they are unaware that virtually all nonextractive industries have decreasing costs.

PART ONE
THE MEASUREMENT OF UTILITY

CHAPTER II. THE THEORY OF UTILITY AND DISUTILITY

A. THE GOAL OF A SOCIALIST ECONOMY

Before we can consider intelligently any of the economic problems of a Socialist society, we must determine the purpose of economic theory under Socialism.

Man's efforts to solve the problem of human purpose have a long history which, in accordance with Comte's well-known law, may be divided into three logical stages. In the first place, from the dawn of history down to our own times there have been religious thinkers who have attempted to solve the problem of the purpose of man and science by trying to divine and state the opinions of supernatural or spiritual powers which they assumed to exist. This method of determining the purpose of science has two major defects. It leads to an extreme diversity of opinion and, furthermore, it provides no method of discovering which opinion is correct.

In the second place, after religious thought had become highly developed, there arose groups of men called philosophers who sought to solve the problem of human purpose by the use of the metaphysical method, which consists in drawing specific conclusions from general principles (major premises) which are thought to be intrinsically rational and valid and, therefore, not to require inductive verification. This method has proven completely unsatisfactory because the conclusions of those who use it depend upon the major premises with which they start, and there is no metaphysical means of determining which premises are true and which are false.

Finally, since the death of Hegel, the last of the great metaphysical philosophers, the task of formulating the purpose of science has been assumed by science itself. Today we use the scientific method itself, the method of observing nature and man and of describing their behavior, to solve this first problem of science itself. Instead of attempting to determine what man ought to want, we observe what he does want.[1] There is a vast difference between the two points of view.

[1] It is true, of course, that once we know what men *do* want, we can say that they ought to use one method of attaining it rather than another, but all scientific use of the term "ought" assumes an already existing purpose, a purpose which exists as a natural fact, like gravitation, regardless of whether priests and philosophers think it ought to exist.

25

Political economy, perhaps due to its late development as a systematic body of doctrine, has always been relatively free from religious and metaphysical reasoning. Economists have long asserted that the purpose of economic theory and activity is to satisfy existing wants, and they have ignored religious and metaphysical ethical doctrines. By some this has been considered to be a reflection upon economics, but actually it is a severe reflection upon religion and metaphysical ethics.

If economics is to be consistently scientific, it must accept as its sole purpose the satisfaction of existing human wants, in so far as these fall within its field. However, it is clear that men possess innumerable wants of all degrees of intensity, and that these wants frequently if not universally conflict with each other. Because of this conflict, the law prohibits the satisfaction of certain wants, and scientists warn against the satisfaction of many others. This does not mean that existing wants can provide no practical guidance to economic theory and practice, or that additional guidance from some other source is needed. It merely means that economics must develop a method of measuring the strength of wants, so that it can direct its attention to satisfying the strongest ones. When the law prohibits the satisfaction of certain wants, it is merely aiding economics to solve this problem, for the legal prohibition of the satisfaction of a want ordinarily means that there are other and stronger wants which conflict with it. Similarly, when a scientist warns against the satisfaction of certain wants he means that such satisfaction would prevent the satisfaction of other and stronger ones. No want can be scientifically condemned unless its satisfaction prevents the satisfaction of more powerful wants.

In the case of a single individual, the determination of the relative intensity of wants is relatively simple and automatic, but in the case of a group of men, where wants experienced by different individuals must be compared, the problem is relatively complex. The solution of this latter problem is the central task of political economy.

Thus far hedonism, the traditional theoretical basis of political economy, has not been mentioned. Is there any conflict between our statement that the purpose of economics is to satisfy existing human wants and the hedonistic principle that economics should strive to maximize the net pleasure income (surplus of pleasure over pain) of the individual? At first glance the answer would seem to be yes, because many human wants are based upon false information and/or unsound reasoning, so that their satisfaction gives less pleasure than anticipated or more pain than pleasure. Economics, it may be argued, cannot aim both at the satisfaction of existing unintelligent wants and at the maximization of net pleasure at the same time. However, this conclusion is unsound. Economics aims at the satisfaction of existing wants, unintelligent as some of them may be, because this will lead to more net pleasure than any other course of action. Improvement in the rationality of human wants will probably continue for an infinite period of time. The fact that these wants are not now perfectly rational does not mean that a science which tries to satisfy these wants has some other purpose than achieving maximum net pleasure. The latter, indeed, is by definition the only rational goal of human activity (that is, pleasure is defined as including everything that pleases man). If it were possible to increase net pleasure by refusing to satisfy certain existing wants, this would be desirable. However, in such a case it would be the duty, not of economists, but of the scientists in whose field of study this want fell to condemn it, and it would then be up to the legislature to pass a law prohibiting its satisfaction. At any given time the economist can assume with reason that existing wants are the best available guide as to what economic goods will give the most pleasure.

This statement of the purpose of economic activity may be translated into conventional economic terminology by using the terms "utility" and "disutility." If utility is defined as that quality common to all economic goods which have the power of satisfying human wants, and disutility as the quality common to all objects, conditions, and services which arouse human dislike, the purpose of economics is to maximize net per capita utility income. Net utility is the surplus of utility over disutility. The idea of per capita income is essential here because individual men will nearly always prefer a maximum per capita income to a maximum national income.

B. THE SIGNIFICANCE OF UTILITY THEORY

There are at least two basic reasons for the fundamental importance of the theory of utility and disutility to the economic principles of a Socialist economy.

In the first place, as already explained, the sole purpose of Socialism is to maximize average net utility income. The only criterion of the soundness or unsoundness of each individual principle of Socialist economic administration, therefore, is the effect of the application of that principle upon average net utility income. The theory of utility and disutility is essential to the use of this criterion. Throughout this treatise the theory of utility will be used to justify the conclusions stated, and the only criticism of them which can be relevant and cogent must be based upon the same grounds. Justice and injustice, morality and immorality, natural rights and divine rights, etc., are all irrelevant as well as meaningless considerations. The only aspect of importance is the effect of a given economic principle upon average net utility income; to determine this, one must be familiar with the theory of utility.

In the second place, from the point of view of formal logic, utility theory is of fundamental importance to the economic doctrine of a Socialist state because it provides the axioms which make possible most of the deductive reasoning of this body of doctrine. All purely deductive reasoning is necessarily futile, witness theology and metaphysics. Deductive reasoning can only be fruitful in the field of political economy if it is based upon certain fundamental premises which are inductive in nature. These primary premises perform the same logical function in political economy as do axioms in mathematics. However, they are inductive in nature, that is, they are generalized statements of observed fact, while mathematical axioms are truths by definition.

As abstract reasoning is the only satisfactory method of dealing with many of the problems of economics—chiefly on account of the complexity of these problems, and the difficulty of turning human society into a laboratory—the primary premises or axioms included in the theory of utility are of great significance for political economy. Any error in a principle of utility or disutility invalidates all conclusions based upon that principle.

Since utility is based upon human wants, the following discussion of utility and disutility opens with a brief consideration of human wants.

C. HUMAN WANTS AND DISLIKES

Human wants and dislikes[2] provide the motives for all human activity and give rise to utility and disutility.

Both wants and dislikes are the products of the evolution of the race and the experience of the individual—in other words, of heredity and environment. Food, water, and clothing have utility because they satisfy hereditary and instinctive wants. Certain types of clothing may have more utility than others, however, due solely to current styles. Such clothing satisfies what may be called an acquired want in addition to satisfying a hereditary want.

Specific wants for consumers' goods are satiable. A finite amount of any such good is sufficient to satisfy completely the want for it. A man needs only a limited amount of food to satisfy his hunger.

Every want goes on decreasing in intensity as it is satisfied, up to the point of complete satisfaction. Continued consumption beyond this point causes disgust or pain in many instances.

[2] Perhaps "diswant" would be a better term. We have used "dislike" to avoid coining another new word.

All specific human wants are competitive, in part at least. That is, the increased satisfaction of one want ordinarily involves a decreased satisfaction of some other want. We cannot devote the same period of time or the same dollar to the satisfaction of two different wants, each of which requires the full period of time or the whole dollar. We must choose between the satisfaction of many different wants at all times.

Specific human wants are unlimited in number. The satisfaction of one specific want immediately creates another want. Civilized man has satisfied some of the wants which are of major importance among primitive peoples, but the satisfaction of these wants has merely created a great number of new, though less intense, wants.

Although unlimited in number, human wants may be classified into a few groups according to the underlying purposes or instincts to whose fulfillment they lead. Just at present it is unfashionable to speak of instincts, particularly detailed minor instincts. The term "drive" has replaced the term "instinct" as a name for the more fundamental hereditary human purposes. There is no need to take part in this controversy here, however. Suffice it to say that no psychologist denies that human beings are so constructed as a result of evolution that sugar tastes sweet and pleasant while quinine tastes bitter and unpleasant; that food, clothing, and shelter are desired because they are necessary to self-preservation, etc. Much of the controversy with respect to the existence of human instincts is purely verbal.

It may be objected that no final explanation of human wants has been given. To say that they are the product of evolution and experience is merely to indicate the nature of a few of the more immediate preceding causes or steps in an endless series of cause and effect. However, only priests and philosophers pretend to give a final explanation for anything. No scientist can do more than describe the immediately preceding causes in an apparently infinite causal series. Since this is all that is necessary for practical control over nature, we need not lament the finite nature of scientific knowledge.

The purposes or instincts which human wants serve are above human judgment. To say that man ought not to desire to live and to perpetuate his kind, for instance, is as meaningless and futile as it is to say that the law of gravitation is immoral. Man is a part of nature and his hereditary drives or instincts are just as much beyond judgment as any other part of nature. However, the specific wants in which these instincts manifest themselves are determined both by native intelligence and by environment, which includes education. They are, therefore, always unintelligent to some degree, for only perfect intelligence and a perfect environment could produce wants which serve perfectly our inherited purposes.

D. UTILITY AND UTILITUM

Any service or commodity which has the power to satisfy a specific human want is said to possess "utility." Such services and commodities are "goods." Utility is a quality, while a good is a tangible object or a personal service.

It is sometimes claimed that utility cannot be measured. But if utility cannot be measured, how do consumers decide what to buy and how do they decide to pay twice as much for one good as for another? There are, of course, irrational influences such as advertising and habit which affect consumers' decisions, but to assert that consumers cannot measure utility is to assert that they cannot weigh their own desires in choosing among different commodities. When a consumer decides to buy one more hat worth ten dollars instead of two more coats worth five dollars apiece, there can be only one rational reason, namely that the hat has more than twice the marginal utility to him than a coat, and he cannot determine this unless he can measure and compare the marginal utility of different goods.

One of the arguments used to support the statement that utility cannot be measured is to assume that a certain good is essential to life and point out that the utility of life itself is infinite. But the assumption itself is unrealistic. There are few goods essential to life. Pork can be replaced by beef and water by milk. Those which are most essential, police protection and drugs, for instance, should not be sold for a price and therefore should be exempt from the application of the pricing and production control principles based upon the utility theory in this chapter.

Utility has no uniform relationship to the average amount of socially necessary labor time required to supply a given article or service. Non-economic goods, such as water, air, sunshine, etc., possess great total utility but involve little or no labor cost. Irreplaceable economic goods, such as land, waterfalls, and minerals, may also possess great utility, both total and marginal, and involve little or no labor cost. It is only in the case of freely reproducible economic goods, and then only as regards marginal utility and marginal labor costs of production, that any close relationship between utility and labor costs exists, or ought to exist.

Although utility is usually defined as the imputed power to satisfy a human want, it is also used to mean the satisfaction which results from the consumption of economic goods. This has often resulted in serious confusion of thought. In this book, therefore, utility will be used only to mean imputed power to satisfy wants.

There is no other word which comes as close as utility to the second meaning, the satisfaction of consumption. Pleasure and welfare are the closest, but they include all human satisfactions and are not limited to those derived from the consumption of economic goods. A new word must therefore be coined to denote this second meaning of utility. "Utilitum" is used in this book since it calls attention to the close relation to utility.

E. DISUTILITY AND DISUTILITUM

Any object or activity which arouses human dislike may be said to possess disutility. Anything which possesses disutility is a "bad."

The same thing may be either a good or a bad, depending upon temporary circumstances. Changes in quantity or frequency, location or time, wants and dislikes—all may serve to change a good into a bad, or a bad into a good.

Disutility, like utility, is used to refer to the actual effect of consumption as well as to the anticipated effect of consumption. Economic analysis would be easier if disutility were used only to refer to the imputed effect of a bad. Hence a new term, "disutilitum," will be used in this book to refer to the actual effect of a bad upon a person.

The two new terms "utilitum" and "disutilitum" permit a more accurate statement of the basic purpose of economic theory. This purpose is to maximize net utilitum, the surplus of utilitum over disutilitum.

Disutility is the opposite of utility, and disutilitum is the opposite of utilitum. The principle that economic control should maximize utilitum is the obverse of the principle that economic control should minimize disutilitum. In the subsequent analysis of these concepts, therefore, specific reference to disutility and disutilitum will be made only when it is desirable to stress this fact or to note some other significant fact about disutility and disutilitum.

I. SOUND VERSUS UNSOUND UTILITY OR DISUTILITY

Utility and disutility may be sound or unsound. Sound utility arises from wants whose satisfaction is desirable, sound disutility from dislikes whose observance is beneficial. Harmful wants and dislikes give rise to unsound utility and disutility respectively.

Human drives and instincts provide only general directives. In his striving to realize these objectives, the individual frequently selects an unsatisfactory method. He attaches utility to articles and services because they are necessary to a certain method of satisfying instinctive ends, and then discovers the method to be unsatisfactory and the utility to have been illusory or apparent only. The same thing is true of disutility.

To illustrate this distinction, we may take the case of a man who desires to buy two different types of medicine, one of which will really benefit him and one of which will not. In such a case the good medicine has sound utility, the bad medicine only unsound utility.

It is perhaps worthy of note that both sound and unsound utility are purely subjective. The difference between them is not that one has apparent and the other real utility. In both cases the utility is apparent, but in one case actual consumption will produce disutilitum while in the other case it will produce utilitum.

If one has an exaggerated idea of the real utility of an article, the utility of that article is part sound and part unsound. The same is true as regards the disutility of a bad.

2. TOTAL VERSUS SPECIFIC UTILITY OR DISUTILITY

Total utility is the total utility of an entire stock of goods. Specific utility is the utility of one unit of this stock or supply. This may be illustrated in a graph as follows:

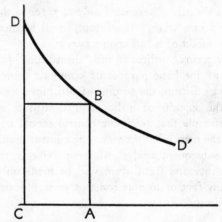

In this graph, which shows a single marginal utility curve DD', the total utility of the supply CA is $CABD$. The specific utility of the first unit of the good in question is DC.

In a similar manner the total disutility of a given quantity of bads differs from the specific disutility of any unit of it.

One of the oldest and most important sources of misunderstanding in economic theory has been the failure to distinguish between total and specific utility. The mercantilists, the classical economists, and Marx himself were puzzled by the fact that although water is more useful to man than diamonds the latter are much more valuable. This paradox cannot be solved by explaining that diamonds cost more labor to produce, for this simply moves the problem one step further back. The real problem is why men carry the production of diamonds to the point where they cost more labor than a given amount of water.

The problem exemplified in the relative prices of water and diamonds was finally solved by the more accurate definition of terms introduced by marginal utility theorists about 1870. The problem arose out of a failure to distinguish between total and specific utility. The total utility of the entire supply of water is infinite since it is essential to life. The specific utility of additional units of water, however, is small because water is abundant. On the other hand, the total utility of the entire supply of diamonds is relatively small because diamonds are luxuries which might easily be dispensed with, while the specific utility of each diamond is relatively high because of the small supply of them.

3. MARGINAL UTILITY OR DISUTILITY

No two units of any good have the same specific utility to any one person. The variation in their utility is clearly shown by the appropriate curve of diminishing utility. The utility of the last unit of any given supply, whether the recipient be an individual or a group, may be called the "marginal utility" of the article or service in question. Likewise, the specific disutility of the last unit of a given quantity of bads may be referred to as the "marginal disutility" of the bad in question.

Orthodox economists have long been accustomed to use the term "economic goods" to describe articles and services which have marginal utility, and the term "free goods"[3] to describe those which have no marginal utility. For this terminology we have substituted the terms "goods" and "bads." All articles or services which possess marginal utility at a given time and place are goods; all those which do not, i.e., all those which possess marginal disutility, are bads.

There is no intermediate condition. An overabundant article obstructs the use of the land on which it lies. Excess land increases transportation and communication costs. An overabundant service annoys the person served.

Many things called free goods by orthodox economists are really alternately goods and bads, or are goods in one place and bads in another at the same time. Sunshine and rain, for instance, are goods whenever they are scarce, and bads whenever they are overabundant.

4. NET UTILITUM AND DISUTILITUM

Net utilitum or disutilitum is the difference between the total utilitum and the total disutilitum caused by the production of a given quantity of

---

[3] The term "free goods" is particularly unfortunate since the things described are no more free than economic goods such as land and water.

goods. When the total utilitum is greater than the total disutilitum, the difference is net utilitum; when it is less, the difference is net disutilitum.

The net utilitum of goods produced by industries with increasing costs may be divided into two parts, consumers' surplus and producers' surplus. The following graph illustrates the meaning of net utilitum, consumers' surplus, and producers' surplus.

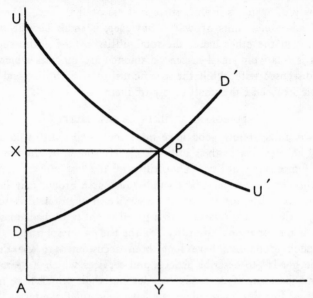

In this graph, UU' represents the utilitum of each unit produced and DD' shows the disutilitum caused by the production of each unit.[4] $AYPU$ represents the total utility of the good in question when the quantity AY is produced. Of this total utilitum a portion is offset by the total disutilitum of production, $AYPD$, leaving a surplus or net utilitum represented by DPU. This can be divided into a consumers' surplus, XPU, and a producers' surplus, DPX. In an industry of decreasing costs, there could obviously be no producers' surplus.

Net utility is the anticipated effect of the consumption of goods. If the net utility is the difference between 100 percent sound utility and

---

[4] The utility and disutility curves shown in the above graph are not supply and demand curves. A utility curve is usually somewhat higher at all points than the demand curve for the same good since a consumer does not make a price offer unless he expects to gain from the purchase, nor does a worker accept a wage offer unless he expects to gain thereby. However, when the plentifulness of a good detracts from its snob appeal, the utility curve may be below the demand curve.

100 percent sound disutility, consumption of the goods in question will yield net disutilitum equal to the previously imputed net utility.

Producers' surplus is often confused with economic rent.[5] The former is utility surplus, the latter a money surplus. The former exists in every industry, the latter only in industries of increasing cost. Every worker enjoys a producers' surplus because the hourly wage he receives is, or ought to be, equal to the marginal disutility of the last hour of labor each day, which is higher than the marginal disutility of any other hour of labor.

F. PRINCIPLES OF UTILITY AND DISUTILITY

Having analyzed and defined various types of utility and disutility, we may now turn our attention to an exposition of the principles of utility and disutility.

The principle of diminishing utility has received far more attention than any other principle of utility or disutility. It states that the marginal utility of any good diminishes as the supply of it increases. The first unit of any good consumed gives more utilitum than any subsequent unit, providing the first unit is large enough, and each additional unit consumed gives less utilitum than the previous one. Since men are familiar with this experience, the marginal utility they attribute to goods diminishes as the supply increases. Of course, this is true only if other conditions remain unaltered.

Of equal importance with the principle of diminishing utility is the principle of increasing disutility, the principle that the marginal disutility of any bad increases as the supply of it increases. The first unit of any bad has less disutilitum, i.e., involves a lower opportunity cost or gives less pain, than any additional unit of that bad, providing the initial unit is small enough; and every additional unit of this bad involves a larger opportunity cost or gives more pain than the previous unit. As disutility is an estimate of disutilitum, it tends to increase with disutilitum.

Both the principle of diminishing utility and the principle of increasing disutility are valid only when limited to a given period of time.

Since the principle of diminishing utility applies only within definite time limits, a different principle of diminishing utility may be stated for an indefinite period of time. Other factors being equal, the marginal utility of a given supply of any good diminishes as the date of its consumption is moved into the future. This may be called the principle of time preference with respect to goods.

The basis of the principle of diminishing utility of future goods is

[5] Later defined as positive rent. See pp. 158–59 below.

quite different from that of the ordinary principle of diminishing utility. Simple diminishing utility is due to satisfaction of wants and consequent decrease in their intensity. Diminishing utility in time is due to the fact that, assuming equal intensity of a want now and in the future, present consumption has more utility than future consumption.

It is possible to attempt to justify this preference for present consumption by citing the possibility of death or a change in wants, but this is mere rationalization. The important fact is that this time preference is a universal attribute of human nature.

An inverse time preference exists in the case of work or effort. The disutility of work is greatest in the immediate present, other factors being equal, and continues to diminish as the work is projected into the future.

Interest may measure either the rate at which the utility of future goods diminishes or the rate at which the disutility of future bads diminishes; or some combination of these two, depending upon the circumstances of the borrower.

The specific utility of a given unit of a certain good to a single individual is not constant; rather it is constantly changing. The desire for a certain food may vary with the condition of the consumer's liver; the desire for a certain article of clothing may depend upon the weather; and the desire for a certain amusement service may alter with every change in the mood of the individual.

It is a corollary of this principle that a given quantity of goods gives the maximum utilitum if it can be consumed at the proper time, that is, when the consumer is most eager to consume it. Hence, consumers should be given freedom as to when they consume goods.

The disutility of a given unit of work or abstinence likewise changes constantly for every individual. On certain days work is almost a pleasure; on others it is extremely unpleasant.

A corollary of this principle is that a given amount of work or abstinence occasions the least amount of disutilitum if it is done at the proper time, i.e., at those times when the disutility of labor or abstinence is at a minimum. This is an argument for permitting each individual to enjoy considerable freedom in determining what days to work or save.

No good has the same utility for any two people. If every individual consumed one orange, no two individuals would get precisely the same amount of pleasure from them. This would also be true if every individual were given a second, third, or any additional orange. The specific utilitum of each second or third or any other orange would be different for each individual.

The principle of differing utility applies not only to individual units of the same good, but also to diminishing utility curves. The diminishing utility curve of a given good is different for each individual. In the case of groups, however, particularly if they are large enough to minimize or eliminate chance variations, the curves may be very similar.

All of the foregoing considerations apply to disutility as well as to utility. The first unit of a given bad has a different amount of disutility for each individual, and the increasing disutility curve for any given bad is different for each individual.

It follows from the principles of differing utility and disutility that equal distribution of any single good cannot maximize the total utilitum secured from it, and equal distribution of a bad cannot minimize the disutilitum produced by it. To achieve these ends, it is necessary to fit the distribution of both goods and bads to individual preferences. It also follows that every increase in the size of the market for a given good may make possible the consumption of that good by someone for whom its utility is higher than its utility to any previous potential consumer. This is an argument for making all markets as large as possible.

Finally, the principle of differing utility may be applied to income as well as to specific goods. A given income possesses a widely varying utility to different individuals, and each increment to income likewise possesses a varying utility for different individuals. This particular application of the general principle of differing utility is unimportant because it is impossible to measure variations in the utility of money incomes to different persons. We must therefore assume that this utility is the same for all persons (see pp. 39–40 below).

I. THE EFFECT OF THESE PRINCIPLES UPON AN ISOLATED PERSON

To illustrate the basic importance of these principles of utility and disutility and their usefulness in the analysis of practical economic problems, we shall explain how they affect the more significant economic decisions of a rational but isolated individual, the familiar Robinson Crusoe of utility theory. We choose a rational Robinson Crusoe because this simplifies the illustration and because the remainder of this treatise is devoted to the effect which these principles of utility and disutility ought to have upon the economic decisions of man living in society.

One of the first and most important economic decisions which a rational Robinson Crusoe would be called upon to make would be that concerning the length and intensity of his own hours of labor. On any given day he would settle this problem by increasing both the length and intensity of his labor until their marginal utility are just equal to their marginal disutility.

It is worthy of special attention that this decision would not be the same on any two days, due to the fact that both the diminishing utility curve of the products of labor and the increasing disutility curve of labor itself vary from day to day and never meet in exactly the same place on different days.

A rational Robinson Crusoe would abstain from present consumption in order to maintain stores available for use in sickness or old age because, due to lower income at such times, goods would have a sufficiently higher marginal utility to compensate for the time preference for present consumption. He would also save some goods in order to increase his supply of capital and thus increase the productivity of his labor. Saving for this purpose would be carried to the point where the marginal disutility of abstinence becomes equal to the marginal utility of the resulting increase in productivity.

The total volume of production is dependent upon the quantity of the three factors in production, land, labor, and capital, which are used. Hence, when our rational Crusoe has determined the supply of labor and the supply of capital, nature having previously determined the supply of land, the total volume of production is automatically fixed, assuming a perfectly rational use of these factors.

The problem of determining how large a quantity of each good and service to produce may be called the problem of the control of production. In the case of our rational Robinson Crusoe it would be solved by carrying the production, and hence the consumption, of each individual good to the point where its marginal utility becomes equal to the marginal disutility of production.

2. THE MEASUREMENT OF UTILITY AND DISUTILITY

If the purpose of Socialism is to maximize net utility income, it is clear that some relatively accurate method of measuring various kinds of utility and disutility must be used. To provide such a method is the function of money and prices, which will therefore be discussed in the following two chapters.

In the case of an isolated individual, all choices are based upon direct sensations of pleasure and pain. With the division of labor which develops in every society, it becomes impossible for the consumer to compare his own pleasure in consumption directly with the disutilitum of production because production is carried on by other persons. Likewise, it becomes impossible for the producer to compare directly the pain and opportunity costs of production experienced by him with the pleasures of consumption experienced by other persons. Moreover, division of labor requires that many men participate in the production of each good; thus, no one of them experiences directly all the disutilitum of production. Prices, therefore, become the chief data for most economic decisions in any advanced society. They take the place of direct sensations of pleasure and pain as the grounds of economic choices. Obviously, since prices themselves are merely indirect measures of subjective sensations, their usefulness depends upon the accuracy with which they measure such sensations, that is, marginal utility and disutility.

3. COMPARABILITY OF UTILITY AND DISUTILITY TO DIFFERENT PERSONS[6]

Since the sole purpose of measuring utility in dollars is to make possible the direct comparison of the utilities and disutilities experienced by different people, it is necessary to consider whether this is possible. A number of contemporary economists have denied that it is possible to measure and compare the utility of a good to different persons.

This is a very radical theory because it means that consumers' preferences usually cannot be measured and compared and should therefore be almost completely ignored under either Capitalism or Socialism. It means that costs should be almost completely ignored because disutilitum experienced by different workers cannot be measured and compared with each other or with the utility of consumption. In other words, it destroys the validity and usefulness of nearly all economic theory, for the chief usefulness of economic theory is as a guide to policies which will maximize net utilitum.

The proponents of the theory that the utility of a good to one person cannot be compared with its utility to another have usually ignored the general implications of the theory. They have used it to criticize individual reform proposals, but have failed to realize that it applies equally to all orthodox justifications of the existing economic system, and they have not hesitated themselves to make numerous recommendations as to what economic policies would promote welfare.

The usual argument advanced to support the theory that the utility of a good to one person cannot be compared with its utility to another, is that one human being can only experience his own sensations, and therefore cannot compare the intensity of his own sensations with those of another person. If he cannot compare his own sensations with those of another person, he is even less capable of feeling and comparing the sensations of two other persons.

[6] Volumes I and II of the *Review of Economic Studies* (1933–35) contain an abstruse discussion of this problem by O. Lange, R. G. D. Allen, H. Bernadelli, and E. H. Phelps-Brown. The views of Bernadelli appear most reasonable. See also J. J. Stigler, "Social Welfare and Differential Prices," *Journal of Farm Economics*, XX (1938), 576; and Frederick V. Waugh, "Rejoinder," *ibid.*, p. 587.

This argument assumes that it is impossible to compare two sensations except by directly experiencing them. The assumption is unjustified.[7] It is possible to compare the sensations of other persons by observing their behavior. Anyone can learn by observing his own behavior that there is a high correlation between his own sensations and his own behavior. He can observe, for instance, that the price he is willing to pay for a good reflects roughly the marginal utility of that good to him. He can learn by talking to other persons that they observe the same correlation between their sensations and their behavior. Hence, it is reasonable for him to assume that by comparing their price offers he can compare their sensations, at least when incomes are equal.

It is sometimes claimed that certain persons enjoy consumption more than others, and that therefore such persons should receive proportionately more income than other men.[8] The critics of the comparability of utility often assume the above claims to be true and conclude that since it is impossible to determine who these more appreciative or greedy persons are, all efforts to compare the utilities experienced by different persons are useless.

All the steps in this argument are questionable. There may be no such more appreciative or greedy persons. Certainly a critic who denies the measurability and comparability of utility is in no position to demonstrate the existence of such persons. Even if such persons do exist, it may be unwise to favor them with higher incomes merely because they enjoy consumption more than other people. They should, of course, be free to produce more than other men, and this freedom alone might raise their earnings much above the average, particularly if there is a positive correlation between productive ability and the ability to enjoy consumption. Moreover, one of the chief purposes of a system of income distribution might be to stimulate production, and the above argument assumes that the sole purpose is to maximize the pleasures of consumption. Finally, even if individuals vary widely in their ability to enjoy consumption and even if the distribution of income could be improved by exact knowledge and use of these variations in sensitivity or greed, it still does not follow that inability to measure and use these variations in this way justifies the abandonment of all efforts to measure and compare utility. It merely

[7] The golden rule would be pointless if knowledge of the sensations of other persons were unattainable. It depends upon the valid assumption that, on the average, other persons experience the same sensations we do under similar circumstances.

[8] It would be equally logical to argue that since some men dislike work more than others, they should be given less work to do without reducing their income. This would be desirable if such differences in dislike of work could be measured and if allowing for them did not reduce indirect utility.

means that the ability of different men to enjoy income should be assumed to be equal.

It is impossible to determine in advance whether a coin will fall heads or tails, but this does not mean that no effort at prediction is possible or worth while. If a thousand coins are spun, about half of them will fall heads up and about half will fall tails up. For the same reason, if there is no way to determine whether an individual's power to enjoy consumption is above or below the average, the logical and useful assumption to make is that he has average power to enjoy consumption. This assumption makes it possible to measure and compare the utility of a good to different persons with more accuracy than any other assumption would give.

G. SUMMARY

The detailed discussion of individual points in this chapter has undoubtedly served to obscure the rather simple but extremely fundamental line of reasoning which integrates this utility theory, and which is the real justification for all subsequent discussion of price determination, cost accounting, and production control. Hence, a brief summary of this chain of reasoning may help both to clarify the present chapter and to explain the purpose of later chapters.

The purpose of economic theory and practice is to maximize net utilitum per capita. Net utilitum is the difference between utilitum (pleasure or satisfaction) and disutilitum (pain or lost pleasure), which cannot be directly measured by the economist. However, utility (anticipated pleasure) and disutility (anticipated pain or loss of pleasure), which are based upon utilitum and disutilitum and are as nearly equal to the latter as the men who directly experience utilitum and disutilitum can make them, are measurable, at least at the margin. For purposes of practical economic control, measurements of marginal utility and disutility are more useful than measurements of total utility or disutility. Hence, it is proper to base economic decisions upon measurements of marginal utility and disutility. To measure them a unit of measurement is essential. Money provides this unit of measurement, and properly determined prices measure marginal utility and disutility in terms of this unit. Accountants add and subtract these indirect measurements of satisfaction and pain, and Socialist economists should use the results of accounting to control production in such a way as to maximize net utilitum (pleasure or satisfaction) per person.

CHAPTER III. MONEY AND BANKING

A. INTRODUCTION

Since the marginal utility and disutility of goods and bads to different men can be measured and compared only in terms of money, it is fitting to pass directly from our discussion of utility to a consideration of the theory of money. The theory of banking will also be discussed in this chapter, for commercial banks are the most important factors affecting the quantity and value of money under Capitalism, and might continue to play the same role in a Socialist economy.

Bourgeois economists have rarely appreciated the outstanding importance of monetary theory in the political economy of Capitalism. They have suffered from the delusion that money is merely a veil which hides but does not seriously affect the actual course of economic developments. As a matter of fact, monetary theory provides the explanation and the remedy for the greatest evil of Capitalism that can be cured without eliminating Capitalism, namely, the business cycle.[1] Many other basic economic problems fall within its scope, also. Under Socialism, however, monetary theory will be of much less importance, both because the monetary system will be greatly simplified and because the effect of monetary disturbances upon the prosperity of the nation will be largely eliminated. For these reasons, monetary theory will not be given the attention here which it ought to receive in any general work on the economic theory of a Capitalist economy.

B. A DEFINITION OF MONEY

A vast amount of confusion in monetary theory has been caused by the continued use of an obsolete definition of the term "money." There was a time only a few centuries ago when what is now called money was

---

[1] The long delay in the use of monetary measures to eliminate the business cycle has done much to stimulate the growth of the world Socialist movement. It has made plausible the Marxian dogma that cycles of increasing severity are inherent in the nature of Capitalism.

While proper monetary control could eliminate the business cycle under Capitalism, this would put an end to periods of abnormally full employment as well as to periods of unusual unemployment. Elimination of business cycles under Capitalism would distribute the great evils of business depressions evenly over every year; it would not eliminate the evils themselves. However, the total disutility of a given amount of unemployment is considerably less when distributed evenly over every year than when concentrated in a few years.

the only thing that performed the functions of money. Today, however, what bourgeois economists call money is used in less than 10 percent of payments in the United States, demand deposits being used in the other 90 percent or more. Money, however, ought to be defined as anything which performs the function of money, that of serving to a significant degree as a means of payment.[2] This is the meaning which we shall use.

Many Socialists have thought that the new society could rid itself of money, and the alleged evils connected with its use, merely by using labor-hours instead of dollars, francs, or marks as units of value. This is an unfortunate illusion based upon the belief that a change in name only will give us a new object. The problem of determining prices in pieces of paper or bookkeeping units called labor hours is just as complicated as the problem of fixing prices in terms of units called dollars and cents. The benefits and evils connected with the use of each unit are the same, provided they are used in the same manner. No object whatsoever is gained by calling one money and refusing to call the other money.

While every means of payment is money, according to our definition, this does not include savings accounts or private credit. Savings accounts, unlike demand deposits, must be turned into money before they can be spent. Savings accounts are merely footsteps left by the passage of money at some past time. They are no more money than any other evidence of investment.

Private credit likewise is not a means of payment; it is a postponement of payment. It cannot increase total sales because it curtails the purchasing power of the creditor as much as it increases the purchasing power of the debtor. However, it may increase the velocity of circulation of money.

C. THE FUNCTION OF MONEY

According to orthodox bourgeois economists, money is a result of the division of labor, and its primary function is to facilitate the exchange of goods made necessary by the division of labor. This theory no doubt helps to explain the historical origin and rise of money, but it is applicable only to an individualistic society and is not valid for a Socialist economy.

The very concept of exchange implies individual production and the need of exchanging the goods of one specialized producer for those of other specialized producers. It applies much more literally to commodities

[2] The qualification, "to a significant degree," is important. Nearly all forms of wealth are occasionally used as a means of payment, but the volume of business transacted with coins, paper money, and demand deposits is probably 99.9 percent of the total.

than to services. Both barter and exchange occur in their purest forms only between individuals. For exchange of this type, money should have intrinsic value; it should be a convenient, durable, valuable, and divisible commodity which can be literally exchanged for its own value in some other commodity. Such money merely serves to introduce uniformity into one of the elements in the primitive barter process.

The displacement of the individual handicraft producer by the capitalist and the rapid vertical integration of industry have steadily reduced the sphere of economic activity within which exchange is necessary. These processes are going on today at a pace more rapid than ever before. Capitalism is eliminating exchange because it is eliminating independent producers. Employees of the same corporation do not exchange goods with each other. State Capitalism might abandon exchange entirely. Exchange no longer exists when all commodities and services are produced by a single producer, the state, for there are no others with whom to carry on exchange—except, of course, foreign producers. Both State Capitalism and State Socialism, in their purest form, eliminate domestic exchange completely and substitute for it the distribution among individual workers of the goods collectively produced by them.

It follows that under Socialism money will not serve to facilitate exchange. It would be as easy to establish a detailed division of labor and a smooth flow of commodities from process to process in a moneyless Socialist economy as it now is to do so in a great industrial plant. True, the cost of the finished products would not be known, and these finished products would have to be divided up among the workers in an arbitrary manner, but exchange would not exist and there would be no obstacle to the division of labor.[3]

In a Socialist economy, a monetary unit would be needed to perform one vital function and money would be needed to perform a second vital function. A monetary unit would be needed to serve as a common denominator making possible the measurement and comparison of different kinds of utility and disutility.[4] All science is based upon the possibility and use of measurement; and political economy, while conceivable in a moneyless state, is nevertheless greatly facilitated by the use of money.

[3] Thus D. H. Robertson is in error when he remarks: "The existence of money then seems to be a necessary condition for any great development of the division of labor. . . . ." *Money* (Harcourt, Brace and Company, Inc., New York, 1922), p. 8.

[4] This is what bourgeois texts mean when they say that money is not only a "medium of exchange" but also a "standard of value." Robertson points out that it is not money itself, but the unit in which money is expressed, that serves as a "standard of value" or as a common denominator for different kinds of utility and disutility.

Unfortunately, a monetary unit does not measure a fixed and concrete thing. An inch or an hour is relatively fixed in value, but a monetary unit is constantly fluctuating. To be sure, the value of money could be made far more stable than it has ever been under Capitalism. But even if a monetary unit were relatively stable in purchasing power, it would still be a very imperfect measure of that which it is designed to measure— namely, subjective utility and disutility. Given a stabilized price level, doubling the total output of goods would double the monetary measure of national income. Because of diminishing utility, however, this 100 per-cent increase in output measured in money would not represent a 100 per-cent increase in either gross or net utility income. Other cases in which totals expressed in terms of money varied independently of totals ex-pressed in utility or disutility might be cited. Defects in the money system of measurement are both obvious and important, but money is nonetheless the best available unit of measure in economics.

Money, or the use of money, makes possible the maximum freedom of choice for the individual as a consumer and as a worker. In the absence of money it would be necessary to divide up economic goods among all consumers in some fairly uniform and arbitrary manner by the use of ration cards or orders. It is true that each consumer might be given a choice between several, indeed many, different ration cards; but it would be impossible to permit anywhere near the degree of freedom of choice made possible by the payment of wages in money.[5]

[5] "The first great achievement of money is that it enables man as consumer to generalize his purchasing power, and to make his claims on society in the form which suits him best. If there were no money, people would have to be paid for their services in kind; and whether they were strictly rationed, or whether they were allowed to help themselves to an unlimited extent, in either case there would be waste. For in the former case they would be encouraged to take more of certain goods and services, and forced to take less of others, than they really required; and in the latter case they would be tempted to be extravagant all round. The existence of a monetary economy helps society to discover what people want and how much they want it, and so to decide what shall be pro-duced and in what quantities, and to make the best use of its limited productive power. And it helps each member of society to insure that the means of enjoy-ment to which he has access yield him the greatest amount of actual enjoyment which is within his reach—it gives him the chance of not surfeiting himself with bus rides or stinting himself unduly of the countenance of Charlie Chaplin.
". . . . Those who have given rein to their fancy in delineating the ideal economic society of the future have often contemplated some system of doles or rationing for the distribution of those staple commodities of which all human beings stand in need. But since even such an ideal society would not be likely to be infinitely rich, the total claim which any individual could make upon it would still have to be limited; and since individual tastes and requirements would presumably continue to differ, people would still have to be given a

It should be noted that the use of money gives the consumer freedom of choice concerning the time of consumption as well as concerning the goods to be consumed. It serves as a claim upon national income which may be exercised at any time.[6]

A further advantage is that the freedom of choice of the seller of labor power, the worker, is also materially increased by the use of money. In the absence of money it would be necessary to compel all workers to do a relatively uniform amount of work in order to secure ration cards. By using money and piece rates, however, it is possible to permit each worker to determine how long or how much work he will do each day. It is also possible to distribute workers among different plants and industries by merely raising or lowering money wages, thus giving the worker complete freedom of choice of occupation and place of work.

Many Socialists have opposed the use of money in a Socialist economy. In some cases their arguments have been purely verbal; that is, they have argued against the use of money and then proposed its use under a different name, such as labor hours. In other cases these arguments have been based upon a confusion of money with capital, or a fear of the possibility of "usury." If money is used in a Socialist economy, it is claimed, private citizens will be able to accumulate money and indulge in usury, thus destroying the economic equality which is the goal of Socialism.[7] This argument overlooks the ease with which a Socialist government could enforce any prohibition of private banking. For instance, the state might

---

certain amount of latitude and discretion with regard to the form in which they presented part at any rate of their claims. In other words, money of some kind—certificates, that is to say, of a general title to real income, to be interpreted and particularized by the individual—would have to persist. The need for money then seems to be a fundamental, if a given volume of productive power—a given poise of mankind in his relations with nature—is to be made to yield the greatest harvest of individual satisfaction which it is capable of yielding." D. H. Robertson, *op. cit.*, p. 6.

[6] This is quite different from serving as a "store of value." Only money of intrinsic value serves this function, and no money of this kind should be used under Socialism.

[7] In *Socialism: A Critical Analysis* (1911), O. D. Skelton, after dismissing as impractical the abolition of money in a Socialist state, remarks:

"The retention of money, however, brings new complications with the possibility involved of lending it at interest and thus perpetuating economic inequality and economic 'exploitation.' Men would differ in their discount of the future then as now. Could the Red Pope succeed better than the Black in the attempt to repress the taking of usury?" (p. 198).

Marx clearly recognized that the exploitation of labor under Capitalism is based, not upon the use of money, but upon the separation of the worker from the tools and materials he must use. See *Capital*, II, 39.

offer small loans at a rate low enough to eliminate all profit, or it might control all transfers of money by requiring them to be made through checks on the state bank. The danger of private usury offers little ground for condemning the use of money under Socialism.

D. THE MONETARY STANDARD

In a primitive economic society, or in one not possessing a stable and powerful government, money must have intrinsic utility since the public cannot depend upon the government's maintaining the purchasing power of money which lacks intrinsic value. It is natural, therefore, that specific commodities should have been used as money long before the introduction of paper or token money. Gold and silver were the favorite. commodities used for this purpose, since they are durable, divisible without loss, universally used, and combine large exchange value with small bulk. Coinage served to guarantee the weight and fineness of these precious metals.

Paper money was first used in the form of a promise to pay gold or silver. After men had used gold and silver for monetary purposes for thousands of years, they naturally came to regard these metals, or at least intrinsic value, as a necessary foundation for all money. Custom is the most convincing logic for the vast majority of men. Not until accidental experience taught them that paper money could retain its purchasing power after the specie reserves behind it had disappeared, did they begin to understand the superfluous character of specie reserves. Even today many monetary theorists still contend that when a nation temporarily goes off the gold standard its money retains a normal domestic purchasing power only because of the anticipated return to a gold standard. Actually, however, the domestic purchasing power of a nation's money has no relation whatsoever to the quantity of metallic reserves behind it. Not only are such reserves entirely superfluous for domestic monetary purposes; they are also very expensive. The twenty-billion-dollar gold reserve of the United States involves a complete loss of the interest on that sum, about six hundred million dollars a year, plus the cost of guarding the hoard.[8] Its sole

[8] One of the many curious features of bourgeois banking theory is the radical difference in the treatment of gold reserves behind the two major forms of bank money. The United States requires a gold reserve behind bank notes much larger than the reserve required behind demand deposits. Moreover, most bank notes are guaranteed 100 percent by the government while demand deposits enjoy only partial protection. Since demand deposits serve as the principal medium of circulation in the United States, being used in about 90 percent of all payments, it would seem that their safety is at least as important as that of bank notes.

possible use is to balance international payments upon some occasions, which could be done far more economically by short-term foreign loans. Over any given period of time, moreover, the balance of payment to foreign nations can easily be altered by proper control over import and export trade, as explained in chapter xx of the present work.

The money used in a Socialist economy should possess no intrinsic value. Paper, tin, or bookkeeping entries will serve as well as gold and silver, and will be much less expensive. No specie reserves should be maintained behind this currency. If a Socialist state is alone in a hostile gold-standard world, as the U.S.S.R. was for a time, there is some justification for a national store of gold and silver to be used to balance international trade and to increase imports quickly in time of war. Even in such a case, however, the national treasure should not be used even ostensibly as a reserve behind the national currency. This is an unnecessary concession to antiquated bourgeois monetary theory.

A Socialist economy should use only three types of money. It should satisfy the total demand for small change by making pennies, nickels, dimes, and quarters out of the cheapest suitable material. The use of nickel, silver, and copper is wasteful because they are too expensive and too heavy. In addition to the necessary supply of small coins, a Socialist economy should possess the proper amount of paper money in convenient denominations. The third form of money should be demand deposits transferable by check. To facilitate proper control of the total supply of money, all demand deposits should have a 100 percent cash reserve behind them. The fallacies involved in commercial banking, which may be defined as the lowering of such reserves below 100 percent, are described below.

The government should pay the costs of coinage and of printing paper money since these costs will be small and difficult to allocate. The costs of maintaining checking accounts and of clearing checks, however, should be charged to depositors. Under Capitalism there is seldom any adequate deterrent to the abuse of checking accounts. Handling checks costs about five cents per check. The number of checks drawn each year would be much smaller if those who occasion this social cost had to pay it.

E. THE PURCHASING POWER OF MONEY

The purchasing power of money is often called the value of money by bourgeois economists. The former phrase is preferable because it does not lead to confusion with the interest rate, popularly known as the value of money, and because, for reasons to be explained later, it is desirable to reduce to a minimum the use of the term "value."

Money has purchasing power over goods in general, over special groups of goods, and over individual goods. Purchasing power over goods in general is what is ordinarily meant when the phrase, "the purchasing power of money," is used.

I. PRICE LEVELS

The purchasing power of money over goods in general is indicated by the price level of economic goods in general, with which it varies inversely and proportionately. When the price level increases by 100 percent, the purchasing power of money declines by 50 percent. The purchasing power of money over every special group of economic goods is likewise shown by a special price level which varies in inverse proportion to it. Hence, the problem of controlling the purchasing power of money is identical with the problem of controlling some price level.

The measurement of price levels involves many technical problems which are not discussed here. No index number or estimated price level is absolutely accurate. Nevertheless, the best available index numbers are sufficiently accurate to make relatively accurate control over the purchasing power of money perfectly feasible. In selecting an index number for this purpose, the primary problem is to choose the index of the right goods rather than to choose the most accurate index.

The purchasing power of the money of a Socialist economy should possess a high degree of stability. Individual prices should rise or fall in such a way as to balance supply and demand, but the price level itself should be relatively stable for a number of reasons.

In the first place, stability of the purchasing power of money is desirable in order to facilitate the operation of the system of production control recommended in this treatise. This system, as explained later, is one of response to marginal profits and losses. Price-level changes distort marginal profits and losses and make a general correction or adjustment of them necessary if they are to serve as guides to production control. Inflation increases all profits and decreases all losses; deflation has the opposite effect. It would be possible to allow for such effects by changing the rules for interpreting profits and losses, but this would introduce an additional and unnecessary complication in the process of production control.

In the second place, stability of purchasing power is desirable in order to make monetary statistics for different periods of time directly comparable without correction for changes in the price level. For instance, figures on national income during different years, or on national wealth at different times, ought to be directly comparable in order to facilitate their comprehension and use by voters.

In the third place, stability of the purchasing power of money is desirable because changes in price levels result in corresponding changes in nominal wages and in the cost of living. This confuses the workers, for they habitually treat changes in nominal wages as changes in real wages, failing to observe and react immediately to changes in the cost of living. Moreover, frequent changes in nominal wages and in the cost of living tend to make family budgets useless, unless expressed in percentages. Whenever the price level changes, every consumer must learn the new value of money and alter his expenditures for each good. This is a gross inconvenience even if properly and promptly effected, and it is, of course, impossible for all consumers to do it properly and promptly.

The purpose of stabilization should determine the selection of the price level to be stabilized. For instance, if the sole purpose is to make statistics of national wealth at different times directly comparable, it is the price level of land, capital goods, and durable consumable goods that should be stabilized. On the other hand, if the purpose is to make directly comparable the national income statistics for different years, the price level of all consumable and capital goods should be stabilized. Obviously, it is easier to decide which price level to stabilize when there is only one purpose to be served than when there are two or more.

In the present instance, stabilization has at least three important purposes. These are: (1) to facilitate the use of profits and losses as guides to proper control of production, (2) to make possible direct comparison of economic statistics for different periods of time, and (3) to eliminate fluctuations in wages and prices which confuse the worker and consumer because they do not correspond to changes in real wages and real costs.

The first purpose noted above can best be served by the stabilization of the price level of consumable and capital end products and services sold for a price, because the production of all such goods should be controlled by profits and losses. Only retail prices or prices paid by the final buyer should be stabilized, since some goods, such as services, have no distinct wholesale price, and since price changes which do not affect the price paid by the final buyer do not affect the total net profit or loss for all stages in production.

As regards the second of the purposes enumerated above, the selection of a price level depends upon which series of statistical data is to be made consistent. We have already noted the two different price levels which should be stabilized in order to make statistics on national wealth and national income comparable at different times. Unquestionably there is some one price level whose stabilization would benefit all statistical series the most; but it is difficult to tell which price level this is. Probably it is the most general price level of all, namely a price level of all transactions, since this is the only one that would be affected by all the prices which enter into statistical data.

The third purpose named, to avoid price changes which confuse the worker and consumer, is best served by the stabilization of the cost of living—that is, of all consumable goods and services. Real wages are not affected by changes in the prices of capital goods unless such changes affect the cost of living.

Since each of the three purposes regarded as most important is best served by the .stabilization of a different price level, it is necessary to choose on the basis of the relative importance of these three purposes, with due reference to the effect of the stabilization of each price level on the two purposes it does not serve so well.

First, let us rate the relative importance of the three purposes of stabilization. Purposes number one and three are undoubtedly more important than purpose number two, since both affect directly the vital problem of what and how much to produce and consume. Moreover, while economic statistics can easily be adjusted for price changes before being published, adjustment of profits and losses is more difficult, and adjustment of wages or market prices by the ordinary worker-consumer is entirely impractical. Since it would be more difficult for the worker-consumer to adjust (deflate or inflate) his wages for changes in the cost of living than it would be for those who control production to adjust profits and losses for changes in the price level, the third purpose is more important than the first.

Considering each of the three price levels selected above with respect to the two purposes for which it is not perfectly suited, we may now note that the price level of all finished consumer and capital goods is so similar to the cost of living that one can be substituted for the other with no marked effect. On the other hand, the transactions price level is quite different from each of the others and hence cannot be used to accomplish purposes one and three.

The outcome of this analysis is that the cost of living is probably the best price level to stabilize in a Socialist economy. The price level of all consumer and capital goods is only slightly less suitable, however.[9]

Thus far we have failed to mention weighting. All prices included in the cost of living, or in any other price level or index, should be properly weighted. That is, they should be multiplied or divided by a factor which will indicate their importance. Weighting of the cost-of-living price level or index should be done in such a way that the proportion of each price to the sum of all prices used will be the same as the propor-

---

[9] In a Capitalist economy it would be much more desirable to stabilize the wholesale price level than either of these, since the chief purpose would naturally be to stabilize profits. The wholesale price level fluctuates much more widely than the cost of living, and these fluctuations affect profits and losses directly.

tion of the value of the annual consumption of the good in question to the total value of all consumer goods sold in that year.

In order to stabilize the purchasing power of money, it is necessary to understand the nature and relative importance of the factors which determine the price level.

The price level is primarily dependent upon four factors, each of which varies independently of the others, but varies in such a way that a certain equilibrium is maintained between them. These facts are most clearly stated in the form of the familiar equation of exchange.

$$M \times V = P \times T$$

In this equation, M stands for the total volume of money, V for the velocity of circulation (the average number of times it changes hands in a given period), P for the price level, and T for the total number of transactions.[10]

While the price level thus depends directly upon three different factors, and each of these in turn upon innumerable others, the volume of money is the most important. This is true largely because M is easily controlled, while the other factors are not subject to direct or accurate control and are, moreover, more stable than M. Under Capitalism both V and T go through marked cycles, but Socialism will eliminate these by eliminating the business cycle.[11] Both V and P also possess definite secular trends which will probably continue under Socialism. Certainly T will continue

[10] Marx was one of the first economists to enumerate these four factors and discuss their relationships (*Capital*, I, 132–40). Apparently he confused "the mass of commodities" with T at certain times. . . . . "If the mass of commodities remain constant, the quantity of circulating money varies with the fluctuations in the prices of those commodities" (p. 134). A page further on, however, he gives a form of the equation of exchange which takes V into consideration and does not confuse "the mass of commodities" with T. ". . . . The quantity of money functioning as the circulating medium is equal to the sum of the price of the commodities divided by the number of moves made by coins of the same denomination." The qualification, "of the same denomination," is decidedly vague, but the context indicates that Marx is referring to the velocity of circulation of money. If this statement is translated into our terms, we have $M = \dfrac{PT}{V}$, one form of the equation of exchange.

[11] Under Capitalism, cyclical fluctuations in V are much greater than cyclical fluctuations in M. Both types of fluctuation are caused by business cycles—or at least are a necessary precondition. However, V is uncontrollable in a free nation, where consumers can do as they please with their funds. Hence we emphasize in this chapter control of M only. This one factor is completely under social control and can easily be altered to offset all changes in V or T, thus maintaining P unaltered or stable.

to increase steadily. However, the effect of any other variations in V and T can very easily be eliminated by proper control of M.[12]

The steady upward trend of T, about 3 percent a year even under Capitalism, will make necessary a proportional annual increase in M. This creation of new paper money required to maintain a stable price level will provide the government with a very considerable source of income. The treatment of this income is discussed in a later chapter.

Nothing can influence the purchasing power of money except by altering one or more of the three factors—M, V, and T. Many bourgeois writers appear to believe that such things as the size of the gold reserve, the balance of trade, the relationship of government income to government expenses, etc., can directly affect the purchasing power of money—i.e., the price level—without altering M, V, or T. These theories are unsound.

The equation of exchange also makes clear that every change in M, the quantity of money, must alter P, the price level, inversely and proportionately, V and T remaining constant. In other words, an increase in the supply of the medium of exchange always causes inflation, while a decrease has the opposite effect, other factors remaining unaltered.

2. BANK CREDIT AND INFLATION

In actual practice, of course, it is impossible to alter M, and hence P, without at the same time affecting V and T. Many bourgeois economists have attempted to use this confusing fact to prove that new bank credit (one form of money) created and placed in circulation by commercial banks does not ordinarily cause inflation. They assert that since new bank credit is ordinarily loaned to producers who use it to create an equal value of new wealth, thus increasing T, no inflation results.

This argument is 90 percent unsound because it ignores the fact that an increase in T must be *proportional* to the increase in M in order to

[12] Marx repudiated the quantity theory of money, the theory that the quantity of money determines the price level (*Capital*, I, 132–40). His repudiation was based, not upon the inexact statement of the theory conventional in his day, but upon the belief that the value, or cost of production, of gold determines its purchasing power. This erroneous doctrine is still held by certain important bourgeois monetary theorists—Cannan, Shaw, and Laughlin, for instance. Of course, the cost of production of gold does have some effect upon its purchasing power, but only because and in so far as it alters the quantity of money. Since the store of gold used for monetary purposes is very large, twenty to thirty times as large as one year's production of gold, and since the quantity of gold is only one factor influencing the quantity of money, the cost of production of gold has no appreciable effect upon the quantity of money or the price level in a short period of time. Rather, the price level determines the marginal costs of gold production, and hence of the amount of gold produced.

prevent inflation. This is clearly impossible, except in very exceptional cases. The income of the United States in normal years is about three times the size of M; its wealth is about ten times M's size. Thus, even if a new bank loan causes an equal absolute increase in the volume of money and the volume of wealth and income, it by no means prevents inflation; it merely reduces it slightly, something like 5 or 10 percent. This point can be made clear by assuming the creation of enough new bank credit to double M as it was in 1929, namely thirty billions, and a simultaneous increase of thirty billion dollars' worth of capital goods as a result of forced saving. Doubling the supply of money would cause a 100 percent increase in the price level, T and V remaining the same. An addition of thirty billions to the national wealth of 350 billions in 1929 would have increased T, in all probability, by much less than 10 percent, because a 10 percent increase in T would require an equal increase in the supply of labor. Moreover, since most bourgeois economists who claim that new bank credit increases T do not even admit that commercial banking increases the supply of physical capital, it is difficult to see how they have any grounds at all for believing that T is increased sufficiently to prevent inflation.

3. METHODS OF CONTROL

Granting, then, that all changes in M have an inflationary effect upon prices and that a Socialist government should stabilize the price level primarily through exercising complete control over M, we come next to the question of the method of control to be used.

In the first place, this control should be vested in the State Bank. That organization should have a Monetary Control Division to carry on this function. This division should employ expert economists and monetary theorists, not practical bankers, and should possess all powers necessary to control the quantity of money in circulation.

There are a number of different methods which might be used by the Division of Monetary Control either to place money in circulation or to withdraw it. Each method has special advantages and disadvantages.

In the first place, newly created money could be placed in circulation by using it as monetary capital and loaning it to various trusts and departments. It could be taken out of circulation merely by calling loans and refusing to reloan the proceeds. Commercial banks increase and decrease the supply of money in this way under Capitalism, but of course there is no national planning. As a result, this alternate creation and destruction of money in the form of bank credit widens rather than restricts natural fluctuations in the price level. However, the advantages and disadvantages of this method of controlling the supply of money are quite different under Capitalism from what they would be under Socialism.[18]

If new money is used as monetary capital in a Socialist economy, the result is the creation of new physical capital, with all the usual benefits of new investment and without any conscious or voluntary individual saving or abstinence on the part of the public. In proper amounts, such new money prevents deflation and thus avoids an increase in real wages without altering nominal wages. The real purchasing power thus taken from consumers may be used to build additional new machinery and erect additional new factory buildings, stores, homes, etc.

The significant aspect of this type of saving is that it is ordinarily unconscious and involuntary. In a democratic state it may be voluntary, in one sense, if the public understands and approves of what is done. It cannot be said to be voluntary under Capitalism, however, because the public is unconscious of the entire process. Workers would not knowingly permit a few private bankers to appropriate the control of and the interest from capital which consists, in the main, of workers' savings.

If a Socialist economy had difficulty in saving and creating the desired amount of capital, it might be expedient to use new money as capital. Saving is easier when it is partly or wholly unconscious. By neglecting to teach its citizens the significance of the process of forced saving, a Socialist government could keep this saving entirely unconscious and involuntary.

On the other hand, if Socialism tends to result in an excessive accumulation of capital, the partly unconscious aspect of this type of saving may prove very undesirable. Oversaving is a real possibility under Socialism since it is probably easier to vote that the nation should save than it is to do the saving personally. The semi-unconscious nature of the type of saving we are dealing with also tends to reduce the disutility of saving and thus to result in oversaving.

Another advantage of placing new funds in circulation by loaning them to trusts and departments is that this reduces the clerical work to a minimum. There would be only a few-score possible borrowers in a Socialist economy, and it would be easy to distribute the new funds among them. The withdrawal of money from circulation by calling loans and refusing to renew them has a similar advantage as a means of taking money out of circulation.

With respect to the effect upon saving and the supply of capital, however, the withdrawal of money from circulation by calling loans has

[18] For instance, it is difficult to increase bank credit and bank loans at the bottom of a depression under Capitalism. It will never be difficult to increase bank loans in a Socialist economy.

advantages and disadvantages just the opposite of those resulting from the expansion of circulation through granting new loans. In other words, it is undesirable when saving is insufficient, and desirable when oversaving occurs. Since, however, the secular trend in production will continue to be upward under Socialism, the need to reduce the supply of money by calling loans would be relatively infrequent. Indeed, any minor degree of inflation could be cured merely by refusing for a sufficient period of time to expand the circulation further.

A second and quite distinct method of placing new money in circulation would be to use new funds to meet the costs of free economic services, usually referred to by Capitalist economists as the cost of government. This would permit a reduction in the tax rates or an increase in the supply of free services. When necessary, money could be taken out of circulation merely by increasing taxes without increasing expenditures.

One advantage of this technique for controlling the supply of money in circulation is that it involves virtually no costs. Taxes must be collected and free services paid for in any case. A change in the tax rate, the sole effect of using new money to meet some of the cost of these services or of withdrawing money from circulation in the above manner, involves no costs at all since it will be as easy to collect a tax of one size as another in a Socialist economy.

A second advantage of varying tax rates in order to control the volume of money in circulation is that it would make possible a direct and immediate effect upon consumers' purchases. In a Socialist economy most taxes should fall directly upon consumers. They would be collected daily in the case of sales taxes, and every payday in the case of income or poll taxes. Thus a change in one of these taxes would almost immediately alter the buying power of the public and affect the price level. This would make possible a very close and accurate control over prices.[14]

It would only be necessary to raise or lower the tax rates in order to offset small and unpredictable changes in the price level. The state could always plan in advance upon using a definite amount of new money to pay for free services, and would only need to change the existing tax rate in order to offset the effect of chance fluctuations in V and T (see page 52). In other words, it would not be necessary to reduce constantly the general tax rate in order to prevent deflation in the price level. The

---

[14] In connection with the use of changes in the sales tax rate in order to control the price level, it should perhaps be emphasized that an increase in the sales tax may be used to lower prices, including sales tax. If the money raised by increasing the sales tax is taken out of circulation, the price level must fall. The higher the sales tax used for this purpose, the greater will be the resulting decline in prices. There is no limit to the price deflation which may be secured through increasing a sales tax.

secular tendency toward deflation could normally be offset by the creation of new money and by its use to pay the costs involved in providing free services and commodities.

The chief disadvantage of placing new money in circulation by using it to meet the costs of free services is that it would almost certainly stimulate unduly the production of free services. If the people do not pay in taxes for every dollar of free service given them, they are likely to underestimate the marginal disutility involved in providing these services. It is easy for a government to be lavish with free goods that cost it nothing except the small pains involved in creating new money.

A second disadvantage of this method of increasing the supply of money is that it may cause the government to be influenced by improper considerations, such as the need for free services, in controlling the quantity of money. If new money is used to pay for free goods, then the government may be tempted to increase the supply of money merely to pay for more free goods.

A third method of alternately increasing and decreasing the volume of money in circulation is that of buying and selling government securities, the "open-market operations" of Capitalism. These are now carried on by central reserve banks primarily in order to control interest rates or gold movements, rather than to stabilize prices; but they are suitable for the latter purpose as well. Unfortunately, it is impossible to determine in advance whether open-market operations alone would be sufficient to stabilize the cost of living.

There should be no government bonds outstanding in a Socialist economy (see page 60). However, the purchase of savings accounts for ready cash would have precisely the same effect as the purchase of government bonds.

The comparison of government bonds with savings deposits helps to make clear the principal disadvantages of open-market operations as a means of social control over the supply of money. If individuals possess bonds or savings deposits, it is because they wish to save, to exchange present funds for an interest income and the possibility of obtaining future funds at any time. Open-market purchase of bonds or savings accounts does not eliminate this desire to save; it merely forces it to use some other channel. That is why it is relatively ineffective under Capitalism as a means of controlling prices. It might be made much more effective under Socialism, since the government would control all means of saving, but its effectiveness would involve a restriction of personal liberty, for people would be forced to spend when they desired to save or vice versa. Hence, open-market operations would be an undesirable means of controlling the supply of money and the price level.

A fourth method of controlling the quantity of money is to create new money and give it directly to the public without demanding any good or service in exchange. Little expense would be involved in the addition of small sums of new money to income payments which must be made anyway. In case of inflation, money could be temporarily withdrawn from circulation by any of the methods previously discussed, but the mere cessation of the issue of new money might be sufficient.

The fundamental advantage of this method of placing new money in circulation is that it does not result in an artificial stimulus either to saving or to the provision of certain types of goods and services. When new money is used as monetary capital, it pushes saving beyond the optimum point, that at which the marginal utility and disutility of abstinence become equal, because it hides or obscures the actual process and disutility of saving by causing unconscious or involuntary saving. When new money is used to finance free services, it has a similar effect upon them. On the other hand, if new money is given directly to consumers, they will spend it for various purposes according to their individual desires, thus stimulating each type of production and saving by the ideal amount only. For these reasons, monthly distribution direct to consumers is the best method of placing new money directly in circulation.

It is now impossible to predict in advance the effect upon the price level of specific changes in the supply of money. By eliminating cyclical changes in V, Socialism will make this task much easier than it now is, and prolonged experimentation will greatly increase our knowledge of the effect of different quantities of new money and of different methods of putting it in use. In the meantime, the Monetary Control Division should merely increase or decrease the supply of money until the desired effect upon prices is produced.

F. BANKING UNDER SOCIALISM

Under Capitalism the relationship between monetary and banking theory is extraordinarily close. Indeed, a large portion of bourgeois banking theory is essentially monetary theory. Hence, money and banking are usually treated in the same chapter of a book on economics, or in the same specialized text or treatise.

In a Socialist economy the situation will be quite different—at least if the principles set forth in this treatise are followed. Banks will no longer create new money and place it in circulation, nor will they make loans or investments. Consequently, banking theory will no longer be monetary theory, or have any close relationship to it. In other words,

there is no particular reason why a treatise on the economic theory of a
Socialist economy should treat money and banking in the same or con-
secutive chapters. A more logical plan would be to discuss banking as
one of many service industries under Socialism. In other words, the care
of money is more closely related to the warehousing of commodities and
to other similar services than to monetary theory. Nevertheless, in this
pioneer treatise on the economic theory of a Socialist economy we shall
follow orthodox practice and discuss banking theory in the same chapter
as monetary theory in order to emphasize the wide difference between the
monetary and the banking theory of a Socialist economy.

Except for the need of emphasizing the great difference between
bourgeois banking theory and Socialist banking theory, it would be unnecessary to devote much space to a discussion of Socialist banking. Socialism will greatly simplify banking theory and practice. Most of the banking theory laboriously developed by bourgeois banking theorists since the
seventeenth century will be useless in a Socialist economy and most of
the practical experience and knowledge of capitalist bankers will be
equally unnecessary. Moreover, the simplicity of the new banking system
is such that no new body of similarly complex theory will need to be developed.

I. ORGANIZATION OF BANKING

There should be only one bank in a Socialist economy, the State Bank.
It should have branches in all parts of the nation, distributed according
to the local demand for their services. The costly duplication of bank
buildings and services so characteristic of Capitalism should of course be
entirely eliminated, each plant or farm community having one banking
office, and one only, located adjacent to or inside the community department store.

These local banking offices should be grouped into local districts and
placed under a local supervisor in much the same manner as chain stores.
Only experience and repeated experiments can indicate how large such
local districts should be. These local districts in turn should be grouped
into a few great regional divisions, such as the twelve federal reserve
districts, directly under the national headquarters.

Thanks to the simplicity and uniformity of banking under Socialism,
the local banking offices would not have very much or very important
work to do. All important problems should be settled at the central office.
All forms should be standardized, all procedure made uniform, all equipment simplified and made as nearly uniform as possible by experts employed at headquarters. The intermediate executives would only need to
check up on local obedience to orders sent out from headquarters. Eval-

uation of the ability of local managers should be based almost entirely upon operating reports submitted by the accounting department. Of course, an effective system of auditing would be of vital importance.

2. FUNCTIONS OF THE STATE BANK

The State Bank of a Socialist economy should cease to perform the most important functions of Capitalist banks, should continue to perform certain other functions of Capitalist banks, and should begin to perform at least three important new functions (see pages 65–66).

In the first place, there would be no need for any type of investment banking under Socialism. By eliminating private corporations and capitalists, Socialism would obviously put an end to the sale of private securities.

Moreover, the sale of government bonds would be unnecessary and undesirable under Socialism. If every citizen were free to deposit his savings in the State Bank and to receive the market rate of interest, less only the costs of handling his account, there would be no reason for the government to offer its securities for sale in order to raise capital. All savings deposits in the State Bank would be entirely at the disposal of the government, and nothing would be gained by converting savings deposits into government bonds. Government securities would be no more secure than deposits in the State Bank, and the rate of interest ought to be the same on both. A rate of interest above or below the market rate would be economically unsound in both cases.

In the second place, Socialism would automatically eliminate 99 percent of the business of trust companies and trust departments of private banks handling the estates of wealthy individuals. Under Socialism there should be no large estates, and the small estates should consist entirely of personal property, government pensions, and deposits in the State Bank, which would require no trust department supervision.

In the third place, the State Bank should not invest or loan any of the funds placed in its care. It should merely credit these deposits to the account of the Bureau of Capital Supply, and thus pass on to this latter organization the task of investing these funds, in order to centralize control over all new investment.

In the fourth place, the State Bank should abandon all commercial banking activities. Commercial banking is the creation by banks of new purchasing power, in the form of either notes or demand deposits. This occurs whenever the cash reserve behind notes or demand deposits is reduced below 100 percent. Commercial banking is not the acceptance of commercial deposits, although this makes possible the creation of demand deposits; it is this creation itself that is commercial banking. A

Socialist State Bank should accept and care for demand deposits, but should keep a 100 percent cash reserve behind them.

Orthodox Capitalist banking theorists accept the social utility of commercial banking. Although their arguments are unsound, few Socialists can refute them. It is therefore appropriate to give at this point a brief statement of the principal orthodox arguments in behalf of the social utility of commercial banking, with their refutation.

The most common argument is that banks put idle money to work. This argument is based upon a false analogy between savings deposits and demand deposits. When an individual curtails his own expenditures in order to create a savings deposit, he does deposit idle or unused money in the bank. Thus the savings bank really transfers idle money from savers to those who can use it effectively. The resulting increase in the volume of purchasing power available for investment purposes diverts the stream of goods and services constantly coming onto the market from buyers-for-consumption to buyers-for-investment, and results in an increase in the total supply of physical capital.

A demand deposit, however, is quite different from a savings deposit. Demand deposits are used to buy commodities in the same way as other kinds of money. Indeed, their velocity of circulation is often higher than that of paper money and specie. Hence, demand deposits do not represent idle money. When commercial banks make commercial loans or investments which lower cash reserves below 100 percent they do not put idle purchasing power or money into circulation; they create new money in the form of demand deposits and put this new money to work.

Most demand deposits are created by mere bookkeeping entries which credit the accounts of borrowers or sellers of securities. In those few cases in which demand deposits are created by the actual physical deposit of tangible specie or paper money in banks, this deposited money is no more idle than the gold and silver reserves behind government paper notes. The specie or currency is merely exchanged for a more convenient form of money—namely, demand deposits—which is created at the moment it is credited to the depositor. To continue to use both the deposited money and the newly created bank-deposit money would merely increase the total supply. It would be equally logical for the government to print an infinite amount of paper money against a small cash reserve on the ground that the reserve is always idle. Reserves may be unnecessary, but they cannot be idle when claims upon them are circulating as money. If unnecessary, they should be abolished, not put into circulation as money to increase the supply of money.

The creation of new money by banks enriches them and their wealthy borrowers just as the creation of new purchasing power enriches counterfeiters. Whoever has the power to create new money possesses a very obvious source of wealth. The only reason why commercial banks do not earn exorbitant rates of profit is that competition forces them to dissipate the larger portion of their gains in unnecessary marble edifices, free services to customers, unsafe loans, and many other costs incidental to getting and keeping their depositors and borrowers. By 1945 the commercial banks of the United States had created about a hundred billion dollars' worth of money in the form of notes and demand deposits. Behind this were gold reserves of about twenty billions. The annual interest income from the difference, eighty billions, amounted to about three billion dollars annually.

A second major argument in favor of the social utility of commercial banking is the plea that commercial banks put idle capital to work. This is based in part upon a mercantilistic confusion of capital with money. Commercial banks do not deal in capital; they deal in money. The two are quite distinct. In part, also, this theory is based upon the false analogy between savings deposits and demand deposits noted above. By transferring existing purchasing power from one person to another, a savings bank may effect the transfer of existing idle physical capital to someone who can use it. This is a very rare consequence.[15] Commercial banks, however, do not transfer money from one person to another; they create it. By causing inflation and stimulating entrepreneurs, they may bring about greater utilization of a given national stock of physical capital, but this is not the process referred to by those who argue that commercial banks benefit society by putting idle physical capital to work.

A third argument in favor of commercial banks is that they benefit society by increasing the supply of money. This plea is inconsistent with the theory of older orthodox economists that banks do not increase the supply of money; but it was very popular among the mercantilists who founded the first commercial banks in both England and America, and as a theory has been repeated intermittently ever since. It is perfectly true that banks do create enormous quantities of money or purchasing power. On this point the mercantilists were far wiser than Adam Smith and his classical and neoclassical successors. Moreover, the creation of new money when it is needed—in other words, when it prevents or lessens a fall in the price level—certainly benefits the national economy by maintaining the profit margin far more than it harms it by the forced expropriation of the wealth obtained by commercial banks and their borrowers through its creation and use. The same may be said of counterfeiters who function

---

[15] Ordinarily those who borrow from savings banks use their funds to buy new commodities and services coming onto the market, not to buy or lease existing capital equipment.

undetected at such times. The trouble with commercial banks is that they ordinarily create money when inflation is already in progress and destroy it after deflation has begun. This is natural, since inflation causes large profits and thus stimulates bank loans while deflation reduces profits and the demand for bank loans. Hence the elimination of commercial banking under Capitalism would sharply reduce the severity of the business cycle, probably by 50 to 75 percent. The real answer to the plea that commercial banking benefits society by creating new money, however, is not a denial of this fact but an assertion that the creation of money is a distinct function which ought to be separated from that of accepting demand deposits. New money ought to be created only in order to preserve a stable price level. If it is created by a commercial bank in order to make possible larger loans to industry and commerce, there will always be a strong temptation to create new money when it is not needed to preserve a stable price level, merely in order to finance business.

It is frequently argued that commercial banks benefit society by economizing the use of gold and silver. Under Capitalism, however, bank money has served to supplement rather than to replace the precious metals in the world as a whole. In a Socialist economy it would be easy to substitute bank credit for specie completely, but it would be equally easy and more desirable to use government paper money as a substitute for specie.

Finally, we may note the plea that commercial banks benefit society by providing an elastic medium of exchange. Actually there is no significant seasonal fluctuation in the supply of bank credit under Capitalism. There is, indeed, a very marked cyclical fluctuation, but, as has been explained, this fluctuation is just the reverse of what is needed. It increases rather than diminishes the severity of the business cycle. Under Socialism whatever seasonal or cyclical changes in the total supply of money are required should be arranged for by the Treasury Department.

We have now covered all the important arguments used by bourgeois economists to justify commercial banking under Capitalism and have found them invalid. Instead of being useful to business, commercial banking is very definitely harmful under Capitalism. It greatly enhances the degree and duration of all cyclical fluctuations in business conditions by making possible marked cyclical fluctuations in the volume of money. It results in compulsory social saving by expropriating the real income of the public at large and turning it over to private capitalists. Interest on the capital saved in this way is paid, not to those who have done the saving, but to the banks.

Under Socialism these evils of commercial banking would largely disappear. No alternate inflation and deflation of bank credit could cause a business cycle because prices would be set low enough to secure full utilization of the factors in production at all times. Since the bank and the trusts would both be socially owned, compulsory social saving could not benefit the wealthy at the expense of the working class.

Why then would commercial banking be undesirable in a Socialist economy? Primarily because it would serve to perpetuate false bourgeois theories concerning the nature and effects of commercial banking.[16] A second reason is that it would divide control over monetary capital and loans between two organizations, the State Bank and the Bureau of Capital Supply. Division of authority over a single economic function is always unwise. A third argument against commercial banking under Socialism is that it would divide control over the total supply of money between the State Bank and the Treasury Department. Finally, as already pointed out, the State Bank would always be under a strong temptation to create demand deposits in order to make possible larger loans.

The State Bank of a Socialist economy should accept time or savings deposits from all citizens, and should pay the full market rate of interest, less only the actual costs involved in handling the account, on all these deposits. The State Bank should not itself invest the funds deposited in it as savings accounts, but should merely credit these funds to the account of the Bureau of Capital Supply.

In the second place, the State Bank should accept all demand deposits offered it, and should handle all checks drawn on these accounts. It should, however, maintain a 100 percent cash (government paper money) reserve behind these deposits, and should make a small charge (equal to the marginal costs involved) for handling each check. A 100 percent cash reserve would eliminate commercial banking, and a charge for cashing checks would hold their use to the optimum level.

In addition to these two major services of modern banks, a few minor ones, such as the purchase and sale of foreign money, the provision of

[16] This appears to have occurred in Soviet Russia. Enormous new industrial plants were financed in part by the loan of reserves behind demand deposits on the entirely erroneous bourgeois assumption that such reserves are "idle" or "unused" capital funds and represent "idle" physical capital available for use. Loaning out the reserves behind demand deposits does increase the capital of the borrower and facilitates industrial expansion, but it does this in precisely the same way as the printing and loan of new paper money would do it, namely by expropriating the possessors of existing purchasing power. Apparently Soviet theorists have failed to grasp this vital point. Thus L. Maryasin, a Soviet banking theorist, explains that "by accumulating the temporarily free funds of our economy, our bank grows together with the growth of our economy. Being the only bank of short-term credit, the state bank concentrates in itself the huge power of the monetary reserves of our entire economy, stimulating with credit instruments the fulfillment of our growing plans" ("Ten Years of Soviet Credit," *Pravda*, June 18, 1932, p. 2, column 3).

safety deposit boxes, and the rendering of certain trust services, might be entrusted to the State Bank.

Three new functions not now performed by Capitalist banks should be assumed by a Socialist State Bank. These are the direct payment of all bills, the preparation of individual income and expense statements, and the analysis of the latter to detect fraud and other crimes.

Under Socialism all business enterprises should collect their debts by mailing bills to the State Bank instead of to the debtor and should receive immediate and automatic payment by the bank instead of voluntary payment by the debtor. This would save the hundreds of millions of dollars it now costs to prepare individual bills, to mail them, to write individual checks in payment of them, to mail the payments in, and to handle individual payments at the creditor's office and at the bank. It would save billions of dollars in bad debts, and would do this without involving any special collection costs.[17]

These savings would be much larger under Socialism than under Capitalism because virtually all retail sales should be credit sales. This principle will be partly justified in a later chapter on marketing. One great advantage of credit sales is that they reduce crime by substituting written bookkeeping entries and bank statements for easily hidden cash transactions. Since credit sales would increase several hundred percent under Socialism, efficiency in the collection of debts would obviously be much more important than it is under Capitalism.

The bills prepared by Socialist trusts would be more honest and accurate than those prepared by Capitalist businessmen because the executives of a Socialist trust could not benefit themselves by overcharging customers and because the larger scale of operations of Socialist trusts would permit the more extensive use of accurate and labor-saving bookkeeping machines. Complaints of customers could be tabulated and counted against the executives responsible.

To secure payment of debts, local branches of individual Socialist trusts should simply send to the local branch of the State Bank a list of their debtors and the amounts due, and the latter should immediately credit the accounts of these trusts and debit the accounts of their debtors by the amount requested. At the end of each month the State Bank should send

---

[17] Reasonable overdrafts could be permitted, upon payment of interest costs involved. Repeated unreasonable overdrafts could be punished by jail sentences. There would be no unemployment or unexpected expenses to justify bad debts and there would be no possibility of escape for anyone guilty of incurring bad debts. Moreover, there would be ample facilities for small or reasonable loans at low rates of interest to all consumers. Under these conditions bad debts would virtually cease to occur.

each depositor a statement of his debits and credits for the month. All complaints concerning individual debits should then be taken up with the trust responsible for them rather than with the bank. All wage and salary payments and other distribution of income should also be made directly through the State Bank for much the same reasons.

The preparation of these periodic statements of income and expense for every individual adult is the second new function which ought to be undertaken by a Socialist banking system. These statements should be far more complete than the personal bank statements characteristic of Capitalism. They could include all important living expenses because there would be only one bank and it would be the ordinary procedure for all payments of over a dollar or two to be made with checks on the State Bank. The individual bank statements prepared by the State Bank ought to classify all expenses into five or ten different groups, such as food, clothing, housing, automobiles, taxes, amusement, and others, and should enumerate the income sources separately.

The third new function of the State Bank should be the examination of these monthly bank statements in order to discover illegal income and expenditures. This sort of inspection would automatically eliminate the possibility of appreciable income from bribery, fraud, or crime in a Socialist economy. By restricting the use of ordinary money to such uses as buying matches, paying carfare, buying theater tickets, etc., the government could make it impossible for anyone to live without a legal source of income and an account at the State Bank. All individuals who lacked such incomes and accounts should be reported to the police and carefully watched. It would still be possible to steal small amounts of money and certain consumable commodities, but the possibility of earning a living in this way would be virtually eliminated at a very small cost because stolen goods could not be sold. Moreover, the chief reasons for crime under Capitalism would no longer exist, since suitable work at good wages would be constantly available for all.

CHAPTER IV. THE DETERMINATION OF PRICES

A. INTRODUCTION

I. THE SUBSTITUTION OF PRICE FOR VALUE THEORY

Value theory has long been considered the heart of political economy. In this treatise, however, a theory of price replaces the conventional theory of value. There are a number of reasons for this change.[1] In the first place, the term "value" is decidedly ambiguous and carries no definite meaning to the layman—if, indeed, it carries any to the specialist in the field of economics. The term value is often used as a synonym for utility. Thus Capitalist economists speak of free goods such as fresh air, pure water, and sunshine as being of incalculable value to mankind. Similarly, they frequently refer to a given article as having a different value for different people. In addition, the term value is often used to mean the natural or long-run average price of a commodity. Thus it is sometimes asserted that wheat or cotton is being sold at a price far above or below its real value. Finally, the term value is very commonly used to mean market price. We say the value of a bond is such and such when we mean that the amount mentioned is its market price.

To make this confusion still worse, the orthodox economist has care-fully defined value in a way which fits none of the above uses. Value is defined as power in exchange, the quantity of one or all other commodities for which a given quantity of a given commodity can be exchanged. Price is then defined as value in terms of money. This latter definition, however, is valid only in an economy where all forms of money are also a commodity, and few such economies exist. Under Socialism money will not be a commodity, hence price will not be a form of value according to this definition.

It should be noted that there are two variations of the above orthodox definition of value, namely, power of exchange over one other commodity or service, and power of exchange over all other commodities and services. The former kind of value can be determined and expressed in arithmetical form. The latter kind of value cannot be definitely determined and arithmetically expressed. This fact alone prevents the latter type of value from being a useful concept to the economist. Science, being based upon measurement, can do little or nothing with immeasurable quantities.

[1] For another statement of this point of view, see Gustav Cassel, *Theory of Social Economy*, pp. 49–52.

In addition to the serious ambiguity of the term value, however, there is this even more important reason for substituting a theory of prices for a theory of value: the economist is interested in prices, not in values. As explained later in this chapter, prices have an all-important role to play in a Socialist economy. True values, such as the value of a pound of raw cotton in terms of butter, have no role whatsoever to play in any advanced economy. Therefore they may as well be ignored by the economist.[2]

2. PRICE THEORY AS RELATED TO ORTHODOX BOURGEOIS AND MARXIAN VALUE THEORY

Although value theory will be replaced by price theory in this treatise, the change is largely verbal. Traditional value theory has been mostly price theory, and the author has no desire to repudiate that body of theory as a whole. The theory of price determination set forth in this and the following chapter is largely an application of orthodox marginal utility value theory to the pricing problems of a Socialist economy.

The complexity and intricacy of analysis possible in marginal utility theory are well known to all students of that body of theory. The following statement of the price theory of a Socialist economy is quite brief and incomplete. Limitations of space are very serious in a work which attempts to cover the entire field of economic theory, and marginal utility theory has already been so well and so frequently stated by orthodox economists that it does not require a restatement here. The plan is to build upon orthodox neoclassical theory rather than to restate it.[3] The

[2] Gustav Cassel, an advocate of so-called "price economics," has explained the emphasis of classical and neoclassical economists upon value theory as partly the result of their belief that an exchange economy without money preceded the present monetary exchange economy, and partly the result of their desire to study the factors which regulate the exchange of goods apart from money, reserving the study of this latter factor to a subsequent chapter. The former belief is erroneous and the latter desire unreasonable.

[3] For able statements of marginal utility theory we refer the reader to such accepted authorities as Menger, Von Wieser, Boehm-Bawerk, Jevons, Marshall, and Pigou.

The theory of imperfect or monopolistic competition is, of course, a far superior description of what happens under Capitalism than is neoclassical economic theory, but for this very reason it is of much less enduring value and of relatively slight help in developing the economic theory of a Socialist economy. What happens under Capitalism, and is described by the theory of monopolistic competition, is not what ought to happen in a Socialist economy. What is thought to be a description of the functioning of Capitalism by neoclassical economists is a false picture of this system, and hence bad "descriptive" economics, but at the same time it is an excellent statement of what ought to happen in a Socialist economy, and hence good "prescriptive" economics.

present treatment, therefore, undertakes only to explain the application of the major principles of marginal utility theory to the pricing problems of a Socialist economy. By adopting the technique here employed, any careful student of this theory will be able to apply other principles of marginal utility theory to these problems and so perfect the application of basic principles here begun. The technique, in brief, is merely that of turning the generalizations of neoclassical marginal utility theory into rules of price determination.

The use of orthodox neoclassical value theory implies a rejection of the Marxian labor theory of value. If Marxian theory were to be applied to the pricing problems of a Socialist economy, it would seem to require prices based solely upon labor costs. Of course, any price, once determined, can be expressed in labor units as well as in dollars. The basic defect of Marxian value theory is that it does not prescribe any technique for deriving prices from labor time. However, a detailed criticism of Marxian value theory is not justified here. This task has already been competently performed by orthodox economists, Boehm-Bawerk in particular, and we refer the reader to these writers for a more detailed criticism of Marxian value theory. In this treatise attention will be concentrated upon new, neglected, or incorrectly solved problems of economic theory.[4]

The real motive which caused Marx to develop and emphasize the labor theory of value seems to have been a desire to prove that all value is produced by labor, and thus to justify the appropriation of the entire product by labor. However, it is possible to concede that rent, interest, and profits ought to be price constituents and still demand that workers in a Socialist economy receive the entire product of industry. Likewise, it is perfectly reasonable to accept marginal utility theory and still claim that the worker creates all wealth and that workers as a class should receive all income not saved. Land and capital, being inanimate, cannot create anything; they are merely tools in the hands of men. Nevertheless, rent and interest ought to affect prices under Socialism, and do affect prices under Capitalism. These are the vital points Marx failed to perceive except when contradicting himself.

3. DEFINITIONS

Price is the power of exchange of an economic good over money. Money itself can possess no price, except in terms of other kinds of money. Money has purchasing power, but no domestic price.

[4] An able summary of the orthodox criticism of Marxian economic theory is contained in Joseph A. Schumpeter's *Capitalism, Socialism and Democracy* (1942), pp. 21–45.

Use of the term value is minimized in this treatise, but where it is used it will mean a sum of prices. Thus we shall speak of the *price* of hats but of the *value* of the total production of hats.

The distinction between market and natural price is useful. Market price needs no definition. Natural price means the ideal or optimum price, the price at which a good should be sold when the entire economic system is in equilibrium and the money costs of producing the marginal unit are everywhere equal to the market price, or fall below or exceed it by an equal percent.

B. THE ADVANTAGES OF A PRICE SYSTEM

The advantages of a price system must be understood before the individual pricing problems of a Socialist economy can be intelligently approached. A few Socialists have rejected the social utility of a price system. There is some evidence that the Russian Communists attempted to eliminate the use of money in the years immediately after the revolution. The bitter attack of the Technocrats upon what they called "the price system" is another indication of the need for an explanation of the functions of this economic institution. In many cases critics of Capitalism identify the price system with Capitalism and assume that the former necessarily involves all the evils of the latter. Certain bourgeois economists, on the other hand, naïvely identify the benefits of the price system with the benefits of Capitalism.[5]

The term "price system" is used here to mean a system in which many, but by no means all, goods are priced in terms of a monetary unit and sold for money, and in which prices help to control production and distribution. A price system may use any kind of money or purchasing power. Most critics of the price system are not really criticizing the price system as defined above; they are merely criticizing one form of money. Whether goods are valued in terms of dollars, labor hours, or kilowatt hours is a purely verbal question. The important problems of monetary theory relate to the method of issuing and controlling purchasing power, whatever its name. Similarly, the problems of price theory relate to the method of fixing prices, regardless of the name of the unit in which price is expressed.

[5] "In common with other business enterprises, public utilities, whether publicly or privately owned, sell their services to consumers at a price. This is, in fact, the characteristic which best distinguishes them from state services. The latter represent, in effect, the economics of communism, while the former are developed and maintained under a system of price economics, which implies the economics of individualism." Martin G. Glaeser, *Outlines of Public Utility Economics* (The Macmillan Company, New York, 1927), p. 7 n.

The function of a price system is to facilitate control over the production of commodities and services and over the distribution of income. A price system does this in two ways. In the first place, it provides invaluable information concerning the marginal utilitum of different goods and concerning the marginal disutilitum of different bads. In the second place, it provides instruments of social control which leave the maximum degree of freedom to each individual both as worker and as consumer. In other words, the prices which are set in any price system become at the same time data concerning utilitum and disutilitum and means of controlling production and distribution. These two functions are discussed separately below.

I. PRICES AS MEASURES OF UTILITY AND DISUTILITY

As already explained, prices largely replace direct sensations of utilitum and disutilitum as soon as a general division of labor arises. An isolated producer can compare directly the utilitum of each good with the disutilitum of the labor required to produce it, but social production resulting from a division of labor makes this impossible. With division of labor, the producer experiences directly only the disutilitum of his own productive effort, which may be only a small part of the total cost of production. He can only estimate the marginal utilitum of his product to whoever consumes it by observing the price he receives for his product. In the same way, the ultimate consumer does not experience directly the disutilitum involved in the production of the goods and services he consumes. He can only estimate this disutilitum by observing the price he pays for them.

Actually, of course, prices measure utility and disutility, not utilitum and disutilitum, but the former are the best indications of the latter, and the sole purpose of measuring utility or disutility is to secure an estimate of utilitum and disutilitum.

When prices are expressed in common units, it becomes possible to compare all kinds of utility and disutility. The utility of an additional raincoat can be compared with the utility of an additional symphony concert or sermon. The disutility of digging ditches can be compared with the disutility of playing the violin. Utility can also be compared with disutility.

It should be noted that price offers also provide valuable data concerning utility and disutility. A demand schedule or a supply schedule contains many price offers but only one price. Nevertheless, the whole demand and the whole supply schedule are useful in the determination of new prices. A demand schedule ought to be used by society in the same way as a personal diminishing utility curve would be used by a rational isolated producer, and a supply schedule corresponds to the increasing dis-utility curve of the latter.

The vital importance of prices as a measure of the marginal utility and disutility of production is due to the fact that all control over production must be based upon them as the only possible measure of utility and disutility. Prices, as measures of utility and disutility, are the sole possible foundation for efficient economic control or management.[6]

While in a Socialist economy prices take the place of, and perform the same functions as, direct sensations of utilitum and disutilitum in the economy of an isolated individual, this does not mean that prices are always accurate measures of marginal utilitum and disutilitum, even when properly fixed and determined.

In the first place, prices may not be properly determined or, if determined in the right way, may not have caused the proper response by producers and consumers. Only when a price serves to balance supply and demand perfectly, and when all producers and consumers have responded properly to existing prices, does it measure accurately both the marginal utility and disutility of the good in question, or either one of them.

In the second place, individuals vary widely in their capacity to enjoy life and feel pain. This means that the same price would represent different amounts of marginal utilitum for different individuals and that the same wage or interest payment would represent different amounts of marginal disutilitum even if incomes were equal. This is a defect in market prices which it is impossible to eliminate since it is impossible to discover the exact amount of pleasure or pain experienced by different

[6] William C. Roper, Jr., has explained the function of a pricing system as an aid to economic management in the following words: "The necessity of an accounting system as a means of judging the efficiency of various methods of production and of various combinations of productive agents, and of securing economic apportionment of these to different employments, has appeared plainly. Equally important for the success of production is an exact comparison of the human agents which direct these combinations. In Capitalist economy able management of economic operations tends to be secured by competition, which eliminates the unfit entrepreneur and makes toward the distribution of ability to the positions for which it is adapted. In the socialized state, only on the basis of exact computation, of accurate comparative costing, can the more able managers be separated from the incompetent, and the higher positions in the productive system be filled with men of the proper talents. By means of a pricing system such as we have outlined, including all productive elements, the collectivist economy can make the necessary comparisons and secure an economically rational distribution of managers among the various branches of production. The difficult matter of managing the enterprise of a socialized state is only solvable when managerial ability can be judged by means of an exact system of pricing and accounting." *The Problem of Pricing in a Socialist State* (Harvard University Press, 1929), p. 511.

individuals. However, sound prices always represent *average* marginal utilitum and disutilitum since among any large number of people the variations tend to cancel out. These average figures are the best obtainable estimates of marginal utilitum and disutilitum. It is far better to use them than to use any other measure or none.

It is often claimed that prices have another defect as measures of marginal utilitum, namely that they are so distorted by inequality of income among consumers that they reflect buying power or income rank even more than they reflect marginal utilitum. This is unquestionably a serious defect of Capitalist prices, for under Capitalism inequality of income is excessive and largely unjustifiable. However, if inequality of income were limited to the amount socially desirable as a means of stimulating production, the fact that an able and well-paid worker could offer a higher price for a good than a less able and relatively poorly paid worker would mean that giving the commodity to the former would do more to increase production and utilitum than giving it to the latter. Thus the higher price offer of the better paid worker would indicate a higher marginal utility.[7]

If wage differentials never exceeded the increased output they called forth, and they should not, they would merely give to the more efficient workers a part of the increase in output evoked by wage differentials. This

---

[7] This is one of the vital points overlooked by Maurice Dobb in the following criticism of "plural voting" or unequal wages under Socialism.

"Unless there were complete equality of reward, 'plural voting' would still remain, if diminished; whereas, if equality of reward prevailed, market valuations would *ipso facto* lose their alleged significance, since money costs would have no meaning. If carpenters are scarcer or more costly to train than scavengers, the market will place a higher value upon their services, and carpenters will derive a higher income and have greater 'voting power' as consumers. On the side of supply the extra 'costliness' of carpenters will receive expression, but only at the expense of giving carpenters a differential 'pull' as consumers, and hence of vitiating the index of demand. On the other hand, if carpenters and scavengers are to be given equal weight as consumers by assuring their equal incomes, then the extra 'costliness' of carpenters will find no expression in costs of production. Here is the central dilemma. Precisely because consumers are also producers, both 'costs' and 'needs' are precluded from receiving simultaneous expressions in the same system of market valuations. Precisely to the extent that market valuations are rendered adequate in one direction, they lose their significance in the other" (*Economic Journal*, December 1933, pp. 591–92).

Dobb also overlooks the fact that it would be possible to combine unequal wage costs with equal wage incomes by interposing between the payer of wage costs and the receiver of wage income a third party who would charge unequal wages and pay equal wages, or by requiring better paid workers to work fewer hours per week. The former method, of course, would prevent wage differentials from serving as incentives to a larger output.

would increase the utilitum of the more efficient workers without lessening that of the less efficient workers. Hence, the inequality of wages due to such differential wages would not destroy the usefulness of market prices as measures of social utility. Rather, it would increase their usefulness for this purpose.

On the other hand, it may be possible to persuade workers to put forth the optimum degree of productive effort without using pecuniary incentives to stimulate them.[8] If this is achieved there will be no inequality of wages to affect prices.

At any given time there is some system of income distribution which alone can permit prices to be perfect measures of marginal social utility and disutility. This involves a certain optimum amount of inequality in income. Any increase or decrease in this degree of inequality serves to distort prices as measures of marginal social utility and disutility.

Certain writers have expressed the fear that under Socialism the state would influence or distort consumer preferences in the same way that advertisers distort them under Capitalism.[9] It is possible to conceive of cases in which this might be desirable; but, if desirable, such conduct could not be indicted for destroying the usefulness of consumer preferences as expressed in market prices. If such conduct is undesirable, voters should repudiate Socialist statesmen responsible for it.

2. PRICES AS IDEAL INSTRUMENTS OF ECONOMIC CONTROL

The second function of a price system is to make possible methods of economic control which leave a maximum degree of freedom to the individual, both as worker and as consumer. As a worker he should be free to choose his own time, place, type, and intensity of labor; as a consumer he should have free choice as to how he spends his net income after taxes. Such freedom for the worker and consumer is possible only under a price system.

Freedom of choice on the part of the consumer is vital because each consumer is the best judge of what commodities and services give him the maximum utilitum at the minimum cost. Without complete freedom of choice, possible only under a price system, it would be necessary for some central authority to plan production. Even if democratically elected, this authority could not be even roughly acquainted with the personal eccentricities of millions of consumers. In the absence of a price system, most goods would have to be rationed to individuals with little regard for their individual tastes. Any compromise with a completely rigid ration is a step

[8] This possibility is discussed in a later chapter on the determination of wages.
[9] M. Dobb, *op. cit.*, p. 592.

toward a price system, since it changes a ration card into a medium of exchange good for different commodities at the option of the buyer.

For as far as we can see into the future, it will be necessary to limit consumption in some way.[10] A price system is the ideal method because it excludes from consumption first those who get the least utilitum from consumption. As the price of any good is raised, those consumers who get the least utilitum from consumption of the marginal unit are the first to cease purchasing it. As the price is lowered, those new consumers who will obtain the most utilitum from the marginal units are the first to purchase them. A price system limits consumption and at the same time distributes the existing supply of each article to those who get the maximum pleasure from it. This presupposes intelligent reaction to prices on the part of the executives of a Socialist economy, but in the absence of a price system it would not be possible at all.

C. CONDITIONS ESSENTIAL TO PROPER PRICING

Before taking up the technique of price determination in a Socialist economy, we must note that certain conditions are essential to proper pricing.

In the first place, there must be some unit in which prices can be expressed—in other words, a monetary unit. A unit of measurement is indispensable if any intelligent effort is to be made to compare marginal utility and disutility.

The second prerequisite for proper price determination in a Socialist economy is stability in the purchasing power of money. If prices are to serve as a means of comparing quantities of utility at different times, the price level should be as stable as possible. A rise or fall in the price level reduces the value of every individual price as a datum for economic decisions.

The third vital condition for price determination under Socialism is individual freedom of choice concerning varieties and quantities of price goods consumed. The function of price offers is to express utility and disutility in commensurable form. Free choice is essential to the performance of this function, for the individual is the only possible measurer and comparer of his own sensations of pleasure and pain. If the individual consumer is not free to buy whatever he pleases, and as much of it as he pleases, he will in many cases not even make price offers. But price offers there must be if a proper price is to be set. Every system of rationing

---

[10] Cassel has made this point the central idea in his *Theory of Social Economy*. He notes that his theory of prices should apply in a properly organized Socialist economy as well as under Capitalism (pp. 128–33).

goods violates this fundamental requirement of proper price determination. It prevents the individual from extending his consumption to the point where marginal utility and disutility are equal. As a result, the price he pays is not an accurate measure of the marginal utility to him of the commodity in question, and consequently the price is not a proper one.

The fourth essential condition of proper price determination in a Socialist economy is freedom of choice on the part of the individual citizen as to what kind of work he does and how much of it he does. The prices of various kinds of labor, and consequently of all the products of labor, cannot be properly fixed unless the individual worker is free to regulate his contribution to the total supply of labor in such a way as to balance the marginal utilitum and disutilitum of labor for him. The worker must have such freedom if the price he accepts for his labor is to be an accurate measure of the disutilitum of labor to him. He is the best, if not the only, judge of his own sensations of disutilitum, and the sole function of cost prices is to measure disutilitum as accurately as possible.

Freedom of consumers to buy what pleases them most, and freedom of workers to choose the jobs they prefer, both require the use of money, as explained in the previous chapter. Therefore, the use of money is an essential prerequisite for sound pricing.

D. THE MACHINERY OF PRICE DETERMINATION

I. THE RESPONSIBILITY FOR PRICE DETERMINATION

In a Socialist economy the supply of nearly all goods will be controlled by nation-wide monopolies. Those which sell their goods for a price will be in a position to determine the prices of their products without fear of price competition. It is true, of course, that buyers play as important a role as sellers in determining prices. The demand schedule is as vital as the supply schedule. What is meant by the statement that these monopolies will have the power to fix prices, is that they will be in the best position to estimate and interpret demand and supply schedules. Each commodity will be consumed by millions of men and produced by a single trust. The latter alone will be in a position to quote prices and to make them effective. While the situation will be different in the case of materials manufactured by one great trust and consumed by only a few others, there will still be good reason to entrust the power of fixing prices to the seller. Prices ought to be fixed by an agency which can make them effective upon the entire supply. Furthermore, the seller should be given full responsibility in order to render bargaining unnecessary, and in order definitely to fix responsibility for prices upon specific agencies.

As explained later, the rent of land and the interest of capital ought to be determined by the supply bureaus in charge of these two factors in production. In the case of labor, however, the general principle that all prices should be quoted by the seller is inapplicable. The price of labor cannot be fixed by the workers. Each organization employing labor ought therefore to decide upon its own wage schedule. Labor is the only good the price of which should not be controlled by a single sales monopoly.

It is important to note that wages ought not to be determined by a bargaining process between representatives of labor and representatives of the employing organization. The entire power to fix wages should be entrusted to the employing trust, and the latter should follow precisely the same procedure in fixing wages that it follows in fixing other prices.

Within each trust the work of fixing prices on all goods produced should be delegated to a special section. Obviously the men in this price section should be carefully trained experts.[11] The function of determining prices ought to be clearly separated from the function of controlling production. The sole function of price determination should be to balance demand and supply; the sole function of production control should be to eliminate both profits and losses. If these functions were not separated, prices might be manipulated to conceal profits and losses. A temporary local scarcity or surplus of goods is less obvious to central authorities than a profit or loss figure in the operating statement, and it is much more harmful to the public.

Separation of price determination and production control would not mean that those who control production would have no influence over prices. By increasing or decreasing the supply of goods they could, in the long run, effect any price changes they desired. The separation of functions would merely compel them to use the roundabout method of altering the supply, instead of the direct method of altering current price quotations. As a consequence, poor production control would result in obvious profits and losses instead of in a scarcity or surplus of goods.[12]

[11] "Mr. Cole proposes to have Socialist prices fixed by a joint Congress equally representative of the State or consumers, and the Guild Congress or the producers. Interference of a body like this in a purely economic arrangement would be uncalled for and worse than ineffective. Prices ought, as advocated in this volume, to be fixed by the accountants in the head offices of the guilds, who would receive statistical information from all the works of the actual cost of labor, cost of materials, upkeep of plant, buildings, etc., in short, all the constituents of price. This is work for experts, and not for a popularly elected assembly." J. H. Smith, *Collectivist Economics* (George Routledge & Sons, Ltd., London, 1925), p. 10 n.

[12] Under Capitalism this desirable separation between price and production control results automatically wherever competition exists and prices are determined in a free market.

In order to secure the desired degree of separation between the functions of price determination and production control, and in order to secure the advantages of large-scale operation and a maximum division of labor in the work of fixing prices, it might be advisable to place the power of determining all prices in the hands of a distinct national organization. The only data required would be information concerning sales, warehouse stocks, and production schedules, for prices should merely serve to equalize sales and supply.

2. THE TECHNIQUE OF PRICE DETERMINATION

As previously stated, the function of price determination, like the function of accounting, should be entrusted to experts trained especially for that work. The following observations deal with the method which they should employ in fixing prices.

Under Capitalism prices are determined either in free markets by the competitive bidding of buyers and sellers, or in the offices of monopolistic producers by arbitrary agreement or decision. Under Socialism all prices should be determined in the latter way. However, obedience to the principles of price determination stated below would result in very different prices from those fixed by Capitalist monopolies.

Two series of data are necessary to proper determination of prices: the consolidated demand schedule and the supply schedule for the good in question.

Obviously, both demand and supply schedules must apply to the same time period. Once these two schedules are available, however, it is a very simple matter to determine what price will equalize sales and supply during a given period of time. The principal task of price experts will be to ascertain demand schedules, since the supply schedule could be prepared by a single producer quite easily.

The simplest and best method of determining the demand schedule for any commodity is to study sales and price records. An analysis of the nature and uses of the commodity is also useful in determining the degree of elasticity of demand. If the article in question is a bolt used only in the manufacture of railroad locomotives, the demand is obviously almost completely independent of price. If it is a popular luxury with a large market still undeveloped, a price reduction will result in a marked increase in demand. Another method of learning something about the demand schedule for any article is actual experimentation with different prices. This is a less desirable method because price variations always complicate the task of controlling production and consumption, but it may be the only method available for discovering the actual demand schedule and hence the economic price.

Since demand schedules are always changing, price determination must always be partly experimental. All that investigation and use of demand schedules can ever achieve is to reduce the limits within which experimental pricing is necessary.

The task of preparing the supply schedule of any given article in a Socialist economy will be relatively easy because of the universality of monopoly and centralized control. Supply is the production schedule at a given price for a definite period, plus any surplus inventory which ought to be sold at this price during the period in question, or minus any desired addition to inventory. Supply schedules should be prepared by those in charge of production, not by the price experts, because production control and price determination ought to be in different hands.

While in the long run supply should always be determined by the average market price, as explained in the next chapter, it need not be affected by minor price variations in the short run. In the case of most price goods, only a very marked change in price would justify an immediate change in the volume of production. In other words, when existing capacity is being fully utilized, as would be generally true under Socialism, the marginal cost of increasing production by one unit would be relatively large and the marginal saving from curtailing production by one unit would be relatively small. Moreover, any price change may be due to temporary causes which would not justify permanent additions to capacity.

The prices of manufactured commodities should be fixed and quoted f.o.b. the point of production. This would serve to allocate the costs of transportation and distribution to those responsible for them.

The prices of agricultural products and raw materials should be fixed and quoted on a delivered basis at the principal markets. This would help to allocate to individual farms the economic rent they create. The price experts of the national trust in charge of wheat production, for instance, should first establish base prices at the principal points of wheat storage and consumption such as Kansas City, Chicago, Los Angeles, Seattle, New York. Then, within the wheat-producing area tributary to each of these centers, all local farm prices should be based upon the central market prices; that is, they should equal these base prices, less transportation and marketing costs. Such a pricing policy would give those farms that are close to market a higher price than those that are distant from the market. This would encourage the more intensive cultivation of the better located farms, and thus reduce the volume of transportation services required. Farm costs per unit of output would rise, but transportation costs per unit of output would fall by more than enough to compensate.

E. PRINCIPLES OF PRICE DETERMINATION

The separation of the function of price determination from that of production control means that prices ought to be set in complete disregard of the costs of production. The function of bringing prices into the proper relationship with costs should be delegated to those who control production. In brief, this means that those who fix prices in a Socialist economy should merely determine market prices, thus performing the function of a competitive market in a Capitalist economy. Natural prices should be the joint result of such pricing and the proper control by producers of the supply appearing on the market.

Those who fix the market prices of a Socialist economy should be governed by the following three rules of price determination, of which the first is by far the most important.

I. THE RELATIONSHIP OF PRICES TO SUPPLY AND DEMAND

The first and most significant principle of pricing in a Socialist economy is that prices should equalize supply and demand. No price which allows any portion of a given supply of commodities or services to go to waste is a proper price. No price which causes any portion of an effective demand (demand at or above the market price) to remain unsatisfied is a proper price.[13]

The supply of any commodity can be equalized with the demand for it by altering either demand or supply, or both at the same time. Prices affect both demand and supply. Under Socialism, as under Capitalism, they should be the sole incentive to increased production and the sole deterrent to increased consumption of price goods. A rise in prices should always serve both to stimulate production and to reduce consumption. A

---

[13] "And as regards the fixing of prices, the socialistic state would soon find that no mathematical formula was of any avail, and that the only means by which it could hope to solve the problem were exact and repeated comparisons between present and future stocks and present and future demand; it would find that prices could not be fixed once and for all, but would have to be altered frequently. Not the theory of averages, but the value of things in exchange would, in most cases, have to serve as its guide in fixing prices; and why should it reject the services of that guide? Why, for example, after failure of the wheat crop, should it not raise the price of wheat, so as to prevent stocks of that grain from being quickly exhausted; or why, after a too plentiful cherry crop, should it not allow cherries to be had very cheap so as to prevent their becoming unfit to eat and having to be thrown away? The socialists want to be too ingenious. They introduce into their system all kinds of things which give unnecessary offense, and which they ought to eliminate as a first step towards making a just appreciation of their principles possible." N. G. Pierson, *Principles of Economy* (Macmillan & Co., Ltd., London, 1902–12), Vol. II, p. 94.

fall in prices should always serve both to reduce production and to increase demand. Thus, it would always be possible to equalize demand and supply by proper price fixation.

It should be noted, however, that over short periods of time demand is far more elastic than supply. A factory cannot be built or enlarged overnight. Once built, it should be used even if it cannot earn a full return upon the capital invested. Under Capitalism much of the immediate elasticity possessed by supply is due to the existence at all times of large quantities of idle plant capacity and large numbers of unemployed men, and to the willingness of Capitalists to increase both when profits vanish. With the capacity production characteristic of Socialism, both of these factors giving immediate elasticity to supply would disappear. Hence, the task of the price experts in the short run would be largely that of altering demand to fit supply. In the long run, however, prices should determine the volume of production as well.

In the case of relatively perishable commodities and of all services, prices must be low enough to move any supply within very short periods of time. Labor, for instance, cannot be stored. Therefore, the supply of and demand for labor ought to be equal during the smallest periods of time. The case of perishable fruits, vegetables, and other foodstuffs is somewhat similar. While these can be preserved for lengths of time varying from one day to several months, there is always a definite and relatively short time within which supply and demand must be balanced if waste is to be prevented.

Even in the case of relatively durable goods, prices should always be low enough to move an entire stock, once produced, even if this requires fixing a price far below the cost of production.[14] This means that the price should be low enough to balance the demand for and supply of this stock within a certain optimum time period. It does not mean that prices must be low enough to dispose of the entire stock immediately. Only in the case of labor is it necessary to dispose of the entire available supply immediately, and, in the case of labor, a price set below cost would not result in any sales, for workers would be free to refuse to work if wages fell below the disutilitum cost of the marginal hour worked.

There is, however, one important qualification to this general principle. In the case of articles which are being constantly manufactured, prices should never fall below the *variable* costs of the marginal unit produced. When demand does not equal supply at this minimum price, stocks should be increased or production curtailed immediately. The producers of all commodities should be aware of this minimum price and should be

[14] Of course, no commodities should be shipped to market when transportation costs exceed their market price at point of destination.

careful not to force prices below it. However, this ought to be the duty of those who control production, not of those who fix prices. The blame for any sale at an uneconomically low price should fall exclusively upon executives in charge of the volume of production and sale, not upon those in charge of price determination.

Not only must prices be low enough to move without waste any supply of goods once produced, no matter what the degree of overproduction, but prices must also always be high enough to restrict demand to supply in case of underproduction. In a word, prices should always be fixed in virtually complete disregard of actual costs of production.

This is inevitable in the case of the three factors in production, for they have no money costs. It is essential in the case of all perishable commodities if they are to be consumed when once produced. It is socially desirable in all cases of scarcity since it limits consumption to those who get the maximum utility from consumption.

2. UNIFORMITY OF PRICES

The second principle to be observed by price experts in a Socialist economy is that prices should be uniform. All purchasers should be quoted the same price for the same good in the same market at the same time. This does not mean that varying transportation costs and other expenses of distribution should not cause price variations from city to city, or from store to store. It does mean that the same good should not be sold at different prices merely in order to tax the buyer according to his ability to pay.

Under Capitalism professional men frequently vary their charges according to the income of their client or patient. The same article is often sold at varying prices in different retail stores, merely because of the varying standards of living in the surrounding retail district. Also an article may be sold at widely different prices upon the basis of inexpensive changes in its appearance or container. All such measures tax the buyer according to his ability to pay. While a Socialist may feel reluctant to criticize such practices under Capitalism, it is nevertheless demonstrable that this pricing practice is unsound in an economy in which the differences in individual income are justified.

The reason is readily apparent. There is only one price which represents the disutility cost of production of the marginal unit, and every buyer must know this cost in order to limit his consumption at the precise point where the marginal utility to him of the commodity in question is just equal to the marginal disutility involved in the production of that commodity. In other words, no attempt to appropriate a portion of any consumer's surplus is justified. Such attempts reduce demand below the proper level, that at which marginal utility to the consumer and marginal disutility to the producer are equal. Because of the resulting rise in price, they also result either in overproduction or in improper monopoly profits.

Uniformity of prices is destroyed, not only by attempts to appropriate for the producer a portion of the consumers' surplus, but also by attempts to appropriate for the consumer any portion of the producers' surplus or economic rent. Thus the treatment of economic rent as a cost of production is sufficiently justified by the advantages of uniform prices. If a farmer using very fertile land sold his crop at the cost of production excluding rent, the result would be great price inequality, for other producers on less fertile lands would have to charge higher prices. But uniform prices for farm products are essential to proper limitation of consumption. No portion of a given supply of grain, for instance, can be sold below the marginal cost of production without increasing the consumption of grain beyond the point at which marginal utility to the consumer equals marginal disutility to the producer. Hence economic rent, while not a disutility cost of production, must be treated as a cost or price constituent in fixing prices.

3. STABILITY OF PRICES

In a Socialist economy stability of individual prices should be a primary interest of those who fix prices and would undoubtedly be far greater than under Capitalism. Price stability is highly desirable for a number of reasons. In the first place, frequent price changes necessitate frequent revision of production plans. The volume of production of each commodity should vary inversely with its cost of production, and directly with its sale price. All fluctuations in either cost prices or sale prices, therefore, make it necessary to revise future production schedules.

In the second place, stability of prices is desirable because it encourages an even rate of consumption. This facilitates smooth and hence economical marketing, and also increases the total utility gained from the consumption of a given quantity of any commodity. This latter fact is explained by the principle of diminishing utility. On the average, the seventh orange consumed on one day gives less utility than the sixth consumed on any other day.

There is a basic and unavoidable conflict between the principle that prices should balance supply and demand, and the principle that they should be stable. If prices are to balance supply and demand at all times, they must react to every small force affecting either supply or demand. If they are to be perfectly stable, they must be unaffected by even the most significant changes in supply and demand. A compromise is necessary in order to resolve this contradiction.

The degree of price stability which is desirable differs widely according to the nature of the good in question. The problem of determining the precise degree of price stability suitable for each good is a difficult one and must be left to the price experts, but it is possible to state certain general principles which should govern the solution of this problem.

In the first place, the optimum degree of price stability depends upon the stability of the supply of the good in question. If the supply varies widely from time to time, particularly if these variations are unpredictable, the market price must inevitably be relatively unstable. Examples of goods in relatively unstable supply are fresh fish, fresh fruits and vegetables, stage and movie hits, etc. On the other hand, if the supply is relatively stable, the price should also be relatively stable. The supply of most manufactured articles is ordinarily quite stable.

In the case of many goods, stability of supply is dependent upon the possibility and cost of storage. The supply of perishable goods in particular is extremely unstable wherever they cannot be stored economically.

One very important class of goods, services, cannot be stored at all. If a house is empty, the service it might be rendering cannot be stored. For this reason, rents should always be low enough to secure full occupancy of all buildings. This means that advertised rents on idle property must be extremely unstable.

In the second place, the degree of price stability that is desirable depends upon the stability of demand. If demand is highly seasonal, or subject to style cycles, or sharply influenced by the weather, prices should be relatively unstable. If demand is highly stable, prices also should be relatively stable.

In a Socialist economy foreign trade would be an important factor causing instability of prices. It will make the supply of commodities subject to importation more unstable and it will make the demand for commodities subject to exportation less stable. At least this would be true if foreign conditions of demand and supply were less stable than domestic conditions.

In the third place, prices ought not to change so frequently that some changes have no appreciable effect upon consumption and production. For instance, if the price of wheat changes every minute of the day, the individual price changes will serve little purpose. A price which stands for a second only, or an hour only, can have little effect upon consumption and production because people have so little time to react to it. All prices should last long enough to have an appreciable and desirable effect upon either demand or supply. In the case of most durable goods this means that prices should remain unchanged at least a week, probably a month or two, and perhaps a year or more at a time.

Price changes are used by many retail stores and producers in the same way as nonuniform prices, in order to appropriate a portion of the consumers' surplus. Department stores are accustomed to sell the first few units of a new article at a price far above its cost, and then to mark prices down steadily until the last units are sold below cost. Publishers sell new books in the same way, and those who market new patented products do likewise under Capitalism. This method of appropriating a portion of the consumers' surplus is unsound for the reasons already given and should not be tolerated in a Socialist economy.[15] All units of a given supply already in existence should be sold at a price low enough to move the last unit. While this can never be predicted exactly, there should be as many errors in the direction of too low an original price as in the direction of too high an original price. Moreover, production of a new good should never be limited merely to secure or maintain a high price.

Under Capitalism price fluctuations are largely due to competition and speculation. The mere nature of a Socialist economy, therefore, would eliminate much of the current instability of prices. Production should be controlled in such a way that overproduction and underproduction will be much less frequent. Every producer would have a monopoly, and this would make price stability more easily attainable. Finally, the elimination of speculation in commodities will help to stabilize prices.

The fact that prices should be far more stable in a Socialist economy than in a Capitalist one must not obscure the vital importance of price changes in a Socialist economy. As is explained at length in a later chapter on production control, price changes and their effects ought to be the sole guides to production.

F. AN ALTERNATIVE SYSTEM OF PRICING

Before leaving the subject of price determination, it may be well to note that there are alternative systems of pricing which go with different systems of production control. The system of pricing developed in this chapter is a necessary foundation for the method of production control recommended in a later chapter. A different method of production control would probably require a different system of pricing. We need not study all these alternative systems of pricing, since most of them go with obviously unsound methods of production control; but the particular alternative pricing system which would accompany the best alternative method of production control, the automatic inventory system of production control,[16] deserves attention.

[15] Of course, prices must be high enough on new products to restrict demand to supply.

[16] For a discussion of the merits of this method of production control see pp. 167–68.

If this system of production control is used, all prices should be based upon the marginal costs of production regardless of the existing relationship between effective demand and effective supply. Instead of being set in such a way as to equalize effective demand and supply, all prices should be set at a level which just covers the marginal costs of production. Production would then be controlled by demand, or rather by the relationship between effective demand and supply. Whenever demand exceeded supply, production would be increased. This in turn would raise the marginal costs of production of goods produced under conditions of increasing costs, so that the eventual effect upon price would be the same, whether the price is raised immediately in order to balance supply and demand (resulting in a profit which stimulates production), or whether price is kept at a low level until production has been increased in response to demand. In both cases an eventual equilibrium which balances supply and demand at the same level by means of the same price would be reached. The vital distinction between the two systems of pricing and production control is that the methods of reaching this equilibrium are different and involve entirely different and distinct systems of determining prices.

The use of prices based upon marginal costs instead of prices designed to immediately balance supply and demand would not invalidate the major portion of the doctrine of this chapter. The first four divisions of this chapter, and likewise sections 2 and 3 under division E, contain little or nothing inconsistent with a cost-of-production system of price determination.

PART TWO
THE PREREQUISITES OF PRODUCTION

CHAPTER V. THE ORGANIZATION OF THE
NATIONAL ECONOMY

A. INTRODUCTION

Under Capitalism there are three distinct types of economic organization and three distinct sciences which cover the field of economic organization. The three sciences are Political Science, Political Economy, and Business Administration. Each of these three sciences has developed or justified a different form of organization. Political science has offered a comprehensive rationalization of existing methods of political organization. Economics has attempted to justify the existing economic organization—or, from the Socialist viewpoint—lack of organization. Finally, business administration has analyzed and studied many different forms of organization suitable for individual business enterprises.

A Capitalist economy is not subjected to any compulsory organization, except in time of war. It is organized, however, by individual self-interest, which leads to unconscious co-operation and creates a certain degree of order and equilibrium in the national economy not only under perfect competition but also under monopolistic competition. Nevertheless, it is proper to charge Capitalism with anarchy. Anarchy is not an absence of organization; it is voluntary organization. The only fundamental differences between Capitalism and Anarchism are these two: (1) that Capitalism functions under the protection of a compulsory political state which Anarchism proposes to abolish, at least as a compulsory organization; (2) that Capitalism results in unconscious co-operation among capitalists, workers, and farmers, while Anarchism proposes conscious voluntary co-operation between members of producers' and consumers' co-operatives which socially own and use all capital.

Socialism will unite the three distinct forms of organization in use under Capitalism into a single system which will replace the Capitalist state, the anarchic Capitalist organization of the national economy, and private business organization. The new economic organization will resemble certain forms of business organization now in use much more closely than existing political or economic forms.[1] Indeed, if it were necessary to explain the new organization in a sentence, the best way would be to say that it will be similar to the organization of a great Capitalist trust like United States Steel or American Telephone and Telegraph, except that the board of directors will be elected by the nation as

[1] This partially justifies Lenin's statement that Socialism would abolish the state.

a whole. In other words, Socialism proposes to replace the anarchy (voluntary co-operation) of Capitalism with an organization which synthesizes the best features of present political and business organization.

The rise of Socialism will reduce the now independent field of political science to a mere division of political economy—an additional reason for retaining the term "political" in the title of the latter science. Under Socialism the problem of determining a form of organization for the state will become a minor part of the problem of determining a form of organization for the national economy. The merger of state and industry will result in the merger of the two independent sciences now dealing with these subjects.

Indeed, the Capitalist state is already an organization devoted solely to economic production. All government services are economic goods. The primary function of the Capitalist state is to produce and distribute economic goods for which it is not wise to charge a money price. In other words, it produces "free" goods while private Capitalists produce "price" goods. In so far as government enters into the latter field it functions as a form of Socialism.

B. PRINCIPLES OF SOCIALIST ORGANIZATION

There are five basic principles of Socialist organization: (1) pure democracy, (2) perfect monopoly, (3) complete centralization, (4) authority from above, and (5) functional organization.

I. PURE DEMOCRACY

Democracy may be defined as a form of government under which a group which comprises or represents the majority has all political power. Of course, the majority can rebel against and, if sufficiently determined, can overthrow almost any government; but this does not make all governments democratic. Democracy requires that there be a peaceful transfer of power from one set of leaders to another at periodic intervals and in accordance with the desires of the majority of adults.

An advanced Socialist economy should possess a democratic form of organization, the chief executives being elected by the majority of citizens either directly or indirectly. The reason for this is very simple. It is not that man has a natural right to be free and self-governing. The philosophy of natural rights is as irrational as all other philosophies. The justification for democracy is that the majority usually has the physical power to have its way if the desire is sufficiently strong. Democratic government is merely the simplest known method for determining which side has the most might. It does not assume that might is right, but it does accept the fact that might is might and that persistent neglect of this fact leads to periodic civil war, hence to economic instability and inefficiency. The elimination of such insecurity and instability outweighs all the disadvantages of democracy, all the evils of control by mediocre minds. Modern industrial societies are so complex that they cannot stand internal strife. A bitter civil war in a state like Germany, England, or the United States would result in starvation for tens of millions and in frightful damage to the national economy.

Another major advantage of democratic control of industry is that it improves the morale of the workers and therefore increases the productivity of labor. Men will not work as hard for leaders chosen by others as they will for leaders chosen by themselves. They believe that leaders chosen by others will divert some or all of the fruits of any additional effort to themselves or to those who appointed them. Hence workers are reluctant to put forth their optimum effort for feudal lords, capitalists, and dictators. Only when working for leaders chosen by themselves do they have the maximum assurance that the gains from increased effort and output will benefit them and not a small ruling clique'or class.

Two important qualifications to the general principle of democracy in a Socialist economy should be noted. In the first place, democracy is an advanced stage of political development and requires certain economic and cultural bases as a foundation. It is as ridiculous to say that a nation like China or India or Russia or Mexico should be democratic as it is to say that a child should display the intelligence of an adult.[2]

Only experience and repeated experiment can enable the social scientist to determine when a nation is ready for democracy, but certain general conclusions are already possible. In the first place, virtually universal literacy is absolutely essential to the success of democracy. In the second place, a certain level of education beyond the mere ability to read and write is necessary. Just what this level is, it is difficult to say. General reading of newspapers and familiarity with political issues would seem to be the minimum. Probably the general possession of a secondary education would be necessary to make democracy work under Socialism. The nominal democracy prevalent under Capitalism only functions because power is really in the hands of the bourgeoisie, most of whom have attended secondary schools. In the third place, a long period of education in democracy is probably essential to success. A nation must be taught the use of the ballot gradually. A sudden change from autocracy or oligarchy to democracy would be difficult if not impossible.

[2] This was one of the great errors of the Russian minority Social Democrats (Mensheviks) in 1917.

The second qualification to the general principle of democracy is this: There is some reasonable doubt as to whether even an advanced nation can change quickly from Capitalism to Socialism without temporarily abandoning democracy. One great division of the world Socialist movement, the Third International, believed that Socialism could be realized in advanced industrial nations already nominally democratic only through the temporary overthrow of democracy and the establishment of a dictatorship of the proletariat. This conviction of the Communist leaders was based largely upon the successful Russian experiment, however, and may well represent an unjustified extension to new conditions of a principle proved valid only under certain past conditions.

While nominal democracy already exists in many advanced nations under Capitalism, there is more oligarchy than democracy in these states. All of the means of communication and education—the press, the radio, the pulpit, the lecture hall, the school system—are owned or controlled by a relatively small bourgeois class, which is thus enabled to dominate the thought of the masses. True democracy can exist only where all political parties and points of view receive their due share of attention in the press, over the radio, in the public schools, etc.

The general principle of democracy has many specific applications, and as to the methods employed in carrying it out, there is occasion for so much difference of opinion that many political problems are bound to arise. Some of these specific applications and problems are now to be discussed.

Universal Suffrage.—Universal suffrage is essential to complete democracy. Although the United States nominally enjoys universal suffrage, about 25 percent of the adult population is not allowed to vote. Negroes are disfranchised through the South; aliens, migratory workers, and new residents are disfranchised everywhere. In some states citizens who have not paid poll taxes or who are dependent upon relief are not allowed to vote. All of these restrictions, which now affect chiefly workers and poor farmers, must be eliminated in a Socialist state.

While universal suffrage ought to prevail in a Socialist economy, every effort should be made to persuade the voters to entrust the actual work of legislation and administration to men far above the average in ability, to men possessing both superior native endowment and superior education. No measure should be adopted which does not have popular approval, but it would be highly desirable to fix educational and native intelligence requirements for all candidates for public office at such a level as to eliminate up to 90 percent of the population. To begin with, laws which merely eliminated the lowest 10 percent might be passed, and later the percentage could be raised as fast as the public could be persuaded of the benefits of such restrictions. In any case, however, an aristocracy of ability must be subject to popular control; otherwise it will be liable to favor its own material interests at the expense of the remainder of the nation.

Proportional Representation.—The representation of every political party in the national legislature should be proportional to its total vote at the previous election. Proportional representation is desirable because it enables small minorities who would not otherwise be represented to secure seats in the legislature. This results in a more complete statement and consideration of both sides of every question. Secondly, proportional representation is desirable because it yields a more accurate representation of the major political parties. Under the present American system of representation it is common for a slight majority in the total vote cast to give one of the major parties an unreasonably large majority in Congress. Thirdly, proportional representation is desirable because, like preferential voting, it gives every voter the feeling that his vote influences the make-up of the national legislature. In the absence of both, many people vote for their second or third choice because they feel that a vote for their first choice would be wasted.

An important demand of proportional representation is that each legislator should represent the same number of voters. One of the most undemocratic features of American government is the gross inequality in the size of electoral districts. The situation is virtually as bad as in England before the Reform Bill of 1832. Almost every state is dominated by a small fraction of its population in consequence of failure to revise electoral districts regularly and because of the fact that Senatorial districts are very unequal in population. The federal government also suffers from this evil. Thus the 110,000 people of Nevada have as much representation in the United States Senate as the 13,400,000 people of New York. Few worse "rotten boroughs" existed in old England.

Regional Representation.—Members of the national legislature should be elected in groups by large regional electoral districts rather than individually by small local ones. This is desirable, in the first place, in order to simplify and improve the system of proportional representation.

The larger the number of representatives from a single district, the easier it is to give proportional representation. Where there is only one representative from a district, proportional representation is impossible, and it must be extremely crude even with two, three, or four representatives. Ten representatives, however, would give representation to any party polling 10 percent of the vote. In order to secure a sufficiently large number of representatives from a single district, it is more desirable to combine many districts into one than to elect many representatives from each old district, for the latter would increase unduly the size of the national legislature.

A much more important reason for regional representation is that local representation fosters provincialism among legislators. Under a system of local representation every legislator is forced to sacrifice the interests of the nation to the interests of his district. If copper is mined in his district, he desires a tariff upon copper imports, regardless of the interests of the nation. If money is being appropriated for any government department, he votes for it if it is to be spent in his district. He is more interested in securing a new post office or other public-works project for his constituents than in balancing the budget, or reducing the national debt. All of the views of legislators who represent local districts are distorted by the selfish interests of such districts. While regional representation would not eliminate these evils, it would do much to reduce them, particularly if candidates were not required to be residents of the regions they represent.

One of the most serious evils resulting from local representation is that it compels legislators to devote much of their time to doing favors for individual constituents. The time of every member of an American legislative assembly is largely taken up with satisfying the personal requests for favors advanced by residents of his district. Regional representation would reduce the political necessity of doing favors for individual constituents by reducing their relative influence, thus freeing the time of legislators for consideration of national issues.[3]

It is sometimes said that local representation is desirable because it produces legislators who are familiar with local problems. This familiarity with the problems of a small district, however, can only be obtained at the cost of familiarity with the problems of the nation; no man can specialize in two fields and become a master in both. Every hour devoted to the study of the petty problems of a small electoral district is one hour less devoted to the vital problems of the nation as a whole. Hence the election of men who devote most of their time to the study of local problems should not be encouraged.

Initiative and Referendum.—Voters should have the power to initiate new legislation and to veto old legislation. The number of signatures required to place an initiative or referendum measure upon the ballot should be small enough to secure the presence of several such measures on every ballot and large enough to prevent an excessive number of them on any one ballot. Perhaps the best method would be to place on the ballot

---

[3] Another method of accomplishing this and other desirable ends is to adopt a rule which prevents a legislature from considering bills involving less than some minimum appropriation, such as $1,000,000.

at each election the five measures having the largest number of supporting signatures.

The national legislature itself ought to have the power to refer proposed laws to the public and should make frequent use of this power. The public should be encouraged to express its opinions on major problems individually. Probably it would be desirable to have a compulsory referendum on, let us say, the five most important measures passed by the national legislature each year. The questions submitted to the voters by the legislature should be designed to determine general attitudes and goals rather than to secure approval for specific laws and details of laws. For instance, the public should be asked to express its general attitude toward prohibition or child labor, but not toward the details of laws designed to carry out such opinions.

Majority Rule.—A majority of the national legislators should at all times have absolute power in its hands. No law or constitutional amendment should require more than a bare majority to give it force. The dead hand of the past in the form of a constitution should not be allowed to overrule the wishes of a present majority. Social inertia is always a powerfull force opposing progress. Every requirement of a two-thirds or three-fourths vote to bring about change simply increases the difficulty of overcoming social inertia because it takes much longer to educate 67 percent or 75 percent of the voters to the value of a reform than it does to educate 51 percent of them, and a more rapid rate of social reform is the primary need of our age.

Frequent Elections.—In order to increase the accuracy with which legislators reflect the views of their electors, more frequent elections are needed. The old Chartist demand for annual parliaments is still sound although a century has passed without its realization. Legislators who are elected for terms of four, five, or six years tend to ignore public opinion until just before the time for re-election. It is for this reason that conservatives who fear the people have ordinarily favored infrequent elections while true democrats have usually demanded frequent elections.

Another significant advantage of frequent elections is that they serve to develop public interest in and study of social problems, thus promoting more intelligent voting.

Continuous Legislative Sessions.—The legislature of a Socialist state should be in continuous session; it should never adjourn except for holidays and brief electoral campaigns. Even under Capitalism legislatures have more business than they can handle and always adjourn with many bills unconsidered and many problems unsolved. Under Socialism the tasks will be still greater.

Short sessions and long adjournments—this system is merely one of the many features of Capitalist democracy designed to prevent change and progress. Conservatives, fearful of the representatives of the people, have built up the myth of the inherent stupidity of Congressmen in order to justify and popularize their opposition to long sessions of Congress. The shorter the session of Congress the less change there can be.

Continuous sessions will make legislation a full-time job. Most Capitalist legislators treat legislation as a part-time job or hobby, and devote the bulk of their time to some other task such as practicing law, running a business, or managing a farm. This inevitably interferes with their work as legislators. National legislation is so important that no legislator should be permitted to engage in any other work for pay or profit.

Direct Primaries.—The candidates of each party for seats in the national legislature should be selected in a direct primary conducted by the national government under a preferential voting system. The chief merit of this method is that it tends to make political parties democratic and responsive to the will of their members.

If direct national primaries are to function well, the voters should not be required to nominate too many candidates. In other words, the size of the legislature should be small enough to reduce party slates nominated by direct primaries to a reasonable length. This means that the national legislature itself should not consist of more than about one hundred members.

Government Payment of Campaign Costs.—One of the prime essentials of genuine democracy is the elimination of financial obstacles to equal participation in political campaigns. All essential campaign costs in both primary and final campaigns should be met by the government. No private expenditures for such purposes should be permitted. Private contributors nearly always want some return from their contribution, and often get it.

To be sure, Socialism would inevitably reduce the gross evils connected with private campaign expenditures since it would eliminate the striking inequality of income characteristic of Capitalism. But this alone would not suffice. Rich men should have no advantage over poor men as political candidates. To this end, newspapers should be required to be impartial in their news stories and to divide their editorial space equally among the competing candidates. All necessary campaign costs, including the living costs of candidates during the campaign, should be paid by the government.

A candidate who spends his time presenting public issues to the voters is performing a valuable educational service, and should be paid his previous wage for this service whether he wins or loses. The number of candidates could be reduced to any desired level by requiring a suitable number of signatures on nomination blanks, by requiring the support of local civic or political organizations, or by running two or more primaries.

A One-Chamber Legislature.—The principal purpose of all second or upper houses of legislatures is to thwart the will of the people as expressed in the democratic lower house. Hence all such chambers or senates should be abolished under Socialism.

Even if both upper and lower houses of legislatures were elected democratically, the result of having two houses would be to make more difficult the passage of all new laws. It always requires more effort to convince two houses of the need for reform than it does to convince one house. The establishment of a one-house legislature would not only facilitate reform by eliminating the undemocratic upper chamber; it would also promote reform by increasing the volume of work accomplished by the legislature.

2. PERFECT MONOPOLY

A basic principle of Socialist organization should be the development of a perfect monopoly in every field of economic activity. It is quite conceivable that Socialism as at present defined—social ownership and operation of the instruments of production—might be organized on a competitive basis, even under a completely centralized national organization. Every industry might be divided into two or more trusts which would compete with each other throughout the nation, and salaries of executives might be varied according to their success in this competition.

Direct competition of this sort ought not to be employed in a Socialist economy because it would result in (1) duplication of services and facilities, (2) unnecessary sales effort, (3) small-scale production, and (4) unfair income differentials.

Direct competition nearly always leads to uneconomic duplication of facilities and services. Competing factories attempt to maintain surplus plant capacity in order to take care of the business they hope to take from their competitors. Competing stores duplicate each others' services and facilities. The classic example of this is the common case of from two to four gas stations on a corner where one of them could do all the business. Competition gives us half-a-dozen milk wagons traversing the same route, two or three newsboys on each corner, a hundred lawyers in a town where fifty would be enough, and so forth. Competition is based upon the existence of unused powers of production. No individual or organization competes for more business when he or it is operating at capacity.

The second basic disadvantage of direct competition is that it always tends to stimulate uneconomic sales effort. Nearly all advertising is unnecessary from the social standpoint, but it increases the income of competitive units more than enough to offset its costs; otherwise it would not be used. Monopolies would have less temptation to indulge in uneconomic advertising than competing economic organizations. The same is true of other uneconomic practices encouraged by aggressive competitive salesmanship (see chapter xviii).

A third serious disadvantage of competition is that it reduces the scale of production below the optimum level. For instance, if the total national production of radios were concentrated in one plant, the cost per unit would be far lower than at present and somewhat lower than if production were concentrated in only two plants. Monopoly alone can make possible production at or nearest the optimum scale of production (see chapter xi).

In the fourth place, competition results in unfair income distribution because it is impossible to create perfectly equal competitive conditions. One store always has a better location than another and there is no practical method for distinguishing perfectly between economic rent and competitive profits. All estimates are rough and therefore unfair because the business which gets the most favorable rent appears to make the largest profit. Similarly, no two factories ever have equally able executives and engineers, and competitive advantages due to superiority of executive or technical staff may cause an unjust differentiation between the wages of equally able ordinary employees in competing plants.

In addition to these four principal defects, competition has other disadvantages. It makes planning more difficult because it increases the independence and the number of economic units. It impedes standardization and simplification. It facilitates uneconomic distribution of the factors in production. It perpetuates anti-social individualism.

The fact that direct competition between business enterprises should be abandoned under Socialism does not imply that other desirable types of competition must be eliminated. Promotion should continue to reward those workers who compete most successfully in the work of production. Piece rates should encourage competitive efforts wherever feasible. Socialist competition between gangs, shops, plants, and industries should be developed. These points are discussed more fully elsewhere (chapter xv).

3. COMPLETE CENTRALIZATION—PRO AND CON

The third fundamental principle of Socialist organization is that control over every division of the national economy should be centralized. The hands of the national legislature and its leader, the chief executive, should hold all the reins of government.

The problem of the proper degree of centralization of control has long divided Socialists. Before 1917, Socialists were classified in groups primarily according to the solution they offered. The Co-operative Movement and the Anarchists looked forward to a highly decentralized organization of society. The Guild Socialists and the Syndicalists compromised by suggesting the establishment of a few score of competing trusts externally independent but highly centralized internally. State Socialism proposed the centralization of all power in the hands of a single central government. Although the rise of Communism has developed a division of opinion among Socialists more basic than that concerning the degree of centralization of power, it has not eliminated these differences of opinion. By its success the Soviet Union has greatly strengthened the case for State Socialism.

We have already noted that one of the major advantages of monopoly is that it increases the scale of production. But even with universal monopoly there may be local or regional monopolies which cannot achieve the optimum scale of production. In such cases these local and regional monopolies should be consolidated into national monopolies and this consolidation would be aided by complete centralization of control in each industry.

In the second place, centralization of control is necessary in order to give full scope to the economies of large-scale management. If it is not advisable to concentrate the entire national production of a good in a single plant, it may be economically desirable to place many district plants under a single management. The economy of large-scale management is one of the chief reasons why competitive Capitalism automatically transforms itself into monopoly Capitalism, thus preparing the way for Socialism. An excellent concrete example of this development is the rapid rise of the chain store. Nearly all of the economies effected are derived from large-scale management. The remarkable competitive success of chain stores demonstrates the efficiency of centralized economic control. Already there are single grocery chains in the United States large enough to perform the entire retail grocery function in nations as large as Belgium, France, Italy, Spain, and perhaps Great Britain.

The principal advantage of large-scale management is that it makes possible a greater division of labor among office workers and executives. Numerous labor-saving office appliances and machines are economical only in a large office. This is particularly true in accounting work, nearly all of which can now be done more cheaply by machine if the volume is large enough.

For executive work the economy of large-scale organization is noteworthy. In an independent retail store one man may function as accountant, buyer, advertising manager, insurance specialist, freight department head, etc. In a medium-sized store or small chain these functions may be performed by separate individuals who, through specialization, eventually become far more competent at their job than any operator of an independent one-man store can be. In a large chain the division of executive labor, and the resulting gain in efficiency, may be carried much further. Instead of one or a few buyers there may be hundreds, each specializing in a certain type of merchandise. Every department of the business, from buying insurance to interdepartmental messenger service, can be entrusted to one or more men who know more about that particular line of work than any other men in the organization. As a result, everything can be done more economically and efficiently in a large organization than in a small one.

A second important advantage of large-scale management is that it makes it possible to give to the ablest executives and specialists control over a larger field of work. There is, for example, some one man who as chief executive of the automobile trust can run that trust with maximum efficiency. At any given time there is only one such person. Under Capitalism such an executive rarely controls an entire industry for the simple reason that almost every industry is divided into several competing units. The situation is the same with respect to technicians and specialists. There is always some one engineer who knows more about high-voltage transmission wires than any other engineer. Under Capitalism he cannot give society the maximum benefit from his knowledge because he can work for only a few power companies. In this fact lies the chief explanation for the enormous differences in efficiency which exist between units of the same industry under Capitalism.[4] Centralization of control would make it possible to raise the efficiency of backward units in each industry to, or somewhere near, the level attained by the most progressive units.

Looked at from the point of view of the individual employee of exceptional ability, this advantage of large-scale management—namely, its chance to get greater returns from ability by extending its field of activity —appears as a greater opportunity for promotion. A large organization offers more opportunities for promotion and promises further advancement than a small organization.

Even though the ablest executive or specialist is not always given the power he deserves, centralization will make it possible to raise the standard of backward units because it will result in uniform accounting methods, more accurate knowledge of relative costs and efficiency, and power to act upon this knowledge. Under these conditions every executive would find it easier to determine the most efficient methods and select the most efficient subordinates.

[4] For a review of the great variations in certain industries see the report of the American Engineering Society, *Waste in Industry* (1921).

Centralization of control and uniform cost accounting will also do much to stimulate competition of the right kind. Mere publicity for comparable operating statistics would do a great deal, but centralization of control will make it possible to act effectively upon the basis of such data and to offer rewards for competitive success in lowering production costs and increasing output. Under Capitalism this is made difficult by the fact that accounting methods are not uniform and it is therefore hard to tell who deserves a reward.

Centralization of control is desirable, in the third place, because it will result in the selection of executives of superior ability. Popular election is a much less efficient method of selecting capable executives than appointment from above. Voters as a class lack both the facts and the ability necessary to make the best selection. In the case of the national legislature, democratic election is necessary to prevent periodic revolution, but this argument does not justify the choosing of subordinate authorities by popular election. Every addition to the number of elected officials increases the length of the ballot and decreases accordingly the efficiency with which democracy functions. The more candidates on the ballot, the less time the voter has to study each candidate and the less he knows about each. It is far easier for the voting public to select one man or one small group of men who will appoint able subordinates than to select able subordinates directly.

In the fourth place, centralization of control is necessary in order to secure co-ordination between different parts of the national economy. Division of authority invariably leads to "passing the buck," friction, and a lack of harmony. A single supreme authority is as essential to a nation as to an army. It is the only method of securing prompt and effective co-ordination of action.

Every efficient private enterprise is characterized by a high degree of centralization of power. In a great Capitalist trust each unit of the trust and every minor executive is subordinate to a single board of directors. Division of authority would cripple the organization. Only in government is division of authority approved, and then only by those who desire to weaken the power of the state.

Uniformity of law is another of the desirable results which will follow from complete centralization of control. Division of authority among the forty-eight states has resulted in forty-eight sets of laws concerning divorce, crime, inheritance, railroad rates, and all the other subjects covered in state laws. Division of authority among counties and cities in the United States has resulted in literally thousands of diverse laws concerning building permits and plans, street traffic, public health, relief, etc. This diversity breeds lawsuits, reduces knowledge of and respect for the law, complicates enforcement, and demonstrates the incapacity of amateur local legislators.

Simplification and standardization of commodities would also be facilitated by centralized control. If retail stores, for instance, are controlled by independent local co-operative or municipal authorities, it may be difficult to get them to agree upon certain standardized fixtures and supplies. Unification of all retail stores into a single organization will result in automatic agreement upon standardized fixtures and supplies.

It should perhaps be pointed out that the need for co-ordination between different parts of the national economy does not imply any need for central planning of production. In chapter vii a method of production control which eliminates entirely any need for central planning of production is recommended.

It is customary for the opponents of State Socialism to charge the latter with an intolerable amount of red tape and bureaucracy. By this, apparently, they mean that complete centralization of control inevitably forces the central executives to determine all questions, no matter how trivial, which face the local management. The result is, so these critics assert, that a mass of red tape develops. Every decision must be approved by so many superior authorities that no problem can be solved simply and quickly, and high executives are overwhelmed by a mass of detail which makes efficient administration impossible.

There are two possible answers to this common criticism. In the first place, experience has repeatedly demonstrated that large-scale or centralized management is more efficient than small-scale or individual management. Thus, in spite of laws and prejudices which favor independent stores, the chain stores have been able to expand much more rapidly than independent stores. The chain store companies operate small-unit stores, and their economies are chiefly those of large-scale management. Their success, like the success of huge Capitalist trusts in many other industries, demonstrates either that highly centralized large-scale management is not bureaucratic or that bureaucracy is consistent with increased efficiency.

The truth of the matter is that red tape and undesirable bureaucracy are not necessary evils of large-scale centralized management. Rather, they are evils to which almost any organization is subject if improperly organized. It is perfectly possible to divide managerial powers and functions between superior and subordinate executives in such a way as to free the former from trivial detail and give the latter full authority to act on matters not deserving the attention of the higher executives. Such should be the policy of a Socialist administration.

It is possible to argue that direct, local governmental or consumer control over local industry is preferable to central control on the ground that the local taxpayer or consumer is directly interested in local government and industry while he is only distantly interested in national government and industry. Bertrand Russell has stated this argument as follows:

Majority rule, as it exists in large States, is subject to the fatal defect that, in a very great number of questions, only a fraction of the nation have any direct interest or knowledge, yet the others have an equal voice in their settlement. When people have no direct interest in a question they are very apt to be influenced by irrelevant considerations; this is shown in the extraordinary reluctance to grant autonomy to subordinate nations or groups. For this reason, it is very dangerous to allow the nation as a whole to decide on matters which concern only a small section, whether that section be geographical or industrial or defined in any other way. The best cure for this evil, so far as can be seen at present, is in allowing self-government to every important group within a nation in all matters that affect that group much more than they affect the rest of the community. The government of a group, chosen by the group, will be far more in touch with its constituents, far more conscious of their interests, than a remote parliament nominally representing the whole country.[5]

It is true that in a large nation there are many local questions in which most members of the national legislature have no direct interest. It is precisely for this reason that they are in a position to decide such questions impartially. Judges and jurors who are directly interested in the cases which come before them are admitted to be biased and, therefore, unfit to pass upon such cases. The same principle should be applied in legislation.

It is also true that in a great many cases the members of national legislatures have no direct knowledge of the local problems which come before them. Neither do jurors possess direct knowledge of the cases which come before them. Both jurors and legislators should become well acquainted with the facts before reaching any decision on the matters which come

[5] Bertrand Russell, *Proposed Roads to Freedom* (Allen & Unwin, London, 1919), p. 133. For another able presentation of the arguments for giving local governments and consumers co-operatives a large share in the control of economic activity, see Sydney and Beatrice Webb, *A Constitution for a Socialist Commonwealth of Great Britain* (1920), pp. 3–26, 213–14, *et passim*. Their viewpoint is undoubtedly colored by the very great achievements of municipal Socialism and consumer co-operatives in Great Britain. However, the chain stores of the United States appear to be even more successful and well-managed than the English co-operatives. The long-continued secular trend towards mobility of population, which has gone much farther in the United States than in England, also threatens the local interest and knowledge upon which both compulsory and voluntary local co-operation are based. Finally, local control of any kind possesses the very real disadvantage of reducing the scale of management below the most economical size.

before them, but the fact that they lack such knowledge to begin with is not a sound criticism.

Finally, it is not necessary or desirable for the national legislature to consider and pass upon minor questions of local interest only. This task should be delegated to local officials of the various trusts and departments. The national legislature should restrict itself to consideration of the most vital and significant questions which are of general interest.

Thus far we have devoted our attention to the arguments for and against complete centralization of control. We shall now turn our attention to some of the corollaries or specific applications of the general principle.

Perhaps the most important result to be anticipated is the elimination of all local self-government. A multitude of individual local government units would be entirely abolished. Only geographical divisions of the great national trusts and departments would remain, and all of their officials would be appointed, directly or indirectly, by the national government.

Another significant result would be the substitution of unity for division of authority in the national government. The American Constitution provides for a division of power among three independent branches of the government: the Congress, the President, and the Judiciary. This is an admirable device for making reform difficult, since it makes it necessary to persuade three independent powers of the need for each new law. It seriously diminishes the efficiency of government because it gives rise to almost constant friction between those who exercise this divided authority.[6] No nation can serve two masters, let alone three. In a Socialist economy, therefore, there should be no division of authority. Either the legislature or the chief executive should be supreme, and the remainder of the government ought to be completely subordinate to it or him. The best solution would be to have the chief executive chosen by and responsible to the national legislature, thus combining in that body supreme legislative and supreme administrative powers.

All judges should be appointed by the chief executive and should be

---

[6] "The chief hurdles which have faced the advance of professional public administration have been certain political philosophies and attitudes deeply ingrained in the American political consciousness. Among these have been the Jacksonian equalization ideas relative to qualifications for public office. The most difficult to efface, however, has been the conviction that honest and capable public administration can be achieved only by dividing the functions of performance up among several different officers and agencies, none being required to co-operate with the other, and each having the power to veto the constructive acts as well as the knavery of the other." J. M. Pfiffner, *Principles of Public Administration*, p. 14.

removable at his pleasure. They should be required to interpret the laws in accordance with the wishes of the chief executive and the majority of the people who support him. Those responsible for the welfare of the nation must possess all authority necessary to fulfill this responsibility.

A third result would be a great reduction in the size of the national legislature. The average size of existing national legislatures is about five or six hundred members. The result is slow and inefficient legislation. The influence of each member is so slight that the public pays little attention to his conduct. In fact, the vast majority of the voters do not know even the names of more than a few legislators. In order to centralize control, speed up legislation, and arouse the interest of the public in the qualifications, opinions, and conduct of each legislator, it is necessary to reduce radically the number to be elected. While no specific number has any demonstrable scientific advantages, one hundred is suggested here to indicate the degree of reduction in size which is desirable. Such a small legislature would be more like the board of directors of a great Capitalist trust than the huge unwieldy legislatures characteristic of Capitalism. In this respect, as in many others, the national organization of a Socialist economy should be modeled upon that of the typical successful Capitalist trust rather than upon the organization of the democratic Capitalist state. Capitalists, who control both business and government under Capitalism, have been sincerely interested in developing a sound organization for their trusts. They have seldom cared to increase the efficiency and hence the power of the democratic state.

4. AUTHORITY FROM ABOVE

Granted the need for a democratic and centralized organization in a Socialist economy, there is still room for discussion concerning the direction or line of control. Should final authority rest at the top, subject to democratic control, or should it rest at the bottom, subject to democratic control? In the former type of organization all executives would be appointed by their superiors—except, of course, the chief executive. In the latter type of organization all executives would be elected by their subordinates, including the lowest executives, the foremen and gang bosses themselves. In the foregoing discussion of the application of the principle of democracy, it was assumed without explanation that the former kind of democratic organization is desirable. This is not a corollary of the principle of democracy, however, and requires a separate justification.

There is a very sharp difference of opinion upon this subject among Socialist theorists. A large number of Socialists assert that "industrial democracy" is a basic and inherent feature of true Socialism, and by "industrial democracy" they mean democratic election of immediate superiors by all classes of workers.[7] They argue that the workers in each shop or working unit are the best judges of the performance and ability of other workers and their immediate superiors. No one else is so intensely interested in the conditions in the individual shop as the workers who spend their lives there. The millions of voters who elect a chief executive know little or nothing about him; the few workers who elect their own foremen know all about him, so it is argued.

In spite of the very real merits of this line of reasoning, authority from above appears to be much superior for a number of reasons. In the first place, the election of executives by their immediate subordinates is likely to destroy or dangerously weaken the discipline necessary in all organizations. If a foreman is elected by the men under him, he may be afraid or unable to demand punctuality, ready obedience, and industry. If he does demand them, he may be replaced by a more lenient individual at the next election.[8]

A second objection is that industrial democracy of this sort may result in the workers' spending too large a portion of their time in committee meetings, election campaigns, and other activities incident to shop politics. Soviet Russia tried shop democracy and found that it consumed too much of the workers' time and attention.

Another objection to shop democracy is that it may result in the election of men with a personality pleasing to others, or with a gift for political intrigue, rather than in the election of the most capable men. Knowledge and ability are frequently found in unattractive men. Indeed, the possession of an unusually pleasing personality seems to make many men feel that they need not labor to acquire expert knowledge in any field, and it reduces the need for industry and study in order to secure promotion. It must be conceded that this same criticism applies to national as well as to shop elections. However, a special method of electing the nation's chief executive which weakens this criticism to a large extent has been proposed. Even if the leaders of the nation were elected by popular ballot, a magnetic personality would have less influence than in a shop election by reason of the far greater distance between the candidate and the voters. The radio and the newspaper are the primary means of conducting national campaigns; in a shop election personal contact is all-important.

[7] However, the term ought to apply to any system of democratic control over industry. If this broader and more liberal interpretation of the term is proper, the system recommended in this treatise is a system of "industrial democracy."

[8] This point is clearly stated in Sidney and Beatrice Webb's *A Constitution for a Socialist Commonwealth of Great Britain* (1920), p. 48.

A fourth point to be made against shop democracy is that it may make difficult the centralization of control advisable in a Socialist economy. One of the important advantages of centralized control, for instance, is that it will enable the central authorities in each industry to use vigorous measures to raise the level of backward plants or units. If these backward units, and there always will be some, are self-governed, and if they elect their own executives who oppose or hamper the introduction of "new-fangled" methods, this process of improvement will be far more difficult than it need be.

A fifth argument against shop democracy is that the interests of any small group always conflict with the interests of society at innumerable points. Short hours and high wages, lax discipline, and waste may benefit one group of workers at the expense of others. Shop democracy would offer a constant temptation to individual groups of workers to benefit themselves at the expense of the working class as a whole.

If a large group of workers and Socialist theorists continue to desire shop democracy after the revolution, every effort should be made to experiment with it on a large enough scale and over a long enough time to determine its real merits.[9] If it works better than any alternative system, the entire national economy should be organized in that way. A Socialist state should always be eager to try out social experiments. In the social sciences no laboratory exists. All important new theories deserve actual testing in a small portion of the national economy before they are rejected or applied to the nation as a whole. There are, of course, some theories that cannot be applied on a small scale, and others which cannot be verified by experiment because of the number and importance of uncontrolled factors. But continual social experimentation should be a feature of a Socialist economy.

While shop democracy is probably undesirable, this does not mean that workers should have no direct control or influence over local shop conditions and policies. Even Capitalism has found trade unions, company unions, and employee representation highly practical and useful. In every shop and plant the workers should be encouraged to offer advice on all questions and should be given control over many minor conditions of real importance to them. If they desire more heat or better light or cleaner toilet facilities, these things should be provided. If they demand unusually high standards, they might well be required to pay for the improvement; but in such matters they should exercise a large degree of control.

[9] This means an experiment with workers numbering millions and lasting a decade or two.

5. FUNCTIONAL ORGANIZATION

The organization of a Socialist economy should be essentially functional in character. The chief executive's immediate subordinates should each be charged with the performance of a single group of related functions. The large nation-wide organizations necessary to perform each of these functions should also be subdivided along functional lines.

The principle of functional organization was first clearly stated and demonstrated by Frederick W. Taylor, the father of scientific management, but was applied by him only to factory and shop management. Taylor defined functional management by saying that it "consists in so dividing the work of management that each man from the assistant superintendent down shall have as few functions as possible to perform. If practicable the work of each man in the management should be confined to the performance of a single leading function."[10]

Many highly centralized governments already exist under Capitalism, but all of these are organized on a military basis. They are divided into provinces and cities, in each of which nearly all governmental functions are controlled by a single provincial or city government. Education, the protection of life and property, public health, housing, and many other functions are all controlled by the same man or group of men. In a state possessing a functional organization, however, each of these functions would be performed by an independent national organization. There would be no local government apart from the local geographical divisions of these national trusts and departments, and each of these would be independent of all the others. The size of the local administrative unit of each trust or department would be determined by the peculiar nature and needs of the organization in question. The Retail Trust might have a local administrative unit for every 500,000 people, while the Department of Justice might require a local administrative unit for every 100,000 people. The important point is that there would be wide variations in the size and number of such administrative units. There would be no common unit for all or many trusts and departments, such as the state, county, city, or plant community.

Legislative powers should be granted to individual trusts and departments wherever this will facilitate proper execution of the functions entrusted to these organizations. For instance, the departments of Health, Education, and Justice should be able to issue decrees having the force of law. Indeed, most legislation should come from functional agencies rather than from a national legislature, the latter retaining power to revise or repeal any laws decreed by such subordinate authorities.

[10] F. W. Taylor, *Taylor System of Shop Management* (1911), p. 99.

Another advantage of granting legislative power to functional experts is that it would greatly reduce the unwieldy legislative burden now resting upon all supreme legislative bodies. Under Capitalism every national legislature is swamped in a sea of proposed bills at every session. None of them even pretend to consider carefully more than a pitifully small proportion of these new bills. Delegation of legislative powers is absolutely essential to prompt and efficient legislation in most fields.

Functional organization is desirable in the nation as a whole for the same reasons that make it desirable in the individual machine shop. It increases the division of mental labor and enlarges the very great gains derived from such division. A mayor or provincial governor who controls public health, education, street repair, police, etc., cannot supervise any of these departments as well as a specialist in that field. Hence each of these functions should be turned over to a national organization specializing in that work. Since this will leave nothing for independent local authorities to do, they can be completely eliminated.

To secure co-ordination of the activities of all trusts and departments operating in a given community or area, local co-ordinating committees including representatives from each trust and department should be established. Problems which cannot be solved by community and area co-ordinating committees should be appealed to regional and ultimately, if necessary, to a supreme national co-ordinating committee reporting directly to the chief executive. Such committees would not constitute a system of local government since they would be appointed by centrally controlled trusts and departments and would intervene only in case of a dispute among these national organizations.

C. SUMMARY OF ORGANIZATIONAL PLAN

Before leaving the subject of the organization of a Socialist economy, it may be well to embody the principles stated above in a concrete plan of organization. The following plan is not meant to be final, but it will serve to summarize and clarify the major principles discussed above. Chart I (p. 110) shows the structure of such a Socialist national organization.

A Socialist economy should be governed by a single, small national legislature of perhaps one hundred members. Major features of the method of election of the legislature should be proportional representation, national representation, annual elections, direct primary, government payment of campaign costs, and universal suffrage. The national legislature should exercise supreme legislative, judicial, and administrative powers. It should be in continuous session and should have power to take any action by a bare majority vote.

CHART I

ORGANIZATION CHART FOR A SOCIALIST ECONOMY

The Electorate
↓
National Legislature
Advisory Staff
{ Health
Education
Justice
Defense
Foreign
Affairs
Finance }
↓
Chief Executive
Advisory Staff
{ Statistics
Research
Accounting
Scientific
Management
Pricing }

1. Division of Professional Services — { Department of Health, Department of Education, Department of Justice }

2. Division of Government Services — { Department of National Defense, Department of Foreign Affairs }

3. Division of Finance — { Department of the Treasury, Department of Social Insurance, Banking Trust }

4. Division of Heavy Industry — { Non-Ferrous Metals Trust, Chemical Trust, Steel Trust, Machine Building Trust, Construction Trust, Automobile Trust, Building Material Trust }

5. Division of Light Industry — { Textile Trust, Clothing Trust, Food Processing Trust, House Furnishings Trust, Printing Trust, Rubber Goods Trust, Leather Goods Trust, Paper Trust }

6. Division of Trade and Commerce — { Transportation Trust, Marketing Trust, Foreign Trade Trust }

7. Division of Vendible Services — { Housing Trust, Amusement Trust, Service Trust, Public Utility Trust }

8. Division of Supply Bureaus — { Bureau of Natural Resources, Bureau of Capital Supply }

9. Division of Extractive Industry — { Agricultural Trust, Lumber Trust, Mining Trust, Oil Trust }

Wide use of both initiative and referendum should prevail. At every election the voters should be given an opportunity to approve or disapprove the major reforms of the preceding year and to force additional reforms upon an inert or hostile legislature.

The chief executive of a Socialist economy should be elected by the national legislature rather than by the voters directly. This small legislative body would consist of superior men who would be in closer contact with the higher officials of the capitol than ordinary voters. They would therefore be in far better position to weigh the merits of various candidates than the public at large. Their choice should be restricted to a limited group of men already high in administrative rank.

The administrative officials of a Socialist economy should be entirely independent of political influence, except in the case of the chief executive and his immediate subordinates. The political success of a certain party should have no effect upon the selection of the other administrative officials. However, since the national legislature ought to be all-powerful, this principle could never possess more than moral or advisory influence. The public could enforce it by turning out a political party which introduces the spoils system, or, if it so wished, it could support a spoils system. This is an inevitable possibility in any democracy.

Every trust or department should have both a temporary political and a permanent professional head. Political heads should not be members of the national legislature. However, each of them should be given legislative powers in the field of his trust or department. Every department or trust should also have wide judicial powers within its special field.

All functions of a Socialist economy should be divided among some two-score great trusts (for price goods) and departments (for free goods). All of these trusts and departments should be subordinate to the chief executive and to the national legislature, but independent of each other. Their local divisions should take over all work now done by independent local governments, which are an evidence of military organization, and hence inconsistent with functional organization. However, co-ordinating committees on which all trusts and departments are represented should exist in each community or area.

Since no chief executive can adequately supervise the work of two-score separate organizations, these should be combined into about ten groups, each under the control of an executive appointed by the chief executive. Similar functions should be grouped together, so far as possible, in order to facilitate supervision.

All judicial functions not entrusted to individual trusts and departments should be exercised by the Department of Justice. The chief executive should have power to remove all judges whose decisions, in his opinion, conflict with the will of the majority of the electorate on matters of principle (but not on matters of fact).

CHAPTER VI.　THE FACTORS IN PRODUCTION

A. DESCRIPTION OF THE FACTORS IN PRODUCTION[1]

The purpose of this chapter is to prepare the way for a discussion of the problems of production by describing the factors in production, and by explaining how to achieve an optimum supply of each factor and an economic allocation among alternative uses.

There are three factors in production: nature, labor, and capital. The first two may be looked upon as primary or original. The third is a secondary or derived factor since it is a product of the combination of the first two. Some orthodox economists consider enterprise as a fourth factor in production, but it is more practical to treat this element as a form of labor.[2]

I. NATURE

All varieties of economic activity require some space, a part of nature, in which to be carried on, and are directly dependent upon nature as a source of raw materials or as a means of production.

Orthodox economists have long used the term "land" to designate the factor in production which is here called "nature." The conventional term, however, has a number of serious defects as the name for the factor in production to which it has been applied.

In the first place, it is used in common everyday speech with a meaning quite different from its definition by the economists. To the layman, land means a portion of the earth's surface used primarily for agricultural

---

[1] For a much more detailed discussion of the subject of this section by an exceptionally lucid writer, see John Stuart Mill, *Principles of Political Economy*, Book I, chapters 1–7. Mill's analysis is as sound for a Socialist as for a Capitalist economy.

[2] "Marshall, in his *Principles*, has endeavoured to set up a fourth class of agents of production, beside land, labour, and capital, namely organization, to the important functions of which in the modern mechanism of production he has devoted several long and suggestive chapters of his book. But, however important it may be to determine the economic role of intellectual progress and of inventions and discoveries (which earlier economists not infrequently confused with capital itself), this classification suffers from the inconvenience that the new agency thus introduced, unlike the old, lacks quantitative precision, except in some special cases. Such a case would arise when organizing talent or technical discovery is incorporated in certain individuals of outstanding gifts or specialized education. But in that case, 'organization' cannot be distinguished from 'labour'; it is only a special form of labour, and has always been so treated." Knut Wicksell, *Lectures on Political Economy* (George Routledge & Sons, Ltd., London, 1934–35), pp. 107–8.

and secondarily for other purposes. It does not include seas and rivers used for fishing, transportation, or the development of power. It does not include deposits of minerals and mines. It does not include rain, sunshine, air, and many other natural events or objects. To the economist, however, all these things are necessary or useful in production, and are, or ought to be, included under the term land.

In the second place, the improved land which is brought to mind by the term land is only partly land. A widely varying fraction of its productivity is due to the investment of capital, an entirely distinct factor in production. Thus the use of the term land by the economist in any but its popular meaning leads to misunderstanding. Nature is a better term, since it has the same meaning in popular use which is given it here in economic theory.

In the third place, nature is a superior term from the point of view of the Socialist since it emphasizes the unchanging and inalienable character of the factor in question. It sounds much more plausible to speak of a landowner than to speak of a nature-owner. The use of the term nature helps to explain the basic Socialist principle that the income from this factor in production ought not to be appropriated by a few private individuals but ought rather to be distributed among all the members of society.

2. LABOR

The second original factor in production is labor, which includes all human effort intended to produce economic goods. No hard and fast line can be drawn between labor and other activities. All human activity is an attempt to produce utility or utilitum. For the most part, economic activity or labor in an advanced industrial society produces economic goods for sale in a market, but it also produces articles and services for consumption by the producer, his family, and his friends. It is difficult to distinguish between the production of services for oneself and noneconomic activity. For instance, a man who shaves himself is performing a service available in commercial barber shops, which therefore may logically be called labor, but the same logic can be applied to many other self-services, such as reading, playing the piano, making love, etc. Few people would be willing to call such activities labor, however. Perhaps the most satisfactory way to distinguish between labor for one's own direct benefit and noneconomic activity, is to base the distinction on the purpose of the performer. If he is chiefly interested in the end-product of his activity, the good produced, the activity may be called labor; while if he is chiefly interested in the pleasure of the activity itself, it may be called noneconomic activity. But many paid workers derive great satisfaction out of their work itself. Therefore, the line between labor for oneself and non-economic activities must continue to be very vague. Labor is no more homogeneous than land. The activity of the watchmaker, the song of the opera star, the sermon of the preacher, the effort of the bricklayer—all are labor. Like different utilities, they have no common denominator other than a monetary unit.

3. CAPITAL

The third factor in production, capital, is a secondary or derived factor, since it can be produced only by use of the two original factors in combination. Capital, indeed, did not come into existence until long after nature and man.

Capital includes all wealth exclusive of nature. All forms of wealth are used to create utility or utilitum. Everything, but labor and nature, that is used to create utilitum is capital. There are, however, two kinds of capital. One kind is used to produce utilitum for the owner or lessee, and the other is used to produce economic goods for consumption by others. The former is consumers' capital; the latter, producers' capital. Houses and automobiles usually belong in the former class, factories and trucks in the latter class.

Acquired skill and useful knowledge, when scarce enough to possess marginal utility, are very important forms of capital. A certain amount of skill is the inevitable result of continuous production,[3] but the great bulk of the personal skill and scientific or technical knowledge which are chiefly responsible for modern civilization is the result of deliberate abstinence. It is past income saved and invested in practice, study, and research in order to increase future productivity and income. Both skill and knowledge are material. They are physical effects wrought upon physical beings. Like other kinds of capital, they may be divided into consumers' and producers' capital. Skill in sport belongs in the former class, except for professionals, and skill in work belongs to the latter class.

Capital is the result of saving, or abstinence. It is a portion of past production which has not yet been consumed. Not only is capital created by saving; it is also maintained by saving. A portion of each period's production must be set aside to repair or replace the capital instruments of production if the existing supply of capital is to be maintained. This is not net saving but it is a part of gross saving.

Money is capital only to the extent of its cost of production. A billion dollars' worth of paper money represents ten dollars' worth of capital,

---

[3] Such skill appears to be a form of capital produced without any abstinence. Actually, it represents past income automatically produced in an unconsumable form. It is capital produced by involuntary abstinence.

and that only when new, if ten dollars is the cost of printing it. Paper money, like bonds, notes, mortgages, patents, copyrights, stock, property deeds, and business agreements, is a claim upon wealth or a share in income but is not wealth itself, except to the extent of its depreciated cost of production.

B. ACHIEVING AN OPTIMUM SUPPLY OF EACH FACTOR IN PRODUCTION

Under Capitalism very little conscious social control is exercised over the total supply of each factor in production. These quantities are determined in an unplanned manner by natural physical and human conditions. But the total wealth and income of a nation are greatly influenced by the quantity of land, labor, and capital available. If a Socialist state is to maximize the production of wealth, it must, in the first place, determine and achieve the optimum supply of each factor in production.

The general principle to be followed in determining the optimum supply of each of the factors in production is that the supply should be increased or decreased until its marginal utility and disutility are equal. This general statement will be elaborated in a discussion of the supply of each individual factor.

It should be emphasized that the size of the optimum supply of one factor in production is dependent upon the quantity of each of the other two. An increase in the supply of one factor increases the marginal utility of the others. Any change in the supply of one factor, therefore, destroys a pre-existing equilibrium (it being assumed that the supply of each factor has been at the optimum level) and makes necessary the determination and attainment of new optimum supply levels. These optimum levels cannot be determined independently. They are three unknowns in a single equation.

1. NATURE

Since the supply of natural agents in a given area is fixed by nature, no problem arises concerning determination of an optimum supply of them or concerning methods of realizing this supply.[4] Of any given supply of natural agents, however, only that portion should be used which returns a rent income. The proper utilization of each natural agent would automatically result if every producer in a Socialist economy extended his

[4] Of course, the supply of land can be increased by the annexation of foreign territory, but this also increases the supply of capital and labor. However, if the annexed land has a relatively small wealth and population, annexation will have the same effect as an increase in the supply of land.

use of it until the marginal cost to him precisely equaled its marginal share in the price of his product.

The total supply of improved land may be altered slightly by reclamation projects and other means. This amounts to an investment of capital, however, and hence should be governed by the rules which apply to the creation and use of capital.

2. LABOR

The supply of labor is far more amenable to social control than the supply of natural resources. While the state cannot create or destroy large numbers of laborers in a short period of time, there is no valid reason why, in the long run, a Socialist government should not alter the total supply of labor in any desired direction and degree.

As explained in chapter iv, the goal of Socialist economic theory is maximum average individual net utilitum. The optimum supply of labor, therefore, is that which maximizes average individual net utilitum.

In estimating the optimum labor supply at any given time, it is important to bear in mind that the supply of natural resources cannot be increased, and that, while the supply of capital can and will be steadily increased, most of this increase would occur even if there were no increase in population. Hence, every increase in population reduces the amount of land and capital per worker. Unless offset by other forces, this reduces the productivity of labor.

The optimum supply of labor depends also upon the relative importance, within the national economy, of industries of increasing and decreasing costs and upon the rate at which their costs increase or decrease. If the supply of labor is below the optimum level, an increase in the supply of labor would lower the cost of living by reducing unit costs in industries of decreasing costs (nonextractive industries) more than it would raise them in industries of increasing costs (extractive industries). It would achieve this effect in spite of the unfavorable effect on labor productivity of the decrease in the amount of land and capital per worker caused by any increase in population.

In order to permit the central authorities to estimate as accurately as possible the optimum labor supply for a given nation, each important division of the national economy should be required to submit a chart showing estimated unit costs for different volumes of production assuming no use of additional capital. The increasing or decreasing costs shown in these charts should be weighted according to the annual consumption of the articles concerned, and then consolidated into a single national chart showing average unit costs for all goods—that is, the converse of the average productivity of labor—for various levels of labor supply.

The low point in this consolidated chart would indicate the optimum supply of labor. This limit should be ascertained periodically in order that a secular trend may be determined. The secular trend is needed since population cannot be changed quickly, and most policies aiming at an optimum labor supply should accordingly be based upon an estimate of some future optimum.

The supply of labor in almost every civilized nation is now much above the optimum level. The truth of this statement is supported by the fact that among the civilized nations of the world the standard of living varies inversely with the population per square mile. In China and India, where population is the densest, wages are shamefully low. In Europe they are much higher. In Australia and North America, where the supply of labor per square mile is far less, wages are still higher. There are other factors, such as the richness of the soil, the industry of the people, and the technique of production, which help to account for these wage variations; but overpopulation can also be proved by comparisons between states where these factors are largely the same. For instance, there are long-established wage differences between England and New England.

The optimum labor supply for any state is subject to great changes, due to improvements in the technique of production. In a nation of advanced technique, such as the United States, where agriculture uses less than one-fifth of the total labor supply and where the number of acres per farm worker is relatively high, increasing costs in agriculture are more than offset by the increasing returns from mass production in industry, transportation, and retail trade. In a nation like China, where 95 percent of the total supply of labor is engaged in a very intensive type of agriculture, increasing costs in that field are only slightly offset by decreasing costs in other branches of the national economy. In the United States, in other words, total national production can be carried far beyond the point where diminishing returns begin to appear in agriculture without increasing the average unit costs of all goods. In China, production can be carried only slightly beyond that point if average unit costs are to be minimized.

The rapid technical progress of the last century and a half has, therefore, enormously increased the optimum level of population in advanced nations. Apparently the same evolution in technique and the same effects upon optimum population levels may be anticipated for an indefinite future period.

The adoption of Socialism would be a great improvement in the technique of production in any advanced state, one which would double or treble the output of manufacturing industry, transportation, and retail distribution. This in turn would double or treble the significance of decreasing costs in these fields and thus justify the extension of agricultural production still further beyond the point where diminishing returns appear. In conjunction with marked improvements in the technique of agriculture itself, these changes might double the optimum population level within a few decades after Socialism has been introduced.

Controlling Hours and Intensity of Labor.—Once the task of determining the optimum labor supply has been performed, a Socialist administration will be faced by the more difficult problem of achieving this optimum level. The total supply of labor at any one time is dependent upon a number of factors. Some of these are proper objects of social control and others are not.

In the first place, if full employment exists, the supply of labor is equal to the amount of work done. This is dependent upon the intensity of effort of the individual worker, the proportion of the population that chooses to work, and the number of hours worked, as well as upon the size of the population. Piece rates and other devices for stimulating the efforts of workers increase the supply of labor. Very considerable increases may result from the movement of women, children, or retired workers into industry. Changes in the hours of labor also affect the total supply of labor, though not in proportion to their degree, since they usually cause an inverse change in the intensity of labor.

The administrators of a Socialist economy should not attempt to regulate the total supply of labor by determining the intensity of labor, the number of women and elderly persons who work, or the hours of labor. Every adult citizen should be allowed to fix his own intensity and hours of labor at the point where the marginal utilitum and disutilitum of work or effort are equal.

The reason for granting this absolute freedom of choice to the individual has already been explained, but is so important that it deserves frequent repetition. The purpose of Socialism is to maximize average net utilitum. Hence each citizen should work each day until the marginal utilitum and disutilitum of labor become equal and then cease working. If he or she works less than this amount, a possible increase in net utilitum is lost. If work is carried beyond this point, the additional labor yields more disutilitum than utilitum and reduces the net utilitum for the day. In order to achieve the desired balance the state must permit each worker to determine the length of his daily work period. No one can measure the sensations experienced by another or determine the time when the marginal utilitum and disutilitum of his labor are equal. The individual can, however, do this for himself and he has a sufficient motive to do so—namely, self-interest.

Since there is a wide diversity in the natural endowment and acquired traits of men and women, there should be corresponding variety in the lengths of working shifts, and a Socialist state should so control economic activity as to permit each worker a wide choice. Under Capitalism no such freedom of choice exists. All the workers in a given plant or industry are compelled to work the same number of hours if they work at all. Under Socialism, however, each large plant ought to be so organized as to give work to men who want to work only four hours a day, to those who wish to work five or six hours a day, and to those who wish to work abnormally long shifts of seven hours a day. Complete freedom of choice is impractical since no two workers are alike and excessive variation in the length of working shifts would increase costs unduly. Nevertheless, it is perfectly feasible to give the great majority of workers a choice between four or five shifts of very different duration. This may increase costs slightly. If it does, the increased costs should be taken out of the wages of those who cause them. If a man who works six hours a day causes less overhead expense per hour of work than one who works two or four hours, he should be paid more per hour. Every worker ought to have a free choice between different shifts, however. The thing to be emphasized is that under Socialism economic activity must be so organized as to fit the needs of man. He must never be sacrificed to the alleged needs of efficiency in production.

Not only should the worker be given a choice concerning his hours of labor; he should also be given a certain minimum choice concerning his intensity of effort. Here again maximum short-run efficiency in production is certain to conflict with maximum individual utility or happiness, and must be sacrificed to the latter. Human nature varies so greatly that an intensity of effort which is ideal for one man destroys the pleasure of living for another. Where the worker uses individual tools and materials, the adjustment problem is easily solved by letting him turn out as much work as he pleases. On an automobile assembly line the problem is more complex, but perfectly capable of solution. The work of assembly can be more or less minutely subdivided so as to vary the task of each individual according to his own wishes. If necessary, different assembly lines can be operated at different speeds so as to give further freedom of choice. The need for freedom of choice of tempo of work would naturally depend upon the amount of freedom of choice concerning the length of the work shift, and vice versa, for each is a partial substitute for the other.

Methods of wage determination have an important effect upon the intensity of effort of nearly all workers and, consequently, upon the supply of labor. If the substitution of piece rates for time wages doubles the output of the average worker—and this has actually happened in many cases—it means that the supply of labor has been doubled. Obviously, therefore, the method of wage payment has a very vital effect upon the size of the optimum population. The more effective the incentives to increased output, the lower is the optimum population.

Controlling the Size of Population.—While in the short run the supply of labor is chiefly determined by the hours of labor, the proportion of the population at work, and the intensity of effort of the average worker, in the long run it is largely determined by the size of the population. Since a Socialist economy should not attempt to control the short-run factors, except by offering an optimum wage for additional output, it must control the supply of labor chiefly by influencing the size of the population.

Every nation ought to assume control over the size of its population. In the absence of any such control, any nation may sink into the frightful poverty of modern India and China. Control of population is a proper function of the state because every addition to the supply of labor, whether due to immigration from some other country or some other world (birth), may increase or diminish the income of every other member of society. To tell a man how many children he may have may appear to be an unjustified interference with personal liberty. If we realize, however, that an additional child may diminish the income and happiness of every other member of society, the justice of such social interference becomes obvious.

Assuming, then, that a Socialist nation should control the size of its population, what measures should it adopt to realize an optimum population? Let us consider first the control of immigration and emigration. Advanced nations can increase their population by permitting immigration from poorer nations. Immigration has the advantage of providing additional labor more quickly and cheaply than any other method. On the other hand, although the biological effects of the intermarriage of persons of different racial stocks are neutral, immigrants ordinarily lower the economic culture and technique of the nations to which they come because they nearly always come from the lower classes of poorer nations. Moreover, immigration deprives the previous population of the very appreciable psychic income it could have derived from supplying the increased numbers of workers through birth and domestic rearing. Rearing children is one of the chief sources of utilitum or human happiness.

A nation which already possesses an optimum population should restrict immigration to negligible proportions. It would always be wise, however, to welcome immigrants of markedly superior natural intelligence, education, or achievement. They would improve the racial stock and also increase the income of the average citizen by supplying superior leadership and professional services.[5]

[5] This exception to the general rule serves to illustrate a significant point. This summary discussion of the factors in production deals with each factor as

While compulsory emigration ought not to be used as a means for relieving overpopulation, a Socialist state would be wise to encourage voluntary emigration when overpopulation exists. The payment of a small bonus or the extension of cheap credit would certainly serve to stimulate emigration and should be used when emigration is desirable. Emigration cannot be looked upon as a major cure for overpopulation, however. The world as a whole suffers from very serious overpopulation, so that the number of countries that need immigrants is very small in comparison with the number of overpopulated nations. Moreover, under Capitalism unemployment usually exists even in those nations which have not yet attained their optimum population, and they are therefore often reluctant to accept immigrants.

The chief means which a Socialist state should use to regulate the volume of population is control of the domestic birth rate. So far as possible, this control should be persuasive only, but compulsory measures should be adopted to deal with an antisocial minority.

For motives other than that of population control, a Socialist state should teach all interested women the best and most scientific means of birth control. This should be done in the public school system. The case for birth control may be clearly stated in economic terminology. The production of children, like the production of anything else, ought to be extended to, but not beyond, the point at which the marginal utilitum and disutilitum of production are equal. Knowledge and practice of birth control are absolutely essential to a limitation of births at this desired point.

Since the utility of children is far greater to some parents than to others, the state ought not to determine absolutely the number of children per family. Only the individuals concerned can estimate the utilitum and disutilitum directly involved. However, the state can estimate the utility or disutility to the remainder of society of an additional child in the average family, and it can transform this estimated gain or loss to other members of the nation into utilitum or disutilitum to the individual parents, thus enabling them to balance the total utilitum and disutilitum of additional children. When a nation has not yet attained an optimum population, it should pay a bonus for each child born. This would greatly encourage births at a small cost. In the United States, for instance, the payment of a bonus of $1,000 per birth would cost only about $3,000,-000,000 a year.

a whole. However, no factor is homogeneous. An oversupply of labor or capital, therefore, is always accompanied by an undersupply of certain kinds of labor or capital and vice versa. It must be emphasized, therefore, that the principles here set forth concerning the control of the total supply of each factor should also be applied to the control of the supply of each kind of labor or capital.

When a nation is suffering from overpopulation, a common situation in the world today, it should establish a tariff on births to protect the existing and future labor supply. The tariff should apply to every child born, unless exceptions are made for eugenic motives, and should be high enough to reduce the birth rate to the desired level. No opportunity to evade this fine or tariff will exist in a Socialist state, since the government will always be able to deduct it from future wages.

A state should not attempt to bring about radical sudden changes in its population unless it has the vigorous support of a large majority of its people. Over a long period of time, however, radical changes can be effected without great cost to any one generation.

The problem of controlling population size is closely related to the problem of eugenics. While the latter question, by general acceptance, lies outside the field of economics, its importance for future economic welfare and progress cannot be overemphasized. A Socialist state should certainly adopt radical eugenic laws as fast as the people can be educated to appreciate their need. The two basic evils which afflict humanity are poverty and poor heredity. The development of industrial technique and the adoption of Socialism will eliminate the former evil. But poor heredity can be eliminated only by breeding out undesirable strains, and this will require many generations to accomplish successfully. The eugenic measures adopted to achieve this result will also increase tremendously the average productivity of labor by eliminating the feeble-minded and other defectives, and by raising the average level of intelligence. Once Socialism has been attained, radical eugenic measures will be the next great reform in the history of society, and the movement for eugenic reform will absorb the bulk of the humanitarian and intellectual forces now devoted to the achievement of Socialism.[6]

3. CAPITAL

The problem of determining and achieving an optimum supply of capital is of particular significance inasmuch as the possession of relatively large stores of capital is the chief feature which distinguishes an advanced nation from a backward nation. It seems probable, indeed, that any backward race can rise to any desired economic level merely by the accumulation of sufficient capital, particularly capital in the form of skill, education, and knowledge.

In the long run, that economic system which provides for the most

[6] For a discussion of the relationship between eugenics and political economy see Pigou, *Economics of Welfare* (4th ed. [1932], London), pp. 91–106. Here as elsewhere, Pigou displays an excessively cautious and conservative attitude towards the advantages of reform.

rapid accumulation of capital is certain to win world-wide dominance, for military reasons if for no other. There is every reason to believe, moreover, that Socialism will surpass Capitalism in its rate of saving.[7]

Despite the more rapid accumulation of capital, the rate of interest will probably rise for a century or more after the adoption of Socialism. Scientific research is steadily creating new opportunities for desirable investment, and Socialism should greatly increase the volume of such research. Moreover, Socialism will markedly increase real incomes, particularly of the more poorly paid workers, and this will tremendously increase the demand for new housing, public utilities, railroads, and all other physical facilities used to satisfy economic wants. Finally, a Socialist government will require vast amounts of capital to build or modernize hospitals, nurseries, schools, universities, libraries, museums, laboratories, concert halls, parks, playgrounds, roads, highways, airports, and other facilities used to provide free services.

Capitalist economists often assume without much discussion that the

[7] "If . . . . the long-prophesied ideal of economists, in which interest will have fallen to a minimum, is tardy in its realization, the cause is presumably to be found in the following circumstances. In the first place, there is the effect of the subjective undervaluation of future needs and overvaluation of future resources, which was observed by Bohm-Bawerk. This in turn is primarily due to the fact that to the individual, the future is always in a high degree uncertain. He does not know whether he himself, or those in whose well-being he is most interested, will really profit by his sacrifices. Moreover, even if capital accumulation as a whole increases production, the return on individual capital accumulation, even the technical return, is uncertain. The enterprises in which capital is invested may perhaps yield large profits if they are very successful; but the chances of such success are not very great. And since, in accordance with the general law of marginal utility, the possibility of a loss of wealth outweighs, for the individual, the prospect of an equal gain, such an enterprise, from the point of view of individual business, must always be regarded as unprofitable unless the chances of gain considerably exceed those of loss. This is probably the general rule. The special inducement which hazardous enterprises offer to gambling or adventurous spirits is a compensation, but operates perhaps more in the destruction than in the accumulation of capital.

"In these respects, however, a collectivist society would afford a much better guarantee for the rapid accumulation of capital than does the existing individualistic society. The capital saved by united efforts would equally benefit all individuals and the whole of society in the future, and the failure of some enterprises would be of little importance, if those which succeeded yielded a correspondingly greater return. Though this is opposed to current opinion, it is precisely in a collectivist society that we should expect a progressive accumulation of capital until production was fully supplied with new capital and the national dividend reached its technical maximum—assuming that interest in the well-being of future generations was not less than in existing society." Knut Wicksell, *Lectures on Political Economy* (George Routledge & Sons, Ltd., London, 1934–35), pp. 211–12.

productivity of capital is equal to the amount which capital can earn in the production of goods to be sold in a competitive market. This over-looks the productivity of capital used to provide free goods or to reduce non-monetary costs such as sickness, accidents, ugliness, boredom, loneli-ness, and other disutilities on which the market places no monetary meas-ure. Under Socialism the productivity of capital will be sharply increased merely by the increased desire of the government and the people to build the facilities necessary to provide free justice, free health, free nursery schools, free playgrounds, etc.; to eliminate most of the existing physical causes of accidents; and to otherwise improve the physical environment.

The cost of creating capital is the disutility of abstinence. The gain from the creation of capital is the increased production of goods made possible thereby. The cost of abstinence is subject to the principle of in-creasing disutility, and the gain from increased production is subject to the law of diminishing utility. The supply of capital is at an optimum level when the marginal utility of capital and the marginal disutility of abstinence are equal. When the supply of capital is below this level, addi-tional abstinence yields net utility and is therefore socially desirable. When the supply of capital is above this level, the marginal unit of absti-nence yields net disutility and is therefore uneconomic.

In a progressive economy the optimum supply of capital is steadily in-creasing. It is, therefore, possible to have an optimum supply of capital and an optimum volume of saving at the same time. The optimum volume of saving is necessary to increase the supply of capital as the optimum supply increases—in other words, to maintain the supply of capital at the ever rising optimum level.

Under Socialism the market rate of interest, established by the Bureau of Capital Supply in a manner to be described later, would measure the marginal utility of capital. If this rate of interest were paid to all savers, and if they were perfectly rational and individually free to control their own volume of saving, each saver would increase his abstinence until its marginal disutility became equal to the marginal rate of interest. This would, therefore, result in an optimum supply of capital and an optimum volume of saving, for the marginal utility of capital and the marginal disutility of abstinence to each saver would be identical.

Compulsory Saving.—If perfect competition existed under Capital-ism, an obvious impossibility, saving would be done voluntarily by mil-lions of individuals. Under modern monopolistic Capitalism, however, most saving is done by governments and corporations, and a majority vote of the citizens or stockholders is all the authority required for such saving. This fact is largely ignored by Capitalist economists who claim that saving is perfectly controlled under Capitalism because each individual carries saving to the optimum level, the level at which the utility and disutility of saving to each individual become equal.

In most cases, the erroneous statement of orthodox economists that something does happen under Capitalism is a good guide as to what ought to happen under Socialism, but saving is an exception to this rule. There are a number of compelling reasons why under Socialism most saving should be social and compulsory rather than individual and voluntary.

In the first place, it is possible that voluntary saving by individuals and corporations is an effective method of accumulating capital under Capitalism only because of the right of bequest and inheritance, and because of the existence of huge unearned incomes which make saving virtually without disutility in many cases. These unearned incomes would disappear or be divided up among the entire working population of a Socialist economy. A Socialist society, moreover, should not tolerate the inheritance of appreciable sums of unearned wealth or income. Inheritance decreases the supply of labor by creating a leisure class, and increases inequality of income. Differences in income due to inheritance are not necessary to stimulate saving, since this economic function can easily be taken over by the state.

State saving and provision of capital is also desirable because it is partially compulsory and would accordingly increase the total volume of saving. Once the majority of voters had approved a certain annual rate of saving, the entire nation would be compelled to assist in achieving this rate. Reckless and improvident individuals who care little about their economic obligations to family and community would be forced to save at the rate determined upon by the majority of voters.

The justification for compelling certain individuals to save is precisely the same as the justification for preventing certain individuals from borrowing as much as they would like to in order to increase their present expenditures. The desire to borrow constantly in order to increase current spending is merely an exaggerated case of desiring to save nothing in order to increase current spending. There is a large minority in every group for whom the present utility of a given income is so much greater than the future utility of an equal income that they must not only be prevented from borrowing excessively but must also be compelled to save a minimum percentage of their income.

Finally, compulsory social saving is desirable because it tends to equalize individual savings and the interest incomes which result from them. It would therefore result in a greater equality of income than voluntary private thrift.

Control over the volume of compulsory social saving should be in the hands of the national legislature or in the hands of the voters themselves.

In the latter case, every voter might be permitted to vote for a specific rate of compulsory saving and the rate receiving the most votes could be adopted.[8]

It would be wise to treat compulsory savings as private savings by crediting them to individual savings accounts on which the market rate of interest is paid. This would aid individual voters in determining the rate of compulsory saving by giving them evidence of the marginal utility of further saving.

Probably the best method of compelling individuals to save would be to levy a uniform and universal income tax. On each pay day the State Bank should debit the demand account of each worker and credit his compulsory savings account by the amount of this savings tax.

[8] After explaining that it is possible to fix either the volume of saving or the rate of interest, and that the determination of one automatically determines the other, H. D. Dickinson continues:

"Two procedures can now be followed [in controlling the accumulation of capital], according as to whether interest-rate or quantity of accumulation is to be taken as the independent variable. In the first case the Supreme Economic Council will fix a certain rate of interest for the year and then earmark the corresponding quantity of capital out of the total social income. In the second case the Supreme Economic Council will fix the amount of capital that is to be raised, and then the ruling rate of interest for the current accounting period will be given [by the consolidated demand schedule for capital]. . . . .

"If interest is to be taken as the independent variable, what principles should be followed in deciding upon a rate of interest? If Cassel's argument in *The Nature and Necessity of Interest* is valid, then the rate of interest depends on the duration of human life" (*Theory of Social Economy*, pp. 241–45).

"Here it is true that the Socialist community cannot determine the exact figure with the accuracy of an individualist community, balancing the attractiveness of perpetuities against that of life annuities. Still, no extreme error in valuation will be incurred if the Supreme Economic Council accumulates until the rate of interest falls to, say, 2 percent and then keeps the rate of interest steady. If the tempo of technical invention increases or if public taste becomes more changeable, the amount of new capital to be raised in a year will increase; if invention or changes in taste fall off, the amount of new capital to be raised will diminish."

A further statement from Dickinson is pertinent here. "If the amount to be saved is to be taken as the independent variable, then the most appropriate formula would be that of F. P. Ramsey ("A Mathematical Theory of Saving," *Economic Journal*, December 1928). It may be objected that the practical application of this formula involves the determination of utilities. Nevertheless, this problem should not prove to be insoluble in a community of approximately equal incomes, given free choice of consumption and the sale of consumption goods at a price in the market. If it can be solved, even approximately, a rate of saving can be determined and then from the demand schedules of the different undertakings a corresponding rate of interest can be found." ("Price Formation in a Socialist Community," *Economic Journal*, June 1933, pp. 244–45.)

Voluntary Saving.—Even if compulsory social saving is adopted, voluntary private savers should be encouraged to assist in the accumulation of capital. Compulsory social saving will increase the rate of accumulation among an improvident minority, just as free and compulsory education raises the educational level of a backward minority; but, like the latter, it should not restrict the attainments of those who desire to achieve more than the average. Incidentally, the provision of free education supported by taxes is merely one form of compulsory social saving, and one long in use under Capitalism.

Private savings might take a number of different forms under Socialism. If workers are to have complete freedom in the expenditure of their income, they must be permitted to save a portion of one period's earnings and spend it in another period. To facilitate and measure such saving, the State Bank should accept savings accounts and pay the market rate of interest. Measurement of such savings is important because they reduce the immediate demand for consumable goods. Payment of interest is proper because this merely passes on to the worker the net gain resulting from his saving.

The most common form of private saving in a Socialist state will undoubtedly be investment in relatively durable consumers' goods such as automobiles, clothing, furniture, radios, books, pictures, household appliances, etc. Indeed, the average worker will possess far more private property under Socialism than he has ever possessed under Capitalism. No limit need be set to saving of this sort.

While private saving in the form of investment in consumers' goods, savings accounts, and insurance should be both permitted and encouraged in a Socialist state, the right of inheritance must be restricted in order to prevent the rise of unearned interest income. If a worker saves a dollar a day out of his wages in anticipation of a trip abroad, he earns whatever interest is paid upon those savings. If, however, he dies unexpectedly, no principal or interest should be paid to his heirs, for they have done nothing to earn this money.

In actual practice, of course, it would do no appreciable injustice to permit the inheritance of sums below a certain minimum—perhaps a thousand dollars. This would permit every worker to inherit far more than the average worker inherits in any Capitalist nation. Moreover, inheritance would be much less needed since the state would pension all dependents unable to work.[9]

Fallacy of Saving by Individual Trusts.—A number of able Socialist

[9] On private property and saving under Socialism see the remarks of Sydney and Beatrice Webb, *A Constitution for the Socialist Commonwealth of Great Britain* (1920), pp. 340–48.

thinkers have suggested that each Socialist trust should accumulate its own new capital whenever additional capital is needed by raising the price of its products above the cost of production.[10] This method of accumulating capital is uneconomic. In the first place, it involves a definite division of control over the volume of saving among the managements of many different trusts. This is contrary to the basic principle of centralization of power.[11] In the second place, the interests of high trust executives and ordinary consumers are apt to be in permanent conflict. A trust executive will usually desire to increase the size of the enterprise under his control, while the consumer will prefer a low price on the goods he buys. Moreover, since trust executives will be less directly subject to popular control than members of the national legislature, they are more likely to disregard the desires of the people with regard to the volume of saving.

In the third place, this method of accumulating capital involves the use of varying sales taxes on the products of different trusts. A rapidly expanding demand might force one industry to use a very high tax, or else fail to satisfy the demand, while at the same time in some stable industry no tax at all would be in use. This is decidedly uneconomic because it involves a distortion of demand. High prices in the expanding industry would destroy demand which might economically be satisfied with capital accumulated in older industries. If it were proper to accumulate additional capital by taxing producers, it would be advisable to tax every industry equally in order that the burden of these taxes would produce the minimum possible effect upon the distribution of demand among different industries. However, for reasons given in a later chapter on taxation (chapter x), few if any taxes should be levied on business.

Involuntary Capital Gains and Losses.—As explained above, the supply of capital in a Socialist economy will be determined chiefly by the volume of past and present compulsory social saving. Private saving will occur, but on a relatively small scale.

In addition to these two factors, however, there would be, under the system of production control which this book recommends, a number of

---

[10] "It [the Socialist Commonwealth] is more likely to arrange, so as to avoid incurring any burden of interest, that each National Board trust should provide in its budget for the year for the execution of the extensions and improvements that it is considered desirable to execute within the year. In this way there would be, in favour of the future, a 'loading' on the cost of production of the commodities or services produced in the year, but (as experience has taught the British Municipal Financiers) a smaller loading than would be necessitated, year in and year out, by the payment of interest and sinking fund of 'borrowed capital.' " *Ibid.*, pp. 347–48.

[11] This principle is elaborated in chapter v, "The Organization of the National Economy."

involuntary capital gains and losses affecting the total volume of capital. All profits or losses due to underproduction or overproduction, for instance, belong in this classification. They should be treated as debits or credits to the capital accounts of the individual trusts, and in the opposite manner by the National Bureau of Capital Supply. In other words, an operating profit made by an individual trust should be debited to the undistributed profit account and credited to the account showing liability due to capital borrowed from the Bureau of Capital Supply. Upon receipt of notice of these entries, the Bureau of Capital Supply should debit its asset account showing advances to the trust in question, and credit its surplus or capital account. After this, the trust should pay interest upon the full balance of its capital account. An operating loss should be treated in precisely the opposite manner—that is, as a repayment of capital. The economic theory behind this treatment of profits and losses will be developed in detail in Part Three. In the long run such operating profits and losses should cancel out.

C. THE ALLOCATION OF THE FACTORS IN PRODUCTION

Having considered the two necessary preliminary questions of how to determine and how to achieve the proper supply of each factor in production, we may now turn to the problems involved in the distribution or allocation of a given supply of each factor among the innumerable alternative uses which are always possible.

The problem of allocating the factors in production among alternative uses may be divided into two parts. In the first place, there is the problem of placing them at the disposal of those economic organizations which can make the best use of them. In the second place, there is the problem faced by the individual organization of determining the best or most economic use for its existing supply. Both phases of the problem of the allocation of the factors in production are at the same time divisions of the general problem of the control of production. This latter subject will be treated in detail in Part Three. In the remainder of this chapter much that is proved in Part Three will be assumed, and attention will be centered on problems peculiar to the allocation of the factors in production.

I. NATURAL RESOURCES

Division Among Individual Trusts and Departments.—In order to facilitate the control and allocation of natural resources, a National Bureau of Natural Resources should be established and given full control over this factor.

The chief function of this bureau should be to lease or rent individual portions of the total supply of natural resources to whatever organization makes the highest bid for their use. It should attempt to maximize its rental income, but at the same time should rarely refuse any bid which is the highest offer at the moment. In other words, it should not use its power to hold resources off the market as a means of raising rental income to a point nearer the level of the real economic rent involved.[12]

The universality of monopoly in a Socialist economy will reduce competition for the use of the factors in production. Under Capitalism, if competition exists, many entrepreneurs are free to bid for each coal mine or city lot, thus forcing rent outlay up to the level of real economic rent. In a Socialist economy, however, there should be no competition for coal mines, and only limited competition for land. Consequently, the rents obtained by the National Bureau of Natural Resources would always fall below the level of economic rent, and in some cases would be purely nominal.

Nevertheless, these rents should serve to set the margins between alternative uses by different trusts and departments at the proper point. For instance, the margin between land used for cultivation and land used for forestry ought to be set at the point where the Agricultural Trust can just afford to outbid the Lumber Trust for the use of land.

This method of distributing the natural resources of the nation among different trusts and departments is sound because rent offers indicate the net utility to be obtained from the use of these natural resources. A trust cannot afford to pay rent for a given piece of land unless it can earn a surplus over other costs sufficient to pay this rent.[13] Since net money income measures net utility, this means that the trust would use the land in such a way as to produce the net utility indicated by the rent offer. The higher the rent offer, the higher the net utility indicated. Hence land and other natural resources should be used by those organizations which offer the highest rent for them.

If competing bidders for the use of natural resources were numerous enough to force up rent payments to the level of real economic rent, several advantages would result. In the first place, all land rent would become a cost of production and none of it would serve to increase profits or reduce losses. As a result, total profits and losses would become more accurate guides to production control. In the second place, a clearer dis-

[12] However, as we shall note in a moment, conservation ^f natural resources may justify holding a portion of them off the market.

[13] In the case of departments with no money income to demonstrate and measure the utility created, rent offers will indicate the net utility which department heads believe will be produced.

tinction between economic rent and other shares in the national income would result. This would facilitate the proper distribution of the national income.

While these two very real advantages would result from the division of a Socialist economy into a greater number of competing bidders for natural resources than proposed in the previous chapter, they would not compensate for the disadvantages involved in a smaller scale of production and management. The disadvantage of not being able to treat full economic rent as a cost in production can be largely offset by carefully distinguishing between marginal and intramarginal profits, as will be explained later on. This distinction would also facilitate the separate treatment of full economic rent as a share in income.

It is of the utmost importance to attain the maximum degree of mobility for each factor in production. Complete mobility makes possible an immediate transfer from a less productive to a more productive employment and thus tends to maximize total national income. In order to achieve the maximum degree of mobility for natural resources, all contracts providing for their use should be terminable at any time by either the Bureau of Natural Resources or the lessor. If the former receives a higher rent offer from a new potential user, and the offer is not met by the present user, the land or resource in question should be taken away from the former user and transferred to the new. Likewise, if any lessor finds such a lease unprofitable, he should have the right to give it up or pay a lower rental. The Bureau of Natural Resources ought to keep the entire supply of valuable land and other resources in use at all times by lowering rents to a level which will secure their use.

The right to terminate leases at any time would not endanger capital invested in fixed improvements on land. The present user would always be free to raise his rent offer to the full value of the land plus the fixed improvements on it. When the land alone is worth more to a potential user than the land plus the fixed improvements is worth to the present user, the transfer obviously is desirable and the fixed capital should be treated as a total loss. If a portion of the bid of the new bidder is due to the fact that it can use the fixed capital as well as the land, the present user and unsuccessful bidder should be credited with the capitalized value of that portion of the bid. In other words, the new and successful bidder should pay the previous user for the value of the fixed investment to it (the new bidder). The difference between this value and the original cost (less proper depreciation) of the fixed capital should be treated as a net loss by the former user.

Division Among Uses Within Each Organization.—The problem of the allocation of natural resources within the great monopolies of a Socialist economy calls for discussion at this point. Within each trust or department, natural resources should be used in such a way as to yield the maximum intramarginal profit, or rent surplus. Being intramarginal in character, this rent surplus should not affect the volume of production, but should indicate the measure of success achieved in the allocation of natural resources within the organization. If the Agricultural Trust, for instance, could secure a larger intramarginal surplus by using certain land for winter wheat instead of spring wheat, it should use this land to produce winter wheat, but should not, on this ground alone, increase the production of wheat. In the same way the building trust should use for apartment houses that land which earns the maximum rent surplus when so used; land which yields the highest rent surplus when used for detached dwelling units should be used for such units only.

Each individual trust or department ought to strive to maximize rent surplus, for rent surplus is net utility expressed in money. Intramarginal costs measure the total disutility of production. Prices measure the minimum, or marginal, utility of consumption. Hence, an intramarginal or rent surplus always represents net utility, and the attempt to maximize rent surplus is merely an attempt to maximize net utility.

This principle, that land should be used for that purpose which yields the largest rent surplus, requires one qualification. The amount of rent surplus secured from any land use depends upon the amount of marginal profit or loss secured. If production is out of balance, if either a marginal profit or loss is being earned, the amount of the intramarginal profit is affected. A monopolistic restriction of output increases marginal profits but reduces rent surplus because it lowers the marginal cost, and overexpansion of production has the opposite effect. Hence it is more accurate to say that each piece of land should be used in the way which yields a maximum total rent when the market price of the commodity produced on that land is equal to the marginal cost of production.

Division Between Present and Future Demands.—The problem of the allocation of the use of natural resources as between different time periods is a part of the problem of the conservation of natural resources. In other words, the restriction of present consumption of natural resources in order to make possible an increased consumption in the future is one method of conservation. But how can we determine to what degree present consumption ought to be curtailed in order to increase potential future consumption? While no thorough analysis of this problem can be undertaken here, it is possible to indicate the directions the analysis must take and to state certain tentative conclusions.

To begin with, it is useful to divide natural resources into two classes, replaceable and irreplaceable. Timber, game, fish, soil fertility, etc., belong in the former class; mineral resources, in the latter. Different principles of conservation for future use must be developed for these two classes of natural resources.

At first glance, it may appear that replaceable natural resources should be replaced as rapidly as they are used up. There are a number of objections to this, however. The supply of a given replaceable natural resource may be so vast and the annual consumption so small by comparison, that no need for conservation exists. Or it may cost more to replace a given quantity of a replaceable natural resource than it is worth. As long as the net gain resulting from the use of a natural resource is less than the full cost of replacing it, the replacement is uneconomic. Conversely, it becomes economic whenever it is profitable.

The problem of the conservation of irreplaceable natural resources for future use involves different factors. The basic consideration is the rate of interest. Other things being equal, the quantity of such resources which ought to be conserved for future use varies inversely with the rate of interest, since the chief cost involved is an interest cost. In other words, a high disutility cost of abstinence makes conservation less economic.[14]

The fact of diminishing utility is the chief reason for conserving irreplaceable natural resources for future use. A given supply of any commodity gives the maximum total utility when its consumption is spread evenly over a given period of time. This fact considered alone suggests that the consumption of a given supply of copper, for instance, should be spread evenly over the period available for consumption. Since this period is infinite, an infinitely small quantity should be consumed each year. However, the preference for present as opposed to future consumption, measured by the prevailing rate of interest, modifies this conclusion. If the utility of consumption a mere fifty years from now is discounted at 4 percent compounded quarterly, it has little present value, which suggests that conservation for more than a very few decades is rarely worth while. The supply of almost every scarce and irreplaceable natural resource promises to last that long without any conservation.

There are still other factors to be considered in determining whether

[14] Pigou has asserted that the rate of interest should be at least partially disregarded, or reduced, when the state evaluates the need for conservation of irreplaceable natural resources (*Economics of Welfare*, pp. 24–29). Even if this were desirable from the long-run viewpoint, which is improbable in view of our rapid scientific progress, it is foolish to urge a democratic state to disregard the real if "irrational" preference of the great majority of its citizens for present consumption. This error is similar to that of certain religious teachers who urge men not to obey their natural instincts. It is impossible for an individual or a state to do what it does not want to do, and the rate of interest is, for the purpose of the present argument, merely a measure of human wants.

to conserve irreplaceable natural resources. One of these is the possibility and cost of substituting some other material. A natural resource should never be valued, even in the future, at a price above the cost of the cheapest, equally satisfactory substitute.

Another factor which is important but immeasurable is the possibility of technical advance which will render the resource in question of little value. This has happened very recently in the case of nitrates used for fertilizer. If Chile had conserved its supply of this natural resource, conservation would have proven uneconomic because of the development of synthetic nitrates.

The considerations noted above clearly suggest that the need for conservation has been overemphasized by the majority of writers who have discussed it. They have understood its advantages, but have not given due weight to the high costs and risks involved.

Under Socialism the fundamental principle of conservation in the case of both replaceable and irreplaceable natural resources is that it is only desirable when profitable.

Conservation of natural resources may be socially desirable and yet unprofitable under Capitalism. Division of control over individual oil pools frequently makes uneconomic drilling profitable to individuals. The risk of forest fires spreading from uncared-for or improperly guarded adjacent holdings may render conservation of timber unprofitable even though it is socially desirable. General property taxes and various other factors have the same effect. With all these disturbing factors eliminated in a Socialist economy, however, desirable conservation should always be profitable.

2. LABOR

The problems involved in the proper allocation of an existing supply of labor are quite different from those involved in the allocation of land and capital. Labor, being animate, requires no national bureau to determine its allocation. Such central control would curtail or destroy the freedom of the individual. The laborer, like the consumer, is a far better judge of his own interests than anyone else when he is in possession of detailed and reliable information concerning alternatives. No outsider can measure the disutility of work to a worker as well as the worker himself. No outsider can measure the utility of additional income to a worker as well as the worker himself. He alone is competent to compare the attractions of different occupations and locations and to determine the allocation of his own labor. The total supply of labor is merely the sum of such bits of labor.

If the individual worker is to determine his own occupation and the place where he will work, he must be granted a degree of freedom and authority unknown under Capitalism. In the first place, he must be given equal educational opportunities, so that he can prepare himself for any occupation for which he is fitted. All costs of vocational education must be met by the state, and students ought to be paid a wage about equal to what they could earn if working.

A more vital and less accepted principle concerning the allocation of labor is that every worker ought to be able to demand work wherever work for which he is fitted is being carried on. In other words, all factories, railroads, stores, mines, and offices should be required to give work to all qualified individuals who ask for it.[15]

Obviously some limitations must be placed upon the right to demand work. Stores, repair shops, and offices employing a handful of workers should not be required to give work to all applicants, although they might be required to promise work within six months' or a year's time. Also, the right should be granted only to qualified employees, except when the new job can be learned in a few weeks' time. However, all unskilled and semi-skilled occupations, in which classes by far the majority of jobs belong, should be open to all applicants.

This principle of the right to demand work has a number of very great advantages. In the first place, it maximizes the freedom of choice of the average worker and thus permits each worker to select the kind and place of work which maximizes his net utilitum. This advantage alone is enough to warrant the change from Capitalism to Socialism. Nine out of ten workers under Capitalism are doing work they do not like and would not choose if they possessed real freedom. Poverty compels them to accept whatever work they can get, whether they like it or not. Once they are employed, the fear of involuntary unemployment prevents them from making any change.

A second great advantage of the right to demand employment is that it makes possible a degree of mobility of labor unknown under Capitalism. At the present time there are enormous variations in the level of wages

[15] Certain bourgeois economists have asserted that Socialism necessarily involves an arbitrary or military allocation of the supply of labor.

"Fundamentally, there are only two economic systems possible, though there may be various mixtures of the two. These two systems are based on two ways of getting things done. One way is to offer a reward for what you want done; the other is to command someone to do it and punish him if he does not" (T. N. Carver, *Current History*, April 1932, p. 2).

Carver goes on to imply that Capitalism represents the former method of getting things done, while Socialism necessarily represents the latter. Of course, there is no basis whatever for this implication. Carver's argument simply indicates the effect of personal bias upon scientific reasoning in the social sciences.

in various industries and regions. For instance, the wages of unskilled labor in the Northern states are from 50 percent to 100 percent above similar wages in several Southern states. The marked immobility of labor which this fact indicates is due partly to ignorance of the higher wages in the North, partly to the costs of transportation, partly to unwillingness to break established ties, but above all, to the risk of unemployment and the difficulty of securing new work of the kind desired. If every Southern worker were guaranteed a job in the North at any trade and place he desired, wages would soon approach the proper equilibrium level which would balance the advantages of working in the North and in the South. Likewise, uneconomic variations in wages between different occupations in the same place would be largely eliminated.

Mobility of labor is highly desirable because it makes possible both a more productive use of labor and a more accurate pricing of labor. If labor were mobile, it would flow naturally from less productive to more productive jobs whenever an appreciable difference arose. This would tend to maximize total national income. Moreover, complete mobility of labor would automatically solve some of the most complex problems of wage determination. It would prevent wages in each occupation or region from moving appreciably above or below their proper equilibrium level. Whenever wages in any one trade or city became too high, outside workers would flock in and reduce them to their proper level, and vice versa when wages were too low. Few justifiable strikes or complaints concerning wage levels could occur in an economy in which wages were automatically regulated in this way by the workers themselves. The right to demand work is as essential to the proper pricing of labor as the right to freedom of choice in making purchases is to the proper pricing of finished consumable commodities.

A third great advantage of the right to demand work is that it would automatically eliminate all unemployment. Every individual who desired work could obtain it at any time. The first objection or question which comes to mind in this connection is, "How could the individual economic unit properly control its use of labor if every worker had the right to demand work in any existing organization?" The answer is very simple. Each organization would be free to manipulate the wages it pays in such a way as to control absolutely its own use of labor. If a hundred new men suddenly demand work at a factory already employing a thousand—an exceedingly improbable event since labor comes on to the market in a regular and predictable manner wherever large numbers are involved—the factory should lower wages and increase production. The decline in wages would reduce the costs of production and lower the price of the finished article until a new equilibrium with a larger number of workers had been attained. An increase in production should always follow a decline in costs, for reasons to be explained later (chapter vii). In summary, any change in the wage rate would affect both the number of workers and the sale of the finished product. Thus, a slight change in the wage rate would usually be sufficient to establish a new equilibrium between the supply of and the demand for labor in any given plant.[16]

Lowering wages is a much more desirable method of restricting the number of employees than refusing to employ certain individuals, for it automatically weeds out those who have the least preference for their present employment. If trusts have the power to lower wages to any desired level, they will be able to employ all those who desire work without incurring a monetary loss. Moreover, since on the average every wage cut will make possible an equivalent reduction in the price of the finished product, these wage cuts will not impoverish workers as a class. Rather they will serve to increase real wages by increasing the volume of employment and by bringing about a more economic distribution of labor.

A further possible objection to the right to demand work is that it will result in an excessive rate of labor turnover. Even under Capitalism, the rate of labor turnover is undesirably high in spite of the difficulty of securing a new job.

The average cost of hiring and training a new worker has been variously estimated at from $20 to $140 (1923 prices) by bourgeois econo-

---

[16] Certain Socialist theorists have specifically condemned this method of controlling the distribution of labor:

"It should also be noted that, in planning to control unemployment, there is one problem that would not be solved so automatically under socialism as under capitalism. The planned society will necessarily have to control the numbers of workers in different occupations, and it must be able to transfer the labor force from one employment to another. . . . . Under present day capitalism, where the propertyless worker is dependent upon his earnings . . . . , the pressure of imminent starvation is the lever that society uses to force him out of those employments in which he is no longer needed, and into those where there is a demand for his services. If the socialist state, by a guarantee of a basic minimum standard of life to all its members, is to abandon the use of so crude a form of coercion, it will necessarily have to devise some other method of bringing pressure to bear upon workers to make labor adjustments in harmony with the interests of the group as a whole." Eveline Burns, "Planning and Unemployment" in *Socialist Planning and a Socialist Program*, edited by H. W. Laidler (Falcon Press, 1932), pp. 29–30.

This statement is questionable. Under Socialism, wage variations would serve to allocate labor much more efficiently than they do under Capitalism, because there would be no danger of unemployment to make workers cling to poorly paid jobs. Far from being a crude form of coercion, wage changes are the most desirable form of "coercion" since they leave more freedom to the worker than any system of individual or group hiring or firing.

mists.[17] The period of training necessary, even in the simplest occupations, before a new worker reaches full output is at least three months. The cost of hiring, the cost of increased wear and tear, the cost of curtailed output, and the cost of spoiled work all go to make up the large aggregate economic cost of labor turnover noted above.

As already indicated, students and young workers should be encouraged to experiment with several different occupations before choosing a permanent profession or trade. Such experimentation is worth the cost of labor turnover involved because the productivity of labor will increase when men and women make more intelligent choices of occupations. However, changing from one job to another after the age of, say, twenty-five should be discouraged by allocating to the worker concerned the full social cost of his action. This might be done by reducing the pay of all new workers over twenty-five years of age for the first few months of their employment at a new type of work. The total reduction in wages should be just sufficient to meet the full cost of labor turnover. A comprehensive system of vocational tests and guidance should also help to reduce the rate of labor turnover by making it easier for workers to find the jobs for which they are best suited.

Another possible objection to the granting of the right to demand work is that certain plants might not have any machinery or capital equipment available to care for an increased number of workers. In order to take on new employees such plants would have to lower wages until old employees left. However, this would be reasonable since it would give the work available to those who wanted it the most. The resulting decline in wage costs would automatically lower prices, create profits, and cause the expansion of capital facilities if the principles developed in later chapters of this treatise are followed. Also, the fall in market prices would permit consumers to spend more money on other articles and thus increase the immediate demand for labor somewhere else.

In order to secure the maximum benefit from the existence of the right to demand work, it would be essential to aid the individual worker in making a wise choice concerning the occupation and location he demands. This could be done in a number of ways. In the first place, newspapers could publish periodically full information concerning piece rates, hourly wages, and salaries in all representative occupations and localities. This would also increase the mobility of labor. The workers would be vitally interested in such information because they would be sure of work at the published rates.

[17] P. Sargent Florence, *Economics of Fatigue and Unrest and the Efficiency of Labour in English and American Industry*, pp. 137–46. This work contains a very complete discussion of the cost of labor turnover.

In the second place, the state should greatly develop the use of vocational tests which indicate the aptitude of the individual for various types of work. Except in the case of the professions, however, such tests should be used chiefly for advisory purposes. The desire of the average person for work suited to his capacities would be a sufficient incentive to proper choice of vocation in most lines of work.

3. CAPITAL

The problem of the proper allocation of capital is relatively simple as compared with the problems involved in the allocation of natural resources and labor. This is true for the reason that capital, in the monetary form[18] in which it is allocated among different users, is homogeneous. All units of monetary capital are alike and should be treated alike. In the case of labor and land, on the other hand, all units are unlike and must be separately handled and priced.

Capital, being, like land, inanimate, must be managed. The entire national stock of capital funds should be under the absolute control of a single organization, the Bureau of Capital Supply. One reason why both land and capital ought to be placed under the control of great national monopolies is that this would lower the unit cost of management by reducing overhead and eliminating duplication of function. It would also simplify the work of those looking for land or capital, since they would need to apply at only one office to cover the entire supply. Finally, unification of control over the entire supply of capital is desirable in order to fix responsibility for this control in one place and secure uniform treatment of all capital and all borrowers.

The Bureau of Capital Supply should handle capital funds only. It would loan capital in the form of money and receive it back in the form of money. The problem of the proper management of specific forms of capital is quite distinct from the problem of managing the total supply of capital expressed in terms of money. Capital goods should be handled by the trusts which produce them and by the trusts and departments which use them. The Bureau of Capital Supply should have nothing to do with individual capital goods.

The principal duty of the Bureau of Capital Supply should be to balance saving and investment and to achieve an ideal distribution of new

---

[18] Money is capital only to the extent of its cost of production, which is negligible in the case of paper, and this capital cannot be directly used by borrowers. However, money is a ticket to or claim upon all goods, and some of these goods are capital goods. It is the allocation of claims upon capital goods that is referred to here.

capital funds among different uses and users by regulating the rate of interest. No appreciable portion of the total supply of monetary capital should ever be idle, since full utilization of monetary capital can be secured at any time by lowering the rate of interest sufficiently. On the other hand, the demand for capital at the prevailing interest rate should never exceed the existing supply of capital, and this could easily be avoided at any time by a sufficient increase in the rate of interest.

Many Socialist writers have objected to the payment of interest in a Socialist economy. This objection is based upon a failure to comprehend the vital economic function of interest. The supply of both monetary and physical capital always has been, and probably always will be, insufficient to satisfy the demand which would exist if no interest were charged for its use. Some method must be used under any economic system to limit the demand for capital to the available supply. Under Capitalism the chief method used is that of charging a rate of interest high enough to balance supply and demand. It is, of course, possible to limit demand to supply by arbitrarily determining which demands to satisfy and which to ignore, but this would result in a very uneconomic distribution of capital among different uses and users. As a method of allocating capital it would be much inferior to the use of an interest charge, for the same reason that arbitrary rationing of consumable goods and services is far less desirable than selling them at prices which balance supply and demand. Charging interest reduces demand to supply by eliminating only that demand which is the weakest, which represents the least potential marginal productivity; for properly determined interest offers are the best available measure of marginal productivity.[19]

[19] Certain bourgeois economists have denied that interest can be properly determined in a Socialist economy.

"Now it is unfortunate that this allowance for interest, the need for which is urgently dictated by economic considerations, cannot be adopted in the socialistic economy. Perhaps this is the most serious objection that can be maintained against socialism. On this account, it requires closer examination.

"When the socialists assert that interest is unnecessary in the socialistic economy because the central authority, which owns all capital-goods, does not find it necessary to pay itself a price for the use of these capital-goods, they unwittingly put their finger on the principal difficulty. Because capital is no longer owned by many private persons, but by the community, which itself disposes of it directly, a rate of interest can no longer be determined. A pricing process is always possible only when demand and supply meet in a market, when the competition of many offerers and demanders, the mutual out-bidding on the part of the buyers and under-cutting on the part of the sellers, leads by trial and error to the gradual emergence of a price, which may be called normal because it is that price at which the available supply, no more and no less, can be exactly disposed of. At present, in the capitalistic economy, interest is determined

Interest, like rent, is a surplus earned by producers. It measures the difference between the total cost of production at the margin where production has been increased without the use of additional capital and the non-interest cost of production at the margin where production is aided by the optimum amount of the most suitable capital goods.

Producers who use capital wisely are able to pay a proper interest rate for its use without raising their prices because this use has lowered their costs just enough to meet the interest charge. The ways in which tools, machines, equipment, buildings, inventories, and other forms of capital lower production costs are too well known to require mention. But the amount saved by the use of capital varies greatly, and new capital funds ought to be invested where they will make possible the largest savings. The best way to achieve this in a Socialist economy is to train all trust and department executives to measure the productivity of capital in their enter-

in the capital market, in which the offerers of capital and the demanders of capital meet in free competition. In the socialistic economy such a process of interest determination would be impossible. There can be no demand and no supply when the capital from the outset is in the possession of its intending user, in this case the socialistic central authority.

"Now it might perhaps be suggested that, since the rate of interest cannot be determined automatically, it should be fixed by the central authority. But this likewise would be quite impossible. It is true that the central authority would know quite well how many capital-goods of a given kind it possessed or could procure by means of a compulsory restriction of consumption; it would know the capacity of the existing plant in the various branches of production; but it would not know how scarce capital was. For the scarcity of means of production must always be related to the demand for them, whose fluctuations give rise to variations in the value of the good in question, in this case capital, even if the supply of it remains constant." Georg Halm, *Collectivist Economic Planning* (George Routledge & Sons, Ltd., London, 1935), pp. 161–63.

This entire argument is so obviously unreasonable that it serves as an excellent illustration of the prejudice of bourgeois economists against Socialism.

The statement that "A pricing process is always possible only when demand and supply meet in a market . . . .," is simply not true, and betrays a total lack of comprehension of the economic functions of a market. All that a market does is to help determine a price which equalizes supply and demand. This function can be performed more accurately by the preparation and use of consolidated demand and supply schedules than by any market. Valuation does not require a market place. As Wicksell has explained (*Lectures on Political Economy*, p. 14), valuation constantly takes place in every economic unit under Capitalism.

Every Capitalist trust has a definite amount of capital and allocates it among different uses by estimating the marginal productivity of capital in different uses. No market is necessary, and the capital "is in the possession of its intending user." It is not necessary to know "how scarce" capital is; it is only necessary to know the quantity of capital available and prepare a demand schedule for it in order to determine the proper rate of interest.

prises and to bid for its use accordingly, and then allocate new capital funds to those who offer the highest bids.[20]

In other words, one vital economic function of interest is to make possible an ideal allocation of capital. This function is just as vital under Socialism as under Capitalism. Socialists may object to the payment of interest to private persons, particularly to those who have inherited their income, but they have no valid reason for objecting to the charging of interest as a means of allocating capital, provided the interest is paid to the state.

There should be one uniform nation-wide rate of interest in a Socialist economy. No distinction should be made according to the length of the loan or according to the risk involved.

The existing supply of capital should always be so distributed between short-period and long-period investments that the marginal productivity of capital in each field is the same. The mere fact that under Capitalism short-term interest rates are different from long-term interest rates demonstrates either that these rates do not measure the marginal utility of capital and therefore cannot serve as guides to the most economic allocation

---

[20] "Unless interest is taken into account in the computing of cost it will appear equally preferable to produce either of two commodities in each of which the same quantity of labour and land is incorporated, although in the case of one of them the expenditure may be spread over a hundred times the period of time that it is in the other. The community will be led to spend its resources on schemes that will only produce consumable goods after centuries, while in the meantime it will suffer penury. . . . .

"To illustrate the problem of interest in a socialist community let us take the case of a railway that has to cross a piece of high ground. Either it may be built in the open with two steep slopes, or it may be constructed with deep cuttings and a tunnel. The first way involves greater cost in operation than the second for the whole time that the line is open; the second way involves a greater expenditure of labour and materials at the time of construction. How can the authority planning the railway balance the extra annual cost of operation against the additional once-and-for-all cost of construction? If the additional construction-cost is only five times the extra annual operation-cost, it is almost certainly worth while to build the tunnel. If it is a hundred times more, the tunnel is almost certainly not worth while. Projected works can be classified according to the number of years' purchase that they require. It is obvious that the community should undertake first those works in which a present outlay saves a large annual cost before proceeding with those that effect a less saving. Equilibrium is obtained by pushing the investment of resources up to the same number of years' purchase in all lines of production. The community must decide upon a certain number of years' purchase (in other words, rate of interest) and apply it as a touchstone to distinguish between feasible and unfeasible undertakings." H. D. Dickinson, "Price Formation in a Socialist Community," in *Economic Journal*, June 1933, p. 243.

of capital, or that capital is improperly distributed between the two different fields of investment.

Interest rates ought not to vary according to risks. The mere nature of Socialism will eliminate nine-tenths of the risks characteristic of Capitalism. As for the risks which do remain, each individual trust should insure itself against them so far as they are predictable or insurable. Losses due to unpredictable risks cannot be anticipated by variations in the interest rate, and therefore should not be included in interest or in any other charge for the use of capital.

The Bureau of Capital Supply should accept or grant all requests for loans at the market rate of interest without questioning the amount or purpose of the loan. Of course, it should always maintain a nice balance between supply and demand by controlling the rate of interest, but this should be the sole means used to reduce demand. The chief executives of each operating trust ought to be far better judges of their need for capital than an official of the Bureau of Capital Supply.

While no restrictions should be placed upon the borrowings of any individual trust or department, the chief executive of the nation and the Executive Committee of the Supreme Economic Council should receive periodic reports concerning the marginal profits and losses of each operating trust and the expenses of each department rendering free services. If any individual trust were continuously and unreasonably guilty of overexpansion, this would result in continuous marginal losses, a signal that the chief executive of that trust should be removed. No borrowing by a trust which did not result in overproduction and marginal losses should be considered excessive, however. In the case of departments supplying free services, the criteria for overborrowing would include the ratio of interest expense to total appropriations for that department, and the wisdom of the investment made. It would be much more ·difficult to detect overborrowing by a department than by a trust.

Mobility of capital aids the economic allocation of capital. To stimulate the rapid flow of capital from less productive to more productive uses, the Bureau of Capital Supply should change the interest rate on all loans at a moment's notice whenever the productivity of capital at the margin changes significantly. If there arises a demand for capital which cannot be fully satisfied by the stream of new savings, the interest rate on all old loans should be raised until a large enough fraction of them is repaid to permit full satisfaction of the new demand.

The only advantage of making loans for definite periods of time at a fixed rate of interest is that this facilitates prediction of future costs. However, the ability to predict costs is of little economic benefit if the predicted costs are not true social costs—in other words, if they are based upon a rate of interest different from the market rate.[21]

The Bureau of Capital Supply need never suffer any credit losses. Every borrower would have state credit behind it, and trusts would have the power of indirect taxation based upon monopoly; hence it could always raise enough money to repay loans or to continue paying interest on them. However, individual trusts should never raise prices for this purpose because prices ought to be based upon present, not past, costs of production. Therefore, every loss of capital by a trust should be treated as a repayment of capital to the Bureau of Capital Supply (see page 182). Departments, on the other hand, should be required to repay all loans or to pay interest on them.

It is sometimes asserted that the effect of the investment of new capital upon certain existing capital investments should be taken into consideration in determining the allocation of new capital. If new capital is invested in machinery which renders obsolete or sharply depreciates the value of existing machinery, for instance, it is claimed that the depreciation of the old machinery should be treated as a deduction from the returns of the new machinery when determining the wisdom of the investment.[22]

This argument is quite unsound. The introduction of new capital equipment should never be delayed on account of its effect upon the value of old capital. In a Socialist economy old machinery should be used only so long as it earns enough to cover the variable costs of production. New and improved machinery should not be introduced until it can lower the costs of production below the variable costs on old machinery, or until the old machinery can no longer satisfy the total demand; but the moment new machinery can reduce the total costs of production below the variable costs on the existing equipment, it should be introduced, regardless of the loss from obsolescence of the old equipment. Obsolescence losses are not real social costs, although they may cause bankruptcy to individual concerns under Capitalism. Value is dependent upon scarcity and would disappear entirely if all goods were sufficiently abundant. Every new invention helps to bring such abundance nearer, and consequently causes a decline in the value of existing capital and consumable commodities. Obviously, such nominal losses indicate a real gain, not a loss, in welfare.

[21] This is one of the many cases in which something that benefits private businessmen under Capitalism is not beneficial to the community. A private businessman obviously benefits from knowing his costs in advance, even if this frees him from the need of making adjustments beneficial to the economy as a whole.

[22] For a clear statement and refutation of this argument see Pigou, *Economics of Welfare*, pp. 163–66.

Closely related to the theory that obsolescence costs should be considered in making new capital investments is the theory that technological unemployment should be treated as a real cost in determining the desirability of new investments. At least one Socialist economist has suggested that under Socialism it would at times be proper to delay the use of new inventions in order to prevent or reduce technological unemployment.[23] This theory is unsound for much the same reasons as the previous theory concerning obsolescence costs. No delay should ever occur in the application of new methods and machinery on the ground of the resulting technological unemployment, which in any case would be negligible if the right to demand work were granted.

One form of capital investment deserves special consideration before this discussion of the allocation of capital is concluded. Investment in scientific research is of peculiar social significance because of the enormous returns it yields. Many individual inventions, such as the Bessemer process or the cotton gin, have saved mankind more money than has been devoted to all scientific research during the past thousand years. There is every reason to believe that scientific research in the future will produce even more profitable inventions.[24]

Under Capitalism the annual expenditure for scientific research amounts to only a small fraction of the optimum total. This is due to a number of causes. The economic gains from new discoveries do not

[23] "Control of unemployment due to this cause (technological change) involves a technique of control over the introduction of new devices, and a willingness to postpone the advantages of new inventions, should circumstances make this necessary.

"But even in a society that held in common ownership the instruments of production an important change in attitude would be necessary if technological unemployment were to be eliminated. In such a society also, due to changes in the rate of growth of population or for other reasons, some periods might be more suited than others to the introduction of new devices. It might thus occasionally be necessary to postpone, or even to forego, some improvement in technique that would undoubtedly make for enhanced production." Eveline Burns, "Planning and Unemployment" in *Socialist Planning and a Socialist Program*, edited by H. W. Laidler (Falcon Press, 1932), pp. 25–26.

E. Heimann argues that technological changes should be curtailed at times because it may require an excessive volume of saving to provide the capital facilities to put the displaced workers back to work (*Sozialistische Wirtschafts und Arbeitsordnung*, pp. 35–37). However, such displaced workers could be absorbed in other industries without any appreciable new investment of capital by a more intensive use of the existing capital facilities, or the resulting temporary unemployment could be distributed equally by reducing the hours of labor for all workers.

[24] For an able statement of the need for more scientific research see J. D. Bernal, "If Industry Gave Science a Chance," *Harper's Magazine*, February 1935 (Vol. 170), pp. 257–68.

accrue to those who make them. In large part these gains benefit consumers rather than producers. Moreover, patents are expensive, run for
a short period of time, are subject to innumerable costly lawsuits, and
ordinarily expire long before a new invention has begun to yield its maximum returns. The original inventor usually lacks the capital necessary
to exploit his invention, and is frequently forced to sell his patent for a
song or yield the bulk of profits earned by it to whoever finances him.
If a new process or invention does prove highly profitable, competitors
are ordinarily able to obtain a patent on the same fundamental idea
by making a few superficial changes or improvements in it.

Finally, most individuals and corporations do not invest in scientific
research because there is never any certainty that a given individual or
laboratory will make a valuable discovery. The total returns from all
scientific research far more than compensate for the total investment; but
this does not apply to all, or even to many, justifiable individual bits of
research. Also, a large share of agriculture, industry, and distribution is
still carried on by small-scale enterprises which lack the resources and
the desire to do scientific research work. As a result, the majority of
research is done by state universities and private endowments—by islands
of socialized capital in a Capitalist sea.

A Socialist government should expand tenfold the annual research
expenditures of even the most advanced industrial nations. Nearly all
of the highest intellectual ability and genius of the nation should be devoted to research either in the social or in the natural sciences. Every
form of economic activity, every trade and occupation, should become
the subject matter of a special applied science and should receive the
attention of a large group of able research workers. Practical problems,
such as those of inventory control and poultry breeding, must receive in
the future the attention which the pure sciences of physics and astronomy
have received in the past.

Obviously it will be impossible to calculate accurately the past or
prospective marginal productivity of capital invested in research. A Socialist state, however, should keep accurate and comprehensive records
of the total productivity of annual research investments. These records
should be used as the basis for planning future investments. Here, as
elsewhere, it will be necessary to make a sharp distinction between total
productivity and marginal productivity. In estimating the utility of employing additional research workers, for instance, the ability of these prospective marginal employees should be given chief attention. They should
not be expected to equal the productivity of the best men already engaged
in research.

Any decision concerning the total annual investment budget for research purposes will necessarily be somewhat arbitrary. However, even an arbitrary Socialist budget should be far more accurate and should come far closer to balancing marginal utility and disutility, than any accidental Capitalistic rate of investment in research. There are very obvious reasons for an enormous increase in this rate, but these reasons are ineffective under Capitalism.

Different methods must be used for estimating the monetary value or utility of research which results in lowering the costs of production of existing goods and for estimating the monetary value of research which results in the production of new consumable goods. When a new process or invention lowers by ten dollars the cost of producing a Ford, the value or utility of this invention can be roughly measured by multiplying the number of Fords produced each year by ten dollars and then capitalizing this annual saving at the prevailing rate of interest. On the other hand, if a new consumable commodity such as the radio is invented, the only possible method of determining the monetary value or net utility of the new invention is to increase production to the optimum (no profit, no loss) level and then estimate the total annual consumers' surplus and capitalize it.

The gain from new inventions cannot be determined from the profits earned in producing them under either Capitalism or Socialism. Profits measure producers' surplus only, and most of the economic benefit from new inventions is inevitably passed on to the public in the form of a consumers' surplus. No entrepreneur is ever able to appropriate more than a small proportion of the optimum consumers' surplus.

Under Capitalism it is frequently asserted that new inventions benefit society by developing new and additional industries and, in consequence, new and additional fields of employment for capital and labor. This argument is quite unsound, for it is the total volume of money coming onto the market and the prevailing price level alone which determine the total volume of employment for capital and labor. Consumers cannot spend money on new inventions without curtailing their purchases of other goods by an equal amount.

PART THREE

THE CONTROL OF THE PRODUCTION OF PRICE GOODS

CHAPTER VII. THE THEORY OF PRODUCTION CONTROL OVER PRICE GOODS

A. INTRODUCTION

The first problem of production control in a Socialist economy is that of determining the total volume of production, the total real national income, in any given period of time.

Under Capitalism the total volume of production varies markedly from year to year, sometimes decreasing by as much as 40 percent in a few years' time and then increasing by 100 percent in an equal succeeding period of time. The total volume of production is nearly always well within the limits set by the supply of the factors in production. At such times, it is determined by the volume of purchases, that is to say, by the supply of purchasing power multiplied by its velocity of circulation. The volume of production, it is true, does not vary exactly with the volume of money purchases, but the direction and extent of its fluctuation are determined by variations in the latter. In other words, under Capitalism the volume of production is determined largely by monetary demand for goods and services.

The situation will be entirely different in a Socialist economy run in accordance with the principles of this treatise. The physical volume of production will not be dependent upon monetary demand, but rather will control monetary demand. As explained in previous chapters, the price of each factor in production, and of each particular part of each factor, should always be low enough to secure immediate utilization of the entire existing supply of that factor. This means that the full supply of each factor in production will be continuously employed. Hence the total volume of production, the national income, will be determined by the supply of the factors in production under Socialism.

Since the various problems connected with the determination and control of the quantity of each factor in production have already been considered in detail, the problem of determining the total volume of production needs no further consideration. This chapter deals only with the problem of controlling the volume of production of individual price goods. This problem may be divided into two parts: (1) the question of what kinds of price goods ought to be produced, and (2) the question of how much of each individual price good ought to be produced.

It is difficult to overemphasize the importance of the theory of control over the production of individual price goods. This is the very heart and integrating center of pure economic theory,[1] and is all the more worthy of emphasis in that it has until recently been consistently ignored by virtually all Socialist theorists. With a few notable exceptions, Socialist thinkers have never even realized the existence of the problem of production control, the true "economic problem."

This chapter is the logical culmination of the theoretical reasoning contained in earlier chapters of this treatise, whose sequence and content were planned to lead up to the solution of the problem of production control. The chapter on utility stated the purpose of a Socialist economy and set forth the nature and principles of utility and disutility. The chapter on money and banking discussed and provided for the common denominator necessary for the measurement and comparison of various kinds of utility and disutility. Finally, in the chapter on the determination of prices there was recommended a system of prices which would measure the marginal utility of all finished consumers' goods and the marginal disutility of all types of labor. The system of production control here presented is based upon the foregoing theory of utility and disutility; it depends upon the use of stable money, and requires the pre-existence of prices which measure marginal utility and disutility.

The theory of production control given below applies only to goods sold for a price. This is an extremely important qualification since most goods might be free goods under Socialism. Control of the production of free goods is discussed in chapter ix.

B. MARGINAL PROFITS AND LOSSES AS GUIDES TO PRODUCTION CONTROL

I. BASIC RULES OF RESPONSE TO MARGINAL PROFITS AND LOSSES

The sole purpose of production control in a Socialist economy should be the maximization of average, and hence of total, net utilitum. The two fundamental principles of production control can easily be deduced from this general purpose.

In the first place, *a Socialist economy ought to produce every good whose production yields net utilitum at any volume of production.* In the second place, *the production of such a good should be increased whenever the production of an additional unit of that good would yield additional net utilitum, and should be curtailed whenever the production of the marginal unit yields net disutilitum.*

[1] "But the theory of value (at least among English economists) is merely a traditional misnomer for the analysis of the output of a single commodity, considered separately." Joan Robinson, *Economics of Imperfect Competition* (1932), p. 16.

These two basic principles of production control can be applied directly by an isolated individual who himself produces everything he consumes, since he can compare directly all sensations of utilitum and disutilitum. In order to make possible the application of these principles in a Socialist economy, however, it is necessary to have a method of measuring and comparing the utility and disutility experienced by millions of different individuals. Such a method was described in chapters iii and iv of Part One. As there explained, money provides a unit of measurement, and prices become fairly accurate measures of marginal utility and disutility if incomes and prices themselves are properly determined.

To permit their practical application in a Socialist economy, it is necessary to translate the two basic principles of production control given above into principles which prescribe the proper reaction to properly determined prices.

It is more difficult to translate the first basic principle into such terms than it is to translate the second. In fact, no perfect translation into a single principle is possible. To say "All goods which can be produced at a profit should be produced" is to give an inexact translation, since some goods which cannot be produced at a profit because of insufficient demand should nevertheless be produced because the resulting consumers' surplus is more than adequate to offset the net disutility represented by the financial loss. An alternative translation is: "All goods whose production at any volume yields a marginal profit should be produced." But this, too, is inaccurate, for the production of such goods may yield a net disutility loss due to the fact that in the case of certain goods requiring heavy capital investments, such as transatlantic cable messages, the cost curve starts much higher than the demand curve.[2]

It is therefore necessary to translate the first basic principle of production control into two principles of reaction to prices. The first is that *all goods whose production yields an over-all profit at any volume of production should be produced.* The second is that *all other goods whose production at any volume creates a consumers' surplus large enough to compensate for the net disutility represented by the over-all net loss should be produced.* Whether a consumers' surplus actually offsets net loss can only be determined by comparing the size of the areas which represent them on a graph.

Both of these principles of practical production control will be quali-

[2] This difficulty might be overcome by defining each good of this type in such a way as to include similar services rendered by methods requiring much less capital. Thus, if messages sent by steamship were considered as the same good as messages sent by cable, the cost of providing the initial unit would be less than its marginal utility.

fied at a later point by (*a*) principles of simplification and standardization, and (*b*) principles of social control designed to prevent the production of products which are considered goods by many individuals but are judged to be bads by the government.

The second basic principle of production control can be easily translated into one simple and universal principle of response to marginal profits and losses: *the output of any good in production should be increased or decreased until its marginal cost (cost at the margin) of production becomes equal to its sales price.*[3] Control over the production of price goods in a Socialist economy will therefore not be more difficult, but far less difficult, than under Capitalism. All that is necessary is to strive to eliminate both marginal profits and marginal losses,[4] to regard the former as evidence of underproduction, the latter as evidence of overproduction.

The marginal profits and losses referred to above are, of course, current profits and losses. Past marginal profits indicate underproduction at some past time; they do not demonstrate present underproduction. To be sure, marginal profits and losses are never known until they too are past profits and losses, but it is always possible to estimate current profits and losses. Production control should be based upon the best possible estimates of actual current marginal profits and losses. In the absence of any known trends or subsequent changes in supply or demand, the most recent data concerning marginal profits and losses are the best basis for estimating actual current profits and losses.

[3] "In an ideal world, price would always be equated to marginal cost to society." R. F. Kahn, *Economic Journal*, XLV (March 1935), 16.

The theory that prices should equal marginal costs was first stated by Jules Dupuit in 1844, but has been largely ignored by later economists. For an able history and restatement of the theory, see Harold Hotelling, "The General Welfare in Relation to Problems of Taxation and of Railway and Utility Rates," *Econometrica*, VI (July 1938), 242–69. See also footnote on p. 000.

As used above and throughout this treatise, marginal cost means cost at the margin and is not affected by changes in intramarginal costs caused by changes in the volume of production. See page 176.

[4] It would be possible, of course, to set any level of profit or loss as the level to be aimed at, and instruct all executives to eliminate all deviations from this desired level. A uniform profit would amount to a uniform sales tax. A uniform loss would provide one means of putting new money into circulation.

One critic, Dr. Calvin Bridges, has suggested that it would be better to call profits surpluses and losses deficits in order to avoid their confusion with the private profits and losses found under Capitalism. This suggestion would also have the merit of partially freeing our proposals from opposition by old Socialists to whom the mere words profit and loss are anathema. The conventional terms, profit and loss, have been retained largely because they make it easier to explain the plan to those who are familiar with the role of profits and losses under Capitalism, and easier too for such persons to comprehend.

The chief principle of production control under Socialism is the principle that the volume of production of each good should be so controlled as to equalize current marginal costs and income. This means that no effort should ever be made to recoup past losses or distribute past profits. Any attempt to balance marginal profits and losses over any period of time would be highly uneconomic because it would always involve further marginal profit or loss. Such profits and losses always indicate imperfect production control; they are always a positive evil since they always represent a distortion of demand and supply. One evil of this sort cannot compensate for or diminish a similar preceding evil; rather, it always involves an additional one.

In other words, marginal losses are not undesirable because they involve monetary losses, nor are marginal profits harmful because they involve unearned and unnecessary profits. Rather, both marginal profits and losses are undesirable because they indicate imperfect control of production and the resulting losses in net utilitum. The recouping of monetary losses out of present marginal profits does not restore the net utility lost as a result of incurring such losses. It invariably causes further and preventable losses in net utilitum due to the imperfect control of production indicated by these marginal profits. In order to permit individual trusts to disregard (in the sense of making no effort to recoup) past marginal losses, it will be necessary for the Bureau of Capital Supply to cover such losses.

In planning the response to a marginal profit or loss, an executive should always allow for the effect which the proposed change in the volume of production will have upon the market price. When production is below the optimum level, it should not be increased to a point which will raise marginal costs to the level of existing market prices. In some cases, a very small increase in production will eliminate a very large marginal profit by causing a sharp reduction in the market price. In other cases, a very large increase in production may be necessary. This depends upon the elasticity of demand. But in every case an increase in output will lower prices and thus reduce the marginal profit.

To enable those who determine the volume of production to estimate the effect upon prices of proposed changes in the volume of production, the price department of each trust should supply them with all available demand schedules and data. The supply schedules prepared by the accounting department will also be of great value in determining production schedules. Indeed, if both supply and demand schedules are accurate, production control will be a very easy matter. The management will merely select that volume of production which will balance marginal cost and market price.

As explained earlier (chapter iv, p. 76), the actual determination of prices should be done by independent price experts. Otherwise prices might be fixed at a point which equals marginal costs instead of at a point which balances supply and demand, and no obvious financial evidence of underproduction and overproduction would exist.

Executives in charge of production control should react to marginal profits and losses only when these exceed a certain minimum amount. While, as indicated in an earlier chapter, Socialist prices should be far more stable than Capitalist prices, there would still be frequent price changes, and production costs of most articles would still undergo almost daily change. Obviously, it would be uneconomic to revise production schedules in response to all such changes in the market price or in the various costs of production. It will be necessary, therefore, in the case of every commodity and service, to determine the minimum changes in prospective marginal profits and losses which justify a revision of production schedules. Variations of less than this minimum should be ignored.

The entire system of production control set forth in this chapter should be applied to each individual article or service. A profit on one article should never be permitted to justify a loss on another. This means that separate cost accounts on every good must be kept. Although the expenditures upon individual cost accounting and production control should never exceed the economic limit, so far as that can be determined, some individual cost accounting and production control is worth while in the case of every good. Concentration of the entire production of each article and service under a single national monopoly will greatly reduce the unit cost of this computation and increase accordingly the limit to which it may be economically developed.[5]

Clearly, joint products are an exception to the rule of individual response. Each group of joint products must be treated as a single article and the profit or loss estimated for the group.

Every response to marginal profits and losses should take into consideration any abnormal or temporary factor affecting such profits. If a war in some other part of the world has temporarily caused the price of copper to soar, production should not be expanded enough to satisfy the increased demand, except so far as this can be done without permanent capital investment. New permanent capital investment in copper mines and smelters should continue to be based upon the normal peacetime prices and demand.

If abnormally good weather conditions reduce the cost per bushel of a given wheat crop below the average level, the marginal profit or loss

[5] For a discussion of the problem of how much money should be spent on cost accounting see pages 189–90.

resulting from this circumstance should not be treated as a sign of under- or overproduction. The number of acres sown to wheat at the beginning of the next season should be based upon average costs and yields over a period of years.

Finally, responses involving investment of fixed capital should be more carefully considered than other responses since it requires a larger and more stable marginal profit to justify them. Whenever unexpected marginal profits first begin to indicate the need of additional fixed capital in a certain industry, a period of waiting to test the stability of the new profits should follow. If the profits turn out to be partly or wholly temporary, or if they tend to increase during the succeeding year or two, the amount of new capital needed can be determined much more accurately.

The importance of a waiting period in such cases varies with the size of the marginal profit involved. The larger the profit, the shorter the period of waiting should be. In the case of new inventions, indeed, the first marginal profits may be large enough to justify an immediate large investment in fixed capital although the full amount needed should never be invested until demand has proved itself fairly stable.

2. THE BUREAU OF ECONOMIC CO-ORDINATION

As explained above, a Socialist state should not use arbitrary centralized planning of production, and each independent Socialist trust should control its own volume of production on the basis of its own marginal profits and losses. Budgetary planning by each trust and department is desirable and consistent with these principles.

In addition, some central co-ordination of the plans of separate agencies would be essential. If each individual trust made its own budgetary plans, there would be need for a central Bureau of Economic Co-ordination to see that these individual plans fit together into a single realizable national plan. It should be the function of such a bureau, not to revise arbitrarily the plans of individual trusts, but to point out conflicts between them. For instance, if the Mining Trust planned to produce a certain definite amount of coal and to sell it at a certain price, those trusts which planned to consume coal ought not as a group to plan to use more than this amount at the price in question. Of course, the production of coal could be increased, but this would raise its price and cause all consuming trusts to change their plans slightly. Therefore, in every case of a conflict between the budgetary plans of different organizations, a compromise would be desirable if feasible.

The Bureau of Economic Co-ordination should rely chiefly on consolidated demand and supply schedules for each and every good in determining whether individual plans of different trusts are reasonably practical. It should have no authority to compel individual trusts and departments to change their plans, but should serve merely to discover and point out conflicts between the budgetary plans of these organizations. Whenever one organization, in response to a marked and apparently significant change in its demand or supply schedule, changes its budgetary plans, it should be the duty of the Bureau of Economic Co-ordination to investigate the probable effect of this change upon other organizations and advise them of its findings. The organization submitting the proposed plan should also be advised of any doubts which the Bureau may have as to the ability of other organizations to provide the necessary supplies, raw materials, labor, etc., or to consume its estimated output.

In the absence of any Bureau of Economic Co-ordination, it would be desirable for the individual organizations to assume the function of comparing future estimates of production. Each individual organization could send a copy of its budgetary plans to all organizations directly affected by it, that is, to all organizations using its finished products or providing its raw materials and supplies. It would then be possible for each individual organization to discover and react to any conflicts between its own estimates and those of other organizations affected by them. However, it would seem probable that a central Bureau of Co-ordination could perform this work more efficiently, since it would eliminate considerable duplication of effort. Such a bureau should also be more impartial than the average trust or department, and could prepare and publish valuable statistics concerning estimated future production.

3. POSITIVE RENT

The principle that the production of every good should be increased or decreased until the marginal cost just equals the market price has two very significant corollaries.

The first corollary is that all industries operating under conditions of increasing costs should yield positive rent, an intramarginal surplus over and above all costs of production. This surplus, called rent by bourgeois economists, would be due solely to the fact that the average cost would be less than the marginal cost and hence less than the market price at the proper level of production. Overproduction might partially or wholly offset this surplus with losses due solely to overproduction, but a rent surplus would reappear whenever the volume of production was restored to the optimum level.

In this treatise the term "rent" will be employed in a wider sense than is traditional. It will be used to describe deficits as well as surpluses which result from the sale of goods at prices equal to marginal costs. The surpluses will be called positive rent; the deficits, negative rent.[6] This will call attention to their common origin. In an individual enterprise, positive rent may be entirely absorbed by payments of land and personal rent—rent outlay—or it may exceed rent outlay and result in a rent surplus. Rent outlay is an opportunity cost; rent surplus is an intramarginal profit.

A rent surplus is earned by some entrepreneurs under Capitalism, but it is relatively unimportant because competition for both men and natural resources raises their prices to levels which turn nearly all positive rent into rent outlay. Under Socialism, however, the lessened competition within individual industries for rare ability and natural resources will turn a great deal of what is now rent outlay into rent surplus. Thus rent surplus will be much more significant under Socialism than under Capitalism.

4. NEGATIVE RENT

The principle that the production of every commodity and service should be increased or decreased until marginal costs are just equal to market prices has another very significant corollary—namely, that all industries producing under conditions of decreasing costs should operate at a loss, negative rent. If an industry operates under conditions of decreasing costs, the marginal cost of production is necessarily below the average cost of production. Under Capitalism such an industry can cover its total costs only by the use of special service charges not related to the volume of use or by charging a price equal to or greater than its average cost of production, and the latter is the usual policy. If it sold its entire output at a price just equal to the cost of production of the marginal unit, it would incur a constant loss. This is impossible under Capitalism,[7] but will be both possible and desirable under Socialism.

[6] H. D. Dickinson used the terms "negative rent" and "positive rent" in this same sense. See his *Economics of Socialism*, p. 108.

[7] Alfred Marshall has suggested that production at a loss in industries of decreasing cost would be possible if the state would subsidize them. (*Principles of Economics*, 8th ed., p. 472). Such subsidies are politically impractical under Capitalism. Moreover, it would be virtually impossible to measure the need for such subsidies in an industry organized on a competitive basis.

Marshall suggests that the money to be used for such subsidies should be raised by taxes on industries of increasing cost. This is undesirable, however, since it would reduce production in these industries below the optimum level. Positive rent is the ideal source for such subsidies.

For a discussion of these points and references to other literature on the subject, see Joan Robinson, *Review of Economic Studies*, I (February 1934), 137–40.

J. M. Clark has pointed out the desirability of reducing prices to marginal costs and has asserted that "a system of public industry is necessary to insure prices down to differential costs." *Economics of Overhead Costs*, p. 448.

The justification for operating industries of decreasing costs at a constant loss is as follows. Marginal costs are the best available measure of the disutilitum of producing the marginal unit. Market prices are the best available measure of the utilitum of this unit to consumers. Hence, any excess of the market price over the marginal cost indicates that the production of the marginal unit creates more utilitum than disutilitum. The goal of Socialism is to maximize net utilitum. All production which yields net utility is therefore worth while, and production yields net utilitum up to the point where marginal costs become equal to market prices.

A graphic presentation of this theory is given below:

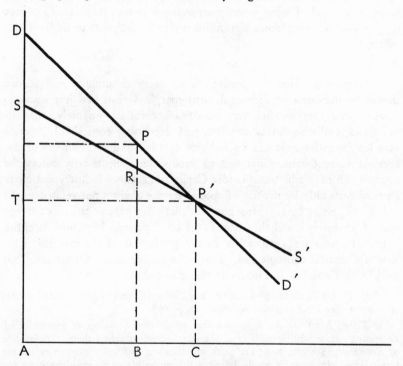

DD' = Demand curve. SS' = Marginal cost curve.
P = Price which equals average cost, when quantity AB is produced.
P' = Price which equals marginal cost, when quantity AC is produced.
PRP' = Net utility gained by increasing output from AB to AC.
STP' = Negative rent which would result from production of the output AC.

Orthodox Capitalist economists have long recognized that in industries of increasing cost, output should be increased to, but not beyond, the point at which the market price becomes equal to the marginal cost of production. According to Ricardo, land rent is merely the surplus income which results from charging for every unit of output a price high enough to cover the cost of producing the marginal or high-cost unit in such industries. This theory has long been generally accepted by bourgeois economists not only because it is true but also because it tends to justify the existence of land rent, a chief source of inequality and private gain under Capitalism.

The equally obvious and logical theory that output should be increased to, but not beyond, the point at which the market price becomes equal to the marginal cost of production in industries of decreasing cost has been stated by very few Capitalist economists, presumably because this theory can be used as a basis for an indictment of Capitalism. It makes clear that industries of decreasing cost, a class which includes virtually all non-extractive industries, should be operated at a loss (negative rent), and this is difficult if not impossible under Capitalism.[8]

The application of this theory would raise the output of all industries of decreasing cost and would lower the output of all industries of increasing cost. Land, labor, and capital shifted to the former industries would be more productive because they would be shifted from uses where they produce no net utility to uses where they produce net utility.

All of these changes in output would reduce market prices. Both the lowering of output in industries of increasing cost and the raising of output in industries of decreasing cost would lower marginal costs and hence prices. Money wages would not fall, however, because the price decline would be due to a more economic use of labor, land, and capital, not to cuts in wages, rent, or interest rates. The sole effect upon wages would be an increase in real wages due to the decline in prices.

The loss which should be incurred by all industries of decreasing cost is of the same nature as the intramarginal profit or rent surplus which should be earned by all industries of increasing cost. Both are due solely to the fact that the marginal cost is different from the average cost of production. Hence the same term, rent, is used to describe both of them. An intramarginal surplus is positive rent. An intramarginal deficit is negative rent. In accordance with orthodox usage, however, the term rent, without a modifier, will be used to mean positive rent, except where it is necessary to emphasize its positive nature.

[8] Fear of this theory is probably the chief reason why bourgeois economists minimize the number and importance of industries of decreasing cost. One sign of this deliberate policy is the fact that cost curves used as illustrations in economics textbooks always turn up. If they did not, textbook writers would be unable to prove that the ideal price is a profitable price under Capitalism.

5. SIMPLIFICATION[9]

Thus far, it has been argued that a Socialist economy should produce any new price good that can be sold at a profit, or at an over-all loss which is offset by the consumers' surplus. There is a very significant qualification of this principle that has not yet been stated. This qualification concerns the number of different varieties of a good which ought to be produced.

It is perfectly conceivable that a million different patterns of gingham cloth might be devised and put on the market. This is actually done under Capitalism, and some quantity of most of these patterns is sold at a profit. The question naturally arises, then, as to whether the Textile Trust in a Socialist economy should produce this enormous variety of gingham patterns. Obviously, the greater the number of patterns, the higher will be the average cost per yard. The plea that Socialism will lower the costs of production of all commodities through simplification has long been popular among Socialists, and unquestionably has a great deal of truth in it. However, there is a conflict between the need for simplification and the principle that every good which yields a profit should be produced.

The principal advantage of simplification is that it increases the scale of production of individual commodities by concentrating production upon a smaller number of articles. The potential increase in the scale of production possible through simplification is indicated by the fact that even under Capitalism voluntary and imperfect simplification in the United States has reduced the number of different types of several commodities by from 60 to 80 percent.[10] The incompleteness of this simplification is indicated by the fact that even after its products had been simplified one industry produced 255,800 different types and sizes of grinding wheels.

Another noteworthy but infrequently stated advantage of simplification is that it focuses the attention of the buyer upon the essential elements of the object under consideration and thereby transfers competition to a field where it has positive social value. Price comparison is greatly aided by simplification. A very considerable part of the extreme variety of types and styles which exists under Capitalism is due to the deliberate efforts of producers to make rational price comparison difficult if not impossible.

If carried too far, simplification may involve certain important dis-

[9] "When a manufacturing company reduces its types and sizes to the least number possible, it is simplification." L. P. Alford, *Management's Handbook*, p. 989.

[10] L. P. Alford, *Laws of Management*, pp. 104–5. See also the numerous publications of the Division of Simplified Practice of the Department of Commerce.

advantages. It may reduce both the amount of experimentation with new products and the consumer's variety of choice below the optimum level. Nevertheless, the advantages of simplification are today far more important than its disadvantages. The often heard complaint of artists and bourgeois travelers that standardization is destroying the individuality of cities and nations deserves little consideration. Poverty is an evil so immeasurably greater than lack of individuality that the latter must be sacrificed to it for many years to come. Granted, then, that simplification is desirable, how can we reconcile the need for simplification with our rule of producing whatever yields a profit? The following principles of simplification provide a partial answer to this problem.

In the first place, simplification of all raw materials, semi-manufactured articles, and capital goods should be carried to the limits set by the needs of industry. The fact that different textile mills use looms of different styles to do the same kind of work does not increase utilitum. The same is true of raw materials and semi-manufactured goods. A certain amount of variety in machinery, tools, raw materials, etc., is indeed necessary to maximum efficiency in doing different kinds of work; but there should be no grades or types of such goods produced solely to distinguish the output of individual plants, or because no central authority has bothered to determine what grades and types are the best.

In the second place, simplification should be carried to a rather high degree in the case of the more practical consumers' goods. Garden tools, kitchen utensils, kitchen stoves, refrigerators, vacuum cleaners, and many other articles belong in this group, which may be called consumers' capital goods. Variety in design is relatively unimportant here because the primary function of such goods is utilitarian. However, once poverty has been entirely eliminated, a good case can be made for artistic variety in the design of such constantly and obviously visible articles as kitchen stoves and refrigerators.

In the third place, finished articles and parts of finished articles not visible to the public eye may be simplified to the limit without any loss to society. In this class belong underwear and the hidden parts of automobiles, radios, houses, etc. The reason for this principle scarcely requires statement. Unseen variety is, obviously, unable to please the public.

A fourth principle of simplification is that, in the case of those articles in which some variety is desirable, no greater variety should be produced than can be offered to each customer. If it is found that men desire a selection of about one hundred different kinds of ties to choose from, the clothing trust should not offer a different selection of one hundred ties in each store or in each community. Much the same variety would suffice for every city and village in the nation. Farmers and villagers have slightly different tastes from city workers, and allowance could be made for this after actual sales statistics had been obtained, but this would not increase greatly the total number of styles to be manufactured. Under Capitalism the number of different styles in men's ties runs into six or seven figures. That is one reason why good ties cost one dollar instead of twenty-five cents.

A fifth principle of simplification is that the consumers of any finished article should have the power as a group to control the variety of that commodity. Every individual consumer of a given article might desire to decrease the variety of that commodity in order to cheapen its price, but all of them might continue so to control their individual purchases of that article as to make every existing style number profitable. In such cases it would be proper for consumers as a group to vote to decrease the variety offered. Under different circumstances it would be proper for them to vote to increase the variety offered. Group action is necessary in both cases in order to make individual desires effective. No individual can secure either increased simplification or increased variety by controlling his own purchases.

In order to give consumers of finished goods an adequate basis for choosing between the economy of simplification and the increased utility of novelty and variety, a Socialist state should acquaint each consumer with the potential savings to be obtained through simplification. Every purchaser of a new automobile, for instance, should be given a leaflet containing accurate and detailed estimates of the price cuts which would be made possible by a reduction in the number of different styles, price-lines, and models, and in the frequency of style changes. This leaflet should also contain estimates of the cost of increasing the number of types and models and the frequency of style changes. The purchaser requires no information concerning the advantage of variety in offering and of style changes, since he himself is the best judge of their utility to him. Every purchaser should be asked to express a preference for more or less simplification, and at periodic intervals these preferences should be tabulated and acted upon by the Automobile Manufacturing Trust. The same procedure should be followed in the case of all expensive merchandise. In the case of medium- and lower-priced merchandise, it would not be worth while to have the consumer vote at each purchase, but similar means should be used to determine consumer preferences and to act upon them periodically.

The greater equality of income which should prevail under Socialism would make simplification of products far easier than it is under Capitalism. At present, for instance, automobiles must be produced to please many different income groups, some of which will be eliminated by

Socialism. Moreover, it is the wealthy classes, especially the idle rich, who are most eager for expensive novelties of all kinds. The elimination of these classes would not only remove the source of the chief demand for novelty and variety; it would also put an end to the universal imitation of the choices of these people by other social classes, including many workers who need bread, housing, education, and medical care more than novelties in clothing.

The total income of a Socialist society will have an important effect upon the desirability of simplification in consumable commodities. So long as the workers live in poverty, filth, and ignorance, as they now do throughout most of the world, novelty of design will be far less desirable than the increased volume of output which simplification makes possible. This is true even in the richest nation in the world, the United States of America. So long as millions of children are undernourished, millions of Negroes are uneducated, and tens of millions of workers live in filthy slums and bleak company villages, the need for a very greatly increased physical output of wealth is far more important than the need for new designs in women's hats. A Socialist administration should provide necessities for all, at any artistic cost, before it devotes any of its resources to increasing the variety and novelty of commodities sold. This economic principle is valid whether or not the voters of a democratic Socialist state choose to apply it. Therefore, Socialist schools should strive to eliminate irrational preferences for style and novelty over necessities.

The style cycle in consumable goods is one of the most wasteful features of contemporary Capitalism. Once the necessities of life have been provided for everyone, the public should be allowed to spend its additional income in whatever way it pleases, but the contemporary style cycle is in very large measure artificial. It is cleverly stimulated by producers in order to increase sales. Hundreds of millions of dollars are spent every year in successful attempts to persuade the public, especially the women, that new styles are more attractive than old ones, and that everyone who fails to follow the style cycle is poor or queer. Once this artificial stimulus is removed, the style cycle will die down to a small fraction of its present magnitude.

6. SOCIAL CONTROL OVER CONSUMPTION

There is another exception to the general rule that a Socialist economy should produce whatever can be sold at a profit and should increase the production of each good until marginal profits have disappeared. Under certain conditions it would be proper for the state to interfere with this system of production control. State interference would be justified: (1) to change uneconomic consumption habits, and (2) to prohibit or restrict the consumption of harmful goods.

Many wants are based upon habit rather than natural preference, and are definitely uneconomic. Once these wants have been altered in a certain way, the total net utilitum of the individual is larger. The food preferences of different races may serve as an illustration. In Japan rice is preferred to wheat, while in the United States wheat is preferred to rice. These preferences developed during a long period when wheat was not available to most Japanese and rice was not available to most Americans. The origin of such habitual preferences can usually be traced back to economic factors, but these preferences frequently continue to exist long after economic conditions have changed and made them uneconomic. If it should suddenly become possible for Japanese workers to buy wheat at a much lower price than rice, they would continue to prefer rice as a basic food for a long time; at least they would not change their diet as rapidly as they should. The meat-eating habits of Americans were acquired when meat was very cheap, but promise to continue indefinitely in spite of the great rise in the relative cost of meat in the last fifty years. Americans acquired the habit of living in detached houses when land was cheap and plentiful, but habit causes them to continue to prefer this type of housing under conditions where it is uneconomic. Many other consumers' habits, based originally upon sound economic reasons but continuing long after these have vanished, might be cited.

In those circumstances where preference is now purely habitual, and where a change in habit would eventually result in greater individual satisfaction, it would be proper for a Socialist government to intervene and attempt to change habitual preferences. The method of intervention which would leave the maximum degree of freedom to the individual consumer is that of granting bounties raised by levying special-purpose taxes. The bounties should be granted for the production of goods and services whose production ought to be encouraged, and the taxes should be levied upon the production of those goods and services whose production ought to be curtailed.

The principles stated above are particularly applicable in the case of new inventions. In order to encourage the rapid introduction of new inventions, a Socialist government should temporarily subsidize the production of all new consumers' goods and services. It would be unnecessary to do this for producers' goods and services, since the government would directly operate industry and could itself introduce new tools and machines whenever desirable.

A government subsidy for all new consumers' goods and services is desirable because the purchase of these items is largely habitual. If ice refrigerators have long been in use, many consumers will continue to purchase such refrigerators even after more efficient and economical electric or gas refrigerators are available. If clothing of a certain material has been habitually worn for many generations, many people will refuse to buy and wear clothing of new and unusual material, even if the latter is cheaper or more serviceable. All new inventions meet a large degree of prejudice and inertia and deserve government subsidies while overcoming these obstacles. Subsidies should not be granted to products new only in design, unless the new style is a necessary result of a new production process which is more economical. Of course, drastic simplification could also solve this problem by eliminating the choice between two styles.

Social interference with production control based solely on profits and losses is also justifiable in the case of certain harmful goods. It is proper for the state to intervene to prevent the purchase of goods having unsound utility. Certain unusually harmful goods, such as habit-forming drugs, dangerous poisons, machine guns, etc., probably should not be offered for sale to the general public at all. In other words, the state should prohibit their consumption. It is to be hoped, however, that this principle will not be interpreted in such a way as to give government officials the power to ban all literature and art they consider obscene or radical, or in such a way as to justify prohibition of the sale of contraceptives.

In addition to certain goods whose consumption ought to be prohibited by the state, there are goods whose consumption is now restricted by excise taxes and should continue to be restricted in a Socialist state. In this group, tobacco, alcoholic liquor, and gambling are of outstanding significance.[11] The method of restriction used should be imposition of an excise or sales tax. This point will be discussed further in connection with the theory of taxation under Socialism.

C. AN AUTOMATIC INVENTORY SYSTEM OF PRODUCTION CONTROL

As an alternative to the use of profits and losses as guides to production control, it would be perfectly possible to use what may be called an automatic inventory system of production control. Under such a system, prices should equal marginal costs, and manufacturing schedules should be controlled in such a way as to maintain specified inventories of all goods. This method of production control has one outstanding advantage in common with the system of response to profits and losses; it places

---

[11] Under Capitalism the principal purpose and effect of the prevailing high taxes on tobacco, beer, and liquor is to place a larger share of the tax burden upon the workers. Unless this harmful effect is offset by suitable measures, the net effect of such taxes may actually be uneconomic.

control over production in the hands of consumers rather than in the hands of an arbitrary planning board. It is, therefore, the best alternative to the use of marginal profits and losses.

However, the automatic inventory system of production control has serious defects. It does not guarantee that temporarily scarce commodities will be distributed to those who will secure the most utilitum from them, namely those who can pay the most for them. It would result in queues in front of stores where temporarily scarce goods were being sold, and this would cause a serious inconvenience and loss of time. It requires a method of pricing different from that which is appropriate for permanently scarce or irreplaceable goods such as land, antiques, and works of art, and would therefore complicate the theory and practice of pricing. For these reasons, this system of production control is not as desirable as the use of properly determined marginal profits and losses.

D. ARBITRARY PLANNING

Socialists have long urged the planning of production on a national scale as a remedy for the major evils of Capitalism and as the proper method of production control in a Socialist economy. Economic planning as a method of production control is not only different from, but quite inconsistent with, the use of marginal profits and losses for production control.

Planning involves control of production by central authorities who plan in advance what ought to be produced and consumed. The use of marginal profits and losses places this control in the hands of workers and consumers, who may determine at any time to produce and consume more eggs and less milk, more radios and fewer pianos, etc. The advantages of complete freedom of choice for workers and consumers have already been explained and need not be reviewed again. However, it is of vital importance to note that arbitrary planning of production, of which the best examples are the Five-Year Plans of the U.S.S.R., always involves a very definite limitation of the freedom of choice of workers and consumers. For that reason a Socialist state should take over and improve the method of production control in use under Capitalism, rather than introduce the use of arbitrary plans.

Plans may, of course, be merely estimates of future sales, and may be revised whenever they do not equal sales. This type of planning, and the budgeting based upon it, is extremely useful under both Capitalism and Socialism. But it is entirely different from the kind of planning illustrated by the Five-Year Plans of the U.S.S.R. The former may be called budgetary planning; the latter, arbitrary planning.[12] What is opposed in this treatise is not budgetary planning, but arbitrary planning. Budgetary plans predict future sales and production; arbitrary plans control them. Arbitrary planning alone is a method of production control. A budget plan merely predicts the results of some alternative method of production control.

It may be argued that democratic election of Socialist officials would assure that arbitrary production plans would provide for whatever the public desired to consume. Unfortunately, this is impossible. Control of production by elected officials is certainly superior to the control of production by an irresponsible dictatorship, but it by no means assures the realization of a plan of production which will give to every citizen precisely those goods which he most desires. The wants of no two individuals are the same, and they change constantly. Every individual desires to consume hundreds of commodities and services, each in a different amount. It is therefore impossible for any government official, no matter how responsive he is to the desires of the public, to discover the desires of his constituents concerning the control of production. Some other method of production control must be used if the national economy is to produce precisely those goods which the public desires and in the quantity it desires.

It should be noted at this point that belief in "production for use" almost universally implies belief in arbitrary planning as the ideal method of production control under Socialism. The League for Industrial Democracy, the American Socialist organization which has done such fine educational work among college students, for a number of years defined its purpose as "education for the new Social Order based upon production for use and not for profit." The trouble with this common Socialist ideal is that it does not tell us how we are to find out what the public needs or what it can use. No two men have the same opinions on this point. Some, for instance, deplore the enormous production of chewing gum, cigarettes, cosmetics, candy, ice cream, etc.[18] Others are convinced that we devote too much of our productive forces to teaching children useless cultural subjects and to maintaining museums. But, if people do not agree as to what society needs, how can a Socialist administration determine what commodities to produce?

[12] Here the word arbitrary means effective or mandatory. It does not imply unreasonableness.

[18] "In replacing the system based on private profit by one based on social use, the community will regulate production according to the importance of social needs; it will considerably restrict the creation of unproductive goods . . . ." (H. Ströbel, *Socialisation in Theory and Practice* [P. S. King & Son, Ltd., London, 1922], p. 38). This implies precisely the type of arbitrary control which a Socialist government ought not to establish.

While production for use, as ordinarily interpreted by Socialists, is an unsound method of production control, it is possible to interpret the expression "production for use" in such a way as to mean production according to the desires of workers and consumers, and to assert that the use of market prices and profits and losses is the best method of determining these desires. This, of course, is what is claimed here; but such an assertion ought not to be used to hide the fundamental difference between the point of view defended above and that which identifies production for use with arbitrary planning.

There are several distinct degrees of arbitrary planning. When completely developed, arbitrary planning includes the universal planning of individual consumption (rationing) and the universal planning of individual work (military organization and control of labor). The so-called "War Communism" which existed in the U.S.S.R. from 1919 to 1921 was a close approach to this type of economy. It is possible to abandon rationing without giving up the military organization and control of labor. This would create a second and much more desirable degree of arbitrary planning. It would be possible, but more difficult and wasteful, to abandon the military organization and control of labor and still retain a complete system of rationing. This would be more difficult and wasteful because rationing would reduce the efficacy of wage differentials as a means of controlling the distribution and productivity of labor. The fourth and least undesirable form of arbitrary planning is one in which both rationing and military control of labor have been abandoned and national planning of goods to be produced alone remains. At this stage, both workers and consumers are free individuals, controlled only by wage and price changes, the effect of which upon profits and losses is disregarded. It is this fourth type of arbitrary planning that exists in the U.S.S.R. today.

The chief purpose of the Russian Five-Year Plans—rapid industrialization—could be more smoothly and efficiently achieved by the use of large subsidies under the system of production control outlined in this book than under the present system of arbitrary planning. It is possible for the leaders of a nation to estimate the need for subsidies in order to industrialize a backward nation, but it is not possible for them to determine the individual goods whose production should be restricted, and the degree to which this restriction should be carried out in order to achieve industrialization. The only economically sound method of restricting production in some industries in order to subsidize it in others is to tax consumers uniformly and permit them to determine the resulting reduction in the production of individual goods.

There is a sharp distinction between a planned economy and planning of production. Any economy which is consciously and rationally designed to serve certain purposes is a planned economy. The Socialist economy described in this treatise, therefore, is a planned economy. However, it does not require the arbitrary planning of production.

Failing to note this distinction, many Socialist theorists have ascribed to arbitrary planning of production important advantages which really belong to the type of planned economy which they advocate.[14] The principal wastes of Capitalism are due to the existence of competition, and would be eliminated by the substitution of monopoly for competition under Socialism, whether or not arbitrary planning is adopted. Monopoly alone would eliminate duplication of facilities and services, preventable over- and underproduction of individual goods, crosshauling of freight, advertising, aggressive salesmanship, etc., and would permit perfect intra-industry co-ordination and full use of budgetary planning. Arbitrary planning would not introduce any new economies; it would merely alter the method of determining the volume of output of individual goods.

Although arbitrary planning ought not to be used to control the volume of production of price goods, it is the only method available for controlling the production of most free goods, and free goods may become more important than price goods under Socialism. These ideas are discussed at greater length in chapters ix and x.

[14] "This [efficiency] means the replacing of the haphazard method of competition with planning, deliberate forethought and judgment in the interest of society as a whole. . . . . Planning and production for social use and not for private gain would eliminate many of the wastes of competition, such as appear in advertising, cross hauls of freight, production of inferior goods, production of luxuries when the demand for necessities is not supplied, over-supply of industrial equipment in certain fields, and the maintenance of a large number of middlemen." B. Mitchell, *A Preface to Economics* (copyright, 1932, by Henry Holt and Company, Inc.), pp. 546–47.

"In such a case [in the absence of economic planning], the national economy would appear to be broken into a number of separate independent undertakings, each of which would not be able individually to determine the needs and interests of Socialist development, and would be guided in its work exclusively by an effort to secure the maximum profit. In other words, in the absence of a planned economy there would reign supreme the same anarchy of production which is found under Capitalism, with all its consequences, crises, waste of productive power, etc." L. Segal and B. Tal, *The Economic Policy of the Soviet Government* (in Russian), p. 104.

CHAPTER VIII. DETERMINATION OF MARGINAL PROFITS AND LOSSES

A. INTRODUCTION

Marginal profits and losses should be the sole basis for control of the production of price goods in a Socialist economy. Although neoclassical economic theory lays great emphasis upon their importance, little serious thought or effort has been given by bourgeois economists and accountants to the problem of measuring marginal profits and losses. Rather, the false assumption has been made that marginal profits and losses coincide with the actual profits and losses calculated by businessmen. In this way, marginal utility theory has been changed into a justification of Capitalism.

In the course of the present chapter, which describes the proper method of determining marginal profits and losses under Socialism, it will be made clear that there is in fact a very great difference between true marginal profits and losses and the actual profits and losses reported in the operating statements prepared by bourgeois accountants. By way of anticipation, however, a preliminary general statement of these differences is desirable.

In the first place, the profits reported by Capitalists often include one or more items which are not even a part of profit as defined by Capitalist economists, and are definitely not a part of marginal profit. Among these items are interest on owned capital, rent on land owned, and part or all of the wages earned by the manager, all of which should be treated as costs of production by a Socialist trust. Failure to treat these items as costs not only inflates Capitalist profits but deflates Capitalist losses.

In the second place, Capitalist costs include *all* costs of production, while marginal costs include only marginal costs. It follows that fixed costs influence Capitalist profits and losses but do not affect marginal profits or losses.

Capitalists are not interested in marginal profits and losses; they are interested in total profits and losses. They desire at all times to maximize total profit, not to eliminate both marginal profits and marginal losses. Thus, even if they knew how to determine marginal profits and losses they would have little use for them. If some socially minded and intelligent Capitalist did decide to measure marginal profits and losses in his business, and to control his output in such a way as to eliminate both marginal profit and marginal loss, it would probably be impossible for him to do so very long. Total losses would eventually cause bankruptcy, and at a time when marginal profits indicated the social desirability of increased production.

Under Capitalism monetary losses are avoided because they involve a net monetary loss to some individual proprietor. In a Socialist economy, however, proper regulation of the supply of money, and proper response to profits and losses by those who control the volume of production, would tend to equalize total marginal profits and losses, so that a monetary loss in one industry would automatically cause or be accompanied by a monetary profit in some other industry. Since the government would operate all industries, it would not need to avoid monetary losses in individual industries in order to maintain its total net income. Financial losses would continue to be undesirable only when they indicated marginal losses.

B. THE PRODUCTION-CONTROL STATEMENT

The operating statement which bourgeois accountants now prepare would continue to be useful in a Socialist economy—improved, of course, so as to treat all costs as costs. Such a statement would be essential to the preparation of individual balance sheets upon which all estimates of national wealth must be based. It would be a record or "accounting" of all funds received or paid out and all values created or destroyed, and would facilitate strict control over these funds and values. However, the profits and losses shown on such an operating statement would have little economic significance under Socialism. They should not control the volume of production, or provide the principal data for such control, as they do under Capitalism.

An entirely new and different kind of operating statement, one which would show only marginal profits and losses, should be prepared by the accountants of every Socialist trust as the basis for production control. To avoid confusion, the new type of operating statement is hereafter called a "production control statement," and the conventional operating statement of Capitalism is referred to as a "financial operating statement."[1] Like a financial operating statement, the production control statement should contain a statement of expenses individually, by groups, and in total; a statement of income; and a statement of the resulting profit or loss. It should nevertheless be quite different from the financial operating statement, for it should record only marginal costs and income and show only marginal profit or loss.

Financial operating statements usually cover one or more plants, each of which produces one or more products. A production control statement should cover only one product, for its purpose would be to aid production control, and the production of each good ought to be separately controlled

[1] "Financial statement" would be briefer, but might lead to confusion with a balance sheet.

if that is possible. In the case of joint products, joint control would of course be unavoidable. Detailed cost reports on individual goods would be far more useful than similar reports on the total marginal profits or losses of entire plants or industries, not only because the former ought to control production, but because small total profits or losses for an entire plant or industry often hide grossly uneconomic marginal profits or losses on individual goods as a result of profits offsetting losses.

Fortunately, bourgeois accountants are already well aware of the vital importance of individual cost reports. All that a Socialist trust needs to do in this respect is to apply the best bourgeois accounting theory. The cost accountants of a Socialist trust should take special pains to supply the management with recent cost data. For each good, formulas should be developed which will make possible an immediate rough calculation of the effect of a given change in any of the major cost elements upon the marginal costs of production.

Recent cost figures are extremely important because in many cases, though not in all, they provide the most accurate basis for estimating the costs of additional or marginal production. Additional production is always future production at the time it is being considered, and its costs are more apt to be similar to current than to past marginal costs. In some cases average costs prevailing over a certain period of time may be better indications of future costs than costs at any given moment, but recent averages are better than old averages covering an equal length of time.

The need for recent cost data justifies the frequent preparation of complete production control statements. Production control statements should be prepared not only at the end of three- or six-month periods, but at least once a month, perhaps oftener in some cases. No control over production should be exercised in the absence of such reports, and the more frequently control is exercised the smaller will be the necessary change in production plans on each occasion.

The frequency of preparation of production control statements should depend upon the good in question. If both costs and market prices are exceedingly stable, the need for frequent reports will be at a minimum. If either costs or market prices are subject to relatively sharp and frequent fluctuations, the need for frequent production control statements will be at a maximum.

In the case of many agricultural crops, one production control statement per season will be sufficient. Winter wheat, for instance, has only one marginal cost for the entire season and the size of the crop is largely fixed, so far as man can fix it, at one time. In the case of freely reproducible articles manufactured from imported raw materials whose price is determined in a world market, however, the situation is quite different and may justify weekly production control statements and weekly changes in production plans.

A consideration of the individual income and cost entries which should appear on a production control statement is now in order. The following discussion does not treat individually all of the almost infinite number of different items which might conceivably appear on such a statement, but only the more important ones, particularly those which should be treated differently in a production control statement than in a financial operating statement, and those concerning whose treatment in a Socialist economy there has been controversy.

Income is discussed first because it ordinarily appears first on an operating statement and because it requires only a brief discussion.

C. THE DETERMINATION OF MARGINAL INCOME

The income shown on a production control statement should be the product of the "f.o.b. factory" price of the item whose cost is being measured, multiplied by the number of units whose cost is being measured. No other kind of income should appear there. Income from the sale or rent of capital goods, raw materials, etc., should appear only on the financial operating statement. There should be no income from investments or interest on bank deposits, since each economic unit should always return all idle capital funds to the Bureau of Capital Supply and since the State Bank should pay no interest on commercial accounts. Appreciation in the value of assets should never be treated as income in the production control statement although it might be so treated in the financial operating statement. Tax refunds and other miscellaneous cash income should also appear on the financial operating statement only.

Marginal income is quite different from marginal increment. The former is the price of the marginal unit, while the latter is the change in total income resulting from the production and sale of one more unit. The production and sale of additional units always reduces the price of the good in question, and therefore reduces the income received on intramarginal units. This reduction may more than offset the income specifically received from the marginal unit. For instance, if Henry Ford were producing 100,000 cars per month and had to reduce his prices one cent per car in order to sell one more car per month, he would lose about $1,000 on the additional car. In any case, marginal increment is always less than the price of the marginal unit, and the fewer the number of producers the greater this difference is. Under Capitalism production is controlled by marginal increment, not by market prices (marginal income). This is one of the major defects of Capitalism.

D. A DEFINITION OF MARGINAL COSTS

Marginal costs are the monetary measure of the additional disutility of producing one more unit of a good. They are the costs of the marginal unit.

Marginal cost must be clearly distinguished from marginal expense, which includes monetary outlays that do not measure real costs. Marginal expense is the change in total expense caused by the production of one more unit.

In extractive industries the production of one more unit at the extensive margin always requires the use of inferior land. This means not only higher real costs at the margin but higher rent on the land previously used, for land rent is merely the difference between the cost of production at the margin and within the margin. This entire increase in land rent enters into marginal expense but not into marginal cost.

There are several other expenses of increased production which are not real costs and do not enter into marginal costs. The use of additional quantities of labor and raw materials ordinarily raises the market price of these goods. The increase in price on the quantities previously used enters into marginal expenses but not into marginal costs because it does not represent a real cost of production.

Similarly, when the increased use of an intermediate good required to expand output lowers the price of that good, the resulting decline in the cost of the quantities previously used would affect marginal expense but not marginal cost. The same reasoning applies also to changes in expenditures due to a reduction in output in both cases. Only changes in real costs at the margin affect marginal costs.

A marginal cost is always a variable cost. It is a cost which varies when the volume of production changes. A fixed cost is always an intramarginal cost. Whether or not a given cost is fixed or variable depends in part upon the volume of production. When a railroad or hydroelectric plant is operating at only 10 percent of capacity, nearly all costs are fixed. On the other hand, when it is operating at 100 percent of capacity, most costs are variable. Throughout industry the proportion of fixed costs to total costs declines steadily as production increases, until full capacity is reached. When a plant is operating at capacity and production must be increased, nearly all costs are variable costs.

Plants and industries differ greatly with respect to the proportion of total expenses which are fixed when production is below total capacity. Under these conditions, industries which use the largest amount of physical capital per dollar of output, particularly capital not suitable to other uses, have the highest ratios of fixed costs; and industries which use the smallest amount of physical capital, particularly capital not suitable for other uses, have the lowest ratios of fixed costs.[2]

Under monopolistic Capitalism, fixed costs have an effect on output the opposite of the effect they should have in a Socialist economy. Fixed costs per unit increase as the volume of production in any industry declines, thus tending to cause a further restriction in production by raising the unit costs which control prices and therefore production and consumption. In a Socialist economy, fixed costs of production should not only never increase prices and curtail production, but should have precisely the opposite effect. Whenever they increase, marginal (variable) costs will decrease, a marginal profit will appear, and, as already explained, production should always be increased sufficiently to eliminate such profits.

E. THE DETERMINATION OF MARGINAL COSTS

The determination of marginal costs is a far more difficult problem than the determination of marginal income. Nevertheless, it is extremely important. The accuracy of production control in a Socialist economy will vary directly with the accuracy of marginal-cost determination.

Only the more important cost items are discussed below, but the kind of reasoning applied to them may be applied to cost items not here discussed. In every case there is just one significant question: Does this cost affect marginal costs at all, partly, or wholly? If it does not affect marginal costs at all, it should never appear in a production control statement. If only a part of it affects them, it should appear on the production control statement only in so far as it enters into marginal costs. If the full amount of a given cost always enters into marginal costs, it should always appear in full on a production control statement.

I. PURE INTRAMARGINAL COSTS

Pure intramarginal (fixed) costs are those which are never affected by a change in the volume of production. Since they never enter into marginal costs, they should always be completely disregarded in considering the wisdom of an increase or decrease in the volume of production.

Rent Surplus.—Rent surplus is a pure fixed cost. Since the time of Ricardo the great majority of orthodox bourgeois economists have taught that positive rent does not enter into the marginal costs of production, but rather is an intramarginal surplus whose amount is determined by the marginal costs of production on marginal no-rent land. In recent years a number of bourgeois critics of this doctrine have pointed out that only

[2] When output is below capacity, the same cost may be variable with respect to an increase in production and fixed with respect to any decrease in production.

a few industries are free to expand by using no-rent land and that the remainder ordinarily expand by using land for which they must pay a rent.

There is considerable merit in this criticism of the Ricardian theory of rent, but it supplements rather than replaces the conventional doctrine. Actually, every industry has both an intensive and extensive margin; that is, it may increase production by using more intensively the land already occupied by it, or it may increase production by extending the area used by it. Obviously, rent never enters into marginal costs at the intensive margin. Whether or not rent enters marginal costs at the extensive margin depends upon the nature of the additional land used to expand production. Every industry is free to increase production by using previously no-rent land, low-rent land, or high-rent land. Many agricultural industries border on land of all three types, and the border may be extended at any point. Other industries are free to establish new and noncontiguous units on any kind of land.

Rent is a marginal cost at many points on the extensive margin of every industry and the degree to which rent enters into marginal costs depends upon the point at which this margin is extended. To the national economy as a whole, however, positive rent is a pure intramarginal surplus since no extension of the total area of land in use ever involves any disutilitum. However, cost accounting should take the industry viewpoint.

From the point of view of the individual industry, positive rent divides itself into two parts, rent outlay and rent surplus. Rent outlay is an opportunity cost which must be paid to secure the use of land. It is a marginal cost since it enters into the cost of production at one or more points on the extensive margin. Rent surplus is the additional rent or intramarginal surplus which accrues to the individual trust. All rent is an intramarginal surplus to the economy as a whole, but only a part of it represents such a surplus to an individual enterprise. Under Capitalism, competition between different units in the same industry tends to turn this rent surplus into a rent outlay, but the monopoly which should prevail under Socialism would turn some rent outlay into an intramarginal surplus in the hands of producing units.

In conclusion, that part of positive rent defined as rent surplus is a pure fixed cost which never enters into marginal costs, but rent outlay does and should enter into marginal costs.

Depletion Charges.—Private owners of irreplaceable natural resources treat the consumption of such resources as a diminution of their capital. Depletion charges are used to build up reserves equal to the reduction in the value of such resources, thus preserving the capital of the owners.

Depletion charges on irreplaceable resources are a part of positive rent, hence an intramarginal or pure fixed cost. If properly determined, they measure the difference between the cost of exploiting valuable natural resources and the cost of exploiting marginal resources, and therefore do not enter into the costs of marginal producers.

Failure to treat depletion charges on irreplaceable resources as a cost of production would not eliminate such costs. Depletion, like economic rent, is a natural phenomenon which can be ignored or misnamed, but cannot be altered or eliminated thereby. Hence, a Socialist mining trust should continue to treat depletion as a cost, but this cost should not be included in marginal costs. The reserves built up in this way should not be retained by the producing trust, but should be transferred to the Bureau of Capital Supply and there treated as a net addition to the total national capital. Depletion charges would thus serve to turn wealth in the form of natural resources into wealth in the form of capital, and would prevent the physical depletion of natural resources from reducing the wealth of the nation.

Depletion charges frequently take the form of royalty payments under Capitalism. Royalties paid by oil and coal companies, for instance, are really a form of depletion charge and should be treated as such under Socialism.

Research.—Under Capitalism the proper treatment of the cost of scientific research is relatively much less important than it will be under Socialism, because under the prevailing system these costs are relatively insignificant. Their tenfold increase as a result of the rise of Socialism will, however, make their proper treatment of more importance.

Expenditures for scientific research are a perfect example of a fixed cost. They bear no relationship whatsoever to the volume of production. The output of radios or electric refrigerators might be increased a hundredfold without making necessary any additional research costs to improve these articles. Of course, a great increase in the consumption of any article makes research on it, or on the method of producing it, potentially more productive, but it does not make it necessary.

Plans and designs are the chief product of scientific research. The cost of all architectural and engineering plans and designs is a pure fixed cost, not affected in any way by the number of times the plans or designs are used. If an automobile plant spends ten million dollars in designing a new model and in drawing up plans for all the new tools and machines required to produce the new model, this cost will not be increased by any increase in the volume of production of the new model. In other words, such costs can never become marginal costs, and hence should never have any effect upon the volume of production. They should appear only on the financial operating statement.

Royalties on patents are one method of collecting the costs of scientific research and invention. In a Socialist economy there should be no patents and no royalties from them, but, if permitted to exist, royalties should appear only on financial operating statements, never on production control statements.

If, by restriction of production, the price of a new invention were raised high enough to repay the capital invested in the preliminary research, consumption of the new product would be reduced to an uneconomically low level, that is, to a level where the specific costs or disutilitum of producing one more unit would be less than the price or utilitum to be received from it. Such a level of production is always uneconomically low because it indicates failure to create potential net utilitum.

Artistic Creation.—The reasoning applied to the costs of scientific research applies with equal force to all costs of original artistic creation. Once a book has been written, the royalties of the author are a pure fixed cost and should never appear on the production control statement. Only the costs of printing one more copy, or the average costs of another edition, should be treated as marginal costs and given a place on the production control statement. This policy would notably increase the reproduction of all existing books and works of art.

The fact that money spent for scientific research and artistic creation should not be treated as a marginal cost of production, once it has been spent, does not mean that funds should be devoted to these purposes regardless of the productivity of the expenditures. No capital funds ought to be invested in scientific research or artistic creation unless there is good reason to believe that such investments will yield consumers' surpluses greater than the market rate of interest; but, once an investment has been made, no effort should be made to restrict the benefit from it by treating it as a marginal cost of production.

The same accounting rule should be applied to the salaries of performers and entertainers whose work has been recorded on phonograph records, music rolls, film, or in other reproducible form. The wage or salary of the performer should not be included in marginal costs because the production and sale of one more recording does not increase the amount of work done by the performer. This principle would hold even if the performer were paid a royalty on each recording sold, for such a royalty would not measure any real marginal cost.

Organization Expenses.—Organization expenses include all nonrecurring expenses involved in the organization of a new business enterprise. Wages paid to those who bring together the men, machinery, and real estate needed by a new enterprise; rent on the office space they use and on the site of the new buildings before they are completed; interest on the capital they use before business begins—all are organization expenses. Taxes and legal fees are important organization expenses today, but should not exist as such in a Socialist economy.

Under Capitalism, organization expenses are treated as a capital investment, the interest on which is a permanent charge against production; or they are treated as a prepaid operating expense and charged off against production in the first few years of operation. Both of these methods of treatment are uneconomic because they tend to raise the cost of production above the true marginal cost, which never includes nonrecurring past expenses. Of the two, the first is the most uneconomic because it results in a permanent distortion of marginal costs. In a Socialist economy, therefore, organization expenses, once incurred, should be treated as pure intramarginal cost. All reorganization costs, model change costs, conversion costs, reconversion costs, and other similar costs should be handled in the same way since they also are unaffected by subsequent changes in the volume of production.

Advertising.—Advertising, of course, will be relatively unimportant in a Socialist economy, but the small amount that is done should be treated as a pure fixed cost. If a million dollars were spent to set forth the merits of an important new invention—and this might be justified—the cost of producing and selling one more unit of this invention should never include any advertising expense. Since the production and sale of one additional unit does not make any additional advertising necessary, it is proper to regard advertising as a pure intramarginal or fixed cost.

Obsolescence.—Obsolescence costs are a pure intramarginal or fixed cost. They are the result of changes in the technique of production, and are never affected by changes in the volume of production. An increase in the volume of production of any good does, to be sure, increase the potential size of obsolescence costs, but this does not make the latter a marginal cost. Since obsolescence costs never become marginal costs, they should never appear on a production control statement.

Losses due solely to obsolescence costs are not a sign of overproduction, as are all marginal losses. Rather, they indicate a new need for increased output, since they are the result of an improvement in the method of production which either improves the product or lowers marginal costs and is therefore certain to result in marginal profits unless production rises.

While failure to cover many fixed costs, such as rent and interest, indicates poor, or at least imperfect, management and should ordinarily be recorded as a black mark against the executives responsible for it, failure to cover fixed costs in the form of obsolescence charges is not an evidence of imperfect management. Obsolescence costs do not represent real disutility costs. Rather, they indicate technical progress and should be placed to the credit of the executives responsible for them. The nominal loss is caused by impairment of the quasi-monopoly and quasi-rents of owners of certain capital goods.

All obsolescence costs should be treated by individual trusts as a re-payment of capital to the Bureau of Capital Supply. This would reduce future interest charges. To the Bureau itself, such losses would represent a net, but at the same time desirable, loss of capital.

Taxes.—Under Capitalism some taxes are pure intramarginal costs, some are alternately marginal and intramarginal costs and some are pure marginal costs. Socialism ought to reduce drastically the complexity and variety of taxes, but there would remain some taxes which do not affect marginal costs and some which do.

Taxes on land rent and other intramarginal costs do not affect the cost of production. Indeed, to call them intramarginal costs is misleading, because such taxes do not increase or decrease intramarginal costs. They merely cause these costs to be paid, directly or indirectly, to the govern-ment instead of to some private person.

Taxes on profit, interest, personal income, inheritance, and private capital also fail to affect marginal costs. They only transfer income or capital from private persons to the government.

Unlike the foregoing taxes, sales taxes do vary with the volume of sales, but they ought not to be treated as marginal costs because they repre-sent no real cost or disutilitum of increasing output. In fact, there should be no price taxes in a Socialist economy, precisely because market prices should equal marginal costs and sales taxes do not represent real marginal costs. Price taxes, to be discussed in chapter x, are prices rather than taxes on prices and do not come under this rule.

Unpredictable Property Damage.—The risk of unexpected and un-predictable property loss due to natural catastrophes will continue to exist under Socialism. Insurance should be used to even out all predictable losses, and such insurance should be treated as a marginal cost when it varies with the volume of production. There will remain unpredictable losses due to fire, flood, earthquake, hurricane, etc., which cannot be in-sured against. Such losses should be treated as pure intramarginal or fixed costs of production and should not be allowed to enter into marginal costs. They should also be treated as a repayment of capital to the Bureau of Capital Supply, or this Bureau should replace the capital lost without debiting the account of the organization concerned.

The same result could be secured by having a single insurance trust which would pay all losses, whether predictable and insured against or not, but would base its premiums on the predictable losses only. The net losses of such an insurance trust should be met by the Bureau of Capital Supply.

2. COSTS ALTERNATELY INTRAMARGINAL AND MARGINAL

We turn now to the consideration of a second group of costs, those which may be either fixed or variable, depending upon the volume of production. When an industry or plant is operating at a level below its capacity, these costs are ordinarily completely intramarginal or fixed, but whenever it becomes necessary to increase the capacity of an industry or plant, these costs become marginal or variable.

Rent Outlay.—Positive rent consists of two parts: rent surplus, which is a pure fixed cost; and rent outlay, which may enter into marginal costs on the extensive margin.

When an industry has once rented a piece of land and has built a plant or made other improvements necessary to its use in a certain way, rent outlay becomes a cost which may be fixed or variable, depending upon the volume of production and the margin (extensive or intensive) under consideration. Whenever it is necessary to use more land, it is a variable or marginal cost, but as long as it is not necessary to use more land, rent outlay is a temporarily fixed or intramarginal cost.

Interest on Fixed Capital.—Interest on capital invested in buildings and equipment is a perfect example of a cost which may be intramarginal or fixed at one time and marginal or variable at another. When capital facilities are incompletely utilized, an increase in production does not increase interest costs, and interest is at such times a fixed cost. When existing-capital equipment is being fully utilized, however, an increase in output makes necessary an increased investment and interest becomes a variable cost.

It should perhaps be stressed that, in accordance with the definition of "fixed" used in this chapter, interest is at times a fixed cost, not because the interest payments are fixed by a contract which makes their payment essential, but because interest does not enter into the marginal cost of production at such times. At present, interest is often called a fixed cost merely because it must be paid.

Depreciation.—Under Capitalism very serious errors are constantly being made in the calculation of depreciation. Among conservative business executives it is considered wise to estimate depreciation at an excessive rate in normal times, and especially during periods of prosperity, in order to accumulate hidden reserves and show a conservative profit statement. Conversely, during periods of business depression it is the practice of many executives to underestimate depreciation charges in order to reduce reported losses.

Any overstatement of depreciation is socially undesirable for a number of reasons. In the first place, it raises the average costs of production and thus restricts total national output or income below the optimum level. In the second place, it results in concealed profits which render government regulation ineffective and mislead many investors. Over considerable periods of time, these concealed profits may restrict production without stimulating investment. In the third place, overstatement of depreciation, when carried on in certain industries but not in others, tends to distort production and consumption. The high prices charged by industries which overestimate their depreciation have the effect of checking consumption in these industries and increasing the demand for products of other industries. This destroys or prevents the desired equilibrium between real marginal cost and market price in each industry, and between the marginal productivity of the factors in production in different industries.

Any underestimate of depreciation, whether intentional or unintentional, is also undesirable. It results in concealed losses, dissipation of capital, and distortion of production and consumption.

For these reasons the executives of a Socialist economy should take pains to secure and use accurate estimates of depreciation costs. The task of preparing accurate depreciation schedules, incidentally, would be greatly simplified by the concentration of this work in the hands of experts in the head offices of great Socialist monopolies.

Occasionally, Capitalist entrepreneurs permit unearned increment due to a rise in the market prices of real estate to offset depreciation charges in whole or in part. This is equally unsound. In a Socialist economy, both unearned increment and depreciation charges should be carefully estimated and independently treated. The former should affect costs only by increasing rent charges, never by reducing depreciation.

Depreciation charges ought to be based on replacement costs alone. If a new invention cuts in half the cost of manufacturing a machine already in use, the depreciation charges on machines in use should be cut in half.[3] The treatment of capital losses due to such inventions is discussed elsewhere. Moreover, the replacement costs used should always be the price of the cheapest capital goods which could be used for the purpose in question. In other words, if at the time a certain factory is erected, brick is the cheapest suitable form of construction, but at a later time cement becomes cheaper, then depreciation charges at this later time should be based upon depreciation of a cement building which would fill the same purpose with equal adequacy.

In most cases when production is not at capacity level, the larger part

[3] One qualification perhaps is necessary here. Depreciation should be based upon the *price*, not the cost of production, of the new machine. Before demand is fully satisfied, there will be a sharp divergence between these two.

of the proper depreciation charge is a fixed cost. Buildings and machinery often depreciate almost as rapidly when idle as when in use. Therefore, when production is below capacity levels, the temporarily fixed elements in depreciation costs should not appear on the production control statement. Such depreciation costs become marginal costs only when it is necessary to increase the quantity of the fixed capital equipment in question in order to expand production. Until this point is reached, only those elements in depreciation costs which are affected by increased production should appear on a production control statement.

Heat and Light.—The cost of heat and light depends upon the number of cubic feet to be heated and lighted and therefore varies with the amount of space used. Like rent outlay, it is a fixed cost whenever a given space is incompletely utilized, and becomes a completely variable cost whenever it is necessary to use additional space in order to increase production.

Certain Insurance, Maintenance, and Tax Costs.—Insurance against certain risks may be either a fixed or a variable cost, depending upon the volume of production. For instance, once a building has been erected, the risk from damage due to some natural catastrophe, or lightning, or fire communicated from outside is little affected by the volume of production carried on. When it becomes necessary to erect a new building in order to increase the volume of production, however, all of these risks and the insurance charges necessary to cover them become variable and therefore marginal costs.

The individual trusts and departments of a Socialist state will be large enough to carry their own insurance. They should set up insurance accounts, debit all losses to them, and credit them periodically with the proper insurance charges. It would be necessary to calculate risks on individual units of capital equipment and on individual processes in order to permit accurate cost accounting.

The insurance accounts of a Socialist trust or department should be in the red as much as in the black. Any permanent accumulation of funds in an individual account would demonstrate that some insurance charges were too high, distorting the real costs of production. Any permanent deficit would prove distortion of costs in the opposite direction.

Maintenance costs made necessary by the passage of time rather than by use, such as the cost of repainting buildings and equipment, may be either fixed or variable. They are not affected by an increase in production which does not make it necessary to build a new plant or install new equipment; but, like rent and interest, they increase whenever it is necessary to expand plant capacity.

As already noted, most costs related to the construction and maintenance of physical facilities are alternately fixed and variable. Some of the free services rendered by the government which should be paid for out of price taxes would benefit users of physical facilities, and ought therefore to be financed by price taxes on such assets. For instance, taxes on real property to support local fire departments would be price taxes of this type and, like other costs involved in the use of fixed assets, would be alternately fixed and variable depending upon the volume of production.

3. PURE MARGINAL COSTS

There are no costs which always vary in precisely the same degree as the volume of production. All costs increase either more rapidly or less rapidly than the volume of production, and many do first one and then the other. In the use of the term "pure marginal costs" there is no implication that certain costs vary directly with and proportionally to the volume of production. Rather, the term designates those costs which are always variable and accordingly always enter into the marginal cost of production. In other words, pure marginal costs are those which, when they occur, should always appear on the production control statement. Pure marginal costs include interest on variable capital; wages and salaries; raw materials, supplies, and power; freight; certain insurance, maintenance, and tax costs.

Interest on Variable Capital.—Every industry uses capital in liquid assets, the need for which varies with every change in the volume of production. Inventories of raw material, goods in process, and finished goods will be the most important form of variable capital under Socialism. Interest on capital invested in such assets is a cost which varies directly with the volume of production and is therefore a pure marginal cost.

Under Capitalism, cash is an important form of variable capital, but it should not be treated as such under Socialism because the real cost of creating cash is insignificant. Interest on unspent loans should therefore not be treated as a marginal cost, even though it varies with the volume of production.

Wages and Salaries.—All wage and salary payments not included under items classified above as pure or occasional fixed costs are pure marginal costs. Direct labor costs vary more closely with the volume of production than do indirect labor costs, but all labor costs are variable. Although administrative salaries frequently do not vary when production is increased, such variance, when it does occur, is due to imperfect determination of executive salaries. Every increase in production increases the amount or importance of the duties of administrative executives, and should therefore increase their salaries if salaries are related to individual productivity. The increase need not be proportional to the increase in production, however, since the burden placed upon executives does not increase as fast as the volume of production. If salaries are independent of individual productivity, as under equality of income, most administrative salaries would be fixed costs, since they would not vary with responsibility; but this is one of the defects of such a system of salaries (see pp. 310–11).

Raw Materials, Supplies, and Power.—Every increase in output makes necessary an increased use of raw materials and supplies; hence the cost of raw materials and supplies is a pure marginal cost. Like direct labor, it is a cost which is not only variable but varies almost in proportion to the volume of production.

The raw material and supply costs which appear on a production control statement should always be based upon current prices. Original costs should appear on the financial operating statement, not on the production control statement.

The cost of power is a perfect example of a pure marginal cost. Every increase in production involves the use of more power, and the increase in power use is ordinarily almost proportional to the increase in output.

Freight.—Freight costs are a pure marginal cost. Every increase in output increases freight costs. They should accordingly be regularly included in marginal costs.

One corollary of these rather obvious facts is that the basing point system of pricing is uneconomic under either Capitalism or Socialism. Under a basing point system, prices are uniform over a given area in spite of differences in transportation costs. This means that different consumers pay the same price although the marginal cost, and hence the marginal disutility of production, is different. Under such circumstances it is always possible to increase net social utility by lowering the price and selling a larger quantity in that part of the market nearest the factory, and by doing the opposite in the more remote parts of the market, for both measures would bring marginal utility and disutility into closer balance. It is impossible to balance marginal utility and disutility unless market prices equal the marginal disutility of production, including freight costs.

As previously indicated, price control and production should be distinct functions handled by different agencies under Socialism. Prices should merely bring supply and demand into balance. Such a pricing policy alone, however, would not eliminate a basing point system of prices. This result would be achieved only if the quantity offered for sale in each place were increased until the market price fell to a point just equal to the marginal cost of production, including freight costs; this would cause prices to vary from town to town.

Certain Insurance, Maintenance, and Tax Costs.—Certain insurance costs are always affected by the volume of production and, indeed, vary almost proportionally with it. The cost of insuring workers against industrial accidents and diseases varies almost proportionally with the volume of output, assuming no change in the technique of production. The cost of insuring inventories of all kinds varies directly with the volume of production, since every increase in output makes larger inventories of all kinds essential. These and other similar types of insurance are pure marginal costs.

Certain maintenance costs, such as those of repairing machinery and replacing worn parts and tools, are pure marginal costs, since they are affected by every change in the volume of production.

Under Capitalism, it is common for businessmen to manipulate their maintenance charges, as well as their depreciation, in order to stabilize their earnings. In periods of prosperity they increase their expenditures for maintenance in order to reduce reported profits, and in periods of depression they reduce their maintenance charges in order to reduce their reported losses. In a Socialist economy, of course, maintenance work and charges should not be controlled in this way but should always be based upon actual needs.

The costs of providing certain free goods paid for out of taxes in a Socialist economy will vary with every change in the volume of production of certain industries. Highway facilities are an excellent example of such free goods. Taxes to cover the variable costs of such goods should be levied in such a way that they will be pure marginal costs to the industries which cause them. In other words they should be price taxes designed to place the cost of certain free services upon those who cause them. If the beneficiary were a producing trust, such taxes would be marginal costs.

Taxes designed to conserve irreplaceable natural resources by increasing the cost of exploiting these resources should also be treated as pure variable costs in spite of the fact that they represent no real cost. Otherwise they would fail to accomplish their purpose.

These observations conclude the classification of costs, the main concern of the present chapter. Next in order is a statement of certain accounting principles basic to the proper determination of marginal costs.

F. THE ADDITION OF MARGINAL PROFITS AND LOSSES

In order to make possible an accurate estimate of success in production control over a period of time, particularly by higher executives not actually engaged in determining weekly or monthly production schedules, accountants engaged in the preparation of semiannual or annual summaries of production control reports should add marginal profits and losses together as if they were all of the same sign. If a certain trust shows a five-million-dollar profit during the first half of the year, and a ten-million-dollar loss during the second half of the year, the final report should not show merely a net loss of five millions. Past losses and profits should either be given in complete detail, or added together as if they were all plus or minus, so that the true extent of the imperfect control of production will be apparent.

Within a given trust, profits and losses made in the production of different articles or services should be treated similarly. They should never be added together so as to cancel and hide each other, but should be shown in detail, or added together as if they were all of the same sign.

G. THE CONTROL OF EXPENDITURES FOR COST ACCOUNTING

The problem of how much money should be devoted to increasing the accuracy of cost accounting is important and complex. Under Capitalism a businessman finds it profitable to devote an additional dollar to cost accounting whenever it seems probable that a loss of a greater amount will be discovered and prevented. Under Socialism, a profit will be as undesirable as a loss of the same amount, since both will indicate an equal degree of maladjustment between supply and demand. Does this mean, then, that under Socialism it will be worth while to spend an additional dollar for more accurate cost accounting whenever it will result in eliminating a profit or loss of an equal or greater amount?

This question must be very definitely answered in the negative. This does not mean that a profit is less undesirable than a loss. It means, rather, that the dollar value of a profit or loss is no measure of its disutility to society as a whole. It is rarely worth while to spend a thousand dollars, or anywhere near that sum, to prevent an equal profit or loss.

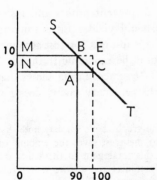

In this figure, the line *ST* represents the price of a commodity *R* for various quantities. Let us assume that the marginal cost of production of *R* is constant. Now, if we assume that the cost is $10.00 and the sales price $9.00, and that production and sales amount to 100 units at $9.00, the trust producing the commodity *R* will suffer a net loss of $100, represented by the rectangle *MNCE* in the above graph. If the installation of a more accurate cost-accounting system enables that trust to price *R* correctly, it will save $100. However, the net saving to society will be far less. It is measured by the triangle BCE and amounts to exactly $5.00. Therefore, it would not be worth over $5.00 to develop and install some system of preventing this loss of $100.

Why is the social loss so much smaller than the pecuniary loss to the trust? The explanation is that overproduction causes the trust to get a lower price on every unit it produces, while the former customers continue to get the same amount of utility from the units they purchase. Only in the case of the excess output is the cost of production greater than utility. Even in the case of these units the utility is greater than their selling price; otherwise no one would buy them. Thus the net loss, obtained by multiplying the total number of units sold by the maximum social loss on the last unit sold, is about twenty times as large as the net social loss, excess of disutility over utility, caused by the assumed degree of overproduction.[4]

The practical conclusion to be drawn from this analysis is that in such cases Socialist trusts should not devote funds to the prevention of profits or losses due to under- or overproduction unless they expect each dollar so spent to reduce profits or losses by twenty times that amount. This figure, of course, is arbitrary. It would be different for each good, depending upon its demand schedule and its supply schedule. For instance, in the above graph the triangle BCE would be much larger if R were produced under conditions of increasing costs, and much smaller if it were produced under conditions of decreasing costs. In order to determine accurately the correct relationship between expenditures upon cost accounting for the purpose of preventing profits and losses and the expected reduction in profits and losses, it would be necessary to make a special study in the case of each commodity.

While expenditures on cost accounting to prevent profits and losses due to an incorrect volume of production should yield returns ranging perhaps from 300 percent to 3,000 percent, expenditures for cost accounting on alternative methods of production would be economic if they had a much smaller effect on profits and losses. If cost accounting shows that one method is more efficient than another, the pecuniary saving does not

---

[4] To illustrate this explanation in terms of the graph above we may note that when the price is raised from $9.00 to $10.00 the trust saves the amount of money ($100) represented by $MNCE$, but of this total gain to the trust, the area $MNAB$ (90 percent of $MNCE$) is merely transferred to the trust from the consumers' surplus of those who continue to consume R. Thus they lose most of what the trust gains, and the net social gain is consequently very small. The consumers who cease to consume when the price is raised from $9.00 to $10.00 also lose the small consumers' surplus measured by BAC. This still further reduces the net social gain, which is now represented by BCE (the equal of BAC).

exaggerate the real utility savings, as in the illustration above. Rather, it underestimates them since it does not include the additional consumers' surplus received by new purchasers.[5]

Since, moreover, such a saving takes the form of a permanent net utility flow, it must be capitalized at the market rate of interest to give a true picture of its present value. If the interest rate be 5 percent, this means that a saving in the cost of production due to more accurate cost accounting justifies a cost-accounting expenditure, really an investment, twenty times as large as the saving. This is quite different from the case of a saving due to more accurate production control made possible by cost accounting, since in the latter case the saving must average several times as large as the expenditure for cost accounting in order to justify it.

[5] This additional consumers' surplus can be roughly estimated, however, by multiplying the increase in number of units produced by one-half of the reduction in cost per unit.

PART FOUR
FREE GOODS

CHAPTER IX. FREE GOODS

A. INTRODUCTION

All economic goods may be divided into two classes; those which ought to be sold for a price, and those which ought not to be sold for a price. We shall call the former *price goods* and the latter *free goods*.[1]

Free goods are not free, in the sense of involving no cost to society, but only in the sense of involving no specific or additional cost to the individual. The group as a whole must pay for all goods distributed gratuitously to individuals.

In the case of certain free goods, moreover, the individual who receives them is actually compelled to pay for them specifically, that is, according to the amount of such goods consumed. Automobile highways, for instance, are free goods, but those who use them pay for them roughly in proportion to their use of them through taxes on gasoline. Such goods, though nominally free, really have much more in common with price goods than with free goods of a purer type.

The importance of free goods is seldom realized by economists. Even under Capitalism between 20 and 30 percent of all economic goods are available to consumers free of charge. Socialism will sharply increase these percentages. Free goods are produced on an immense scale by all Capitalist governments, and on a considerable scale by private philanthropists. The state is by far the largest producer of economic goods in every industrial nation, and most of the goods it produces are distributed gratuitously. Every dollar of taxes goes to pay for the production of some free good. Every charitable or religious donation serves the same purpose. The combined total is enormous. One reason for the failure to appreciate the importance of free goods is probably that they are largely intangible, i.e., services rather than commodities.

Thus far in this treatise, price goods have received more attention than free goods. Part Three, "The Control of Production," develops a theory of production control, most of which is obviously applicable only to price goods.[2] It is impossible to use marginal profits and losses as guides to production control in the case of commodities and services which are distributed free of charge.

[1] In orthodox bourgeois economic theory, the term "free goods" has an accepted meaning different from that given above. It means costless or noneconomic goods, such as sunshine, water, air, etc.

[2] However, the theory of simplification developed in chapter vii applies to free goods as well as to price goods.

Part Four is devoted to the theory of free goods. The present chapter deals with the problem of determining what goods ought to be distributed gratuitously, the problem of controlling the production of such goods, and some practical details concerning the provision of free goods.

B. THE DETERMINATION OF FREE GOODS

The first problem with respect to free goods is that of determining what goods ought to be treated as free goods. Free goods have been defined above as those economic goods which ought to be offered to consumers free of charge. But what goods ought to be made available to consumers free of charge?

This subject has been dealt with by bourgeois economists under a different name. The problem of determining what services should be provided by government and what services by private initiative—i.e., the problem of setting limits to government activity—has long perplexed Capitalist economists, and they have been unable to arrive at any mutually satisfactory agreement on this point. Nominally, this problem will cease to exist under Socialism since the government will carry on all economic activity. Actually, however, it will continue as a major problem, for it will still be necessary to determine what goods and services should be distributed gratuitously and paid for out of taxes, and what goods and services should be sold for a price. Under Socialism, this problem will be essentially a continuation of the old question of the proper limits of governmental activity, for Capitalist economists—at least those of the liberal or laissez faire school—have always assumed that the government should produce and distribute only those goods which ought to be distributed gratuitously.

In order to decide whether any specific good is a free good—that is, whether it should be distributed gratuitously—one must understand both the general case in behalf of price distribution and the nature of the exceptions to this general case. The general case for a price system—which implies price distribution—has already been stated in detail, but a review of that important argument may be helpful here.

I.   THE ADVANTAGES OF PRICE DISTRIBUTION

Economic goods are by definition scarce, the quantity available being insufficient to satisfy the demand for them in the absence of any price. The consumption of such goods may be restricted by the use of rationing as well as by charging a price, but the latter is a much superior method of exercising control, since it reduces consumption by eliminating first those consumers who derive the least utilitum from the marginal unit. This reduces waste and misuse of goods because it is those consumers who have the least need for a good who are most apt to waste or misuse it.

In the second place, price distribution is ordinarily desirable because it facilitates the control of production. Properly determined prices make it possible to measure both the marginal costs, or disutility, and the marginal value, or utility, of production. In the absence of any measures of these quantities, sound production control is difficult. Goods will be produced which cost more than they are worth, and other goods which ought to be produced, because their production would cost less than they are worth, will not be produced at all. Thus, prices aid intelligent production as well as intelligent distribution of goods.

In the third place, price distribution is essential to some methods of stimulating the efforts of the individual worker. Piece rates and other forms of differential wages are today the best method of stimulating production, and they would be useless if all goods were distributed gratuitously. Every extension of the list of free goods tends to reduce the effect of pecuniary incentives to production. It is true that other incentives are available, and these will be discussed in a chapter on wages, but pecuniary incentives may be needed for some time to come.

In the case of individual goods, the importance of the first two advantages of price distribution, control over demand and control over production, varies directly with the elasticity of demand. If the demand is highly elastic—that is, if demand is greatly affected by price changes— price distribution is vitally important. If the demand is relatively inelastic, free distribution of price goods is least harmful because it has little effect upon the volume of consumption.

It is often assumed that the waste resulting from free distribution of a good is equal to the value of the additional goods which are demanded as a result of free distribution. This assumption is erroneous, since the additional goods yield considerable utilitum to those who consume them, which is measured by the price at which each increment could be sold. Moreover, if the same productive power were used to produce additional quantities of goods with a higher marginal utility, the marginal utility of the latter goods also would decline as output rose. Hence, the money cost to producers of the additional goods required under free distribution is much greater than the real social cost of free distribution. Price distribution, like cost accounting (see pp. 189–90), is only justifiable when the dollar saving is much greater than the dollar cost.

2. THE ADVANTAGES OF FREE DISTRIBUTION

In spite of the very important advantages of price distribution, there are a large number of cases in which free distribution of commodities and services is economically desirable because the advantages of free distribution outweigh the disadvantages. We shall now turn our attention to these advantages.

One significant difference between the advantages of price distribution and the advantages of free distribution deserves note. The former apply to all goods subject to price distribution, while many of the latter apply only to special groups of free goods.

In the first place, free distribution of certain goods is desirable because it increases the consumption of goods whose consumption ought to be increased. Many consumers are not good judges of the utilitum to them of certain commodities and services. To the extent that the state is a better judge of such matters, it may be justified in distributing these goods gratuitously in order to increase their consumption. In a democratic state, free distribution does not increase consumption beyond the level which a majority of the voters think desirable, but it increases consumption by a minority beyond the level which individuals less educated or intelligent than the average voter think necessary under price distribution. Thus, free provision of education increases its consumption by many people beyond the point at which they would cease to buy it if they had to pay its full cost. On the other hand, free provision of education does not, and should not, prevent individual parents in advance of the majority of voters from buying more educational advantages for themselves or their children than are provided free of cost by the state.

A second major reason for free distribution of goods and services is the desire to provide greater equality of opportunity for both children and adults. If the child of a poor laborer receives less education or medical attention than the child of a successful engineer, he starts the race of life under a real handicap, a handicap that can be partially eliminated by provision of a certain minimum of free education and medical care for all children. Here again, such a minimum should serve to raise the consumption by a poor or backward minority without limiting consumption by a well-to-do or progressive minority.

A third important reason for gratuitous distribution is the social significance or value of certain conditions which can only be ensured by such distribution. Community health, for instance, has an economic value to every individual. We cannot afford to permit communicable diseases to occur and spread merely because the individuals concerned refuse or are unable to spend sufficient money for prevention, segregation, and cure. Therefore, society should pay the full costs of the prevention, segregation, and cure of communicable diseases. A similar argument applies to all other types of disease. If society permits the individual to lose his productive power, temporarily or permanently, merely because the cost of medical care seems to him to be, or actually is, too high it must take upon itself the burden of supporting that individual and his family. It is much more economical to provide free medical attention for those who require it than to pay for their maintenance when sick and unable to work.

A fourth advantage of free distribution of goods is that it always reduces the cost of raising the money to pay for them. In other words, taxation is a much more economical method of allocating costs to users than sale at a price. For some goods, the saving is quite significant.

In the case of public highways, for instance, the cost of maintaining toll houses and collectors on all roads would be considerably greater than the cost of raising an equal sum of money by taxation. Similarly, the necessary costs of postal service and suburban transportation could be collected much more economically by taxation than by selling stamps and collecting fares.

The inconvenience caused to the public by requiring them to pay for commodities and services is a major part of the full social cost of price distribution. By eliminating this cost, free distribution may confer an important benefit. In the case of inexpensive and frequently purchased goods, the inconvenience of immediate payment may be considerable in relation to the total cost of the goods. For instance, the inconvenience of having to find or purchase a stamp in order to mail a letter is frequently far greater than the monetary cost of the stamp. The collection of highway tolls would undoubtedly occasion an inconvenience to travelers much greater than the burden of the toll itself. Payment for such services by taxation involves no inconvenience to the individual since he merely writes out a check for a larger sum when he pays his taxes or pays a higher price for gasoline which he must stop and purchase anyway.

A fifth advantage of free distribution is that in the case of certain goods it increases consumption and utilitum without occasioning any increase in the cost of production. If a service—radio broadcasting, for instance—is worth rendering, and if it costs as much to supply the service to a thousand as to a million people, charging a price for the service will reduce consumption greatly without lowering costs. For this reason, all such services should be rendered gratuitously. This is merely an extreme application of the principle, developed in an earlier chapter, that in the case of freely reproducible goods, market prices should on the average just equal marginal costs.

Finally, free distribution of goods is advantageous in certain cases where it is difficult or impossible to allocate costs or charge a price. Radio broadcasting is an excellent illustration of such cases. It is difficult or impossible to determine how much individual listeners use their radio sets. Hence, it is proper to meet the costs of radio broadcasting out of taxes.

One unsound argument in favor of free distribution of goods deserves mention here. Some writers have urged that necessities be treated as free goods, presumably in order to equalize real incomes. But the best way to equalize real income is to equalize money income. Most of the advantages of price distribution would continue to apply after all income differences had been abolished. For instance, price distribution checks waste; hence, such distribution will be desirable long after equality of income has been achieved.

3. GOODS SUITABLE FOR FREE DISTRIBUTION

Free goods may be classified in two ways: according to the reason for treating them as free goods, or according to the nature of the good. Since in many cases there are several reasons for free distribution, the second basis of classification is used here.

Education.—The term "education" covers the largest and most significant group of commodities and services which should be treated as free goods.

Elementary education (from age six to age fourteen) is already a free good in advanced Capitalist countries. Of course, there are still many children who receive less than eight years of elementary education, notably the children of southern Negroes and sharecroppers in the United States; teachers are too few, and the number of elementary school teachers in the most advanced public school systems ought to be doubled or trebled; but the principle of free elementary education is already generally accepted under Capitalism.

To free elementary education, Socialism ought to add free preschool and kindergarten education, free secondary education, and free higher education. The many advantages of preschool education (from age two to age six) are already generally recognized by progressive students of education. These years are the critical years in the formation of character and in social adjustment, and few mothers are competent to guide children wisely during these years. Moreover, it is very wasteful of labor to have one mother devote her time to one or two children only. Mothers with special abilities which fit them for the care of children under six should receive professional university training and should be charged with the care of a group of children of this age. These specially talented and professionally trained teachers should, of course, be given physical facilities, such as playrooms and toys, which the individual mother could not afford. Such a preschool system of education not only would provide superior care for children but would free millions of women for more productive and often more agreeable work in industry. To facilitate this end, all public schools should keep children long enough to permit their mothers to do a full day's work (five or six hours) in industry every working day in the year.

Secondary and higher education is partly subsidized by government in the United States, but most of the cost must still be borne by parents. The government pays the tuition costs of most high-school and college students, but it does not pay the living costs, which are usually much higher than tuition costs. A Socialist state ought to pay both tuition costs and living costs for all students over the age at which young people are permitted to leave school and go to work.

Free secondary and higher education is absolutely essential to any real equality of opportunity for young people, and equality of opportunity is in turn essential to the proper selection, training, and use of the most able professional and administrative personnel for both industry and government.

Free education is also desirable because many parents and students are not good judges of the value of education to themselves and to society. Many parents are willing to sacrifice the long-run interests of their children to their own short-run comfort. Many parents cannot afford the costs of higher education for their children. Moreover, many if not most of the benefits of higher education accrue to employers, neighbors, and other persons outside the family circle. Parents ought not to be required to pay for these benefits to the community even when they are willing to do so.

Finally, if higher education is really free, it will not be necessary to pay educated men an income high enough to repay with interest the costs of their education. This will reduce inequality of income without reducing incentives to efficiency. It is obviously unfair to pay professional men higher wages than they would otherwise earn merely because their parents could afford to buy them an expensive professional education not available to others.

Newspapers constitute one of the principal means of adult education. It is impossible to vote intelligently without reading a newspaper. Since intelligent voting is of the greatest importance in a Socialist society, the government should do everything in its power, including paying for the publication and distribution of newspapers, to facilitate it. The elimination of virtually all advertising from the press of a Socialist nation will increase the cost of newspapers to the public and markedly curtail their use unless free distribution is undertaken.

Probably the state should also undertake the publication and free distribution of at least one magazine covering the social, economic, and political questions of the day, in order to permit the voter to obtain a complete and impartial discussion of them. All scientific, technological, and trade journals are also primarily educational and should therefore be financed by the government.

Another service, at least partly educational, which should be provided without charge is that of radio broadcasting. There are three good reasons for treating radio broadcasting as a free good. In the first place, the educational value, which will be much greater under Socialism, would partly justify such treatment. In the second place, it is difficult to collect a price for listening to radio broadcasts.[3] Finally, and most important of all, radio broadcasting is a service whose cost is independent of the number of listeners. There is no economic reason for curtailing the number of listeners, and there is a very good one—the entertainment or education offered—for increasing their number. Charging a price for radio use would decrease the number of listeners, and therefore the real income created by broadcasting, without reducing the cost of broadcasting.

Museums and libraries likewise belong under the general heading of education. They are already treated as free goods under Capitalism. A distinction might be made between museums and libraries having a purely or largely cultural value and those useful for vocational or social education. Only the latter deserve state support on the ground of their educational value to the masses. However, since art museums aid in the vocational training of certain workers—namely, artists—and should be provided for that reason alone, they might as well be opened to the public free of charge in order to increase the total utility derived from them.

Health Services.—After education, health services are probably the most important group of economic goods which should be provided free of charge. A certain minimum amount of medicine, hospital care, medical attention, dental treatment, etc., should be treated as a free good in a Socialist economy.

This minimum should be the highest minimum that a majority of voters will approve, and those who desire more than this minimum amount of health service should be free to buy more. At the present time, there are each year in the United States at least 400,000 unnecessary deaths which could be prevented by proper health care. This country ought to spend upon health services at least 10 percent of its national income, as compared with the 2 percent it now spends. Medical science has made marvelous progress in recent decades, but most of the potential benefits from this progress are still unachieved because of the ignorance, apathy, and poverty of those who most need medical care.

Free provision of health services would greatly increase the consumption of them. Most workers cannot afford proper medical care today, and

---

[3] This might be done indirectly, however, by means of a small sales tax on radio tubes.

those who can afford it often stay away from the dentist and the doctor in order to save money. Moreover, among those who can afford medical care and do go to the doctor, some reject the recommended operation or treatment because they suspect the doctor is merely trying to increase his fees, a practice not unknown in the medical profession.

Free health services for children would do much to create the complete equality of opportunity which has long been an American ideal. A child who receives insufficient or improper medical care is often handicapped for life. Many studies have shown that children who do badly in school or on the playground can often be helped by proper glasses, hearing aids, diet, gland treatments, and many other kinds of dental and medical care which they are not now receiving.

Free health care would materially increase the productivity of labor by improving the health of the average worker. Millions of American workers now suffer from lowered vitality caused by such easily preventable or curable diseases as tuberculosis, malaria, hookworm, syphilis, gonorrhea, and abscessed teeth. In addition, millions of workers have physical defects such as poor eyesight, partial deafness, and hernia, which have not been properly treated or corrected and which therefore reduce their productivity to an unnecessary degree.

Finally, health services ought to be provided free of charge because many of the benefits of health care accrue to the public. The prevention and cure of infectious diseases protects all taxpayers against the risk of infection. The treatment of noninfectious diseases protects all taxpayers against the risk of having to support disabled workers and their dependents. It is much cheaper to cure the sick than to support them after they have become permanently unemployable.

Justice.—The term "justice" covers a third group of services which should be treated as free goods in a Socialist economy. It includes all services necessary for the proper interpretation and application of law. In other words, all lawyers, as well as all judges, should be paid by the state rather than by the individual.

Justice should be available without any cost whatever to the individual, for two reasons. In the first place, free provision of court and legal facilities will increase the use of them by those who ought to use them. Under Capitalism innumerable illegal acts are endured by private citizens, simply because it is cheaper to endure them than to prevent them or secure damages through legal action.

In the second place, justice should be provided without charge in order to increase equality of opportunity. Charging a price for legal action gives the wealthy man a great advantage over the poor man. The man who hires a fifty-thousand-dollar lawyer has an enormous advantage over the man who can afford only a cheap lawyer. All men should be equal before the bar of justice, and this requires provision of free and equal legal aid to all. In brief, justice is not justice if it is sold to the highest bidder or if a price is charged for it.

Protection of Life and Property.—Protection of life and property is still another group of services which should be rendered without charge in a Socialist economy. These services have already been recognized and treated as free goods under Capitalism. They include the services of firemen, policemen, the army, the navy, lifeguards, forest rangers, lighthouses, etc.

Protective services should be rendered gratuitously, chiefly because it is impossible to allocate their costs to those who benefit from them. No accountant can determine whose house would have been robbed in the absence of certain police activity. Free provision of protective services also benefits society by increasing the consumption of them, and by promoting equality of opportunity.

Personal Income Insurance.—A Socialist state should provide free income insurance against all risks to every citizen. In other words, every individual should be guaranteed continuance of his income in case of accident, illness, unemployment, or death. All worthy temporary or permanent dependents should receive adequate insurance benefits. All unworthy dependents should be confined in appropriate institutions.

Insurance is advantageous to the individual because it converts unpredictable and serious losses into small uniform annual costs. It increases the marginal utility of money income (and the real goods purchased with such income) by taking money away from the individual when his income is high, and its marginal utility therefore low, and returning it to him when his income is low, and its marginal utility therefore high. The costs of providing insurance, excessive as they are under Capitalism, do not offset the advantage gained by exchanging income with a low marginal utility for income with a high marginal utility.

Unfortunately, when insurance is voluntary those who need it the most buy it the least because they are poor, ignorant, shortsighted, or bad risks. Capitalist life insurance companies, for instance, spend millions of dollars a month giving examinations designed to exclude persons who have physical defects from getting insurance. Yet it is precisely these bad risks who most need life insurance.

Insurance benefits the community even more than it benefits the individual. When a father without life insurance dies, his children must ordinarily be supported by relatives, neighbors, and taxpayers. All who need insurance and fail to secure it eventually become burdens upon the community. Poverty due to loss of uninsured incomes causes crime, disease, insanity, vice, and ignorance, and seriously reduces the productivity of labor. All of these consequences diminish the income and welfare of those who carry insurance.

Since one man's failure to carry insurance injures not only him and his family but every other member of the community, the other members of the community are not only justified in compelling him to carry insurance, but would be foolish not to do so. Treating insurance as a free good amounts to making it compulsory, for everyone will accept free insurance benefits and as taxpayers they must pay for free insurance whether they want to or not.

Another advantage of making insurance a free good is that this would drastically reduce the cost of providing it. Under Capitalism the principal costs of providing insurance are advertising and selling costs. The first year's premium usually goes to the salesman, and most policies lapse after a few years. Making insurance a free good would automatically eliminate such selling costs and at the same time would increase by several hundred per cent the amount of insurance in force. Moreover, the cost of collecting and paying premiums would be reduced by 90 percent because premiums would merely be added to taxes, which would cost no more to collect if they were increased to cover the costs of free insurance.

Treating insurance as a free good has other less obvious advantages. By making insurance universal, it would increase equality of income among adults and equality of opportunity among children, which in turn would promote democracy and social stability.

Free insurance for every person against all risks would involve no significant real cost to the community. Insurance merely redistributes the costs of losses which would occur anyway. Fire insurance, for instance, does not cause fires; it merely redistributes the costs of fires. The only necessary real cost of insurance is the expense of collecting premiums and paying benefits, and this is much less than the real gains from insurance. Hence complete insurance against all risks would cost little under Socialism, and this cost would be offset many times by the advantages resulting from universal and adequate insurance.

Public-Utility Services.—The services of sewer systems have long been treated as a free good under Capitalism, presumably because they contribute to public health. However, there are other justifications for this policy. The marginal costs of serving one more home after a sewer system has been built are so small that any price based upon average cost would discourage use unduly. Moreover, it is difficult to measure the use of a sewer system by each user. Finally, free provision of sewers saves the cost of keeping an account for each user, mailing monthly bills to users, and receiving and cashing millions of individual payments.

The same considerations apply in varying degrees to other public-utility services, and would probably justify treating some if not all of them as free goods.

Water is perhaps the closest analogy to sewer service. It is essential to public health, the marginal cost is far below the average cost, and the costs of measuring use and collecting monthly payments are high in proportion to marginal cost. Moreover, free provision of water would not increase consumption unduly since the cost of water has little effect on domestic use.

Free provision of gas and electricity would have most of the advantages noted above, although the connection with public health is much less direct and significant. However, free provision of these goods would increase their use greatly because they can both be used for cooking and heating. If either gas or electricity were free and coal and wood were not, all homes connected with gas or electrical utilities would use gas or electricity instead of coal and wood for heating. Such a shift may soon become economically desirable, but it is probably not desirable now except in special cases. Moreover, since heating costs are large costs and differ widely in different homes and in different parts of the country, it may be desirable to have them always met by the consumer. It would be possible, however, to provide electricity and/or gas free of charge for domestic non-heating uses. Local experiments with this policy would certainly be desirable, and might demonstrate that this policy should be adopted for the country as a whole.

Telephones provide services which are not essential to health, except for securing medical advice and service in an emergency. Moreover, since additional calls make more complex and expensive central office equipment necessary, marginal costs do not behave as they do in other utilities. On the other hand, the cost of keeping records on local calls is so large relative to the cost of such calls that private telephone companies long ago abandoned the practice of charging for them individually. This indicates that provision of free local telephone service for domestic users would not increase use unreasonably and would probably be economical. Long-distance calls are an entirely different matter. Obviously they should not be free because the demand for them is very elastic.

Utility services of all kinds should be free only to domestic consumers. In a Socialist economy, all business enterprises would be so large that it would be economical to measure their use of each utility service and collect a proportionate charge. This practice would have the merit of contributing to accurate cost accounting and pricing.

Certain Transportation Services.—While most transportation services should be treated as price goods, a number of transportation services should be rendered free of charge. The justification for such treatment varies from case to case.

First-class postal service should be treated as a free good because the demand for such service is highly inelastic.[4] Moreover, free first-class mail service would save all costs to the postal system involved in printing stamps, selling stamps, postmarking letters, etc., and all the inconvenience to the public of having to buy and use stamps. These gains would more than offset the costs of handling the additional business created by free provision of first-class postal service.

Streets and highways, trails and walks, should be open to the public free of charge, largely because it is too much of a nuisance to collect tolls from all who use them. Another reason is that the collection of tolls frequently discourages use without reducing costs. Once a highway has been built, it might as well be used by ten thousand cars a day as by a hundred cars a day since additional use by light cars does not injure a highway.

A third type of transportation service which should probably be treated as a free good in a Socialist economy is local transportation by bus, streetcar, elevated, or subway lines. Free service would eliminate the expenses of collecting fares, speed up the service, and increase the ease and convenience of all local transportation. It would not lead to a large increase in the demand for such service, since the principal cost of all local transportation to the consumer is the time consumed, and since the demand for local transportation is chiefly determined by other factors than its price.

Finally, a Socialist state should permit and encourage travelers to make use of all empty freight carriers, whether trucks, freight cars, or ships, as a means of free transportation. This would not appreciably increase the cost of moving such empty carriers, and would serve both to decrease the demand for more expensive service and to facilitate low-cost traveling.

Governmental Services.—In conclusion, it is well to note that such purely governmental functions as legislation and administration are economic services in the free-goods class. They have an economic cost, and an economic utility which is their sole justification. They must be rendered gratuitously because it is impossible to place a price upon them and collect it from voluntary purchasers. Those who do not buy them would receive most of their benefits anyway. Hence their purchase must be made compulsory and their cost must be met by taxes imposed upon all citizens.

---

[4] Direct mail advertising, of course would scarcely exist in a Socialist state, and so would not be increased by free postal service.

C. CONTROLLING THE VOLUME OF PRODUCTION OF FREE GOODS

The problem of determining the volume of production of free goods is quite different from, and considerably more complex than, the problem of determining the volume of production of price goods. As noted previously, the proper solution of the latter problem is to fix a price which covers marginal costs and then permit consumers themselves to determine their own volume of consumption. This method, obviously, cannot be applied to free goods.

Two different methods should be used for controlling the production of free goods. In the case of certain goods for which the demand is highly inelastic, it will be advisable to produce whatever supply is consumed. First-class postal service, local transportation, justice, elementary education, ordinary medical attention, etc., belong in this class.

In the case of free goods for which the demand is relatively elastic, it will be necessary for the national legislature to determine the individual and/or national ration. Higher education, research, library service, newspapers, protection of life and property, highway construction, radio broadcasting, etc., belong in this classification. The undoubted fact that there will be wide disagreement among legislators as to the proper volume of production of each of these goods does not in any way discredit this method of controlling production, for all individual users will be free to buy more of most of these goods, and should be encouraged or compelled to consume their share of the free supply.

D. COMPULSORY CONSUMPTION

One of the principal advantages of free distribution is that it increases the consumption of goods which ought to be consumed more liberally. It is only fair to state, however, that this end may be achieved even more completely by a very different method; namely, by compulsory consumption. This method has already been almost universally adopted as a means of increasing the consumption of elementary education, and should be applied to some other goods, such as medical attention. Under Capitalism, such goods ought to be free as well as compulsory because many working-class families cannot afford to pay for them. Under Socialism, of course, no such difficulty would exist, for wages could be fixed at a level high enough to cover the cost of these goods.

If consumption of any good were compulsory in a Socialist economy, there would be no need to make it free in order to increase the use of it.

Under Socialism, free provision of compulsory goods could only be justified on other grounds, such as the difficulty of allocating costs or the nuisance involved in collecting them. There is also the consideration that the major advantages of price distribution, proper limitation of consumption and control of production, would no longer exist in the case of goods whose consumption is compulsory. However, price distribution would still serve to allocate costs to those responsible for them, and this might justify charging a price for free goods whose consumption is compulsory.

CHAPTER X. TAXATION

A. INTRODUCTION

Taxation may be defined as the raising of money by means other than borrowing, to pay for free goods. In the absence of free goods, no taxation would be necessary. The proper rate of taxation is determined at the same time that the volume of production of free goods is determined since all free goods should be paid for out of taxes.

The above definition of taxation is broad enough to include the creation of new purchasing power and the use of the profits of state enterprises. It does not include the levying of taxes to pay for capital goods. This is compulsory social saving rather than taxation.

Under Capitalism a number of different basic types of taxation, and an almost infinite number of varieties of each basic type, have been developed. There seems to be a general belief that many small taxes are felt much less than one large tax designed to raise the same total amount. The truth of this belief is doubtful; but whether it is true or not, a Socialist economy should use a single general tax to raise all funds needed over and above those brought in by special-purpose taxes. A single tax is desirable for this purpose since it will make it possible for taxpayers to have a more accurate idea of the burden of taxation and hence to regulate this burden more intelligently. Special-purpose taxes are desirable, not because, but in spite of the fact that they break up the total tax burden into smaller parts. If there were no special purposes to be achieved, it would be highly desirable to raise all tax funds by a single, universal, and very distinctly felt direct tax, hereafter called the general revenue tax. The tax system of a Socialist economy should be far simpler than the tax system of any existing Capitalist state. Certain taxes which from the point of view of a Socialist are highly desirable under Capitalism are definitely undesirable in a Socialist economy, and vice versa. We cannot apply to a Socialist economy the principles of taxation developed either by bourgeois or by Socialist theorists for a Capitalist state.

B. SPECIAL-PURPOSE TAXES

Special-purpose taxes are taxes levied to accomplish some special purpose other than the raising of revenue. For convenience in description and analysis they may be divided into: (1) sales taxes on individual goods, (2) taxes on private wealth and income, and (3) other special-purpose taxes.

1. SALES TAXES ON INDIVIDUAL GOODS

The effect of all sales taxes on individual goods (excise taxes) is to restrict consumption, and accordingly production. They should be levied only on specific commodities or services whose consumption it is desirable to restrict.

The reasons for which it is desirable to limit consumption may be divided into two classes. A special-purpose tax may be imposed on individual goods in order to limit consumption, either (1) to prevent production from being extended beyond the optimum point—the point at which marginal utility and disutility become equal—by placing the costs of free goods upon those who consume them in proportion to their consumption of them (in other words, by using special-purpose taxes to perform precisely the same function that is performed by market prices); or (2) to limit consumption of goods deemed harmful to the consumer—that is, to reduce consumption of such goods below the level considered to be the optimum level by consumers who pay no sales taxes.

A tax on gasoline to raise money for highway construction and maintenance is an example of a special-purpose tax designed to perform the same function as a market price. A tax on alcoholic beverages is an example of a tax designed to reduce the consumption of a commodity generally deemed harmful. The former reduces the consumption of highway facilities only to the optimum point; the latter tax is added to a fair market price and holds production well below the usual optimum point, the point at which marginal utility and disutility as measured by unadjusted money costs and prices become equal. The former is a "price tax," not because it is a tax on prices, but because it serves the function of a price. The latter is a "restriction tax," not merely because it restricts consumption—all taxes do this—but because it holds consumption well within the limit deemed the optimum by free individuals who pay only a market price for the good in question.

a) PRICE TAXES

Since price taxes perform the same function as prices, they are desirable only in cases where prices would be desirable if feasible. There are two good reasons for using a price tax in place of a price, (1) to reduce the costs of paying and collecting a price, and (2) to make collection of a price possible where it could not otherwise be collected. The tax on gasoline is an illustration of the former; a tax on radio tubes to raise money for radio broadcasting would be an illustration of the latter.

The criterion to be used in determining whether a free good requires a special tax is whether or not the gain from levying the special tax exceeds the cost of levying it. The gain is a reduction of consumption to the optimum level. If demand is inelastic, this gain will be slight. If the value of one year's output of the good in question is small, the gain will be small. A special price tax is most likely to be worth its cost in the case of free goods, the annual cost of which is large, and the demand for which is elastic. In addition to its cost of collection, every special price tax has the disadvantage of further complicating the system of taxation and thus confusing the taxpayer and voter.

Perfect and Imperfect Price Taxes.—Price taxes may be divided into two classes, perfect price taxes and imperfect price taxes. A perfect price tax is one which, if put at the right level, performs perfectly the function of a price—namely, the function of placing the costs of production precisely upon those who cause and benefit from them.

A tax on gasoline to pay the costs of road construction and maintenance is an illustration of a perfect price tax. If properly set, it places the costs of road construction and maintenance upon those who benefit from it in proportion to their use of the roads. Of course, the term "perfect" is used in a relative sense only. No tax performs the function of a price absolutely perfectly.

In certain cases it may be wise to impose special price taxes when they perform a part but not all of the function of prices. For instance, it might be advantageous to meet the costs of a local improvement or service by imposing a tax which falls only on people who live in the locality in question. Such a tax would tend to place the costs of the local improvement or service upon those who benefited from it, but it would not do it at all perfectly. Such taxes may be called "imperfect price taxes." There would be much more scope for them in a nation with local self-government than in a nation without. It is also possible to apply imperfect price taxes to other than geographical divisions of the population. For instance, the cost of caring for victims of automobile accidents might be met out of taxes on automobiles.

Imperfect price taxes are also justifiable as a means of enabling local governmental units to increase their own supply of free commodities and services above the level fixed upon for the country as a whole.

If the nation determines to spend two hundred dollars a year on the education of each child, for instance, no local government should be free to reduce this amount, but all should be free to increase it by levying local taxes—imperfect price taxes, which place the burden of the additional free services roughly upon those who benefit from them. All money raised for education should be spent by the central government, but local governments, if they exist, should have power to levy imperfect price taxes to augment the expenditures of the central government in their area.

All funds raised by price taxes should be spent solely for the benefit of those who pay them. The proceeds of gasoline taxes levied in New York City should not be spent upon new roads in Utah or Nevada. Price taxes collected in rich areas should never be spent in developing poorer districts. By definition, price taxes are taxes which are suitable only where prices ought to be charged—in other words, where the beneficiary ought to pay the full cost of the service rendered.

Price Taxes Necessary Under Socialism.—There are several important price taxes which should be used in a Socialist economy. First and foremost is a tax designed to make those who use through roads and highways pay the marginal costs occasioned by their use. A gasoline tax probably comes closer than any other single tax to accomplishing this purpose, but it should perhaps be supplemented by some other special tax, such as one on tires, oil, or the gross weight of vehicles in order to impose on heavy vehicles a burden more accurately proportioned to the wear they cause on highways. The ideal is a single tax, or combination of taxes, which makes all different types of vehicles pay in exact proportion to the wear they cause. A vehicle tax alone is very unsatisfactory for this purpose, since it does not vary according to the number of miles the car is driven.

A tax on all vehicles based on the number of miles driven multiplied by the total average loaded weight might be even better than a gas tax as a measure of damage done to roads and highways. Perhaps private car owners could not be trusted to report mileage correctly, but all state organizations could be relied upon and speedometers in private cars might be sealed. Another alternative is that a gas tax might be applied to private car owners and a ton-mile tax to government vehicles.

Minor roads in the country or city whose chief function is to give access to certain property should be paid for out of taxes upon that property. A small share of the cost of main roads also should be met in this way. Otherwise, property situated on main roads would obtain the same access to highways as other property, and without paying anything for it. Taxes on such property should be sufficient to pay for the kind of road which would have been built in the absence of a through road.

A special imperfect price tax to meet the costs of local urban transportation should be levied if such service is a free good. While it is impossible to devise a special tax which would fall upon those who benefit from free urban transportation services in exact proportion to their individual benefit, it is possible to limit the tax to those who can benefit from these services by raising all the funds for a community system of transportation from taxes on that community. In other words, special taxes to allocate the costs of free transportation services are feasible because these costs can be allocated geographically if not individually. The tax used for this purpose should probably be a poll tax on persons over ten years of age. It should not be a tax on income, house rent, or purchases, since the individual's use of free local transportation services will not vary in direct proportion but probably in inverse proportion to his income, rent, and purchases. The poorer paid workers will be most likely to use free street-car service rather than their own automobiles.

Certain types of compulsory insurance, notably fire and industrial accident insurance, should be financed by compulsory payment of premiums· which vary with the risk involved. Such premiums tend to promote the reduction of risks by placing a dollar-and-cents value upon risk reduction. Taxes to finance compulsory insurance which vary with the risk involved are perfect price taxes.

b) RESTRICTION TAXES

We may now turn to the consideration of the second of the two chief varieties of special-purpose taxes on goods, namely, restriction taxes. These are not levied in order to reduce consumption to the ordinary optimum level, the level to which consumption falls when the consumer pays a price equal to the marginal costs of production, but in order to reduce consumption below that level. They are levied upon goods and services which are considered physically harmful. The justification for them is that in such cases the state is a better judge of utilitum than the individual consumer and the cost of enforcement is less than the gain. Whether this justification is sound or not, restriction taxes will always exist in democratic states because the majority will always be in position to exercise control over the minority.

In the absence of complete prohibition or complete toleration of such goods, a Socialist state would levy restriction taxes upon habit-forming drugs, alcoholic drinks, organized prostitution, gambling, tobacco, coffee, tea, soft drinks, candy, and similar goods. This is not the place to weigh the utility of such restrictions, many varieties of which are popular but difficult to enforce in Capitalist America. Under Socialism they will be much easier to enforce.

2. TAXES ON WEALTH AND INCOME

Special-purpose taxes may also be levied on private wealth, or on the transfer of title to wealth by inheritance or gift. Proper determination of wages and salaries under Socialism would greatly reduce the need for such taxes as a means of preserving the optimum degree of equality of income and opportunity, but a real though reduced need would remain. In time of war, for instance, capital levies on capital in the form of durable consumers' goods would serve to bring about a more even distribution of such goods among consumers and thus reduce the need for war-time production of them. The acquisition of wealth by gift or inheritance should be limited at all times to personal property valued at not more than the equivalent of one year's income.

Personal-income taxes would not be needed to increase equality of income under Socialism if wages and salaries were properly determined. It is much more rational to pay workers the income they ought to receive to begin with than to pay them more than they ought to receive and take back some of this income later by means of a progressive or selective personal-income tax. However, personal-income taxes might be needed to raise revenue even though they should not be used to equalize income.

3. OTHER SPECIAL-PURPOSE TAXES

In addition to special-purpose taxes on individual goods and on wealth and income, there are other types worthy of mention. In certain countries taxes are already levied upon bachelors in order to encourage marriage and the rearing of a family. Under Socialism special taxes upon large families will be far more desirable in most countries than special taxes upon childless individuals, since overpopulation is far more common than underpopulation. This point has been discussed in an earlier chapter (page 121).

Taxes might be used to control immigration and emigration. Taxes on immigrants would not only reduce the volume of immigration to any desired level, but would also furnish some or all of the capital required to provide homes and capital facilities for use by immigrants. Taxes on emigration would also reduce the number of emigrants to any desired level.

Duties on imports and exports are special-purpose taxes of great importance under Capitalism, but should not be used under Socialism. In those relatively few cases where a tariff on imports is beneficial, the same result can be achieved by a subsidy to domestic producers—a method which has the great advantage of making the social costs of protection obvious.

Special taxes on the cutting of timber, the mining of scarce metals, the extraction of petroleum, and on other similar extractive industries might be used to conserve irreplaceable natural resources. In a previous chapter on the factors in production, however, the need for such conservation was questioned.

The creation of new money by the state is a special-purpose tax. The purpose should be to stabilize prices, employment, and profits. New money ought not to be created to provide the government with funds (see pages 56–58). The creation of money is a tax because it transfers real purchasing power from the public to the government.

Other special-purpose taxes which belong in this classification might be mentioned, but the above illustrations will suffice to indicate the nature and importance of such taxes.

C. THE GENERAL REVENUE TAX

Virtually the entire rent and interest income of a properly organized Socialist economy will flow directly into the hands of the state, either through the supply bureaus or through other similar organizations. The reader may then naturally inquire: Why should the state not use this income to provide free goods, instead of levying taxes to raise funds for this purpose? This question is all the more pertinent and reasonable since the above suggestion offers one, and perhaps the best, solution of the difficult problem of how to distribute rent and interest income among the citizens of a Socialist state.

In 1940 the wealth of the United States was about $350,000,000,000, and the national income about $78,000,000,000. Assuming a 5 percent average return on wealth, we find that rent and interest amounted roughly to 20 percent of the entire national income. If a similar rate prevailed in a Socialist economy, rent and interest might provide all or most of the funds needed to pay for the free goods whose costs were not met by special-purpose taxes.

Why, then, should a Socialist economy not use rent and interest to meet the costs of free services not covered by special-purpose taxes? In the first place, all positive rent and some interest would be required to offset negative rent. In the second place, the use of interest to defray the costs of free goods would prevent the voters from feeling directly and vividly the personal disutilitum involved in furnishing funds to pay for free services. If the government is permitted to use the entire national rent and interest income, or as much of it as it deems proper, to pay for free goods, the production of these goods is likely to be carried beyond the optimum point. If voters do not have to give up the marginal dollars spent for free goods, they will not know the disutility cost of providing the marginal units of free goods, and therefore will not be able to determine the optimum point at which the production of such goods should be limited.

Another reason for not using rent and interest income to meet the costs of free services rendered by a Socialist government is that such use would prevent a more exact allocation of the costs of free goods to those who cause and benefit from them. The costs of certain free goods should be allocated to consumers through prices taxes in order to permit each consumer to control his own consumption of these free goods wisely. If rent and interest were used to pay the cost of such free goods, this cost would fall equally on all consumers and therefore would not serve to restrict the consumption of these free goods to the optimum level.

1. THE CASE FOR A POLL TAX

There are three general taxes any one of which might serve as the general revenue tax of a Socialist economy. These are an income tax, a sales tax, and a per capita or poll tax. Since economic rent and interest would accrue directly to the government, there would be no need to tax them.

Of these three alternative types of general tax, the type which undoubtedly has the least appeal to the average Socialist, namely the poll tax, would be the best general revenue tax under Socialism.

Socialists have long supported differential income taxes under Capitalism because such taxes tend to lessen the injustice of Capitalism. This stand is entirely justified as a temporary policy under Capitalism, but it would have no justification in a Socialist economy. Under Socialism all incomes should be fixed at ideal levels at the time they are paid. If this is done, any alteration of their relationship to each other by income taxes would destroy the ideal relationship already existing between them.

This point is so important that it will stand restatement and illustration. If piece rates on a certain type of work are properly determined, they will give to the more efficient workers an incentive sufficient, but no more than sufficient, to persuade them to carry their personal production per day to the optimum level, the point at which the disutility of turning out one more piece a day is just equal to the utility to society of having that piece produced. An income tax affecting only the more efficient workers, or affecting them more sharply than other workers, would obviously reduce the usefulness of such ideal piece rates. It would allocate an unduly large share of the overhead costs of government to the last unit produced by the more efficient workers and an unduly small share of such overhead costs to the units turned out by the less efficient workers. As a consequence, the efforts of inefficient workers would be unduly stimulated and the efforts of efficient workers would be depressed.

Both income and sales taxes reduce the real reward of marginal effort by taking away from the worker a part of the wage paid for producing the marginal unit. Hence they reduce the marginal effort of workers and the total volume of production. This is desirable only when production has been carried beyond the optimum point at which the marginal utility and disutility of labor are equal.

The costs of free goods which should be met by a general revenue tax may be compared with overhead costs in a factory. They are a kind of social overhead costs. They do not vary in direct proportion to the volume of production. Indeed, with a given population, land area, and capital, the demand for free services, and accordingly their cost, would be affected scarcely at all by minor changes in the total amount of work done. If, however, an additional hour of work done does not increase the costs of free services, the real wage received for this unit of work ought not to be diminished by an income or sales tax. Either tax would prevent wages from measuring accurately the net marginal utility of labor and would, consequently, prevent proper voluntary control of the supply of labor by individual workers. A head tax does not suffer from this defect; consequently, the substitution of a head tax for an income or sales tax would increase the total supply of labor, the total physical volume of production, and the total net utilitum of a Socialist economy.

The costs to be met out of the funds raised by a general revenue tax in a Socialist economy are principally the costs of education, health, justice, social insurance, and similar services. An efficient worker who turns out twice as many pieces a day as a relatively inefficient worker will not use any more of these free services than the latter individual. He ought not, therefore, to be expected to contribute any more toward the costs of education, health, justice, etc., than the inefficient worker. Under Capitalism it is desirable to compel the rich, living on an income from inherited or unearned wealth, to pay for the education of the workers; but under Socialism it will not be desirable to compel the more energetic, industrious, and able workers to contribute to the costs of educating the children of inefficient workers. The purpose of compulsory and free education will then be to compel the less efficient worker to spend a minimum sum on the education of his children, not to shift these costs to more able workers.

The costs which are to be met by the general revenue tax vary almost directly with population. The parents of ten children will cause the state about three times as much expense for education, health, justice, etc., as the parents of two children.

A poll tax which applied to children as well as adults would place more of the costs of raising children upon parents and would free adults without dependent children from bearing a share of the costs of raising the children of other parents. If overpopulation existed and no eugenic control had been established, a poll tax which applied to children as well as adults would be desirable, since it would reduce the birth rate. However, differences in the number of children per family ought to be determined by eugenic considerations alone, and the best way for the state to try to achieve this would be a system of monetary penalties and rewards. If such a eugenic system is used, there should be no other conflicting system of penalizing or rewarding large families and a poll tax should apply only to adults.

A poll tax is also desirable since it compels women who do not earn their living to contribute their proper share to the cost of those free services which benefit them as much as anyone else. An income tax reduces the incentive for women to earn their own living because it reduces the net reward for working. A per capita tax offers a definite incentive to them to earn their own living.

The theory that taxes should be based wholly or partly on ability to pay is entirely unsound. It is just as unreasonable to allocate taxes according to ability to pay as it is to allocate any other cost of production in this way, or to fix market prices on a similar basis. The purpose of cost allocation and price fixation is to allocate costs to those who cause and benefit from them. Taxation is merely the method used to allocate the costs of free goods provided by the state.

All costs of free services not covered by special-purpose taxes should be met by a uniform poll tax on adults. This head tax might be collected in installments monthly, quarterly, or semiannually. Each installment should be deducted from wage and salary payments without asking the consent of the individual. Monthly or even weekly tax collections or deductions would probably be desirable, since the poll tax would be large—perhaps 10 to 20 percent of the average income in the United States.

If all wage and salary payments passed through the State Bank, tax deductions could easily be made by the bank and credited directly to the national treasury. If some wages and salaries were paid in cash, it would be necessary for the employers to make tax deductions from the wages paid.

2. Income Tax Versus a Sales Tax

As explained above, a poll tax is more desirable than an income or sales tax as a means of meeting the costs of free services not met by special-purpose taxes. However, Capitalism has developed in Socialists an intense dislike of head taxes, and this prejudice will undoubtedly linger on for some time after the justification for it has vanished. For this reason, a Socialist state is likely to use income or sales taxes during its early years. It is worth while, therefore, to note the relative merits of these two kinds of taxes.

One advantage of the sales tax over the income tax is that the former is collected from the ultimate payer in small daily installments while an income tax must be collected in much larger amounts at relatively infrequent intervals. This advantage is not a very great one since income taxes could easily be collected every pay day—as they are now in the United States.

It is claimed that a sales tax is superior to an income tax since it is collected only when the consumer has money and is therefore able to pay it. The recapture method of collecting income taxes, so freely used under Capitalism, gives this argument some merit, but it would have no validity in a Socialist state if income taxes were deducted from all wages, salaries, and other incomes before payment. Income taxes would then be due only when the individual had funds to meet them. Incidentally, this method of collecting income taxes would eliminate all possibilities of income-tax evasion, the prevalence of which under the prevailing system is one of the chief disadvantages of income taxes as compared with sales taxes.

A second real advantage of a sales tax is that it is cheaper to collect than an income tax. Prices must be determined and collected whether or not a sales tax is levied. The addition of 10 percent, or some other percentage, to all prices would not increase the cost of price determination appreciably, nor would it be more expensive to write out sales checks and monthly bills for larger sums than for smaller sums. Since all retail sales of commodities and services would be handled by three or four great trusts, the cost to the Treasury Department of determining and collecting a sales tax would be infinitesimal.

On the other hand, the collection of an income tax, while it would involve more expense than a sales tax, would be much more simple and economical than it is under Capitalism. Each trust and department would merely turn over to the Treasury Department a fixed percentage on its entire payroll and other income disbursements.

A word concerning these other income disbursements is in order. If an income tax applies only to wages and salaries, it falls entirely on one factor in production, labor, and it distorts both demand and supply by raising the price of this factor. It follows that an income tax should affect the incomes from, and prices of, all factors equally. If an income tax is levied, every department or trust ought to be required to pay the same tax on its marginal rent and interest costs as on its payroll. However, a large share of economic rent would take the form of an intramarginal surplus or profit on which it would not be necessary to levy a tax because such a tax would not affect marginal costs.

If all free and price goods were produced and distributed by a single trust, all cost payments would be income to some consumer and this income would approximately equal total sales. In such a case, a nonprogressive income tax and a sales tax would amount to the same thing—namely, a tax on gross income. From the point of view of the entire economy, they amount to this in any case.

3. Tax Exemptions

All taxes levied in a Socialist economy should be universal; that is to say, they should apply to all goods or persons in the class being taxed. No exemptions should be granted to individual goods or persons. A tax exemption has precisely the same effect as a subsidy of equal amount. Subsidies may be justified in certain cases, but they should always be granted in an obvious and visible form. Although tax exemptions have precisely the same purpose and effect as subsidies, few people realize this fact. Thus, many individuals may be found who will approve of tax exemption for church property but would vigorously oppose the granting of subsidies to religious sects. Voters and legislators are hardly ever aware of the cost of tax exemptions, but they watch subsidies very closely and hence are much more apt to limit them to the proper amount.

In addition to tax exemption for churches, many other forms of tax exemption exist under Capitalism which ought not to exist in a Socialist state. Tax exemptions for philanthropic institutions, private schools, local governmental units, children and other dependents, earned incomes, etc., should be abolished and, if government support is desirable, should be replaced by subsidies.

D. BORROWING AS A MEANS OF PAYING FOR FREE GOODS

Under Capitalism, governments frequently borrow from their citizens the funds used to meet the costs of rendering free services. Under Socialism, the government might borrow from private citizens or from the Bureau of Capital Supply for such purposes.

A Socialist state should never borrow money to meet the ordinary expenses of rendering free services since this would result in the dissipation of capital. All rent, interest, and wage costs not representing investment of capital should be regularly met from current taxes or rent and interest income. All funds used to provide capital equipment, however, should be obtained from the Bureau of Capital Supply, and the departments which use such funds should pay permanently and regularly the full market rate of interest upon them.

It would be perfectly possible, of course, for taxes to be set at a rate high enough to provide funds for both current expenses and capital investment. In this case, the tax rate would involve an element of compulsory social saving. This is undesirable as it would distort both present and future costs of the service in question and would obscure and decentralize the accumulation of capital.

In other words, borrowing from the Bureau of Capital Supply is more desirable than direct saving because, in the first place, the former policy would set up interest costs as a permanent charge against free goods and would take saving out of the costs of such goods. This would result in a more accurate determination of the real costs of providing free services. When government departments own their own plant or facilities outright, they are likely to disregard interest costs or figure them too low.

In the second place, borrowing from the Bureau of Capital Supply is desirable because it would help to concentrate control over the accumulation, the supply, and the allocation of all capital in the hands of a single organization. Centralization of control and elimination of duplication of function ought to be two of the chief aims of a Socialist state.

The same principles of government borrowing which apply in time of peace should apply in wartime. All wartime increases in current expenses should be met out of higher taxes, and only investments of permanent value should be paid for from the proceeds of loans made by the public or by the Bureau of Capital Supply. All funds which can be borrowed can also be appropriated by direct taxation.

Under Capitalism it has long been customary to meet the bulk of the costs of war from the proceeds of bonds sold to the bourgeois class. In subsequent decades these bonds are retired, or at least the interest is met, from the proceeds of taxes which fall largely upon the working class; namely, import duties, liquor taxes, tobacco taxes, salt taxes, public-utility taxes, etc.[1] Bourgeois economists frequently claim that this is done in order to prevent a single generation from paying the entire costs of a war, but this is both a misstatement of purpose and a misstatement of possible effect. Food, clothing, and ammunition used in World War I could not have been produced if it had not been paid for at the time. Taxes used to retire war bonds merely serve to transfer money from one member to another of the same generation. In other words, it is impossible for a subsequent generation to pay the costs of an old war. The real purpose and effect of war bonds under Capitalism is to transfer as large a portion as possible of the costs of war to the working class.

[1] The development of income taxes has changed conditions somewhat, but not until all taxes fall on the incomes of the bourgeois will this analysis be entirely false.

PART FIVE

THE THEORY OF MANAGEMENT

CHAPTER XI. THE ORGANIZATION OF PRODUCTION

A. INTRODUCTION

The next three chapters are devoted to the theory of management under Socialism. Obviously only a brief summary of the most novel and/or significant principles is possible.

Fortunately, Capitalism has created a very highly developed theory of scientific business management, most of which can be carried over with little change into a Socialist society. The chief task of Socialist leaders will be to run the national economy as efficiently as the best-managed capitalist trusts are now run. This will require a new theory of how to co-ordinate the activities of different producing units, not a new theory of how to manage an individual business unit.

In the field of business management the chief defect of Capitalism is that the manager of every independent business unit is free to ignore or violate the theory of management already developed under Capitalism and already applied by the executives of most large trusts. The great majority of small businessmen have never been taught the principles of scientific management. Moreover, it is difficult to apply these principles to a small firm. Socialism will promote scientific management by placing over all minor business executives, higher executives who have been thoroughly trained in scientific management. The chain-store systems have demonstrated under Capitalism that this is both feasible and profitable.

The present chapter deals with those problems of management which are most important at the time a new production unit is being organized. However, they continue to be significant as long as that unit is in existence.

B. FACTORS IN PLANT LOCATION

The problem of proper plant location under Capitalism has been repeatedly and thoroughly discussed by bourgeois economists.[1] Since the major portion of their analysis is equally valid for a Socialist economy, there is no need to develop a new or original theory of plant location under Socialism. However, it may be well to explain how Socialism will alter certain factors which influence plant location.

[1] See Alfred Weber's *Theory of the Location of Industries*, translated by C. J. Friedrich, and *Plant Location*, by W. Gerald Holmes. Weber's work is the more scholarly and exhaustive, Holmes's work the more lucid and readable of the two.

The basic principle of plant location is that a plant should be so located as to reduce to a minimum the average price of the finished article to the purchaser at the point of consumption. The principal factors which affect this price and therefore the location of plants, are: (1) the cost of raw materials; (2) the cost of labor; (3) the cost of distribution; (4) the cost of fuel or power; (5) the cost of plant facilities.

All of these costs vary from location to location, and according to the nature of the industry involved. Socialism will modify these costs in several ways.

I. FREIGHT RATES

In the first place, Socialism should change drastically both the average level and the relationship to each other of freight rates. This would affect all of the costs noted above, particularly the cost of raw materials and the cost of distribution.

The enormously complicated railroad-rate system in use under Capitalism is designed to tax the shipper, not according to the cost of the service rendered, but according to his ability to pay. Rates vary directly with the value of the commodity transported. The shipper of a carload of silk goods has to pay many times as much per mile as the shipper of a carload of coal, but the cost of the service rendered by the railroad is about the same in the two cases. This rate discrimination serves to increase greatly the total revenues of the railroads but is quite unsound from the standpoint of society as a whole. The economic evils of the present freight-rate structure will be discussed in a later chapter on transportation under Socialism. At this point it is necessary to anticipate one conclusion stated there, namely, that the same rate should be charged for the same service regardless of the value of the commodity shipped.

Such freight rates would have a very important influence upon the location of productive enterprises in a Socialist economy. Under Capitalism, freight rates are far lower on raw materials than on finished products, because of the higher value of the latter. This is a vital factor favoring plant location near markets rather than near sources of raw materials. Freight rates based on cost of service will result in the location of plants nearer the sources of raw materials and supplies, for the total weight of the raw materials and supplies is much greater than the total weight of the finished products. Location of plants as close as possible to the sources of raw materials and supplies reduces total freight costs to a minimum. By encouraging the transportation of raw materials, existing freight rates greatly increase the total volume of freight to be hauled, without thereby increasing the physical volume of production.

The freight rates prevailing under Capitalism increase the concentration of industry in large cities in two ways—by offering uneconomically low rates on the shipment of raw materials, and by giving the cities preferential rates on the shipment of both finished goods and raw materials. Since the cities are important markets for finished goods, railroad rates which make the transportation of finished goods more expensive than the transportation of raw materials favor the location of factories in large cities, for such a location makes it unnecessary to ship some finished goods to market. Moreover, in the period of real competition between American railroads, large cities were able to obtain preferential rates because they were served by two or more competing lines. Government regulation has merely solidified the rate structure developed during this period; it has not fundamentally altered it. The result is that large cities still have unjustifiable freight-rate advantages over other possible locations for industry. Socialism should end this discrimination, and such reorganization would tend to decentralize industry.

2. LABOR SUPPLY

Another factor influencing plant location which will be changed by Socialism is the mobility of labor. At present, a shoe manufacturer is very likely to build a new shoe plant in Boston or St. Louis principally in order to be near an existing supply of skilled shoe-plant workers. In a Socialist economy, the existing location of skilled labor will have much less influence upon the selection of new plant sites. Labor will be more mobile. Cost calculation will be more accurate, and the results will be acted upon more promptly and decisively. It will be much more feasible to move skilled labor to a new community whenever this will result in a significant decrease in the cost of production. If the prevailing rate of pure interest is 2 percent, an investment of $150,000 in transferring skilled workers to a new community will be worth while in order to cut annual production costs by the small sum of $3,000.

New factories are nowadays built in already densely populated areas, not only to be near a supply of skilled or cheap labor, but also in order to be near adequate existing housing facilities. Few private employers build the housing used by their workers, and private builders rarely agree to provide new housing for a new plant. Under Socialism the location of existing housing will be much less important as a factor in determining plant location. New housing will be built immediately wherever it can be used, and the construction of new housing will ordinarily be planned and carried out at the same time as the construction of new production facilities.

Under Capitalism, uneconomic concentration of industry and population in large cities is the result of a sort of vicious circle. Workers dependent on industry for their livelihood must locate near existing places of employment. New plants, largely dependent upon an adequate labor supply, must locate near existing sources of labor. Neither worker nor employer is likely to move to a new and better location unless its advantages are very great.

All of this merely indicates the evils of Capitalist individualism and division of authority. In a Socialist society, labor, housing, and factories will all be centrally controlled and co-ordinated.

3. CLIMATE

Climate affects certain production processes, and for this reason has already influenced the location of a few industries, such as the production of moving pictures. Its chief effect, however, is upon the health and happiness of the worker and his family, and this effect has been largely ignored by Capitalists. A Socialist state ought, therefore, to pay special attention to this factor in planning the location of operating units of both trusts and departments.

By voluntary emigration in large numbers to the Southwest and the Pacific Coast, American workers have already demonstrated a widespread desire to escape the harsh climates of states in which American industry and government are now chiefly concentrated. Florida and the Southern states as a whole also have a better year-round climate than states north of the Mason and Dixon line and east of the Rocky Mountains. If good jobs at Northern rates of pay were freely available in these areas, as they ought to be under Socialism, many more Americans would voluntarily move permanently to the Pacific and Gulf Coasts. If transportation were provided free of charge to those planning a permanent move, even more Americans would move to these areas. Such a subsidy to migration to sunnier climates would be well justified since it would improve the health, productivity, and happiness of the American people.

Most Americans still live north of the Ohio and east of the Mississippi chiefly because their forefathers landed there as poor immigrants unable to pay for transportation into the interior. Slavery and its evil consequences, most of which still endure, kept them out of the South and the extreme difficulties of transportation long kept even the well-to-do out of the Pacific Coast area. When industry developed in the Northern and Eastern states it merely chained to these areas a large population which had never had a chance to make an intelligent choice of a place to live.

It is true, of course, that the coal and iron and other natural resources played a part in the location of certain industries in the Northern states. However, the steady decline of transportation costs and the continuing rise in the American standard of living makes the location of natural resources less important, and the health and welfare of the worker and his family more important every year, as factors in determining the location of industry. These trends will be accelerated by Socialism.

Moreover, there are many large enterprises located in the Northern states which are not dependent upon local natural resources to any significant extent and which should be moved bodily to the South, the Southwest, or the Pacific Coast. Among these are the rubber-tire industry, the textile industry, the clothing industry, the insurance companies, the shoe industry, the universities, and most departments of the federal government. Indeed, such a transfer would place many of these industries much closer to the sources of the raw materials they use (cotton, wool, rubber, oil, lumber, etc.).

Although the firm offer of steady jobs at Northern wage levels and free transportation would undoubtedly increase considerably the already existing migration of workers to the milder climates of the South and West, these measures alone might not be sufficient to achieve an optimum volume of migration. People who have never been to California cannot always appreciate its advantages, and even if they do they may be restrained by social and family ties from migrating. Hence, it might be desirable for a Socialist government to use additional means of promoting this migration—for instance, publicity and direct subsidies.

Within a century after the establishment of a Socialist government in the United States, the area north of the Mason and Dixon line and east of the Rocky Mountains should have lost 90 percent of its population, and the small population which remains should be almost exclusively engaged in extractive industries. A similar but less drastic population decline should occur in the Southern states which border on the Mason and Dixon line and in other southern areas where the climate is relatively cold in winter or hot in the summer. The great bulk of the American population should then be located in Arizona, New Mexico, California, Oregon, Washington, and Hawaii.

The illustrations used above apply to the United States, but every large country has some areas which possess a relatively mild and healthful climate. In every large country, therefore, a Socialist government should plan and achieve a more desirable distribution of its population among climate belts.

4. OTHER FACTORS

A factor hindering proper plant location under Capitalism is the division in ownership and control of individual industries. To return to the case of shoes, if the manufacturers of the raw materials, findings, supplies, and machinery used in the production of shoes are already concen-

trated in two or three centers, it will probably pay any new shoe manufacturer to build his plant in those established centers. He will be able
to carry smaller inventories and to secure supplies, parts, and repairs much
more quickly than if he were to locate somewhere else. It might be
economically very desirable to move the entire industry to a different part
of the nation; but as long as each unit of the industry is necessary to the
others, and separately owned, it will be difficult to get the various proprie-
tors to move as individuals or as a group. This is the reason why many
industries remain concentrated in a few cities where they originated, long
after they ought to be transferred, in part or wholly, to entirely different
locations. Under Socialism, however, each industry will be able to act
and move as a unit whenever this is economically desirable because each
industry will have a single central management.

Not only will central control over a given industry alter the conditions
determining plant location under Socialism; unified control over all industries will also alter the factors controlling the location of individual
plants. The location of units of two or more different industries will be
determined by a single executive whenever these units are closely related
to each other. For instance, the location of power plants and the location
of plants which use their power will be determined at the same time by
the same experts, so far as possible. This will result in a more desirable
location of all the productive units concerned. Since nearly all plants are
dependent upon other plants for materials or markets, this means that the
location of all plants should be decided at the same time by the same
experts. While this will be impossible to achieve at any one time, it will
be possible to determine an ideal plan of plant location for all industries,
and then work steadily towards the relocation of industry.

Socialism will entirely eliminate certain minor factors affecting plant
location under Capitalism. Variations in state and local laws, particularly
those concerning taxation, affect plant location at present, but should not
exist under Socialism. Hence, under Socialism no plant will be located in
a certain state or city in order to escape regulation of the hours of labor
and wages, or in order to evade income taxes prevailing in other regions.

Under Capitalism, special inducements are frequently offered by local
communities or Chambers of Commerce in order to attract certain industries or plants. This practice, of course, should cease with the introduction
of Socialism. Still another minor factor affecting plant location under
Capitalism is the ease of securing capital. One of the reasons why American industries remain or locate in New England and the Middle Atlantic
states is the fact that interest rates are lower there. Under Socialism,
interest rates should be the same throughout the nation.

Other minor factors affecting plant location under Capitalism will lose part or all of their influence under Socialism. The preference of the owner of a given factory for his native city as a home will cease to affect plant location. The ready access to commodity exchanges and competitive markets, which is a noteworthy advantage of location in a large city under Capitalism, will lose nearly all of its significance in a completely integrated Socialist economy. The complete elimination of the necessity of competitive sales efforts will deprive city factories of very real advantages and promote decentralization.

C. PLANT LOCATION AND CITY PLANNING

Under Capitalism the average city worker spends about an hour a day, and from ten to twenty cents, for transportation to and from work. This is due to the fact that cities grow up accidentally rather than according to plan, and to the practice of concentrating dwellings in one part of town and factories in another. In a Socialist society, every city should be planned so that workers will be able to live as close as possible to the plants in which they work. Factories should not be grouped together in the dirtiest and ugliest part of the city. Each plant should be separated from the others and placed in the midst of a small community of workers' dwellings. The factory building should be a thing of beauty, showing the same architectural and landscaping care now devoted to the finest public buildings and private homes. A community of individual homes and apartments (the workers should have free choice between the two) housing up to 25,000 people can easily be grouped around a single plant so as to permit workers in the most distant homes to reach the plant in a fifteen-minute walk. This would save both the time and the money now devoted to transportation to and from work. If these savings were used to increase production instead of leisure, the total output of city workers should rise by about 10 percent.[2] If they were devoted to leisure or education an even larger though intangible benefit would result.

Since every worker should be able to get work of any kind wherever he wants it under Socialism, all the members of a family should be able to find the kind of work they want in the same plant community in the great majority of cases. A large factory offers work of many kinds and workers would therefore have a wide choice of vocation in each plant. Moreover, next to each large plant there should be a shopping center

[2] The average American worker spends one hour a day, and ten cents, to go to and from his work. Eliminating this money cost and saving an average of thirty minutes a day per man for thirty million urban workers would yield a total national economy (estimating time at one dollar an hour) of over $4,000,000,000 a year.

offering a wide variety of jobs. Dwellings close to the boundary between one plant community and another should be reserved for families with members working in both communities.

Offices should be treated in the same manner as manufacturing plants. The main national and regional offices of all trusts and departments should be grouped together or divided up into units employing from five to ten thousand workers, and each unit should be made the center of a separate plant community with its own retail facilities, professional offices, bank, etc., and with all employees housed within a one-mile radius of their place of work.

D. DIVISION OF LABOR

If each worker produced everything he consumed, no division of labor would exist. As soon as and in so far as he uses buildings, roads, tools, supplies, materials, and other capital goods in whose production other workers have participated, division of labor exists. It began, in all probability, with a simple division of tasks between men and women. As primitive tribal life arose, there was added an elementary division of labor among men, who became priests, chieftains, soldiers, hunters, and artisans. Every subsequent advance in methods of production has brought about a further degree of human specialization, until today we may see scores of men performing separate operations on each part used in the assembly of a manufactured product.

The development of the division of labor has by no means ceased even though in a few cases it may have been carried too far. The problem of determining the optimum division of labor on work under his control is a problem which is constantly before every business executive under either Socialism or Capitalism. He is free at any time to increase or decrease this division of labor. He must reach a definite decision on this point and must review it periodically. In order to reach such decisions, he must, of course, experiment with different degrees of division of labor. Hence he ought to be familiar with the advantages, disadvantages, and natural limits of the division of labor.

In his frequently quoted discussion of the division of labor, Adam Smith set forth its advantages in these words:

This great increase in the quantity of work, which, in consequence of the division of labor, the same number of people are capable of performing, is owing to three different circumstances: first, to the increase of dexterity in every particular workman; secondly, to the saving of the time, which is commonly lost in passing from one species of work to another; and lastly, to the invention of a great number of machines which facilitate and abridge labor and enable one man to do the work of many.[3]

The principal advantage of the division of human labor is undoubtedly the great increase in skill and speed which it makes possible in two different ways.

In the first place, the division of labor reduces the number of the operations which each worker must perform. The worker therefore performs each of these operations much more frequently, and he learns to perform them more skillfully and more swiftly. Practice makes perfect only when the division of labor results in sufficient practice. This is even more true of mental than of physical labor. The more complex and difficult the work, the greater is the increase in skill resulting from a proper division of labor. Specialization among college professors, doctors, lawyers, and executives is therefore even more fruitful than specialization among factory workers.

In the second place, the division of labor increases the skill and speed of workers of all kinds because it permits the workers to specialize in that kind of work for which he is best suited by heredity and training. In a completely unspecialized economy, all men would do the same kind of work. Division of labor makes it possible for some men to specialize in mental work and others in physical labor, for some to specialize in bricklaying and others in plastering, and so on. There is just as much difference between the abilities of different men as there is between different soils and climates. Suiting the job to the man is therefore as productive as suiting the crop to the land. Neither could occur without division of labor.

The second advantage mentioned by Smith, "the saving of the time which is commonly lost in passing from one species of work to another," refers to the time lost in laying down one tool and picking up another, getting out new materials, moving from one work place to another, and so forth.

The third advantage mentioned by Smith, the stimulus to the invention of new machinery, is in the long run even more important than the increase in the dexterity of the workmen although it causes no comparable immediate increase in productivity. The division of labor stimulates invention by so simplifying operations that even an ordinary laborer can occasionally devise a machine to perform them, and by greatly increasing the dexterity and ability of those who specialize in the work of invention. When a technological problem is split into numerous sub-problems, each of which is assigned to a specialist, the effect is to bring the study within

[3] *Wealth of Nations*, Book I, chap. i.

the capacity of lesser brains, at the same time making very much easier the synthesizing work that has to be done by a brain of greater power.

There are several advantages of the division of labor which were not mentioned by Adam Smith. In the first place, it greatly simplifies work by dividing complex processes into their constituent parts. We have just noted the effect of this simplification in the field of technological research. It also greatly reduces the amount of education, training, and experience necessary to provide competent workers. Where the same amount of time and money is still devoted to training, the benefits derived from this preparation are markedly increased. All of the advantages of the division of labor, of course, can be treated either as reducing total cost or as increasing total output.

Since simplification of work reduces the amount of training necessary to develop good workers, it makes it much easier for workers to move from one task to another. This increase in the mobility of labor results in more equal wage rates for different tasks, plants, and cities, and decreases the inevitable losses from the displacement of skilled workers by labor-saving machinery.

Simplification and standardization of labor processes also make possible the use of piece rates and other forms of incentive wages, since they enable executives to measure the amount of work done by workers. Every increase in the division of labor renders the piece-rate system more efficient.

Division of labor makes possible the maximum utilization of unusual ability. The subdivision of complex work processes into their constituent parts makes it possible to concentrate the efforts of the limited supply of unusually able men upon those constituent parts which deserve their attention.[4] A great scientist who has to write his own letters, cook his own meals, and manufacture his own equipment is obviously being forced to waste much of his time.

Finally, the division of human labor makes possible a corresponding division of the work performed by capital and land. Without division of labor, the manufacture of specialized tools admirably suited to each specific kind of work would, to a large extent, be uneconomic. Without division of human labor, it would be impossible to use the best wheat land for growing wheat, the best cotton land for growing cotton, the best potato land for growing potatoes, and so forth. These advantages are very great.

The most important disadvantage of the division of labor is the cost

[4] To the Capitalist entrepreneur this advantage assumes a different form. It enables him to hire cheap unskilled labor to do work formerly done by relatively costly skilled labor.

of marketing goods and services. In the absence of any division of labor, all trade would disappear. The sole function of commerce is to make possible a division of labor.

It has been estimated by bourgeois economists that the costs of marketing goods and services now equal the costs of producing them. As used here, marketing includes the selling activities of producers, jobbers, wholesalers, and retailers, and all transportation services. The latter alone amount to one-tenth of the national income of the United States.

The introduction of Socialism will reduce the costs of marketing by from 50 to 80 percent. Most marketing costs are due to competition and individualism. Every merger and every new trust or chain-store system reduces them somewhat. Socialism will continue this development to its natural conclusion, and thus reduce greatly the chief disadvantage of the division of labor.

While an increase in the division of labor between companies and regions ordinarily causes an increase in marketing costs, this is by no means an inevitable result of all increases in the division of labor. If a factory has not yet developed the optimum degree of division of labor for its existing volume of production, it may increase its division of labor to this optimum level without increasing marketing costs. Vertical integration of independent firms permits an increased division of labor and at the same time reduces marketing costs. It is only when an increase in the division of labor is achieved through horizontal combination or vertical disintegration that it increases marketing costs.

Moreover, the costs of wholesale and retail distribution are the chief items in total marketing costs, and these are not affected by increases in the division of labor on goods already produced outside the home. Transportation costs and handling costs of brokers and other middlemen and processors are the only costs increased by a further division of labor between firms and regions on such goods.

The second important disadvantage of an increased division of labor is the increased cost of handling and moving materials and goods in process inside the factory or producing unit. This is an intra-plant equivalent of the increased marketing costs which develop outside the plant. When each worker specializes upon an operation or process, it is necessary to move the work-in-process through the hands of many workers and through many departments.

It is sometimes asserted that specialization deforms the worker physically and mentally by developing him along one line or in one capacity at the expense of all the others. The harm may come from the overstrain of certain muscles and nerves, or from the lack of use of the others. A partial answer to this charge is that it does not describe a necessary result of the division of labor, but a result of overwork and neglect of proper exercise and recreation. Where division of labor places an undue strain upon certain muscles and nerves, the hours of labor should be reduced and workers should take care to properly exercise their other muscles and nerves during leisure periods. However, the need of providing for this necessity must be recognized as a disadvantage.

Many writers have charged that the division of labor makes work excessively monotonous and uninteresting. The high turnover of labor typical of most factories is sometimes blamed largely upon the monotony of work caused by a minute division of labor.

There is undoubtedly a measure of truth in this charge, at least in the case of certain individuals. For some people, a task which is quickly learned loses interest quickly. Nevertheless, the charge that an extreme division of labor renders work monotonous and uninteresting has probably been overworked. Most of this criticism has been made by students and intellectuals who are certainly not representative of the working class in their reactions to monotonous and highly repetitive work. There seems to be a very strong possibility that large numbers of workers actually prefer work of this kind because, once learned, it becomes pure habit, involves no new problems from day to day, and leaves the mind free for more congenial thoughts, even during the hours of labor themselves. In many cases where the individual actually prefers this kind of work, he will refuse to acknowledge it, just as many people refuse to admit that they enjoy reading the *Saturday Evening Post* more than Shakespeare. In a Socialist economy, moreover, those workers who really do dislike highly repetitive work would be free to choose any occupation that pleased them.

If there really are a large number of workers who are willing to sacrifice a portion of their income in order to avoid work which they consider too repetitive and monotonous, special efforts should be made to permit them to do less repetitive work. They should even be permitted to engage in old-fashioned handwork if they desire. The workers who enjoy this kind of work, however, must bear the costs of the resulting decline in output. If consumers prefer handwork, a portion of the higher costs may be passed on to the consumer, but in all probability most of the decrease in efficiency will have to be offset by corresponding wage cuts.

A very simple method of reducing the monotony of repetitive work for those who suffer from it would be to permit daily, weekly, or monthly changes from one kind of work to another. Repetitive processes and much semiskilled work are so easy to learn that many workers might master two or three different jobs and change periodically from one to another. For instance, a girl who operates an adding machine in the morning might sell toys in the afternoon, or a man who inserts bolt No. 121 in a Ford chassis in the morning might drive a delivery truck in the afternoon. Every facility should be offered individual workers to secure such a variation in routine, but obviously the worker benefited should bear all costs involved. However, such periodic variations of routine might actually increase output by relieving the strain upon certain nerves and muscles. Careful scientific experiments are needed to answer this question and to determine the optimum degree of variation in routine.

It has long been recognized that the division of labor is ultimately limited by the extent of the market, for the latter fixes the maximum potential volume of production of a given good in a given plant. The factors which determine the extent of the market, and which restrain the division of labor within the ultimate limits set by the extent of the market, have received less attention.

There are two principal factors which largely determine the extent of the market: namely, the costs of transportation and the diversity or variety of goods and services produced. Every reduction in transportation costs broadens the market for a commodity produced in a given place, and thus makes possible an increase in the division of labor. Every increase in the variety of commodities produced, whether due to the appearance of a new model of an article already in use or to the introduction of an entirely new article, reduces the volume of demand for articles previously in use and diminishes the potential degree of the division of labor. If all men wore a single style of hat summer and winter, the market for this hat would be a hundred times as large as the market for any hat now produced. If only one kind of automobile were produced and sold in the United States, the extent of the market for this car would be about four times as large as the extent of the market for any car now produced.

The extent of the market merely sets the ultimate or potential, not the actual, limit to the division of labor. Under Capitalism, nearly all markets are supplied by a greater or lesser number of competing producers, each of whom consequently has a volume of production far less than the extent of the market would permit. Competition is incompatible with a full development of the division of labor. Only under a system of perfect and universal monopoly can the division of labor be carried to the ultimate limit set by the extent of the market.

Even within the limits of a single producing organization, the division of labor is rarely developed to the fullest possible degree. Sometimes production is divided between two or more plants when concentration in a single plant would make possible a greater division of labor and reduced costs of production. In nearly all cases the division of labor is insufficiently developed in individual plants because of ignorance on the part of the management. In the last quarter-century an enormous increase in the division of labor has occurred, a very large part of which might have been adopted much earlier. In other words, it was human ignorance, not the extent of the market or the scale of production, which had previously prevented the adoption of this division of labor. The same situation continues to exist today. The average Capitalist producer does not spend one-tenth of the money which he ought to spend on research on further division of labor. Indeed, most producers do no research work on this problem whatsoever, but merely imitate their competitors.

The general principle which should govern the division of labor is that it should be increased until the last increment of it causes more disutilitum than utilitum. In practice, monetary costs must represent disutilitum and monetary savings must measure utilitum. Since different units of the division of labor are not homogeneous, every unit must be treated as a marginal unit and its utilitum and disutilitum measured and compared in monetary terms.

The division of labor should unquestionably be carried a great deal further in a Socialist economy than it has ever been carried in the most advanced Capitalist nations. By simplifying the variety of goods produced, by reducing transportation costs, and by eliminating competition, Socialism will enormously increase the extent of all markets and thus raise the optimum level of the division of labor.

In order to take advantage of both old and new opportunities for an increased division of labor, a Socialist economy ought to carry on constant and large-scale research in the methods of dividing labor processes into their simplest parts. The change from Capitalism to Socialism will make desirable very large temporary expenditures upon this type of research, due to the resulting sudden creation of great opportunities for a further division of labor; and this research work should be continued permanently at a level far above that existing under Capitalism. The division of labor has done more to increase the productive powers of labor than any other one thing, except the invention of machinery, and the greatest progress in the division of labor has occurred only in the present century. A method of improving production which has accomplished such marvelous results in the past deserves far more attention and scientific investigation than it has ever received under Capitalism.

One important reason why private capitalists have failed to devote the proper amount of attention to increasing the division of labor is that in a competitive society the benefits of any increase in the efficiency of production accrue largely to consumers. This is particularly true in the case of improvements in the division of labor, as it is impossible to patent and monopolize such ideas even for a short while. Since private profit is the sole motive to production, and since only a fraction of the gain resulting from an increased division of labor accrues to the capitalist who develops and introduces it, there is little incentive to research or improvement in the division of labor.

E. SCALE OF PRODUCTION

The scale of production is largely distinct from, and may vary independently of, the scale of organization or management.[5] A single organization or trust, possessing a complete monopoly of the production of automobiles, for example, may produce all cars in a single plant, or it may divide its production among many plants. However, there is a relationship between the scale of production and the scale of management because, while the scale of production may be any fraction of the scale of management, the scale of management cannot be less than the scale of production.

The scale of production in any industry has two aspects: (*a*) vertical integration, the grouping together in one plant of successive stages in production; and (*b*) horizontal integration, the grouping together in one plant of those working at a single stage in the production of a good. The scale of production may be very large in one respect, and very small in the other. Thus every successive operation on each part of a Ford car might be performed in a separate plant, while at the same time all work at each stage of production might be carried on in a single plant. Under such circumstances, vertical integration of production would be at a minimum, but horizontal integration would be at a maximum.

I. ADVANTAGES OF LARGE-SCALE PRODUCTION

The advantages of large-scale production may be divided into two groups: those that apply to vertical integration, and those that apply to horizontal integration or mass production.

Vertical integration increases the scale of management in the individual plant, and thus helps to make possible the important advantages of large-scale management. In the second place, it reduces the cost of transporting parts from one process to another. If all parts are produced in separate plants, they must be shipped from the point of production to the point of assembly. This involves the costs of packing and unpacking, loading and unloading, freight charges, accounting entries, etc. On the other hand, if all parts are manufactured in a single, properly designed

[5] The problem of the proper scale of management or organization has already been discussed in chapter v, pp. 99–101.

plant, they are at or near the correct assembly point when they are completed. In the third place, vertical integration reduces inventories to a minimum. If parts are manufactured in separate plants, both the parts manufacturers and the assembly plant must maintain stocks of all of them. Manufacture and assembly of parts in a single plant makes possible a direct flow of parts to the assembly lines, and reduces inventories to the minimum necessary to prevent a stoppage of the assembly lines.

Finally, vertical integration lowers the cost per unit of product for all subsidiary services and overhead costs other than management. Heat, light, space, repair work, janitor service, the service of the personnel department, etc., can all be provided more economically for a large plant than for a small plant.

Turning now to the advantages of horizontal integration, the concentration of work at a given level of production in a single plant, we may note that this does even more to increase the scale of management than vertical integration. Horizontal integration does not require an increase in the number of basic managerial divisions because it does not increase the number of technological processes; it merely gives to each existing division a greater volume of work to supervise.

In the second place, horizontal integration lowers the cost per unit of all subsidiary services and overhead costs other than management, just as vertical integration does. In the case of horizontal integration this applies particularly to buying and selling costs and to the expenses of the receiving and shipping departments.

In the third place, horizontal integration makes possible a very great increase in the division of labor. This advantage is largely peculiar to horizontal integration. It does not follow from vertical integration, except in the field of management and in the provision of certain subsidiary services required by several successive steps in production.

Finally, mass production makes possible a greatly increased use of labor-saving machinery. If machinery is to be used to the greatest advantage, it must be used continuously, and this requires mass production. A large factory is able to use machines which save only a fraction of a cent per unit of output but which are profitable on account of the volume of production. Mass production makes possible a division of labor among machines and the designing of special new machines for many processes not previously performed by machines.

The advantages of large-scale production described above apply to every increase in the scale of production. There is no limit to the *internal* economies resulting from large-scale production, except perhaps in extractive industries, particularly agriculture, where an indefinite increase in the scale of production eventually requires the use of inferior resources.

All nonextractive industries operate under conditions of indefinitely diminishing internal costs.[6]

2. DISADVANTAGES OF LARGE-SCALE PRODUCTION

While every increase in the scale of production results in lower internal costs, it does not necessarily result in lower total costs (internal plus external) to the consumer. In many cases an increase in the scale of production raises external costs enough to increase total costs.

In the first place, every increase in the scale of production due to horizontal integration increases the necessary transportation costs involved in the distribution of the product. If all the bricks used in the United States were produced in a single plant, the internal costs of production (the costs of operations performed inside the plant) would be at a minimum, but the transportation costs involved in distribution would be at a maximum and would much more than offset the saving in internal costs.

The importance of this disadvantage of large-scale production varies widely according to the nature of the product. It depends largely upon the value per pound of the product in question. If the value per pound is low, as in the case of steel, cement, and brick, the above-mentioned disadvantage is of great importance and may be sufficient to justify division of production among many local plants. If the value per pound is relatively high, as in the case of clothing, shoes, furniture, and jewelry, this disadvantage is much less important and may not offset the advantage of complete concentration of production in a single plant.

A second significant disadvantage of horizontal integration is that it nearly always involves an increase in the necessary costs of transporting raw materials, semimanufactured materials, and supplies from their source to the manufacturing plants. If all pigs were slaughtered and packed in Chicago, the internal plant costs would be at a minimum, but the freight-in costs would be at a maximum. Every decrease in the scale of production due to the establishment of a new regional or local meat-

---

[6] The great majority of bourgeois economists have failed to recognize this fundamental principle. Thus Pigou writes: "Internal economies reach the limit at different points in different kinds of industry—but always long before the individual establishment has grown to any appreciable fraction of the whole industry of which it is a part" (*Economics of Welfare*, p. 220).

On the other hand, Florence insists that the logic of organization requires the concentration of production in units of the largest size; and that it is only avoidable human failings which result in smaller plants. (*The Logic of Industrial Organization*, p. 11.) For a similar view see Mooney and Reiley, *Onward Industry*, p. 308.

Joan Robinson discusses the nature of some economies of large-scale production in her *Economics of Imperfect Competition*, pp. 333–43.

packing plant would increase internal plant costs and decrease freight-in costs.

The importance of this second disadvantage of large-scale production depends largely upon the location, supply, weight, and bulk of the raw materials and supplies concerned. For instance, if the raw materials to be used are abundant and widely scattered, as in the case of clay, sand, wood, and petroleum, this second disadvantage of large-scale production will be relatively unimportant because the necessary raw materials will ordinarily be close at hand and large-scale production will involve only small increases in transportation costs on raw materials. On the other hand, if the necessary raw materials are scarce and widely scattered, the opposite will be true.

It is sometimes asserted that production should be divided among many small plants scattered through the countryside in order that workers will not need to live in huge and assertedly unhealthful cities. This may be desirable, but the proper criterion of plant size automatically takes such factors into consideration. It would be uneconomic to build small plants in the country simply because a few intellectual or artistic individuals think the workers ought to live there. If, however, the workers actually prefer to live in small rural communities, properly determined wages will be sufficiently lower in such communities to cause the erection of factories there. On the other hand, if the wages made possible by the location of plants in large cities attract all workers into the cities, it will be because, weighing the relative advantages of rural and urban life, they choose the city. In this respect, as in many others, the goal of a Socialist administration should be effectual freedom of choice, not the control of the many according to the ideals of a few.

3. OPTIMUM SCALE OF PRODUCTION

The optimum scale of production is that which yields the lowest average prices to consumers at the point of consumption. Whenever a question concerning the optimum scale of production in any particular industry arises, it will be necessary to estimate the effect upon net costs to the consumer of all the advantages and disadvantages listed above. In many cases experimentation with plants of different size and location will be required in order to solve the problem. Since conditions change constantly, this process of experimentation must be unceasing.

Under Socialism the scale of production in all industries will be much greater than it now is under Capitalism. In the case of innumerable highly manufactured articles, all production should be concentrated in a single national plant. In small nations such as Japan, England, France, and Germany, the manufacture of nearly all articles, heavy and bulky as well as light and valuable, should be concentrated in single plants. In the United States, Russia, Canada, Australia, China, and India, there will be more reason for local manufacture of heavy and bulky commodities.

Innumerable serious obstacles prevent the realization of the maximum economies of large-scale production under Capitalism. The prejudices of the petite bourgeoisie cause governments to pass laws against mergers and combinations, and to use force to break up the more successful trusts such as the original Standard Oil Company. Corporation income-tax laws, social-insurance laws, wage-and-hour legislation, and many similar laws discriminate against large concerns. Many states prohibit corporations from engaging in agriculture, law, medical practice, and other economic activities in order to protect small business. Inertia and ignorance prevent innumerable small producers from attaining the economies possible through mergers and combinations. Small independent producers work long hours for a negligible reward, and forego interest on their capital in order to stay in business. The desire to justify high prices causes the great trusts to leave small high-cost marginal producers in the field. Naturally, these obstacles to large-scale production will cease to exist in the new society.

F. COMBINATION OF THE AGENTS IN PRODUCTION[7]

One of the problems which constantly face every business executive is the problem of how to combine land, labor, and capital in the most productive manner.[8] Any business executive in a Socialist economy will be free at any time to order, or at least to suggest, the use of more or less of any factor in production in the work which he supervises. The general principles which should govern the combination of the factors in production form the subject matter of this section.

First, however, it is well to recall that the practical business executive is not dealing with three homogeneous factors in production, but with the varied individual forms of these factors. In other words, he always faces concrete problems in which labor assumes the form of accountants, salesmen, truck drivers, etc., and land and capital assume equally specific forms. His constant problem is whether to hire more or fewer foremen,

[7] For a much more detailed discussion of this topic see J. D. Black, *Production Economics*, chaps. xi, xii, xiii.

[8] An earlier chapter (chapter vi, "The Factors in Production") dealt with this problem in its most general and simplest form, namely as the question of what ratios should exist between the total supply of land, capital, and labor.

more or less space in a certain building, more or less equipment of a certain kind—not more or less of land, capital, and labor in the abstract. The innumerable concrete forms assumed by the three factors in production will be referred to hereafter as "agents in production."

In dealing with these concrete problems the economist must be careful not to interfere with or take over any of the functions of the engineer or applied specialist in the field concerned. He cannot say that a cotton mill should maintain a definite proportion between the number of spinners and the number of spinning machines of a certain type. He can only develop general principles to aid in determining this specific ratio.

On the other hand, the fact that the engineer alone cannot determine the proper combination of the agents in production is worth emphasizing. Technical efficiency is distinct from, and may run counter to, economic efficiency. It is not worth while to save labor and materials unless this results in lower costs or a net addition to consumers' or producers' surplus. The proper technique of production in any industry is dependent upon cost relationships and may be changed at any time by a change in cost relationships, particularly by a change in the relationship between the interest rate and local wages.

This point deserves to be stressed because many radical thinkers, notably the Technocrats, have assumed that engineers can solve our economic problems better than economists and businessmen. Acceptance of this error is also probably one of the basic reasons why so many who believe in economic planning fail to see the difficulties involved. They assume that economic production is a purely technical engineering problem, once the quantities to be produced have been decided upon.

Discovering the proper combination of the agents in production is a problem of cost reduction. The general principle to be followed is that the agents in production should be combined in such a way as to reduce average unit costs to a minimum. This principle is an obvious corollary of the fundamental doctrine that properly determined costs are the best measure of disutilitum.

The chief difficulty in the application of this principle arises out of the fact that most producers use many different agents of production, all of which may vary in quantity and quality independently of the others. The number of these variables does not make it impossible to determine with approximate accuracy a definite least-cost combination, but it does complicate the problem.

The problem of determining the least-cost combination of the agents in production may be divided into two parts: (1) the determination of the least-cost *quantitative* combination, and (2) the determination of the least-cost *qualitative* combination of the elements in production.

I. THE LEAST-COST QUANTITATIVE COMBINATION

The only method available for discovering the least-cost combination of the agents in production is the experimental method. Actual experiments must be made with all possible combinations and the results carefully tabulated. The general principles which govern all scientific work should govern these experiments. They should be carried on by special research workers wherever possible.

The principle of diminishing returns has long been known to, and emphasized by, bourgeois economists. It has frequently been restricted to the effect of constantly increasing doses of labor and capital upon land, but it applies with equal truth to every possible combination of both the factors and the agents in production. In other words, whenever two or more agents in production are combined and the quantity of one remains constant while the quantity of the other or others steadily increases, the returns per physical unit of input of the varying agents begin to decrease after a certain point has been reached.

The principle of diminishing returns is really a principle of increasing and decreasing returns. In other words, as one agent is varied in quantity, the output per unit of the varying agent first increases and then decreases. Indeed, in certain cases the output first increases, then decreases, and finally increases again before beginning to diminish permanently. Thus the principle of diminishing returns in its broadest form ought to be called the principle of varying returns; it should be stated merely as the rule that when two or more agents are used in production and the quantity of one of them is varied, the returns per unit of the varying agent vary.

In order to determine the least-cost combination of agents for the production of any good, it is desirable to prepare graphs showing the effect of variations in the quantity of each agent used when the quantity of the other agents used remains fixed. Separate graphs should be prepared for different combinations of the fixed agents.

Obviously, it will be both unnecessary and impossible to prepare graphs of this kind for all possible quantities and combinations of the fixed elements. Attention should be centered on those combinations which preliminary or exploratory work shows to be nearest the least-cost combination. Only when the least-cost combination has been roughly located will the more careful and intensive study of combinations be worth while. Attention should also be centered on those agents which account for large shares in the volume of the output. There are usually two or three agents which between them account for the bulk of the cost of production. These should be investigated more thoroughly than such minor agents as heat or light in a factory.

The principle of diminishing or varying returns refers to physical quantities of output. In order to discover the least-cost combination of agents, it is necessary to introduce an independent factor, prices. It is obviously more desirable to economize in the use of an agent of production when that agent is selling at a high price than when it is selling at a low price.

Since prices vary continually, while the relationships between different physical combinations and total physical outputs are relatively constant, data concerning the latter may be prepared for continuing use with changing price data in order to discover the current least-cost combination. If data on the relationship between varying physical combinations and total physical output are available, the least-cost combination may be ascertained at any time by multiplying all quantities by their market prices. This will give the total cost, which divided by the product, will give the unit cost. The least-cost combination is that which gives the minimum unit cost.

Whenever buildings or other fixed improvements are planned, some prediction of the most economical combinations of the agents in production in the future is essential, since physical facilities are an agent in production and ought to permit a least-cost combination of these agents.

Since future prices are always uncertain, it is never possible to predict accurately in advance the proper combination of the elements in production. Studies of price trends will be helpful, and should always be used by men who are planning future combinations, but their use will not make perfect prediction possible.

2. THE LEAST-COST QUALITATIVE COMBINATION

Thus far we have been dealing with the problem of the proper combination of the agents in production upon the assumption that they are relatively homogeneous—that is, sufficiently homogeneous not to invalidate our discussion and conclusions. Actually, however, certain agents in production, such as wheat land and managerial ability, are decidedly heterogeneous. No general relationship between a given quantity of land or ability, other agents in production, and total output—in other words, no universally applicable curve of increasing and decreasing returns—can be discovered.

To eliminate this significant defect in the previous analysis, several methods are available. In the first place, it is possible to treat each grade or quality of an agent as a separate agent in production. If carried out literally, this suggestion would involve an infinite increase in the number of agents, but a rough classification of different qualities into groups, each of which is to be treated as a distinct element, would make this method practical. Certainly it would be much more accurate than an analysis of combinations which completely neglected differences in quality.

A second method, less desirable than the first, would be to treat heterogeneous elements in the same way as homogeneous elements, and to perform enough experiments to get the average effect of variations in the quantity of heterogeneous elements used. This would provide some foundation for the determination of the quantity of such elements to be used and would probably be a satisfactory method in cases where the heterogeneous element in question has little effect upon the total output.

It should be noted that the essence of these methods is to collect qualitative differences into groups which can then be treated as distinct agents in production and their combination determined in the same way as the quantitative combination of other agents. There is, however, another method of approaching the problem of combining agents possessing significant qualitative differences within themselves. If the qualities of heterogeneous agents are graded according to their productivity, it is possible to state a significant general principle concerning their combination. This principle is that like grades of agents in production should be combined with like grades of other agents in production.

To illustrate this point let us assume that wheat land, wheat seed, fertilizer, tractors, tractor drivers, wheat-farm managers, etc., can be divided into two groups according to productivity—the more-productive *A* group and the less-productive *B* group. Under such circumstances, all the *A* land should be farmed with *A* equipment, seed, and fertilizer, by *A* men, before any *A* equipment is used on *B* land. If the classification is properly done, each agent will be subdivided so that there will be just enough *A* men and equipment to farm the *A* land, and no more.

The reason why the best men and other agents in production should be assigned to the best land is that this gives maximum scope to their productivity. If a new plow turns a furrow 10 percent deeper than any plow previously in use and· thus increases the value of the crop by 10 percent at a relatively small increase in cost, this new plow should be used on the most fertile land; for then the resulting 10 percent increase in crop value will be a far higher absolute gain than if the new plow is employed on the least fertile land in use. In other words, a percentage increase amounts to the maximum absolute increase only when it applies to a maximum base.

The universal application of this principle deserves special emphasis. Not only should the best seed, plows, fertilizer, and other equipment be used on the best land, but the best teachers should devote their full time to the best students, particularly in higher institutions of learning. The most skillful and dexterous machine operators in all factories should be given the newest and best machines to operate. The highest executives ought to have the most efficient stenographers and secretaries. The most capable fishermen should be given the best fishing boats and equipment, and so forth throughout the entire national economy.

Under Capitalism no effective method of combining like qualities of agents in production is in use. The self-interest of the entrepreneur dictates such a combination, but in most cases the entrepreneur either does not understand the dictates of his rational self-interest, or lacks the means to obey them if he does understand them.

Each trust and department of a Socialist economy should adopt effective measures to assure constant and permanent observance of the principle of the combination of like qualities of agents in production. This means, in the first place, that all heterogeneous elements must be analyzed, classified, and graded according to their productivity. In the second place, it means that all trust and department executives must be taught the significance of the principle and required to apply it.

One qualification of the general principle of combining like grades of agents in production must be made. Certain types of new machinery do not result in a proportional increase in output but merely reduce the costs of doing a certain kind of work. Thus a new type of plow might be invented which does not increase yield per acre, but merely reduces the cost of plowing. There would be no advantage in using such a plow on good land instead of on poor land. This applies to all differences which lower cost but do not affect the volume or the quality of the output. Gradation of the agents in production for the purpose of aiding the proper combination of them should, therefore, be based entirely upon differences which affect the value of the output and should ignore differences which affect only the cost of the service rendered by the agent.

CHAPTER XII. THE SUPERVISION OF PRODUCTION

A. LEADERSHIP

The present chapter is devoted to the problem of selecting able executives and to those problems of management which become important after an enterprise has been started, and which are not a part of the Taylor system of scientific management described in the chapter to follow.

Orthodox bourgeois economists have largely ignored the problem of selecting economic leaders. They assume without justification that success in fair competition is the typical basis of executive authority under Capitalism, and they ignore or deny the predominant importance of inheritance of wealth and of the control of proxies by corporation managements. Bourgeois economists assume that Capitalism is desirable and relatively permanent, and they consider the selection of many leaders by inheritance to be an inherent feature of Capitalism.

It is difficult to overemphasize the importance of able leadership in a Socialist economy. Wise leadership is more essential to efficient economic activity than extensive organization or perfect equipment. This maxim is not new to economic theory, although it has been more fully appreciated by students of military strategy than by economists.

The decisions of the chief executive of a great trust frequently result in mistakes costing millions of dollars or in improvements saving equally large sums. That is why under Capitalism the chief executives of a few great trusts are paid salaries and bonuses amounting to more than a million dollars a year. The elimination of Capitalism, by eliminating nearly all the risks of modern business, will reduce the nominal monetary significance of the decisions of the chief executives of large undertakings; but at the same time it will increase the real economic significance of their decisions by permitting them to focus all of their remarkable talents upon business problems, such as those of cost reduction and efficient organization, which really involve the welfare of the people.

I. PERSONAL QUALITIES OF LEADERS

It is difficult to define the personal qualities essential to able leadership. Obviously, in a Socialist state the inheritance of wealth and social position will not continue to play their present dominant role. Equality of educational opportunity is an essential preliminary requirement for any efficient selection of leaders.

Mental ability, as shown by intelligence tests, is the most important

quality to be sought in business executives. Probably minimum requirements in this respect should be set for all executives, varying according
to their rank. Thus, if executives above a certain rank make up only one
percent of the total working population, they might well be required to
rank in the upper ten percent of all workers in intelligence. Only long-
continued experimentation can show just how high or low these minimum
intelligence requirements should be.

Health, of course, is a personal quality which greatly increases the
effectiveness of business executives. The minds of healthy men are clearer
and capable of longer and closer application than those of less healthy
individuals. However, quality of thought is far more important than
quantity. A small but definite superiority in intellectual capacity may
more than offset a very marked difference in health. The number of
invalids and semi-invalids who have attained high positions in the artistic
and scientific world is a striking commentary upon the relative importance
of health and intellectual ability.

Under Capitalism, a sales personality, the quality of being able to
make friends and dominate others, is probably more important for success as an executive than any other attribute. The presidents of the great
American trusts and monopolies are above the average in intellectual
endowment, but by no means remarkable in this respect. Their outstanding quality, where their position is not due to inheritance or influence,
is that of personal magnetism and force. This is especially true in old
and stable organizations where the chief executive has risen from the
ranks. It is much less true in those cases where the chief executive is a
successful entrepreneur, as in the case of the Ford Company. Here intellect
is probably much more significant.

Personality is a dominant factor and intellect a relatively minor factor
in determining business success under Capitalism, partly because of the
enormous importance of salesmanship. Native intelligence and technical
training are of great value in the field of production, but they count
for relatively little, at least as compared with personality, in the field of
selling or marketing the product. Marketing costs, moreover, are on the
average as large as production costs.

A graduate of a technical school or university, even if he be far above
the general level in native intelligence, receives a salary little above the
wage of a skilled laborer. A successful salesman, usually on a lower
level in both native intelligence and education, may easily earn five or
ten times as much as the engineer. Under Capitalism, the ability to
persuade consumers, retailers, or wholesalers to buy one brand of canned
peaches instead of another brand is far rarer, and therefore far more
valuable than the ability to produce canned peaches efficiently.

The importance of salesmanship and the sales personality pervades the entire Capitalist economy. Unskilled laborers who have the energy and personality to go out and get jobs earn a larger wage than more efficient and industrious workers who are less effective personal salesmen. Professional men who have social graces and a pleasing personality obtain more clients and patients than other professional men who lack these gifts but who are nevertheless better trained and more able than the former.

2. MEASUREMENT AND PUBLICITY

Socialism will inevitably diminish the importance of sales personality as a factor in success and thus increase the relative importance of productive achievements and ability. Nevertheless, it will still be possible for a high executive to promote those men under him whose personality he likes, rather than those who are superior in native intelligence and productive achievement. To reduce this possibility to a minimum, a Socialist state should take great pains to develop and apply what Sydney Webb calls the principle of "measurement and publicity." That is, the state must develop methods of measuring and evaluating the accomplishments of executives wherever possible. In certain types of work this will be impossible, and in such cases native intelligence as shown by intelligence tests should be largely relied upon. In many large and stable industries, however, it is entirely practical to develop performance tests. Once developed and applied, of course, the results should be made public in order to justify promotions and in order to stimulate Socialist competition.

While no exhaustive analysis is possible here, a few methods of testing performance may be suggested. In the first place it is necessary to secure statistics concerning significant and commensurable aspects of the work done. In transportation a large number of statistical series concerning such things as ton-miles per locomotive, ton-miles per car, daily car-loadings, maintenance costs per mile, etc., are already prepared.[1] Similar statistical series may be developed in all basic industries. Once collected, these statistics must be weighted and combined in such a way as to give a single index number which best reflects the efficiency of operation. This

[1] Of course, costs per ton-mile are the best index of total operating efficiency, but this can be applied only to the chief transportation executive, not to minor officials in charge of specific functions.

Such indices of operating efficiency would of course be affected by personality traits of executives. A popular executive will secure better co-operation from his subordinates and fellow executives than will an unpopular executive. The purpose of using such indices should not be to eliminate personality factors, but only to eliminate the influence of those personality traits which would not promote efficiency under Socialism.

index number should then be used in comparing past and present results and in evaluating the work of different executives. The way to refine profit and loss figures so that they measure the efficiency of production control has already been explained. Promotion should always be based largely upon the index of operating efficiency, past marginal profits and losses, and intelligence tests.

The principle of measurement and publicity should be applied, not only to subordinate executives, but also to entire industries and the nation as a whole. Certain fundamental indices of economic welfare, similar to those on business conditions under Capitalism, must be worked out and published periodically in order that the voters will have a scientific basis for appraising the work of the dominant political party and its leaders.

3. TWO RULES OF EXECUTIVE WORK

The value of leadership can be greatly increased by an intelligent application of two rules of executive work. In the first place, executives should concentrate their time and efforts upon the most important problems of the unit under their control. In the case of high executives, particularly, it is of vital importance that they leave to subordinates the solution of all but the most significant problems. No high executive should ever be pressed for time or overburdened with work. The very importance of his position and the problems he solves demands that he have more freedom, more leisure, more recreation, and more time than subordinate executives. To give him the time for unhurried and carefully-thought-out decisions, it is necessary to reduce the work given him to the minimum. All but the most important problems must be handled by his subordinates. Visitors must be ruthlessly denied the privilege of seeing him.

The rule that executives should concentrate all of their time upon the most important problems of the work under their control differs somewhat from the principle of exceptions. L. P. Alford asserts that "managerial efficiency is greatly increased by concentrating managerial attention solely upon those executive matters which are variations from routine, plan or standard."[2] This principle is of decided merit, but it is not true that all important problems arise out of "exceptional" or unanticipated behavior. The problem of cost reduction is ever present and parts of it are always of vital importance. Moreover, many exceptional or unexpected developments do not deserve the attention of a high executive. Only the important exceptions deserve his attention. However, a combination of the "exception principle" with what we may call the "principle of relative importance" should be decidedly useful.

[2] Alford, *Laws of Management*, p. 74.

In this connection it is important to note that the frequent charge that Socialism involves "bureaucracy" and "red tape" is based upon an assumption that Socialist executives will not apply the principle of relative importance. If local and subordinate officials are given the power to make routine and relatively unimportant decisions on their own initiative, as they should be, and if superior executives concentrate upon important and exceptional problems, no cause for complaint concerning bureaucracy and red tape will exist.

A second basic principle of executive work is that free use should be made of expert opinion whenever the executive faces technical problems. This rule is of particular importance for the general executive who must supervise the performance of various distinct functions within a given organization. It is less important for the functional executive, for he is presumed to be an expert himself on most matters under his control.

B. THE MAINTENANCE OF DISCIPLINE

The maintenance of discipline among workers and executives will be as necessary in a Socialist society as under Capitalism. This does not mean that false contemporary, social, or disciplinary standards must be retained. For instance, efficient production does not require workers to call executives "Sir" or "Mister," while they themselves are addressed by their first names. Separate washrooms, coatrooms, and dining halls for executives tend only to turn necessary occupational differences into unnecessary social castes, and should not exist in a Socialist plant. On the other hand, a reasonably prompt obedience of workers to superiors is absolutely essential to efficiency in production. Everything necessary should be done to develop this degree of respect for authority among all workers and executives. To this end, all executives should be given the power to reward, and perhaps to penalize, the workers under them.

The principal method of developing obedience and co-operation among all workers and executives should be intensive education in school. This should be supplemented by adult education through newspapers, magazines, posters, radio programs, moving pictures, and all other publicity channels.

Many instances of disobedience are the result of personality conflicts and can be ended by the simple expedient of placing the worker under a different supervisor. If a supervisor has an unusual number of such cases among his subordinates, the supervisor himself is probably unfit.

Obedience and co-operation among workers can be promoted by the use of periodic rewards for good conduct, including promotion, bonuses, and special privileges. It is usually more effective to reward good conduct than to punish bad conduct. If penalties are used, they should be of such nature that they affect only the worker and do not punish his innocent dependents. Overtime work without pay, loss of medals and honors, publicity, and loss of vacation are penalties of this type.

Discharge, the penalty most frequently employed under Capitalism, should not be used as a penalty at all under Socialism. Discharge merely shifts the responsibility to some other employer or results in wasteful unemployment. A worker should be transferred to a more suitable job if he is unable to perform his duties properly and if personnel experts state that he would be more productive and happier as a result of the transfer. Indeed, such transfers should be made whenever the above reasons exist, regardless of the conduct of the worker.

It is just as foolish to discharge a worker for disobedience as to discharge a soldier for disobedience. Work and military service are both duties which no one should be allowed to escape.

Serious behavior problems should of course be treated in special institutions, just as insanity is; but this should never be described as or considered a form of punishment. Insurance benefits equal to full-time wages should be paid throughout the period of such treatment. The dependents of a worker should not suffer any loss in income because of disobedience on the part of their breadwinner.

C. SOCIALIST COMPETITION

While Socialism will eliminate a great many socially undesirable forms of competition, such as advertising, sales effort, adulteration of products, and stimulation of style cycles, it need not eliminate any desirable form of competition, such as efforts to reduce costs, increase individual productivity, and develop new and superior products. Indeed, a Socialist government should make every effort to stimulate all desirable types of competition.

The very nature of a Socialist economy will facilitate the perpetuation and development of desirable forms of competition. Under Capitalism the consumer serves as a judge of the competitive success of competing firms. He indicates his judgment by placing his patronage with the firm he considers most successful. However, the individual consumer is a decidedly poor judge of competitive success. He is influenced by advertising and sales effort. He does not take the trouble to make an accurate and scientific comparison of the goods and prices offered by all competitors. He does not know whether the favorable prices he pays are the result of underpayment of workers, long hours of labor, or the absence of health, accident, and old-age insurance, or whether they are the result of superior efficiency.

On the other hand, when every unit of a given industry is a part of a single Socialist trust, the top executives of that trust will be in an ideal position to determine the efficiency of each unit of the industry. They will have full knowledge of all relevant facts concerning wages, equipment, cost of raw materials, prices received, quality of product, etc., and will be in a far better position than consumers to determine real competitive success.

Every Socialist trust should promote Socialist competition—that is, socially desirable competition—between groups of workers or units of industry. Every worker should belong to a competitive group or "industrial team," and every such team should take part in an annual or semi-annual tournament with all other teams in its own industry and the nation. The final events in this national industrial tournament should be widely publicized and the winners suitably honored. If the tournament is properly managed, it may take the place of the World Series and other similar sporting events as an object of public interest.

In order to make competition possible among all teams, it will be necessary to assign carefully determined handicaps and to measure all results in comparable terms such as percentages of cost reduction and increase in output.

To stimulate interest in the lower brackets of the tournament, some reward should be offered for success in every stage or bracket of the tournament. Even within teams defeated in the first stage of competition, rewards might well be distributed to the individual members of the team who make the best record. Membership in a select honor group such as a shock brigade might serve this end. So far as possible, all rewards should be nonpecuniary.

D. HOURS OF PLANT OPERATION

The proper method of determining the hours of labor for workers has already been discussed in chapter vi (pages 118–20). The hours of plant operation, however, may vary independently of the hours of labor, and thus require a separate discussion.

In a Socialist economy the majority of workers will probably work a five- or six-hour shift, resting every third or fourth day. The problem of hours of plant operation, therefore, is a question of whether to use capital facilities only during these limited periods, or to attempt to exploit them more fully by using more than one shift a day and more than three days in a four-day week.

The economy to be obtained through increased utilization of a limited supply of capital is obvious. A 100 percent increase in the hours of operation of existing plant capacity has virtually the same effect upon the volume of production as a 100 percent increase in the number or capacity of existing plants. Moreover, the former method of increasing production requires no abstinence or saving, and can be adopted whenever desired, while a 100 percent increase in the capacity of existing plants involves heavy abstinence costs and may take many years to accomplish.

However, all increases in the hours of plant operation create disutilitum. Two, three, four, or more shifts a day cause the workers positive disutilitum by disturbing their periods of rest and sleep, and by reducing the opportunity for social intercourse and amusement during free hours. Night work, particularly, has a high disutility cost.

Since attempts to use the facilities of production more than one shift a day result in both increased utilitum and increased disutilitum, and since no outside observer can experience these effects, the problem should be solved by passing on to the workers the full gains and costs incurred and permitting them to balance the two and reach a free decision concerning the merits of increased or continuous plant operation. In other words, those who work at night should be paid higher wages which accurately reflect the saving in overhead costs achieved through night work. If these savings increase the wages of the night shift so much that night work becomes more popular than day work, then these savings should be shared with the day workers in such a way as to equalize the demand for jobs in all shifts. The important point is that night work is worth while whenever it makes possible wage increases which attract the required number of men and women to night work.

In regard to running two shifts a day, it should be noted that the gains are so large in comparison with the costs that no hesitation in introducing a two-shift regime need be felt. This fact has been recognized by certain Capitalist writers. Lord Leverhulme explained that if the ordinary factory runs two six-hour shifts instead of one eight-hour shift a day, the same wages can be paid for the shorter work day as for the longer work day, even if the production per worker declines in proportion to the reduction in the hours of labor, a highly improbable consequence. His argument assumes that fixed costs are equal to varying costs and that they are not increased by working two shifts a day.[3] Under Socialism, of course, a double shift would reduce hours from a smaller maximum to a smaller minimum.

To avoid the necessity for a one-hour meal period, the day shifts under a multi-shift regime might well be reduced to five hours. The in-

---

[3] Leverhulme, *The Six-Hour Day* (1918). See also P. S. Florence, *Economics of Fatigue and Unrest and the Efficiency of Labour in English and American Industry* (1924), pp. 214–16.

creased pay for night work and the greater disutility of such work might make a four-hour or three-hour night shift popular. Two five-hour, two four-hour, and two three-hour shifts would permit a twenty-four-hour schedule for most plants. As previously explained, however, workers should have a choice between shifts of two or three different lengths at all times.

Temporary scarcity of a given commodity often results in high prices for the capital instruments used in the production of that commodity. This is especially true if a long period of time is necessary to duplicate these capital instruments. In such cases, the scarcity value of the capital instruments makes night shifts and twenty-four-hour operation all the more desirable, and justifies the payment of unusually large bonuses or wages in order to persuade men to work at night. When it is not already the general rule, twenty-four-hour operation should be one of the principal means of ending shortages of specific commodities.

Precisely the same method should be applied to determine whether mines, farms, and factories should operate on Saturday, Sunday, and other civil or religious holidays. Every productive organization should give its employees complete freedom in their choice of off-days. However, if more than one-seventh of them choose any one day, the wages paid for work on that day should be raised until either the number of men who desire the day off is reduced to exactly one-seventh (or two-sevenths, if the average worker takes two days a week off) or until wages cannot be increased any further without causing the variable costs of production to exceed the market price of the commodity produced. This measure would probably eliminate the economic waste caused by all general holidays without exercising any compulsion. It would merely permit those who help eliminate such wastes to gain the entire benefit of this waste prevention, or the share of it necessary to call forth their efforts.

Giving workers the full gains from such waste prevention may not be sufficient to secure full utilization of all capital on traditional holidays. In that case, no compulsion should be used, for the individual is the best judge of utilitum and disutilitum to him; but enough plant departments, or machines, should be operated on holidays to give work at higher than normal wages to all those who desire to work. These individuals could rest on other days, when wages would be lower.

The proportion between variable and fixed costs differs from industry to industry. If it averaged 50-50, the average holiday wage could be 100 percent above weekday wages in order to secure steady use of all capital. In all probability, a wage increase of much less than this proportion would serve the desired end. If not, and if there is any scarcity of labor on holidays, then those industries in which the proportion of fixed expenses to variable expenses is the highest should be operated first with the limited supply of labor. In some industries this proportion is so high that a 200 percent or more increase in holiday wages would be justified in order to secure steady operation. In industries using little capital, only a very small increase in wages would be justified in order to secure uninterrupted operations. These same factors should also help to determine whether continuous twenty-four-hour operation of a plant is desirable throughout the week.

Holidays are evils inherited from Capitalism. Respect for them will slowly disappear in a Socialist society as religion and nationalism, the forces behind nearly all existing holidays, slowly die out. The payment of large, but not uneconomic, bonuses for holiday work will do much to destroy them. A Socialist state should abandon the practice of declaring new holidays, and should use other measures, such as special commemorative newspaper issues and radio programs, for honoring national heroes and historical achievements. Religious holidays should not be enforced by a state which tolerates all religious opinions, including atheism. Religious freedom implies that each worker should be free to decide whether or not he will work on Sunday or any other religious holiday.

E. PREVENTION OF INDUSTRIAL ACCIDENTS AND DISEASES

One of the outstanding evils of Capitalism is the huge number of workers who suffer from industrial accidents and diseases.[4] This is all the more worthy of criticism since it is almost entirely preventable.

In 1928 the Committee on Safety and Production, of the American Engineering Council, published the results of a careful investigation of this subject, and concluded that the majority of industrial accidents in the United States could and should be prevented at a relatively small cost. Indeed, it stated that "maximum productivity is ordinarily secured only when the accident performance tends toward the irreducible minimum."[5]

The fact that accidents and cases of industrial disease can be greatly reduced at a small cost has been repeatedly demonstrated in individual plants under Capitalism.[6] By placing a small fraction of the total costs of industrial accidents on the owners of industry, workmen's compensation

---

[4] An industrial disease is the visible and serious cumulative effect of a long series of invisible minor industrial accidents, such as the injury done to the lungs by each grain of silica inhaled.

[5] American Engineering Council (Committee on Safety and Production), *Safety and Production*, p. 35.

[6] Alford, *op. cit.*, pp. 208–14.

laws have given a profit motive to accident prevention, and have notably reduced the number of accidents. This again proves the possibility of preventing accidents.

One of the basic principles of accident and disease prevention is that all cases, including minor ones, should be recorded and carefully analyzed. This should be done for all cases, outside of as well as during hours of labor. When they have been properly recorded and classified according to type and cause, a comprehensive investigation into methods and costs of eliminating individual causes should be undertaken. Human nature and normal human errors should never be treated as causes. Only preventable causes should be tabulated and investigated.

Under Capitalism the proper method of preventing industrial accidents and diseases is to place their full cost upon the owners in whose plants they occur. As long as accidents cause no losses to the owner, he will do little to prevent them. Even if he felt kind-hearted and philanthropic, competition with less sentimental producers would force him to neglect accident prevention unless he had a monopoly.

Under Socialism the costs of industrial accidents and diseases should be fully borne by those plants and industries in which they occur. No system of insurance which places any of this burden upon plants not responsible for it should be used. The purpose of compensation under Socialism should be not only to invoke the cost-reduction motive in the drive against accidents and disease but also to measure the cost of these evils and to restrict consumption of products whose manufacture involves unusual danger to human life. Here, as elsewhere, allocation of costs to products and individuals who benefit from them reduces these costs to a minimum.

Once the costs of industrial accidents have been ascertained, allocated, and classified according to cause, and once the cost of eliminating individual causes has also been ascertained, the problem of accident and disease prevention is simply one of the comparison of cost to be saved with the cost to be incurred.

The task of estimating the cost of accident prevention will ordinarily be much easier than the task of estimating the cost of industrial accidents and diseases, particularly when death occurs. The costs in wages lost, hospital expenses, interruption to production, etc., are fairly easy to estimate, but the human pain caused by accidents and the worry caused by the possibility of accidents are virtually immeasurable. The value of a human life, moreover, is entirely incommensurable.

The economic value of a human life to society cannot be measured by capitalizing the earnings of the individual in question. If an individual consumes all that he earns, society suffers no appreciable economic loss from his death. If, however, he has been using half of an earned income of $2,000 a year to support dependents deserving support, or has been saving an equal sum, his death puts the burden of support of the dependents in question upon society or deprives society of his annual savings. These sums can be capitalized to measure his value to society and thus to aid in determining the proper expenditure for accident reduction.

While it is impossible to measure the value of human life, the cost charged to individual plants for each fatal accident should not be less than the charge for the most serious nonfatal accident, an accident which would require full support of the victim and his dependents for life. Probably, also, it should not be more, for such a charge would be $100,000 or greater.

Under Socialism, the cost charged to the plant in which an accident occurs should be entirely distinct from the compensation granted to the injured worker or his family. The cost charge to the plant should ordinarily exceed the compensation, for the latter is but one of the costs of industrial accidents. In cases where a fatally injured worker has no dependents, no compensation should be paid to his heirs. Instead, the entire charge should be paid to the state. In other words, compensation should be based solely upon needs. Cost charges, however, should be uniform and should be based upon average total costs involved.

F. STABILIZATION OF PRODUCTION

Under Capitalism there is a high degree of seasonal fluctuation in the output of many industries. In some cases this is due to natural and unpreventable causes, as in the canning industry. In others, it is due to the uncertainty of demand and to seasonal consumption. A Socialist administration should adopt special measures to reduce seasonal fluctuation of the latter kind. If consumers buy straw hats only in the spring and summer, for instance, this is no reason why straw-hat factories should operate only six months a year. The entire annual consumption should be carefully estimated in advance, and then produced fairly evenly through the twelve months of the year.

Producing goods for a seasonal market in advance of the selling season would increase interest and inventory costs, but it would reduce the costs of seasonal unemployment and seasonal shifts in employment by more than enough to compensate. Under Capitalism, employers bear only the former costs. The burden of unemployment falls upon the workers and the government. Hence, employers have little interest in reducing seasonal unemployment and turnover.

In those industries in which seasonal fluctuation in production is unpreventable at an economically justifiable cost, all of the additional expenses caused by the seasonal nature of the industry, including transportation costs and lost wages, should be paid by the employing trust and passed on to consumers in the form of higher prices. This would reduce the consumption of the products of seasonal industries to the optimum level at which market price covers full marginal costs.

G. BUDGETARY CONTROL

As explained previously, a Socialist state should not plan production ahead of time, in the manner commonly assumed to be characteristic of Socialism. Instead of producing in accordance with a plan, a Socialist economy should produce in accordance with popular demand as reflected in marginal profits and losses. Each trust should be relatively free of central authority in regard to production control, although a central Bureau of Economic Co-ordination should be established to co-ordinate the independent estimates of future production made by individual trusts.

While arbitrary centralized planning of production should be minimized, planning in the sense of budgetary control over individual economic units should be far more common, detailed, and accurate than it is under Capitalism. Every trust and department should use a system of budgetary control such as that employed by the best-managed Capitalist trusts. The consolidation of each industry into a single large monopoly would facilitate the planning or estimating of future production by eliminating competition. Even under Capitalism, giant monopolies like the Bell Telephone System are able to plan or predict their activities much more intelligently than producers operating in highly competitive fields.

Budgetary control is based upon an estimate of future sales which is made in both physical quantities and monetary terms. The former is used as a basis for planning the purchase of raw materials, capital improvements, labor force, etc. The latter is used to plan expenses, bank loans, and investment of idle funds. Whenever actual sales significantly exceed or fall below the estimates upon which the budget is based, both the estimated sales figure and the budget items are revised.[7]

While the sales estimates upon which all budgets are based should be prepared by expert statisticians, the estimates of individual department expenses necessary to the estimated volume of production should be made by the department heads concerned, and should then be co-ordinated into a single plant budget. As a measure of division of labor, it might prove

[7] For an able summary of conventional budgeting procedure, see L. P. Alford, *Management's Handbook*, pp. 1269–1312.

economical to have all sales estimates made by a single national statistical office.

Budgetary control is very valuable as a means of planning each detail of production and as a means of controlling expenses. Expert statisticians can estimate future sales far better than general executives or individual department heads. This enables the latter to make more intelligent preparation for future production. A budget also serves to co-ordinate the work of independent department heads by causing them all to plan on the same volume of production.

H. COST ACCOUNTING AND STATISTICS

Cost accounting has already been discussed in considerable detail in earlier chapters, particularly in chapter viii, "The Determination of Marginal Profits and Losses." Both cost accounting and statistics should be more widely used and more elaborately developed under Socialism than under Capitalism. The theory of cost accounting and statistics has, of course, been highly developed under Capitalism, but few capitalist enterprises have made use of the best accounting and statistical theory. Moreover, the very nature of competitive Capitalism makes uniform methods and full publicity almost impossible to achieve, and both of these are essential to the optimum use of accounting and statistical reports.

The chief executive of a Socialist economy should require the use of standardized accounting and statistical definitions, forms, and principles by all trusts and departments. This does not mean that the same accounts should be set up and the same reports prepared by every economic unit, but that all units engaged in the same economic activity should set up the same accounts and prepare the same reports. Moreover, the accounts and reports of units engaged in different activities should be as uniform as the needs of these units permit. Thus, accounts such as depreciation and insurance, and report items such as number of employees and hours of labor, should be uniformly defined and interpreted by all reporting agencies.

Uniformity of accounting and statistical reports would increase their usefulness to a very marked degree. It is impossible to discover which of two or more producers of the same good is earning the largest profit or producing at the lowest cost if all of them use different methods of calculating depreciation, obsolescence, inventory losses, overhead costs, and so forth. Under Capitalism a retail store which reports a 10 percent profit may be earning much less than a retail factory which reports a 10 percent loss. Such misleading profit and loss statements make it impossible to determine where additional capital should be invested, when wages should be increased, what method of production is most efficient, and so on.

Statistical reports which are not prepared in a uniform manner are equally misleading. Thus, one company may report a small accident rate because it defines accidents in one way, while another company with a lower rate may report a high accident rate because it uses a broader definition of accidents. Under Capitalism, the best statisticians are compelled to spend most of their time detecting and making estimates to compensate in a rough way for differences in statistical methods which should not exist in a Socialist economy.

All economic decisions ought to be based upon accounting and statistical reports. Hence the value of comparable figures secured from properly and uniformly prepared reports is very great. The preparation of such reports under Socialism would be made easier by the introduction of more suitable units of weight, capacity, size, distance, and money. The traditional units in use in English-speaking countries, such as the foot, rod, acre, league, mile, fathom, shilling, etc., are all inexcusably complicated, confusing, and unsuited to the needs of rapid calculation. Their use increases the cost of production in every American industry.

A Socialist economy ought to use that system of weights and measures which would reduce the costs of calculation to a minimum, other factors being equal. It is almost universally admitted, even by bourgeois writers, that the metric system is superior to the conglomeration of different weights and measures used in English-speaking nations.

It has been charged that the adoption of the metric system would involve huge obsolescence losses, but there is little justification for this claim. The size of manufactured articles ought to be determined by the needs of those who consume them, not by the system of weights and measures. A change in a unit of measurement, therefore, need occasion no change in the actual weight or size of manufactured goods unless a change is desirable for other reasons. And if the actual size of the product remains the same, the machinery now used to make it will not be rendered obsolete by a shift to the metric system.

The calendar also should be made the subject of careful scientific study and should be reformed in the manner best designed to aid the preparation and use of accounting and statistical reports. The advantages of calendar reform for accounting are so great that certain large Capitalist trusts have already adopted reformed calendars for their own accounting. The chief purposes of calendar reform should be to divide the year into equal and readily divisible periods, and to create a uniform calendar for every year. No hesitation should be felt in changing the number of days in the week. Perhaps ten months of thirty-six days divided into six six-day weeks or thirty-six long weeks of ten days, with a four- or five-day year-end week, would be desirable since ten is an ideal number for division. Every month should begin on the same day in the week and should contain the same number of days. This would permit the comparison of output in one month with output in another month without making any calculation to allow for differences in the number of days in each month. For the same reason, the number of holidays in each month should be the same.

The use of numbers to identify articles, places, and persons is already common under Capitalism, but every company and government agency has its own independent system. For instance, the catalogue numbers used by General Electric are different from those used by Westinghouse, and the identification numbers used by the FBI are different from social security numbers. Moreover, all of these individual systems are incomplete since none of them covers all articles or all people. A Socialist state should introduce a complete system of identification numbers which would cover every article, place, and person and should require the use of this single national identification system by every trust and department.

A uniform identification system for all tangible economic goods would make it possible to add together all inventory reports by individual trusts and departments and arrive at a consolidated national inventory of consumers' goods and capital goods which would include a detailed breakdown of each general class into the smallest subclass used by all individual reporting units. It would also make it possible for any buyer, seller, or other person to refer to any individual commodity by number without having to give a long verbal description.

A uniform system of identification numbers for persons would make it possible to keep all accounting and statistical records concerning people in a more economical manner, since numbers are shorter than names; they need never be the same for two people, and can be more easily handled by bookkeeping and statistical machines. Moreover, payroll records, bank statements, tax payment accounts, and other similar records prepared by different trusts and departments could be more easily used to check each other if all of these records used uniform identification numbers instead of names.

Identification numbers may be planned in such a way as to reduce their average length to the minimum or in such a way as to give the maximum information about the person or thing identified. If they are to be as short as possible, and thus facilitate recognition, repetition, and memorization, identification numbers should have the maximum number of variations in each digit place. In the case of automobile numbers, the number of variations per digit place has already been increased 240 percent by the use of letters as well as numbers. This makes it possible to assign distinct numbers to 1,336,336 cars without using more than four digit places.

The use of other symbols, such as $+$, $-$, $\triangle$, $\square$, and $\perp$, as alternatives in each digit place would further shorten the average length of identification numbers.

On the other hand, identification numbers might be used to describe as well as identify persons or objects. For instance, thé first characters could be an individual's initials, and each succeeding symbol in the number could be designed to tell something about him—sex, year of birth, place of birth, etc. Such identification numbers might be even longer than straight arithmetic numbers, but they would make unnecessary the recording in other punch-card columns of the information contained in the identification number, and they would also help police and other persons to determine whether identification numbers actually belonged to people claiming them.

Prolonged scientific experiments will be necessary to decide which type of numbering system is best for each use. Short numbers may be most useful where quick recognition is important, as on automobile license plates, while information numbers may be the most useful on articles sold at retail.

In order to facilitate the preparation of national statistical reports and the conduct of scientific research, a Socialist government should establish and keep up to date a central statistical file which consolidates all the information available in local, regional, or national trust and department files. For instance, the central file on persons should include every living person, and every deceased person of whom any useful facts are known, and should include all information about these persons available in the records of local health offices, churches, unions, banks, police, schools, employment offices, insurance companies, income-tax offices, employers, and other local offices. This information should all be punched on punch cards suitable for machine tabulation, and one or more duplicates should be punched and returned to local or regional files for various uses. Such files would be of great value for a wide variety of purposes such as the preparation of vital statistics, planning eugenic reform, determining the causes of disease and crime, catching criminals, writing history, and so forth.

Complete centralized statistical records on the location and use of all economic goods, the volume of production, marginal and average costs, and all other statistical data useful for central control or scientific research should also be maintained.

CHAPTER XIII. THE TAYLOR SYSTEM OF SCIENTIFIC SHOP MANAGEMENT

A. INTRODUCTION

Scientific shop management is used here to mean that body of managerial theory developed largely by F. W. Taylor and his immediate disciples and designed primarily for application in manufacturing plants. It is concerned largely with the control of shop operations in an established plant. However, some of its basic principles would be applicable in large factory farms, retail stores, mines, lumber camps, and other production units.

The term "scientific" is applied to shop management, not because it is more scientific than the theory of general management, but because usage has already given to the managerial theory developed by Taylor and his followers the term "scientific management."[1] The term "shop" has been introduced to help distinguish the principles of scientific management developed by Taylor from other equally scientific principles of management.

[1] The following quotation indicates the very definite meaning of the term "scientific management" and also constitutes a recognition by a Socialist of the importance of this theory under Socialism.

"There is yet a newer and greater source of economy which we owe to the competitive system, and which may likewise be transferred to use in industries under public control, viz., scientific management. This may perhaps be regarded as a development of cost accounting from the passive attitude of merely recording the cost at which the goods are actually being produced, to the active investigation, by a scientific method, of all possible means of reducing the costs of manufacture. From the point of view of technical efficiency scientific management is the supreme art of production by human labour and machinery, in which all knowledge of organization and all natural science is called in to aid the industrial organizer. His object is to find the most advantageous adjustment of machines to the capacities of the workers, having in mind the kind of goods required. A most detailed study of the individual differences of different workmen is undertaken, and each is allotted to the kind of work in which he can naturally excel. Every tool, every instrument of measurement and every machine he handles is worked out in detail with the utmost care, so as to be perfectly adapted to the special task for which it is intended. Numerous ingenious automatic contrivances are utilized for registering work done and also the fatigue experienced by the operating workmen. The planning and supervision of the routine work are divided amongst a number of men on a functional basis, and they become specialists in design, in adjustments of tools, in routing of work, and so on." H. Stanley Jevons, *Economic Equality in the Cooperative Commonwealth* (Methuen & Co., Ltd., London, 1933), p. 89.

One of the major reasons for setting scientific shop management apart and discussing it separately is the fact that it is a comprehensive and well-knit body of theory developed by a small group of men who deserve special recognition. The theory of scientific management constitutes one of the most significant contributions to knowledge made by American thinkers, and Frederick W. Taylor deserves recognition as one of the greatest of American scientists.[2]

The Taylor system of scientific shop management possesses enormous potential economic significance. Specialists in this field are convinced that the application of the principles of scientific shop management will double the output of industry. Frank B. Gilbreth, one of Taylor's ablest disciples, has asserted: "We have never seen a case in our work where time study and analysis did not result in more than doubling the output of the worker."[3]

Unfortunately, owing to the relative unimportance of efficiency in production as compared with efficiency in selling under Capitalism, owing to the inertia, ignorance, and insecurity of private entrepreneurs, and owing to the small scale of production typical of many industries under Capitalism, the benefits of scientific shop management have as yet been secured in very few plants, probably less than 10 percent of the total in the most advanced industrial nations.

In a Socialist economy every executive who would be benefited thereby should be thoroughly grounded in the basic principles of scientific management. Moreover, every producing organization should have as a part of its executive personnel a staff of highly trained specialists in this field, who would devote their full time to the development and application of its principles to the work of the plant in question.

[2] Few Americans have even heard the name, Frederick W. Taylor. A son of petty bourgeois parents, with an education above that of the ordinary worker, he went to work for the Midland Steel Company as an unskilled worker in 1875, and rose rapidly from one position to another until he was foreman of a machine shop. In this capacity he determined to eliminate "soldiering" and inefficiency among his men, and his efforts in this direction were the beginnings of his life-long devotion to the cause of efficient production or scientific management. Although his thinking was always colored by the profit psychology of his employers, Taylor was one of the first to realize that management alone was responsible for virtually all of the huge waste and inefficiency characteristic of industry in his day as in ours. Never a scholar or systematic thinker, he developed his practice chronologically far in advance of his theory, and left much of the work of logical systematization and exposition to his immediate disciples, who, fortunately were men of unusual ability and made many real contributions to the incomplete practice and theory of scientific management left them by their leader.

[3] Gilbreth, *Primer of Scientific Management* (1912), p. 12.

B. THE THEORY OF SCIENTIFIC SHOP MANAGEMENT[4]

Conventional unscientific systems of management leave to each worker the final responsibility for doing his work as he thinks best, with little help and advice from the management. Because of this freedom and individualism it is not necessary or customary for laborers to work in accordance with the rules and laws of a science or art. In nearly all occupations the science which underlies each act of each workman is so great, and amounts to so much, that the workman who is best suited to actually do the work is incapable, through insufficiency of either education or natural intelligence, of fully understanding this science without the guidance and help of those who are working with him or over him. If work is to be done in a scientific manner,

. . . . the management must take over and perform much of the work which is now left to the men; almost every act of the workman should be preceded by one or more preparatory acts of the management which enable him to do his work better and quicker than he otherwise could. And each man should daily be taught by and receive the most friendly help from those who are over him, instead of being, at the one extreme, driven or coerced by his bosses, and at the other left to his own unaided devices.

This close intimate personal co-operation between the management and the men is of the essence of modern scientific or task management.[5]

Taylor classified the new duties to be assumed by the management under a system of scientific management as follows:

First. They develop a science for each element of a man's work, which replaces the old rule-of-thumb method.

Second. They scientifically select and then train, teach, and develop the workman, whereas in the past he chose his own work and trained himself as best he could.

Third. They heartily co-operate with the men so as to insure all of the work being done in accordance with the principles of the science which has been developed.

Fourth. There is an almost equal division of the work and the responsibility between the management and the workmen. The management takes over all work for which they are better fitted than the workmen, while in the past almost all of the work and the greater part of the responsibility were thrown upon the men.[6]

---

[4] The following statement of the principles of scientific shop management is based largely upon Taylor's own writings, and those of his immediate followers, particularly Gilbreth.

[5] Frederick W. Taylor, *Principles of Scientific Management* (Harper & Brothers, New York and London, 1911), p. 26.   [6] *Ibid.*, pp. 36–37.

In the following pages these duties will be explained in more detail. Since the fourth point in the above outline really restates the fundamental idea of which the first three are specific applications, it need not be explained separately.

I. JOB OR OPERATION ANALYSIS

The first and most important principle of scientific shop management as outlined by Taylor is that the management must "develop a science for each element of a man's work, which replaces the old 'rule-of-thumb' method." This principle is of vast significance because it involves a complete change in the methods used by all trades and all workers. It requires the application of science to the everyday labor performed by all workers, and is therefore the most potentially productive of all the principles of scientific shop management. Taylor has explained the need for this application of science to the existing methods of work, as follows:

In an industrial establishment which employs say from 500 to 1000 workmen, there will be found in many cases at least twenty to thirty different trades. The workmen in each of these trades have had their knowledge handed down to them by word of mouth, through the many years in which their trade has been developed from the primitive condition, in which our far-distant ancestors each one practiced the rudiments of many different trades, to the present state of great and growing subdivision of labor, in which each man specializes upon some comparatively small class of work.

The ingenuity of each generation has developed quicker and better methods for doing every element of the work in every trade. Thus the methods which are now in use may in a broad sense be said to be an evolution representing the survival of the fittest and best of the ideas which have been developed since the starting of each trade. However, while this is true in a broad sense, only those who are intimately acquainted with each of these trades are fully aware of the fact that in hardly any element of any trade is there uniformity in the methods which are used. Instead of having only one way which is generally accepted as a standard, there are in daily use, say, fifty or a hundred different ways of doing each element of the work. And a little thought will make it clear that this must inevitably be the case, since our methods have been handed down from man to man by word of mouth, or have, in most cases, been almost unconsciously learned through personal observation. Practically in no instances have they been codified or systematically analyzed or described.[7]

Every operation which is repeated often enough to make its improvement worth while should be carefully observed, studied, and analyzed by competent management engineers. The operation should be subdivided into its component parts and each part made the object of both time and

[7] *Op. cit.*, pp. 31–32.

motion studies. Every alternative method of performing the operation should be similarly studied.

In this analysis, time study and motion study[8] are of particular importance. Each operation should be timed as a whole with a stop watch, and then each component part of the operation should be timed. Likewise, each alternative method as a whole and each alternative component part should be accurately timed. Motion study consists of visualizing or charting each motion made by different workers in performing an operation in each of several alternative ways, and then eliminating all unnecessary motions, providing for the full use of both hands, and substituting less tiring for more tiring motions wherever possible.

Taylor summarized the work of operation analysis as follows:

First. Find, say 10 or 15 different men (preferably in as many separate establishments and different parts of the country) who are especially skillful in doing the particular work to be analyzed.

Second. Study the exact series of elementary operations or motions which each of these men uses in doing the work which is being investigated, as well as the implements each man uses.

Third. Study with a stop-watch the time required to make each of these elementary movements and then select the quickest way of doing each element of the work.

Fourth. Eliminate all false movements, slow movements, and useless movements.

Fifth. After doing away with all unnecessary movements, collect into one series the quickest and best movements as well as the best implements.[9]

As a result of reading, observation, analysis, research, and time and motion studies, the management engineer should be able to devise a standard method of performing the operation which eliminates slow and unnecessary movements and makes use of the best possible technique. The same type of intensive scientific research should be applied to tools and devices used by the worker in performing any operation. There is always a large number and variety of each type of tool, but there can be only one for each worker which will help him perform a given operation in the most efficient way. In many cases a new and superior tool must be designed.[10]

[8] Taylor used the term "time study" to include both time and motion study, while Gilbreth used the term "motion study" to include both ideas. It is better to treat them as separate methods or steps in job analysis, as is done here.

[9] *Op. cit.*, pp. 117–18. For a more detailed discussion of operation or job analysis, see *Motion Study* by Frank Gilbreth. This is one of the very ablest works on scientific management.

[10] "Scientific management requires, first, a careful investigation of each of the many modifications of the same implement, developed under rule of thumb; and

Once a careful, scientific analysis of the operation has been completed, the management engineer should prescribe standard methods, tools, and devices. A standard is simply a carefully thought-out method of performing an operation or a carefully drawn specification covering an implement, a material, or a product. The idea of perfection is not involved. The standard is simply the best yet devised. Improvements in standards are inevitable and are to be encouraged. However, standards require certain safeguards. Workmen ought not to be permitted to alter them at will. They should be changed only by experts in job analysis after due consideration of new suggestions by workers or after new research.

Scientific management requires careful scientific investigation of the proper intensity and duration of labor for each operation or task and for each individual. There is a certain ideal intensity and duration of labor for each individual in each occupation and this should be determined as accurately as is worth while.

Under Capitalism, the worker rests one day in seven because of a custom based upon religious superstition. No scientific study of fatigue was made as a basis for the decision that workers should rest one day in seven. A Socialist state should conduct the research necessary to determine whether workers should rest one day in two or one in ten or any intermediate combination. The same sort of research should be conducted to determine the proper hours of labor per day at different kinds and intensities of work and for different individuals. The length and frequency of vacation periods should also be made the subject of careful study.

2. SELECTION AND TRAINING OF EMPLOYEES

The second new function or principle of scientific shop management noted by Taylor is that the management should "scientifically select and then train, teach and develop the workman, whereas in the past he chose his own work and trained himself as best he could." This principle is less important than the first and third.

Scientific management includes the scientific selection of employees. Intensive research must be undertaken to discover what physical and mental qualities aid the performance of each type of work. Once these qualities are known, definite requirements must be established. These requirements, of course, must not be too high or too unusual to permit an adequate supply of labor at reasonable wages, and a wide freedom of choice of occupation by the individual. But, they ought to help each

second, after a time study has been made of the speed attainable with each of these implements, that the good points of several of them shall be united in a single standard implement, which will enable the workman to work faster and with greater ease than he could before." Taylor, *op. cit.*, p. 118.

worker to find the job for which he is best suited and in which he will accordingly earn the highest wages. No worker has the time or initiative to experiment with all possible types of work in order to find that for which he is best suited. The establishment of specific physical and mental requirements for each type of work should help the individual ·by restricting the possible field of experimentation and preventing the worst failures, but it should not eliminate or unduly restrict freedom of choice of occupations.

The rapid rise of personnel work and personnel departments in the United States in recent years is undoubtedly partly due to the emphasis of scientific shop management upon proper selection and training of employees. Under Capitalism, however, all personnel work is grossly distorted by the private-profit motive. Personnel departments attempt to attract able employees, whether or not such employees are relatively best suited for the work in question, and they attempt to weed out applicants for work who are relatively low in ability, even when such individuals are better suited for the work in question than for any other kind of work. In a Socialist economy the efforts of personnel workers should be devoted to helping all workers, those below the average in ability as well as those above the average, to find the work for which they are best fitted.

All standard job methods developed as a result of scientific analysis of individual operations and implements should be written down as clearly and lucidly as possible on instruction cards, which should be issued to the worker with each new job order. Every worker should then be trained to do his work in accordance with these instruction cards. In order to introduce the use of new standard methods and implements, it may be necessary to employ special teachers. Once standard methods have been introduced, however, the task of training new and old employees to do their work in the prescribed manner should be handed over to the functional foreman.

Under Capitalism it is necessary for each plant which has introduced scientific management to continue to retrain all new employees in its own improved methods. Under Socialism, however, all plants doing the same work should use the same standard methods and the state school system should assume the burden of teaching standard methods to workers before they enter industry.

3. IMPROVEMENT OF MANAGEMENT

The third major principle of scientific shop management, as stated by Taylor in his brief summary quoted above, is that the management should "heartily cooperate with the men so as to insure all of the work being done in accordance with the principles of the science which has been developed [by job analysis]."

This is a very vague and unsatisfactory statement of the remaining functions of scientific shop management, and betrays Taylor's weakness in logical exposition and systematization. However, it contains a clue to the third basic principle of scientific shop management.

The first and second basic principles involve improvement of methods and improvement of employees respectively. The third basic idea of scientific shop management may be briefly summarized as improvement of management. While all three principles, being parts of scientific shop management, contribute to this end, the type of improvement included under the third principle is most appropriately called improvement of management.

Taylor and his followers have developed many specific methods of accomplishing this result. Only the most significant of these are covered in the following pages.

Incentive Wages.—Perhaps the most important single principle of scientific shop management is the rule that incentive wages should be introduced wherever possible. The adoption of this single principle frequently increases output by 50 to 100 percent.

The reason for this is rather obvious. As long as workers are paid by the hour or day, they may care only about the number of hours or days worked. As long as a group of workers is paid uniform wages, each member of the group may consider it unnecessary to turn out more work than the least productive member of the group. In the absence of strong nonpecuniary incentives, uniform wages tend to reduce the productivity of all workers to the level of the least productive worker. Group pressure or opinion frequently supplements natural laziness as a force tending to reduce productivity to the minimum acceptable level. If an ambitious worker attempts to produce considerably more than the average of his fellow workers, they sabotage his work, appeal to him personally, or use physical violence in order to reduce his output to the average level. The universal fear of unemployment under Capitalism causes workers to reduce their output in order to make work and wages last as long as possible for them, or in order to create jobs for their unemployed fellow workers. This factor, of course, would not operate in a Socialist economy. Nevertheless, incentive wages might still be necessary in order to persuade workers to put forth their optimum efforts, at least until a new generation of workers reared under Socialism has been taught to respond to nonpecuniary incentives.

There are a number of different types of incentive wage or salary payments—individual bonus, group bonus, commissions, differential time wages, individual piece rates, group piece rates, etc. Even co-operation and profit sharing are in essence merely methods of incentive wage payment. Ordinarily, however, individual piece rates are the type of incentive wage recommended by students of scientific shop management.

Since the determination of piece rates is part of the determination of wages in general, piece rates will be discussed in more detail in a later chapter on wages (see pages 315–20).

Central Planning.—A basic principle which may be included under point three, "The Improvement of Management," is that all shop work should be planned by and controlled from a central planning department. Stated in these simple words, this principle may seem self-evident. It is true that a certain amount of central planning is inevitable, and has always been present in industry. Scientific shop management, however, demands a great extension of the amount and degree of central planning. To achieve this, it proposes that this work be taken out of the hands of the chief executives and the shop foremen and placed under the control of a special department established for that purpose.

There are, of course, types of industry in which the character of the work is so simple, the variety of products so small, and the volume of production so large and uniform that little central planning and routing is necessary. Mass production at a uniform rate eliminates the need of shifting workers and machines from one use to another, of providing workers with tools, materials, and instructions for each new job lot, of co-ordinating production so as to eliminate lost time for both workers and machines, etc. Mass production will naturally be far more prevalent under Socialism than under Capitalism. Nevertheless, there will still be a wide opportunity to use the type of central planning developed by Taylor and his followers. Wherever it is necessary to shift workers and machines from one job to another at frequent intervals, central planning will be desirable.

The basic idea involved in central planning is a further division of labor. Central planning relieves the worker of all clerical and executive work. He no longer has to decide what work to do, what work-place or machine to use, what tools, materials, and supplies to obtain, etc. All these decisions are made for him by the planning department, and communicated to him on printed forms. When filled in and returned to the planning department, these forms provide full information concerning the work done in the shop. In addition to making all decisions for the worker, the planning department must take care to provide all equipment and conditions necessary to the proper performance of the work.

By assuming these functions, the planning department relieves the worker of the work he is least qualified to perform and permits him to concentrate on the work he is best qualified to perform. The work of which he is relieved is handed over to full-time specialists in that sort of work, to men better qualified by natural aptitude, education, and experience for this work. In addition to these advantages of the division of labor, central planning results in more co-ordination between the work of different men and different departments or shops, and gives the management more accurate knowledge concerning the time required to fill orders and the condition of all work in process.

The following summary of the work involved in central planning is taken from a chapter entitled "Control of Shop Operations," by H. K. Hathaway in *Scientific Management in American Industry*.

The work of a central planning department may be divided into two major functions: (1) predetermining what is to be done, how it is to be done, what facilities and materials are to be employed, and when it is to be done; (2) providing and bringing together at the right time the material, the facilities, the requisite information and the qualified worker.

The first of these—the predetermination of what, when, and how—starts with the provision of drawings, specifications, models or samples, the object of which is to show, in a manner that will preclude the possibility of error or misunderstanding, the nature of the article to be produced or the service to be performed. . . . .

When the basic information as to what is to be done has been provided, the next step is to determine how the work is to be done, what facilities are to be utilized, and what materials will be needed at each stage of the work. This would include what are in most instances of Scientific Management regarded as two distinct major functions of a properly organized planning department, namely, routing, and the preparation of detailed instruction cards defining the manner in which individual operations are to be performed. The latter of these two functions, or stages, in the planning or work is in reality a continuation of the first.

These two functions of planning call for the previous establishment of certain features of the Taylor system that are essentially preliminary and auxiliary to the functions in question. . . . . (1) rearrangement of machinery or such other equipment as may be necessary to facilitate the storage of materials (jobs ahead) at the various workplaces so as to permit great independence in the use of machines and of personnel, and so on; (2) the establishment of a store room and a system for its operation, or, as today few plants are found totally lacking in this respect, the development or modification of existing store rooms and systems to meet the requirements of routing and of centralized control; (3) development of the order system—including shipping orders and manufacturing orders; (4) development or modification of the balance-of-stores or stock-record system so that it may not only be a record of transactions and of what is on hand in the store rooms, but also a live agency regulating the procurement of materials and feeding work to the shop; (5) provision of suitable information relating to the product to be manufactured, in the shape of drawings or specifications, showing as a basis for routing the materials required and what is to be done; (6) standardization of machinery, tools and other facilities, and the availability in the planning department of codified data in regard thereto.

The second phase of planning-room control covering the bringing together at the right time of facilities and workers, would include: (1) the work of the balance-of-stores (or stock-ledger) clerk, which has for its object the maintenance of a proper supply—adequate but not excessive—of all materials or parts, whether purchased or manufactured, that should be regularly carried in stock; (2) the procurement of any materials that are not carried in stock and hence must be obtained specially for the work being planned; (3) the order-of-work function which includes the assignment of workers to machines or work places and their transfer as fluctuations in the amount of work ahead of the various machines or work places may necessitate; the scheduling of jobs to be done at each machine or work place in accordance with their relative importance; recording progress on each job and seeing that it moves from operation to operation without undue delay, and last but by no means least in importance, taking whatever steps may be necessary to straighten out the trouble whenever anything does go wrong. This might be called the executive phase of planning. . . . .

Inspection.—A third principle of scientific shop management which may properly be discussed under improvement of management is the principle of adequate inspection.

Scientific shop management increases the importance and necessity of inspection. Incentive wages ordinarily cause workers to sacrifice quality for quantity, unless adequate inspection occurs. Moreover, inspection is also vital as a method of discovering variations from standard operating methods and conditions.

Inspection should be extended to the rate of progress of work. The planning department should keep track of the progress of all work and investigate all delays. This type of inspection should make possible improvement as well as maintenance of standards.

Functional Organization.—Improved management is also brought about under scientific management by adoption of a functional form of organization. Under previous systems of management a military form of organization prevailed. The smallest unit of organization in each plant was under the control of a single foreman who performed all managerial functions for his shop or gang. Taylor introduced a system of "functional foremen" which divides up the necessary managerial work among specialists, each in control of one function of management. The principal functional foremen in an industrial plant should be the following:

P (*a*)   Route clerk, and order-of-work clerk (production supervisor)

P (*b*)   Instruction card clerk (methods supervisor)

P (*c*)   Time and cost clerk

S (*d*)   Disciplinarian

S (*e*)   Gang boss (preparation supervisor)

S (*f*)   Speed boss (instructor or shop-method supervisor)

S (*g*)   Repair boss (maintenance supervisor)

S (*h*)   Inspector (quality supervisor)

P (*i*)   Balance-of-stores clerk[11]

Some of these functional foremen ought to work in the planning department and some in the shop; the former have been marked with a *P* and the latter with an *S*. This indicates how much of the work formerly done by shop foremen is done by the planning department in a shop operating under scientific management.

This list of foremen is more a list of functions than of functional foremen. It is common practice, particularly in small plants, to hand over two or three or more of these functions to a single individual. The list should not be regarded as standard or universally accepted. Different exponents of scientific management have different ideas about the number and importance of these functions.

Each functional foreman has charge of all the men in the shop so that every worker has a number of foremen directly over him. The functional foremen all learn to do their special work much better than any single foreman who must perform all of these functions. Division of labor is of even greater value in executive work than in manual labor, and its utility in the latter field is well known. Under the traditional plan of management, each foreman has so many functions and duties to perform that he has to depend largely upon the individual workman to guess for himself as to which is the best way to do the work. Under scientific management functional foremen know enough about their functions to be of far greater assistance to the men under them than the ordinary single foreman can be.

[11] F. B. Gilbreth, *Primer of Scientific Management*, p. 17.

PART SIX

THE DISTRIBUTION OF INCOME

CHAPTER XIV. RENT, INTEREST, AND OTHER NON-WAGE INCOME

A. INTRODUCTION

As a program of radical economic reconstruction Socialism includes two principal proposals. In the first place, Socialists propose a complete reorganization of economic activity in order to eliminate the enormous wastes of competition and individualism. The method suggested is the establishment of a perfect and efficient monopoly in every industry, and the co-ordination of the operations of these monopolies by a supreme national authority. Thus far this book has been devoted almost entirely to an elaboration and explanation of this first proposal for basic Socialist change.

In the second place, Socialists propose a radical change in the existing system of income distribution. They desire to reduce inequality in earned incomes and to eliminate all unearned incomes;[1] or, where this is impossible, as in the case of land rent, to distribute this income in such a way as to avoid creating or increasing differences in individual income. It is this second basic proposal of Socialism which is discussed in the next two chapters.

The two basic proposals of Socialism described above may be achieved independently of each other. It would be perfectly possible to eliminate competition and individualism—in other words, to establish a perfect monopoly in every industry—without altering to any appreciable degree the distribution of the national income among classes and individuals. Certain tendencies in this direction may be found in the theory and practice of most Fascist parties. Moreover, as Marx so clearly pointed out almost a century ago, competitive Capitalism inevitably tends to evolve toward monopoly Capitalism. The only Capitalist feature of pure monopoly Capitalism would be the distribution of income.

On the other hand, it is perfectly possible to achieve the second proposal of Socialism, less inequality in the distribution of income, without any alteration in the wasteful competitive organization of industry. If all land and capital were owned by the government and leased to private entrepreneurs for the maximum return obtainable, if personal rents were appropriated by means of income taxes, and if inheritance taxes were sufficiently high, a very Socialistic distribution of income might easily be achieved without any change in the competitive organization of industry.

[1] The elimination of certain earned income, namely, personal rent, is also desirable (see pp. 321–22).

Thus, either of the two basic proposals of Socialism may be achieved without the other.

The distribution theory of orthodox Capitalist economists is concerned primarily with the determination of the amount of the four principal shares in income—rent, interest, profits, and wages—and with the determination of the portions of such shares accruing to individual units of land, capital, enterprise, and labor under Capitalism. Very little attention is given to the problem of determining the proper distribution of this income among individuals. That is the chief reason why most of what bourgeois economists have to say concerning the determination of rent, interest, and wages is valid under Capitalism and will continue to be valid under Socialism.[2] The primary task of Socialist distribution theory is not to refute or replace bourgeois theory concerning the determination of rent, interest, and wages, but to develop a new theory concerning the ideal distribution of rent, interest, and wages among individuals.

The criticism of bourgeois distribution theory may be stated in a different way. Under Capitalism, a share in income has two functions to perform. In the first place, it acts as a cost of production, and therefore should balance the supply of and the demand for the productive agent whose price it is. In the second place, each unit of income becomes personal income to some individual, and should serve to distribute income among individuals in an ideal manner.

Capitalist economists have usually overlooked this inevitable duality in the function of Capitalist shares in income. They have tacitly assumed that since the payment of land rent serves to balance demand and supply for all types of land, its receipt by the private land owner is socially desirable. They state or imply that since tickets to a concert by Caruso must be sold at a high price in order to restrict demand to supply, the receipt of an enormous income by an individual like Caruso is socially desirable. In a word, they believe that the problem of the pricing of the factors in production is identical with the problem of the proper distribution of income among individuals. Actually, they have developed a distribution theory which is a relatively sound theory of pricing the factors in production, but a very unsound theory of the proper distribution of income among individuals.[3]

In this chapter, by contrast, the sharp distinction between the problem of pricing land and capital and the problem of distributing rent and interest among individuals will be stressed. In order to do this, it is neces-

---

[2] Obviously, this is not true of bourgeois theories of profit. They may be valid under Capitalism, but certainly not under Socialism.

[3] Of course, this is but one of many errors traceable to the false assumption that economics should be descriptive rather than prescriptive.

sary, wherever possible, to divide the Capitalist process of income distribution into two distinct steps, the pricing of the factors in production or final cost determination and the distribution of income. Each of these steps is subject to control and alteration independently of the other.

The question of when it is feasible to set up two different steps in the pricing process in order to separate the determination of final costs from the determination of individual income is considered later on in connection with a discussion of the distribution of the income from the factors in production (pages 290, 298). The conclusions may be summarized here, however. Land and capital can be controlled in such a way as to distinguish between final cost determination and the determination of individual income. In the case of labor, however, the difficulty and cost of making such a distinction render it impractical in the great majority of cases. But not in all. Personal rent can and should be denied to workers earning more than a maximum of perhaps $10,000 per year.

Another defect of bourgeois distribution theory deserves mention. Bourgeois economists are in the habit of saying that land rent is produced or earned by land, that interest is produced or earned by capital, and that wages alone are produced or earned by labor. Since both land and capital are inanimate, however, it is a serious misuse of language to assert that they produce or earn anything. Man alone is a dynamic, active, intelligent force in economic activity; hence man alone can be said to earn or produce anything. This is a valid interpretation of the famous Marxian principle that labor produces all value, though it is not what Marx actually meant.

While labor alone can be said to earn or produce value, it is perfectly true that the amount of value produced by an individual worker, or by all workers, depends upon the amount and nature of the capital instruments available. Labor alone produces value, but it can produce much more value by using modern machinery upon fertile or well-located land, than by using primitive implements on poor land. In the complete absence of land, labor could produce no value whatsoever; in the complete absence of capital it could produce very little.

B. DETERMINATION OF RENT AND INTEREST

The proper determination of rent and interest as costs of production in a Socialist economy has already been explained. In chapter iv, "The Determination of Prices," a general theory of pricing was developed. In chapter vi, "The Factors in Production," this theory was applied to interest and to rent outlay. In chapter vii, "The Theory of Production Control over Price Goods," the nature of negative rent and rent surplus was stated. At this point, therefore, it is sufficient merely to summarize what has already been said concerning the determination of rent and interest.

Positive rent is a surplus which results from the sale of goods produced under conditions of increasing costs for a uniform price equal to the marginal cost of production at the optimum volume of production. Positive rent may be divided into personal rent and land rent, according to the cause of the increasing costs which give rise to it, or into rent outlay and rent surplus, according to the manner in which it is collected.[4]

The theory of distribution of income among the factors in production is properly regarded by bourgeois economists as merely a special application of general price or value theory. Under Socialism, general price theory should guide the determination of most final costs, i.e., rent, interest, and wages. The sole important exception to this principle occurs in the case of rent. With universal monopoly there would be few bidders for most pieces of land and for many talented workers like Caruso or Chaplin. This would make perfect pricing of land and talented workers impossible, at least by the conventional method of discovering the single price which balances supply and demand. It would therefore be necessary to use two different means of measuring and collecting total positive rent.

In the first place, every trust and department should be required to pay a rent high enough to secure the use of whatever land or talented workers it desires. This rent payment, which we have termed rent outlay, would always be higher than any other user could afford, but in the absence of adequate competition among producers, it would usually be far below full positive rent.

In the second place, therefore, some method of determining this rent surplus must be developed, and each trust yielding such a rent surplus must be required to make a supplementary rent payment to the Bureau of Land Supply. This supplementary rent payment should be equal to the full rent surplus, less any negative rent arising within the trust in question. It is perfectly possible for certain divisions of a trust to yield a rent surplus while other divisions yield a negative rent. Only the net rent of the entire trust should be turned over to the Bureau of Land Supply.

The supplementary rent payment might be determined by the Bureau of Land Supply, by the individual trust, or by a committee composed of representatives of both. Probably the latter method would be the best.

[4] A third form of rent, quasi-rent, the surplus due to the scarcity of the best capital equipment, is sometimes mentioned by bourgeois economists. This is not a true rent, since it can easily be eliminated by the increased output of scarce machines. It is really a temporary monopoly profit due to the scarcity of these machines.

Supplementary rent payments should be fixed at the end of each accounting period and should be based largely upon the pure intramarginal surplus or profit earned in that period. By pure intramarginal profit is meant the profit due solely to the fact that intramarginal costs (including rent outlay) are lower than marginal costs. In other words, such profits should not be affected by profits and losses due to change in appraisal of assets, profits and losses due to imperfect control of production, uninsurable accidents, and the like.

Such a method for the determination and collection of positive rent surpluses could not be applied to departments. Since they would provide their goods without charge, no intramarginal profits would arise to indicate the existence and amount of rent surplus. Failure to measure and collect such rent surpluses would not be a serious evil, however, since they would be small. Large rent surpluses would arise only in agriculture and other extractive industries under the system of renting land proposed in this treatise. Personal rent surpluses would be as large in departments as in trusts, but in both they would probably be relatively small. Failure to collect rent surpluses from departments would mean a reduction in the total, but not in the marginal, costs of the free services they render.

Interest is a price charged for the use of capital in order to balance the supply of and the demand for capital and in order to aid the rational allocation of capital among different borrowers. Interest does not measure the total increase in production or real income made possible by the use of capital.[5] A huge consumers' surplus accrues to those who borrow and use capital. Interest amounts to less than 10 percent of the total income of the United States at present, but the destruction of all capital in the United States would reduce the national income by at least 99 percent.

It is possible to charge a price for the use of capital only because capital is scarce. It is scarce because some saving causes disutilitum. Many people would save without any interest incentive, and some would pay for the privilege of being allowed to save, but the marginal units of capital must result from painful abstinence or there would be no limit on the supply of capital. Under Capitalism the payment of interest to private individuals is necessary in order to persuade marginal savers to abstain from consumption.

[5] Interest has been defined as "the income which capital returns to its owner whether he lends it or employs it himself in his own business" (T. N. Carver, *The Distribution of Wealth*, p. 213). If the owner of capital uses it himself, however, the resulting income or increase in income is not all interest; most of it may be profit. Interest equals the marginal, not the total, utility of capital to any individual owner.

Interest measures neither the total increase in production made possible by the use of capital, nor the total disutility cost of supplying the existing volume of capital. When properly determined, however, the interest rate does measure the utility of the marginal or least-useful unit of capital, and at the same time measures the disutility involved in supplying the most costly or marginal unit of capital. All other prices do the same.

In a Socialist economy, interest should be directly determined and collected by the Bureau of Capital Supply. This Bureau should establish a rate of interest just high enough to balance the total supply of and demand for capital. It should require demand schedules from all who borrow capital, and should combine these individual demand schedules into a single consolidated demand schedule in order to facilitate the determination of a rate of interest which will just balance supply and demand. At any given time, supply will be relatively fixed, and even in the long run it will never be subject to rapid or unforeseen fluctuations, for the process of saving is necessarily slow and large-scale destruction of capital is very infrequent.

While the interest rate should be directly fixed by the Bureau of Capital Supply, the basic factors which actually but indirectly control the rate of interest should be much the same as they are under Capitalism. The rate of interest should continue to be determined by demand and supply and by the factors behind them. The demand for capital ought to be governed chiefly by the cost and the usefulness of available capital instruments, and these in turn will be constantly altered by new inventions[6] and by changes in the supply of labor.

The factors behind the supply of capital will be somewhat different under Socialism, however. The supply of capital will be determined by the national legislature directly, and by the majority of the voters indirectly, instead of by individual savers as under Capitalism. However, the chief incentive to additional saving will still be the interest to be earned upon this additional capital.

The response of the general population, or the majority of voters, to this incentive will continue to be determined by the disutility of saving, and this, in turn, by the native intelligence, education, foresight, etc., of the general population. Most of these basic factors affecting the demand for and supply of capital have been carefully discussed by bourgeois economists and so require no detailed treatment here.

[6] Certain inventions, by lowering the cost of existing capital equipment or displacing more costly equipment, will serve to decrease the demand for capital. On the other hand, the development of new machines which replace labor, rather than more costly equipment, will tend to raise the rate of interest.

C. THE DISTRIBUTION OF POSITIVE RENT AND INTEREST[7]

No explicit theory of the distribution or division of positive rent and interest among individuals under Socialism has been advanced by most Socialist writers, but many of them have taken a very definite stand against treating land rent and interest as costs of production. This attitude has a significant but indirect bearing upon the distribution of rent and interest.

Rent and interest, or their equivalents, would continue to exist and to be distributed among individuals even if they were not treated as costs of production, and their distribution would depend upon the pricing policy followed. If prices were the same as they would be if rent and interest were treated as costs, in accordance with the price theory supported in this treatise, rent and interest would accrue initially to those who work where it is earned. Since different industries and enterprises give rise to widely varying amounts of rent and interest, this would create new and unearned differences in incomes. If wages were determined in accordance with the principles developed in this treatise, however, such an initial distribution of rent and interest could not result in permanent unearned differentials in wages; for any unearned wage differences would attract additional labor to favored industries and plants and thus automatically eliminate themselves, the end result being an equal proportional increase in all wages. But this would involve an uneconomic shifting of labor from more productive to less productive jobs. In effect, rent and interest would have been used to subsidize the employment of labor in less productive jobs because they would offset the losses which would otherwise have resulted from this uneconomic shift of labor.

Failure to treat rent and interest as costs of production would result in a quite different distribution of rent and interest if market prices were based upon wage costs alone, as many Marxists have recommended. This price policy would pass on to consumers all savings made possible by ignoring rent and interest as costs, and would consequently distribute rent and income among consumers. The amount received by each consumer would depend upon the goods purchased. Those goods whose costs had previously included large sums for rent and interest would be most cheapened, and persons who purchased them at the new low prices would receive a relatively large share of rent and interest. On the other hand, those goods whose costs had included small rent and interest charges would be little affected in price, and people who purchased them would receive little rent

[7] For an interesting mathematical treatment of the subject of this section, see Enrico Baronne's "The Ministry of Production in the Collectivist State" in F. Hayek's *Collectivist Economic Planning* (London, 1933), pp. 274–76.

and interest. Since different consumers spend their income for different goods, an unequal and unjustifiable division of rent and interest would result from this method of distributing rent and interest. Moreover, prices based on wage costs only would have a distorting effect upon the production and consumption of different goods. In effect, rent and interest would be used to expand beyond the optimum point the output of all goods produced by industries using above-average amounts of capital and land.[8] This method of distributing rent and income, implied in the Marxian treatment of costs and prices, is clearly uneconomic.

These are the two methods of distributing rent and interest implicit in traditional Socialist price theory. Failure to treat rent and interest as costs may result in one method or the other, but both are uneconomic. Hence it is better to treat rent and interest as costs of production, collect them, and distribute them among individuals in a conscious and rational manner.

I. PRIMARY DISTRIBUTION

Both positive rent and interest should be distributed in two stages, a different method of distribution being used at each stage. The first stage and its method of distribution may be called "primary distribution," the second stage of distribution and its method may be called "supplementary distribution."

The method of primary distribution ought to be different for rent and interest, as well as being different for primary and supplementary distribution.

Positive Rent.—The primary use or distribution of positive-rent income should be to cover negative-rent costs and thus permit industries of decreasing costs to extend production to the proper level. In the first place, within each trust, rent surplus—that portion of positive rent not paid out for the use of land and talented workers—should be used to cover negative rent, and only the net rent surplus or deficit should be transferred to the national treasury. If there is a net negative-rent cost, this should be covered by the treasury. In the second place, the treasury should use its positive-rent income to offset its payments on account of negative rent. Only that portion of positive rent remaining after payment of all costs due to negative rent should be used for supplementary distribution.

It is conceivable that in certain Socialist economies there would be no surplus positive rent left for supplementary distribution, and that it would be necessary for the treasury to meet a net rent deficit. This seems unlikely, but only actual experiment can settle this question.

[8] See chap. vi, pp. 140–42.

Interest.—The primary use of interest-income should be to pay interest to individual adults on the capital they have saved. In a Socialist economy, the volume of saving should be determined by the central government, and each worker should be required to save whether he desires to or not. The bank account of every worker should be periodically debited by a sum equal to 10 to 30 percent or more of his income during the period, and this sum should be credited to the savings account of the Bureau of Capital Supply. Only as a voter should the individual have anything to say about this minimum amount of compulsory saving. He ought to be permitted to save additional sums in a voluntary manner, however.

While the bulk of all saving ought to be compulsory, it should not be unrewarded. Every individual should receive the market rate of interest, less handling costs, upon his entire savings, compulsory as well as voluntary. This would give each worker a measure of the marginal utility of capital and thus permit him as a citizen to act more intelligently in the control of the volume of saving and capital. It would also give to every worker a steadily growing interest-income which, together with his share in the supplementary distribution of rent and interest, would make him independent in his old age. If the government required every worker to save 20 percent of his wage-income, for instance, at the end of forty years' work each worker would have accumulated a sum equal to eight years' wages. The interest on this sum alone at 6 percent would provide an income equal to about half his average wage-income. In addition, each worker over sixty should be granted his share in the supplementary distribution of rent and interest whether he continued to work or not.

The payment of interest on compulsory savings would virtually render old-age pensions unnecessary. The size of the income in old age from interest on compulsory saving could be greatly increased by the redeposit of all interest earned before the age of sixty. The government might require this in order to increase the interest-income of the elderly, but it would have the undesirable effect of preventing young and middle-aged workers from feeling most completely the marginal utility of saving.

Whatever the form of the income paid to elderly people, this income should under no consideration be conditioned upon retirement from work. Elderly people should be offered no inducement to cease being productive. Any inducement of this sort lowers the total supply of labor below the optimum level at which the marginal utility and disutility of labor are equal. A gradually increasing interest-income is the ideal safeguard for old age because, among other things, it never offers an inducement to cease working. Even an old-age pension should be paid, whether or not the recipient continues to work.

Another very desirable feature of an interest-income for the aged is that it is so obviously an earned income that it has no appearance of charity. Pensions are less satisfying to the aged since they do not represent payment for a specific and necessary service in such an obvious manner as interest-income.

Payment of interest to all who have saved voluntarily or under compulsion will only distribute a minor fraction of the total interest-income of a Socialist economy. The bulk of the capital is most advanced nations has been saved by individuals who are no longer living. Every year under Capitalism more capital is inherited than saved.[9] The more advanced and stable the economy, the larger is the proportion of existing capital which has been created by past generations. The major share of the national interest-income will probably continue under Socialism to be earned on capital accumulated by past generations, in spite of the increased rate of saving. This interest surplus will be subject to supplementary distribution.

2. SUPPLEMENTARY DISTRIBUTION

Two methods of primary distribution, one for positive rent and one for interest, have been described. One method of supplementary distribution will suffice for both rent and interest. Before this method is explained, it is necessary to analyze a plausible but unsound method of supplementary distribution.

A Uniform Proportional Increase in All Wages.—The share of the national income which takes the form of rent or interest is dependent, among other things, upon the amount of work done. Every increase in the supply of labor serves to increase both rent and interest, and every decrease in the supply of labor has the opposite effect. Moreover, all rent and interest is produced by labor.

On these grounds it may be argued that surplus rent and interest should be divided up among those who work, according to the value of the work done by each individual. Such a method of distribution would result in an equal ratio of increase in all wage and salary payments; that is, the result would be similar to that obtained if rent and interest were not treated as costs but prices were nevertheless properly determined.

The distribution of rent and interest among wage earners as a uniform proportional increase in all wages is undesirable for a number of reasons, some of which have already been stated. In the first place, while the amount of rent and interest is affected by the amount of work done, both rent and interest are primarily determined by other factors, notably the nature and amount of the land available and the supply of capital.

[9] Including depression years, savings average less than 10 percent of peacetime national income in the United States; inheritance of capital (exclusive of land) exceeds 20 percent.

In the second place, distribution of rent and interest as a uniform proportional increase in wages would enhance the absolute differential between the wages of different workers; it would constitute an unequal distribution of income. But an equal distribution of a *given* income always serves to maximize the total utility derived from it, and rent and interest are given incomes unaffected by the manner of their distribution.

A third, and by far the most significant, objection to this method of distributing rent and interest is that it would distort the market price for labor by adding to it a portion of land rent and interest. The market price for labor ought to measure as accurately as possible the marginal utility of labor, permitting the individual worker to control his hours and intensity of labor in such a way that the utilitum and disutilitum of the marginal unit of his work may be equal. If some rent and interest were added to the wage he receives for this marginal unit of work, the additional rent and interest would cause him to increase his hours or intensity of labor beyond the optimum point. In other words, all workers would perform additional extramarginal labor which involved more pain than it would be worth, because this would give them an additional share in rent and interest, more than sufficient to compensate them for this net disutility. To society as a whole, however, this additional labor would be uneconomic as it would involve disutilitum in excess of the utilitum created. It would be economic for the individual, because it would increase his share of rent and interest, but it would be uneconomic to society because it would produce net disutilitum.

It is true that each additional hour of labor increases both rent and interest, but this increase occurs at the expense of the wages received by those already employed. The worker who does an additional hour of labor increases social income only by the amount of his wages. If at the same time he raises rent and interest, and lowers the wages of those already at work, this is only because of a change in the relationship between the demand for and the supply of each of these factors in production. No real increase in national income other than that indicated by his additional wages occurs.

Under Capitalism, the mere fact that land rent and interest accrue to private landlords and capitalists irrespective of the amount of work they do prevents the distribution of rent and interest from increasing the apparent marginal utility of labor beyond its true level. The volume of rent and interest earned does vary with the number of hours worked, but since it accrues to only a few fortunate individuals it does not increase the monetary reward for labor, the only indication of the marginal utility of labor. Under Socialism, however, rent and interest should be divided among workers. Hence arbitrary distribution, irrespective of the number of hours worked, is necessary in order to prevent distortion of the marginal wage of labor.[10]

Equal Distribution Among All Workers.—In order to prevent the supplementary distribution of rent and interest from altering the marginal wage of labor, that portion of rent and interest subject to supplementary distribution should be divided equally among all wage earners, regardless of the number of hours worked or the value of their labor. Only wage earners should receive a share in this distribution, because they alone produce rent and interest.

One important qualification may be necessary. If supplementary rent and interest are distributed equally to all wage earners, irrespective of their hours of labor, certain men may refuse to work more than some nominal minimum such as an hour a day. Their share in the equal distribution of supplementary rent and interest, in combination with their small wages, might give such people a sufficient income. Under Socialism, rent and interest subject to supplementary distribution might amount to 10 percent of the national income. Under such conditions it would be possible, by working one hour a day, to earn about 30 percent as much as a man who worked six hours a day. To reduce this kind of injustice to a minimum, it would appear to be necessary to establish some limit, such as three hours a day, with the provision that a worker who worked less than this limit would not receive a full share of surplus rent and interest income. On the other hand, it certainly seems unreasonable to make an individual work even one hour a day if the wage of that hour has less utility to him than an additional hour of leisure. The joker here is the fact that the utility of the wage depends upon the volume of income already guaranteed to the individual. Certainly no individual without other income should be forced to work beyond the point at which the utility of the wage received equals the disutility of earning it. However, in the case of workers enjoying an unearned income, the distribution of which lowers the marginal utility of labor, it does seem fair to require a certain amount of work before full participation in unearned income is permitted. Probably a minimum requirement of perhaps three hours work a day should be established. Those who work only one or two hours a day might be given one-third or two-thirds of the full equal share.

This minimum should be set at about half of the average freely chosen number of working hours per day. This would leave a wide range of choice concerning number of hours to work within which supplementary

---

[10] The advantages of disassociating social dividends, as well as any general-purpose tax, from the differences in earned income are explained by Abram Bergson in *The Structure of Soviet Wages* (1944), pp. 19–22.

rent and interest payments would not affect marginal wages, and would still prevent those who worked an abnormally short period from receiving a full share in supplementary rent and interest distribution.

The method of supplementary distribution of rent and interest proposed above may seem entirely unnecessary. It would certainly simplify things if all surplus rent and interest remaining after primary distribution were turned over to the national treasury. This would save the cost of distributing surplus rent and interest to private individuals, and might entirely eliminate the need for and the cost of collecting a general tax. In view of the obvious advantages of such a policy, it may be well to repeat in summary form the two arguments already advanced (page 216) in favor of distributing all rent and interest among individuals and levying a general tax.

One reason is that the use of rent and interest for this purpose would have all the evils of indirect taxation. Taxpayers would be less able to sense and control the cost of free services. The second reason for levying a general tax, rather than using rent and interest, is that by means of a poll tax, the cost of free goods could be allocated according to benefit in those cases where such allocation is desirable, while the use of rent and interest would divide the burden among workers in relative equality regardless of the number of their dependents (see pp. 217–19).

D. OTHER NON-WAGE INCOME

While rent, interest, and wages constitute the three basic elements into which all costs and all income may be divided, there will be certain types of government income in a Socialist society which will be either a mixture of these elements or a mere transfer of existing capital. We turn now to a consideration of the nature and distribution of these special forms of state income.

I. PROFITS AND LOSSES OF INDIVIDUAL TRUSTS

At the end of every accounting period each Socialist trust will show some profit or loss. These profits and losses may be due to over- or under-investment, to errors in production control, to reappraisal of assets, to imperfect measurements of rent and interest, to unexpected price changes, and to other such factors.

Whenever excess capacity results in idle facilities or in unduly low marginal costs, a loss which may be attributed to overinvestment will occur. Whenever the marginal cost is above the optimum level by reason of insufficient production capacity, a profit in the nature of a quasi rent on existing facilities may be earned. Such a rent is different from land rent or personal rent in that it indicates undercapacity and underinvestment.

In addition to losses due to overcapacity and profits due to undercapacity, there will be losses due to overproduction and profits due to underproduction, both of which indicate imperfect production control. If the price received for its product is above the marginal cost of production, the producing trust will earn a profit due to underproduction. If the market price is below the marginal cost of production, the trust will incur a loss due to overproduction.

Each trust will earn a paper profit whenever the market value of its assets increases and a paper loss whenever this value decreases. Frequent reappraisal of all assets would be essential to proper cost accounting since all cost estimates should be based upon current costs of materials, supplies, capital, equipment, etc.

In spite of the differences among them, these profits and losses would all merge into a single net profit or loss for each trust.

The total profits of all trusts would about equal the total losses of all trusts if prices were stable. Hence no problem of distribution arises with respect to these gains and losses; it would merely be necessary to cancel them off against each other through a central control account.

The reason why total net losses and total net gains would roughly cancel out is readily explained. If all trust managers aim at a perfect balance between marginal costs and market prices, they will make as many errors in one direction as in the other, and these chance variations will approximately cancel out by equaling and offsetting each other. Profits and losses due to reappraisal of assets will also tend to cancel out, provided the price level is relatively stable. A decline in the price of one raw material must be offset by a rise in the price of some other raw material if the price is to be stable.

A net profit earned by an individual trust would increase its monetary capital and should be treated as an additional advance from the Bureau of Capital Supply or should be paid directly to it. Net losses should be treated as repayments of capital to the Bureau. This treatment of net profits and losses would not appreciably alter the total assets of the Bureau of Capital Supply, since net profits and losses would equal each other, but it would alter the capital accounts of individual trusts which did not immediately pay their profits into the Bureau or secure additional loans to cover their losses.

While no distinction between the varieties of profit and loss noted above need be made in distribution theory, the distinctions are important for purposes of production control. Each kind of profit or loss should be individually calculated and stated on the production-control statement or the financial operating statement. Marginal profits and losses only should appear on the former but all should appear on the latter.

The above discussion applies also to profits and losses resulting from the use of price taxes, which should serve the same function as prices.

2. INCOME FROM THE CREATION OF MONEY

Under Socialism all income from the creation of purchasing power should accrue to the state. It is impossible to estimate accurately either the absolute or relative amount of such income in a Socialist state, but the quantity of money should increase at about the same rate as production, or from 4 percent to 6 percent a year. The quantity of money in the United States in 1946 was close to $100,000,000,000. Obviously, therefore, income from the creation of new purchasing power would be a significant source of income to a Socialist state.

The problem of distributing such income was discussed in an earlier chapter on money and banking (pp. 56–58). The method of distribution inevitably affects the price level, and for that reason the selection of a method must be based upon the needs of price and monetary control. In the discussion of price control, therefore, it was recommended that the income from the creation of new money be distributed directly to the public as a sort of social dividend.

As previously indicated, such income is a mixture of rent, interest, and wages. This fact is most apparent in the case of a static economy, where all new money causes inflation, which expropriates a portion of all rent, interest, and wages, and transfers it to the agency which creates the new money. Although the growth of production offsets partly or wholly the inflationary effect of new money in a dynamic economy, the income from the creation of the new money is of precisely the same nature as in a static economy. In the absence of the new money, all real wages, rents, and interest payments would rise,[11] in consequence of a fall in the cost of living. The creation of new money prevents in whole or in part this increase in real wages, rent, and interest by transferring it to the agency which creates the new money. The issue of new money, in other words, always involves a tax upon all existing wage, rent, and interest incomes. Hence, the income from such issues is merely a mixture of expropriated rent, interest, and wages.

Such being the case, it is logical to argue that it should be divided into these component elements and that each element should be distributed in the manner proper to that element. This would be possible because the shares of each element in the income from the creation of new money

[11] This is not always true under Capitalism, for falling prices tend to cause depressions, but it would be true under Socialism.

would be roughly the same as the relative shares of these elements in the total national income, and the latter could be readily ascertained. If this were done, about one-third of the income from the creation of new money would probably be added to rent and interest, and distributed as such, and about two-thirds added to wages. The portion assigned to wages could be distributed as a uniform proportional increase in the wages of all workers.

On the other hand, it seems likely that the economic cost of dividing the income from the creation of new money into its basic elements and using two different methods of distributing these elements, would be greater than the benefit to be derived from this refinement of distribution. In other words, it might be better to add this income to supplementary rent and interest and distribute them all as a social dividend, though this would cause money wages to be some 4 to 6 percent (a percentage equal to the rate of increase in national income) below their proper level.

If it is decided to distribute a portion of this or any other income, as an addition to wages, one economical method of doing so would be to divide the given sum among all trusts, departments, and other economic divisions according to their payroll, and instruct them to make a uniform proportional addition to all wages paid. This would save the cost of preparing and mailing out additional individual checks or credit slips. Another efficient method for achieving the same end would be to instruct the State Bank to increase all wages and salary deposits during a certain period by a certain fixed percent and debit the national treasury for the total of such credits.

3. INCOME FROM CERTAIN SPECIAL-PURPOSE TAXES

Under Capitalism many special-purpose excise taxes, such as those on beer, tobacco, and tea, are set at an excessively high level in order to increase their yield. A similar result might occur under Socialism if the revenue from such taxes were used to pay the costs of free services. In order to avoid this danger, it would perhaps be well to distribute the revenue from most special-purpose, non-price taxes among the general public and raise all funds necessary to meet the costs of free services from a single general tax. Price taxes, of course, should be set in accordance with the general principles of price determination and should never be raised merely to increase state revenues. No tax can serve two purposes at the same time when these purposes conflict with each other, and raising revenue conflicts with all the special purposes that special-purpose taxes should serve.

Special-purpose excise taxes increase the cost of living and lower real wages since they are sales taxes on widely used commodities. They lower real wages slightly below the optimum level, which just equals the marginal utility of labor, and consequently reduce the supply of labor and the volume of production below the proper level.

The most important argument against distributing among the people the proceeds from special-purpose taxes is that it would involve considerable additional bookkeeping work unless it is possible to add these revenues to other types of income, such as rent and interest, which are to be distributed among the people. If no other revenues are to be so distributed, the cost of setting up and administering a special system for the distribution of revenues from special-purpose taxes would be grounds for serious objection to such a distribution.

Inheritance taxes are special-purpose taxes, but the revenues from them ought not to be distributed at all, since this would involve the dissipation of capital. Rather, they should be turned over to the Bureau of Capital Supply and treated as a transfer of capital funds from a private person to the state. In most cases, such taxes would merely involve the return of government bonds to the state or the cancellation of savings deposits.

CHAPTER XV. WAGES

A. INTRODUCTION

Several phases of the problem of determining wages in a Socialist economy have already been considered. In chapter iv, "The Determination of Prices," the general principles which should govern pricing were set forth. Since one theory of wages under Socialism is that wages should in most cases be equal to the market price of the labor involved, these general principles of pricing could be applied to the determination of such wages.

In chapter vi, "The Factors in Production," the use of wage rates as a means of determining the total supply of labor and as a means of allocating that supply of labor to different uses was developed. A theory of the division of income into rent, interest, and wages, was outlined and applied to wages. In this chapter, therefore, only the theory of the division of rent, interest, and wages among individuals remains to be discussed.

Finally, the subject of wage determination was partly covered by the discussion of piece rates in chapter xiii, "The Taylor System of Scientific Shop Management," because piece rates have always formed a major division of that subject. Indeed, it is quite possible that students of scientific management have done more than orthodox economists to develop a sound theory of individual wage determination.

Under Capitalism, wages serve two purposes. As costs they help producers to economize, and as income they help to determine individual shares in the national income. In many cases, however, no single sum can perform both of these functions properly. A sum which best serves to guide production, results in an excessive private income. Therefore, in such cases at least, a Socialist economy should separate the determination of labor costs or prices from the determination of wage-income.

The term "price of labor" will be used here to mean the cost of labor to the purchaser of it, and the term "wage," will be used to mean the income received directly from his labor by the worker. In some cases, the price of labor should be identical with the wage of labor, and in some cases it should not.

This chapter deals only with the determination of nominal or money wages. Under Socialism as under Capitalism, real wages, the buying power of nominal wages, will depend upon both nominal wages and the price level. Real wages cannot be fixed by the executives who control nominal wages, as these executives have no control over the price level.

They should give no thought to real wages, therefore, but should confine their attention to the proper determination of money wages.

The general level of real wages is determined largely by the technique of production and the per capita supply of natural resources and capital. Real wages in Japan are higher than real wages in China or India because the technique of production in use in Japan is greatly superior to that in use in China or India. On the other hand, real wages in France and Argentina are much higher than real wages in Japan, largely because of the differences in natural resources and capital, or, in other words, because of the overpopulation of Japan.

There are only three important methods which may be used to increase real wages. First and most important of these is the improvement of the technique of production. Scientific research offers infinite opportunities for the reduction of costs and the increase of real wages. Secondly, it is always possible to increase real wages by accumulating additional capital. Since scientific knowledge is a form of capital, this second method really includes the first. Thirdly, it is usually possible to increase real wages by increasing or decreasing the total population until an optimum population is attained. This amounts to changing the relationship between the number of workers and the supply of wealth.

While real wages are chiefly dependent upon two factors, the technique of production and the relationship between population and the supply of capital and natural resources, both of these factors, particularly the former, have many casual factors behind them. Almost every subject discussed in this treatise affects real wages. The purpose of all economic theory is to maximize net-utility income per capita, and this ordinarily varies directly with real wages. Whatever increases one, nearly always increases the other.

Real wages and nominal wages do not necessarily vary together under Capitalism. Real wages may decline in periods of business recovery when nominal wages rise, and may rise in periods of recession when nominal wages decline. In a Socialist economy, however, real wages and nominal wages would always vary together, both directly and proportionately, if the price .level were stabilized in the manner prescribed in chapter iii, "Money and Banking." With such price stabilization, every increase or decrease in nominal wages would mean an equal increase or decrease in real wages, since the cost of living would not vary.

One of the principal merits of Socialism is that it would sharply reduce the inequality of income prevailing under Capitalism by eliminating all private income from land, capital, speculation, and business profits, most of which is unearned inherited income.

Socialism should also notably reduce the inequality of wages characteristic of Capitalism. This could be done in two ways: (1) by removing certain monopolistic restrictions upon the supply of labor available for the better paid jobs, and (2) by curtailing or entirely eliminating the use of wage differences as a means of allocating labor to different industries and as a means of stimulating workers to increase their output.

B. THE ELIMINATION OF MONOPOLY AS A CAUSE OF WAGE INEQUALITY

Under Capitalism there is an undue variation in the wages paid to different classes of labor and to different workers within each class because of monopolistic restrictions on the supply of certain kinds of labor. In the United States, wages in 1940 ranged from 50 cents a day for unskilled Negro women workers in the South to $12.00 a day for skilled white workers in the North. Such an unreasonable difference in wages is due to a number of different kinds of monopolistic factors, none of which should exist in a Socialist state.

In the first place, men and women receive unequal wages, even for the same work, under Capitalism because of restrictions on the employment of women. A woman teacher is ordinarily paid $1,200 a year for work for which a man would be paid $1,600. Frequently they work side by side in the same school, doing identically the same work. This inequality is due to the fact that, in relation to demand, the supply of women workers is larger and is increasing faster than the supply of men workers. Superstition, prejudice, and custom give men a near monopoly in many better-paid occupations. In a Socialist economy, however, women ought to be free to do any work for which they are qualified. They should be allowed to work at men's wages in every trade and every industry in the nation. If too many apply in any one plant, the wages paid both men and women should be lowered until the correct total labor force is achieved. Women should have equal opportunities in trade and professional schools. In other words, all existing educational and wage discrimination against women should be eliminated.

A second important monopolistic cause of wage variations under Capitalism is the cost and difficulty of securing vocational training. This limits artificially the number of workers who are qualified for skilled work and raises their wages unduly. In a Socialist economy, all vocational education should be free, and students over eighteen in vocational schools should be as well paid as unskilled workers. This would have two effects. First, the wages of skilled labor would not have to be high enough to pay for the time and capital devoted to acquiring skill. (The employing trust should, however, be required to pay for the cost of this training so that the cost of skilled labor to it will not be below the total economic cost of such labor.) Secondly, this free vocational training would so thin the ranks of unskilled labor and so increase the supply of skilled labor that the present difference between the wages of skilled and unskilled labor would largely disappear.

A third important cause of the excessive difference in the wages of skilled and unskilled labor under Capitalism is the selfish Capitalistic policy of artificial monopoly followed by many trade unions and by professional associations such as the American Bar Association. Many unions of skilled workers have adopted measures which artificially restrict the supply of labor in their trades. These measures take various forms. Sometimes the number of apprentices is rigidly restricted. Frequently a large initiation fee is charged to reduce the number of union members. Occasionally unions simply refuse to accept new members unless they have "pull," i.e., are sons of present union members. These measures are effective only when the union is strong enough to enforce a closed shop, but many unions have a closed shop now. The cost of high wages secured through such measures falls chiefly upon the consuming public, largely composed of other wage earners, for the employers usually raise the price of the finished product enough to offset the increased wage costs. The relatively high cost of housing and the persistence of slums in American cities are partly due to the high monopoly wages in the building trades which are maintained by measures of the type noted above. Similarly, the high cost of medical care is partly due to the monopolistic policies of the American Medical Association—for instance, its efforts to prevent exiled German doctors from practicing in America. In a Socialist economy, no trade union or other organization of workers should be allowed to raise its own wages by means of such monopolistic practices.

A fourth important monopolistic cause of uneconomic wage differentials under Capitalism is the ignorance of the worker concerning wages and opportunities for employment in his trade in other cities and plants. Many Southern mill workers in the United States do not know how much higher wages are in New England than in the South. Many farm laborers in the South do not know that farm wages are much higher in the North and West. Even if they are aware of these higher wages in other districts, they do not know where and when jobs are available, or whether they could obtain them if they applied for them. A Socialist state should maintain a national employment service to make all of this information available to workers without cost. This service should enable a Negro in Alabama to secure any job he is qualified for in any part of the country at the wage prevailing there, simply by asking for it. This would increase the mobility of labor and have a very great tendency to iron out wage inequalities due to chance and ignorance.

In order to further increase the mobility of labor the national employment service or the State Bank should offer to loan money to cover the cost of moving from one job to another. There would be no danger of credit losses on such loans in a Socialist state, and they would tend to reduce uneconomic geographical variation in wages to a minimum.

C. EQUAL VERSUS UNEQUAL WAGES

The elimination of inequalities in income from land, capital, and business profits, and the elimination of wage differences caused by labor monopolies, would remove the worst evils of economic inequality. However, it would be possible, and many Socialist thinkers have argued that it would be desirable, to go still further and eliminate all inequality in income. The advantages and disadvantages of this final step toward equality will now receive consideration.

Unequal wages may serve either or both of two entirely distinct but very significant purposes. They may be used (1) to control the distribution of labor among different trades, plants, shifts, etc., and/or (2) to stimulate production by proportioning wages to individual output.

I. Unequal Wages and the Allocation of Labor

The problem of the proper distribution of labor among different trades, plants, and shifts in a Socialist economy has already been treated in detail in chapter vi, "The Factors in Production."

In chapter vi it was noted that every change in money wages in a given market affects labor in two ways; first, by altering the supply of labor; secondly, by altering the demand for it. The distinction between wages and the price of labor made earlier in the present chapter makes it possible to restate this fact and say that the use of labor may be altered in two ways; first, by varying its wage; secondly, by varying its price. Neither of these methods used alone, however, would permit sound allocation of labor. With equal wages, no amount of variation in labor prices would secure a proper allocation of labor, because price charges do not affect the number of job applicants. With equal labor prices, no amount of variation of wages would suffice to secure this goal, for the reason that price changes alone affect the demand for labor of a given type.

Other methods are available for controlling the distribution of labor. Workers might be ordered to work in certain trades and plants, and might be shifted from one to another in an arbitrary or military fashion. This method is highly undesirable because it curtails the liberty of the individual, and because it renders impossible the accurate measurement and balancing of the personal marginal utility of wages and the marginal disutility of different kinds of labor by the individual worker, the only person who can possibly achieve this balance. It is also possible to control the allocation of labor in a nonmilitary way without using differential wages. Assuming equal money wages, it would be possible to control the distribution of labor by altering the hours of labor, the required intensity of labor, or the conditions of labor. Of these alternatives, the most feasible is that of altering the hours of labor, for they are most easily measured and altered according to temporary needs, and workers have a clear understanding of the effect of small changes in the hours of labor.

These alternative methods have one major advantage over wage differentials as a method of controlling the distribution of labor. They do not cause inequality among dependents of wage earners. Even the most justifiable of wage variations tend to affect dependents unfairly. Still, variation of the hours of labor is probably less desirable than variation of money wages as a means of controlling the distribution of labor, both because it might decrease unduly the total number of hours worked and so reduce the national income, and because it takes control of the hours of labor out of the hands of the individual workers. Since the workers themselves are the best judges of the net disutility or utility of each hour of labor, it is they who should control their hours of labor. The latter argument is valid, of course, only if each worker is able to decide how many hours a day he will work, a privilege workers do not have today.

Wage differentials would not have to be very large to persuade workers to distribute themselves in the proper way among different trades, plants, and regions if the mobility of labor were increased and safeguarded as it should be under Socialism.

Wage differentials used solely to control the distribution of labor between various trades, plants, shifts, and localities, and no greater than necessary for this purpose, do not result in real economic inequality, except for dependents, so long as each worker has complete freedom to choose his own place and kind of work. If he chooses a job with a low wage, it will be because for him the total net psychic income from that job is greater than from any other. High wages do not mean inequality when every worker is free and able to earn them. In such cases they indicate a higher disutility of labor or a lower nonmonetary psychic income[1] for the marginal worker whom it is necessary to attract into that industry.

[1] Total psychic income includes that secured from wages; nonmonetary psychic income excludes it.

The total psychic income received by individual workers doing similar work for similar pay varies widely. This kind of economic inequality is inevitable. No system of payment can eliminate it because it is unmeasurable.[2] However, wage differentials or variations in the hours of labor used to control the allocation of labor do tend to reduce it by offsetting the other advantages and disadvantages of individual jobs.

II. Unequal Wages as Incentives to Optimum Production

As explained above, unequal wages may be used as incentives to optimum production, whether or not they are used to control the distribution of labor. It would be perfectly possible to equalize the average level of wages in all occupations, locations, and plants, controlling the distribution of labor among them by varying the hours or intensity of labor, and at the same time to use wage increments within each of these groups to provide incentives to optimum production.

Unequal wages used solely to control the distribution of labor serve not to increase but rather to decrease the inevitable differences in workers' psychic income. On the other hand, unequal wages designed to stimulate production, necessarily serve to increase existing inequality in psychic income. Since workers differ widely in their productivity, pecuniary incentives to increased production enlarge differences in output and, accordingly, in wages and psychic incomes.

a) THE CASE FOR EQUAL WAGES

The principal arguments in favor of equal wages, and against the use of unequal wages to increase production, are four in number.

Equal Treatment of Dependents.—The first, most important advantage of equal wages, and one seldom if ever mentioned, is that equal wages do not result in undeserved inequality among children and other independents of wage earners. We may concede, for the moment, that workers deserve incomes above the average if they can earn them. Workers, however, make up less than half of the population. In order to pay these workers unequal wages, it is necessary to give unequal incomes to the dependents of these workers, to wives and children who have done little or nothing to deserve such discrimination. The children of an inefficient worker must be penalized in order to penalize their father. The children of an efficient worker must be given special undeserved privileges in order to reward their father for his superior work. This makes it impossible to achieve equality of opportunity for children. The strong caste lines evident among women under Capitalism are largely based upon the differ-

[2] See pp. 36–38.

ing incomes of their husbands or fathers. The use of unequal wages in a Socialist economy would result in a similar evil. It would be much less serious, of course, due to the social appropriation of rent, interest, and profits, but it would still be a very real evil.

To summarize, the principal defect of a system of incentive wages is that it rewards and punishes helpless children and other dependents for the ability or lack of ability of the family breadwinner. If unequal wages are worth while, it can be only because their advantages more than compensate for this serious evil. The disutility of such injustice, however, cannot be measured and balanced against the increased productivity resulting from piece rates. Hence the decision concerning the relative merits of the two systems will always be a personal and subjective affair.

This objection to unequal incomes can be met satisfactorily by devising a type of income or reward which can only be received by the worker who earns it. For instance, the more productive workers might be rewarded by reducing their hours of labor without cutting their pay, by improving their conditions of labor, by granting special honors or medals to them, and by promoting them to positions of greater power.

Equal Treatment of Workers.—The second significant advantage of equal wages over incentive wages is that they do not base the income of the individual worker on factors beyond his control. They do not penalize workers who are below the average in efficiency or productivity, nor do they reward workers above the average in these respects. Since the productivity of the individual is largely determined by heredity and childhood environment, both of which are beyond the control of the individual adult worker, it is manifestly unjust to reward or punish him according to his productivity.

If certain men inherit rare and valuable physical and mental abilities, nature may deserve a reward, but the fortunate individual deserves none. Indeed, justice would seem to require that those who are endowed by nature with more than an equal share of health, beauty, and intelligence should receive a less than equal share of the good things produced by man, for unjustified inequality arouses indignation in every sensitive and intelligent observer.

The entire philosophy of Capitalism is based upon a false religious assumption, that of the freedom of the will. In spite of great differences in heredity and environment, the great majority of men and women are presumed to control their own actions so that they can be virtuous and industrious if they so desire. It is this belief in freedom of the will that causes men to punish vindictively those who violate the law. It is this false assumption that enables Capitalist apologists to justify the gross inequality of Capitalism. If a man is poor and miserable, it is a due punishment for sin and idleness, they preach. If he is wealthy and comfortable, it is merely a proper reward for his virtuous and industrious conduct. Of course, orthodox thinkers admit exceptions, but they believe that these principles apply to the great majority of cases.

There is no need at this point to deny that ability and industry lead to wealth under Capitalism, or that they might lead to wealth in a suitably designed Socialist economy. What must be denied is that a man deserves a reward for being able and industrious. No one thinks that race horses deserve high rewards for their swiftness. But men and horses are precisely similar in this respect. Some of them are born able, or fast, and some of them are not. Some of them are trained in a manner which improves their ability or speed, and some are not. The vital point is that neither horses nor men deserve special rewards for their heredity or past environment. The able man deserves high wages in this world and heaven in the next no more than the fast horse.

It should be carefully noted, however, that the foregoing reasoning does not deny that men and horses both respond to tangible rewards or incentives. This important fact is discussed below.

To summarize this point, unequal wages reward some men for childhood advantages and inherited abilities and punish other men for lacking these advantages and abilities. Unequal wages enhance and perpetuate the undeserved inequality created by nature and nurture.

Nonmonetary Rewards.—A third important argument in favor of equality of wages is that it may be possible to induce nearly all men to work as hard as they ought to work without using incentive wages.

Some men require no special incentive whatsoever. Particularly in a Socialist economy, where every man would be free to apply himself to that specific kind of work for which he is best fitted, many men would find sufficient reward for optimum output in the pleasure of work itself.

Even under Capitalism, the majority of great deeds are done by humble inventors, artists, scientists, and thinkers for the sheer joy of doing difficult and stimulating work. For superior men in all fields the utility or pleasure of work well done is the greatest incentive to doing fine work. Nor is this characteristic peculiar to a few exceptional men. The artisan in every line of work secures real satisfaction from work well done.

In addition to enjoying good workmanship as an end in itself, men desire respect and praise, especially from neighbors and fellow workers, and respect and admiration can be secured by industry and good workmanship. This incentive to maximum production will not only continue to operate under Socialism, but will be far more effective, since ability and industry will be more important bases of social gradation. Under Capitalism, a fine workman may feel humble before a poor one because the latter has inherited a higher economic and social position. Under Socialism, popular judgment concerning the value and character of an individual will be based upon his economic productivity much more than at present, for the major conflicting bases of evaluation—inherited income, undeserved educational advantages, and unearned income—will have been destroyed.

To encourage public recognition of and respect for superior productivity, management should grade each worker according to his volume of output or personal ability, and the grades should be periodically posted on a public bulletin board or published in the plant paper. Special chevrons, badges, medals, or cups should be awarded periodically to those who excel in productivity and ability.

Formal honors of all kinds should be extensively used in a Socialist economy as a reward for outstanding work and as an incentive to increased effort. The Soviet title "Honored Artist of the Republic," for instance, gives great pleasure to most of those who bear it, and stimulates thousands of artists to increase their labor output in the hopes of earning it. On the other hand, this title costs society nothing. It involves no disutility. An increase in wages paid to artists may result in lower wages for all other workers, but the award of an honor cannot injure them in any way.

A powerful natural incentive to industry and efficiency which would continue to influence workers even if monetary rewards were abandoned is the desire for power. The great majority of men are eager to be promoted to positions which increase their authority. Indeed, so strong is this desire in ambitious individuals that they will accept a reduction in income in order to secure a position of greater authority. At every election thousands of successful lawyers and business men demonstrate their willingness to sacrifice income for power. If promotion were used throughout all branches of a Socialist economy to reward industry and efficiency, men would have another effective stimulus to optimum productivity in the absence of wage incentives.

If these incentives to industry and good workmanship prove insufficient, a number of other nonmonetary incentives might be offered. For instance, the use of better-quality clothing might be restricted to the more industrious and capable workers, as is the custom in the Army and Navy today. Longer vacations, earlier retirement, and shorter working hours might also be used to reward the most deserving workers. Special privileges with respect to choice of work place in a plant or office, choice of lunch hour, use of executive dining room and rest rooms, choice of vacation period, and many other similar privileges might be granted to outstanding workers.

Maximum Utility from Given Income.—The fourth and well-known advantage of equal wages is that, because of diminishing utility, an equal distribution of a given national income results in the maximum total individual utility income. If two boys have two oranges each and if one orange is taken from the first boy and given to the second, the first boy loses more than the second boy gains because the second orange eaten gives more pleasure than the third. This conclusion is based upon the assumption that the curve of the declining marginal utility of oranges is about the same for both boys. While this might not be true in this case, it is a sound assumption for income or goods in general (see pages 39–41).

An individual who receives an income of $1,000,000 a year gets very little additional pleasure from the last $990,000. The social appropriation and relatively equal distribution of this surplus income would enormously increase the pleasure obtained from it. If social appropriation, by reducing the incentives to production, were to cut in half such surplus incomes and the production they measure, the equal distribution of the reduced surplus would still give far more pleasure than the receipt of the entire surplus by the individual who produced it.

The Difficulty of Measuring Productivity.—A common argument against unequal wages is the difficulty of measuring differences in individual productivity. It is relatively easy to measure the output of men doing piecework under identical conditions, but this is not the usual situation. It is very difficult to measure differences in the output of two lawyers or schoolteachers. Yet the greatest differences in wages exist in those occupations in which it is most difficult to measure differences in output. A fast worker on piecework rarely earns three times as much as a slow worker, yet one lawyer may earn a hundred times as much as another.

There are two considerations which weaken the force of this argument. In the first place, payment of equal wages would not eliminate the need for accurate measurement of the value of the work done by each individual as a basis for cost accounting. In the absence of correct pricing of labor and proper cost accounting, there would be no equilibrium between the demand for and supply of each kind of labor; and consequently labor would not be used most economically.

The second consideration which weakens the above argument is that while it is impossible to develop a perfectly accurate measure of productivity or a perfectly just system of incentive wages, it is quite easy to fix wages which serve far better than equal wages to measure productivity and provide incentives to production. The impossibility of achieving perfection is never a sound reason for rejecting a step toward this goal.

b) THE CASE FOR INCENTIVE WAGES

Let us turn now to the arguments in favor of using unequal money wages as a means of increasing the productivity of labor.

Increased Production.—The principal argument in behalf of incentive wages is that they increase total production and total utility income. Repeated experiments in innumerable Capitalistic enterprises have demonstrated that piece rates are remarkably effective in increasing production under present conditions. The results vary widely, but it seems probable that the application of a sound piece-rate system to workers previously paid ordinary day or time wages will increase production by somewhere between 50 percent and 100 percent in the great majority of cases.[3] Probably the advantage of piece rates over pure Communism is appreciably greater, since even under Capitalistic time wages a man may work hard in order to achieve a higher time wage.

The reason incentive wage systems increase production may be explained as follows. An isolated individual, or one working for himself, increases his productive efforts to the point where the utility and disutility of his work become equal. Until he reaches this marginal point, every additional unit of effort yields a net surplus of utility over disutility. If a man works for time wages, however, his utility income does not vary automatically according to his efforts. Hence, he has insufficient incentive to increase his efforts to the proper level.

We have already noted that a 100 percent increase in production does not mean a 100 percent increase in net-utility income. In the first place, the last units of wealth produced have much less utility than the first units, as is clearly stated in the principle of diminishing utility. In the United States the second half of the average man's income probably gives him less than half as much utility as the first. In the second place, the additional disutility involved in earning the second half of his income probably is much larger than the disutility involved in earning the first half of his income.

Nevertheless, the real net utility of a 100 percent increase in physical production must not be minimized. As long as the great majority of workers live in poverty, ignorance, and ill health, as they now do in most countries, there will be a very great need for a higher productivity of labor.

The effectiveness of monetary incentives in increasing the productivity of labor is greatest in the case of unskilled labor and labor for which piece

---

[3] Bourgeois economists hold that wages are determined by the marginal productivity of labor, but ignore the vital fact that the marginal productivity of labor is determined by the method of wage payment.

rates are suitable. It is least in the case of professional work and other work for which piece rates are not suitable. Hence, if a compromise between equal and unequal wages is necessary, it might be desirable to retain unequal wages only for unskilled labor and labor for which piece rates are suitable. Under Capitalism it is inequality of wages at higher levels that causes the greatest harm, in spite of the fact that at these higher levels inequality of wages has the least effect upon the productivity of labor.

Identity of Wage and Price of Labor.—If all workers doing similar work in one plant were paid the same hourly wage, and if output varied from worker to worker, as is inevitable in most cases,[4] it would perhaps be necessary to establish for each worker a labor price (distinct from wage price) which would measure his output, appear in the cost accounts of the plant in question, and play a part in determining marginal profits and losses.

Such a determination and use of labor prices might be needed to restrict the demand for superior workers and increase the demand for inferior workers. In the absence of such differing labor prices, each plant might strive to employ only superior workers or might by chance secure an unusual proportion of such workers, and the marginal costs of different plants and plant divisions would then be determined by their relative success or failure in attracting the superior workers. This would reduce the usefulness of marginal costs as measures of managerial efficiency and as guides to production control.

Properly determined unequal wages perform two vital functions under both Capitalism and Socialism: (1) they serve to control the supply of labor and its allocation, and (2) they enter into costs and help to determine the volume of production and the demand for each good. If wages were equal in a Socialist economy, it would still be desirable to determine and use differing labor prices in order to help determine the production costs of individual goods and thus control production and demand. This would involve the use of two sets of figures, wages and labor costs, and would increase clerical costs and the complexity of wage control and accounting. Unequal wages, which make labor costs and wages identical, possess the advantage of eliminating these additional costs and complexities.

It would be possible, of course, to develop a simple system of fixing

---

[4] Where the speed of the conveyor or machine determines the pace of the worker, or where it is possible to count the pieces produced, it will be possible to fix uniform tasks and require every worker to perform them and no more. In such cases wages and labor costs can be made identical by requiring the same output from all workers.

labor costs. For instance, the cost charged for the use of a worker might be increased 4 percent for each year of vocational education and 1 percent for each point by which his I.Q. exceeds 100. Or each worker might be periodically rated by his supervisor and these ratings used both to promote competition and to fix labor costs. Although such methods of fixing labor costs would yield only rough approximations, little more can be said for the differential wages now used as labor costs. Only in the case of piece rates do present unequal wages come close to measuring the productivity of individual workers.

Even a simple system of using labor prices would require fixing a price for each worker, keeping records of both wages and labor prices, and transferring the net difference between wages and labor prices to the government treasury. It might, therefore, be better to make no effort to fix and use labor costs, and to minimize the resulting distortion of marginal costs by requiring each plant manager to hire all applicants with proper training regardless of their individual abilities. If every plant had a typical random selection of workers of different productivities, average labor costs for marginal production in large plants would not be significantly distorted by differences in labor productivity due to selection of workers.

c) SUMMARY AND CONCLUSIONS

Equal wages have the great merit of eliminating unequal treatment of dependents, who have done little or nothing to justify such discrimination. Equal wages do not reward or punish men for hereditary qualities, childhood advantages or disadvantages, and other circumstances over which they had little or no control. Equal distribution of a given national income results in more satisfaction (net utility) to consumers than any other possible distribution of that income. Finally, there are many non-monetary incentives which could be used to persuade men to be industrious and efficient.

On the other hand, unequal incentive wages have repeatedly demonstrated their power to increase output very markedly wherever piece rates can be used, and they would make it unnecessary to determine and use a separate price for the labor of each worker.

The relative force of these arguments depends upon the size of the national income. In a country where the workers have only a bare subsistence wage, as in India and China, the need for incentive wages to increase output is at a maximum and the harm of unequal wages to workers and dependents is at a minimum since the inequality caused by incentive wages is at a minimum. In a comparatively wealthy country such as the United States or Great Britain, on the other hand, the need for incentive wages to increase output is much less and the injustice to workers and dependents of unequal wages is more serious because the resulting inequality of income is greater and more obvious.

Similarly the advantages of incentive wages in increasing output have been best demonstrated in the case of wage workers doing piecework, and are least proved in the case of salaried workers and executives. Yet inequality is now far greater among salaried workers than among piece-rate wage workers.

Under Capitalism the salaries of executives and professional men are determined largely by custom or arbitrary decision rather than by the importance of the position or the productivity of the individual. The president of one trust may receive a salary and bonus of $1,000,000 a year while the president of another equally large and successful trust receives only $100,000 a year. A fashionable doctor may be paid $100,000 a year while a research scientist who has discovered a new drug which will save a million lives is paid only $10,000 a year. A jazz-band leader may earn $500,000 a year while a composer of rare genius is paid $10,000.

It is possible that every promotion of an executive or professional worker should carry with it a small increase in salary, as in the Army or the Navy, in order to make promotion more attractive. But it is obvious that salary differentials larger than those now existing in government service do not measure differences in productivity and are not necessary to increase competition for promotion. The desire for promotion among military officers and government officials is already as intense as it ought to be, and would probably remain so even if present salary differentials were drastically reduced. As explained previously, nonmonetary incentives are so strong among men in executive and professional activities that few if any monetary incentives are needed.

Even under Socialism it would be difficult to determine by scientific experimentation whether equal or unequal wages result in greater net utility income for the nation as a whole. It would require two- or three-score years to condition a new generation in such a way as to make a fair test of equal wages possible, and by that time other conditions would have changed so much that it would be difficult to measure the change in per capita income caused by the new wage system. Workers taught from childhood that incentive wages are fair and necessary will react quite differently to equal wages than workers taught from childhood that equal wages are fair and practical.

It is particularly hopeless to try to test the effect of equal wages by introducing them in only a few enterprises, when the best workers are free to transfer to other enterprises which continue to offer them wages much above the average. It is only on a national scale that equal wages can be tested.

Although the foregoing discussion casts serious doubt upon the need for unequal wages in the United States after Socialism has been firmly established for a few decades, it would probably be wise to retain piece rates and small salary differentials throughout the period of transition from Capitalism to Socialism and to re-educate the adult population to Socialist ideals and methods. After this period has passed, additional steps towards equality of income should be tried, and subsequent policies should be based in part upon the success of these experiments even though this success will be difficult to measure.

The above conclusions apply only to the use of unequal money wages to increase the productivity of men doing the same kind of work on the same shift in the same plant or production unit. The use of wage differences to attract the proper number of men to each occupation, shift, and plant may be desirable even if men doing the same kind of work on the same shift in the same plant are paid equal wages.

D. THE DETERMINATION OF UNEQUAL WAGES

As indicated above, differences in money wages should be used for some time at least after the introduction of Socialism (1) as a means of attracting the proper number of workers into each trade, plant, and shift, and (2) as a means of inducing workers to be more productive. There is no analytical problem involved in determining wage differences necessary to achieve the first purpose, since it will be necessary only to determine by experiment which differentials actually do achieve this purpose.[5] On the other hand, the problem of determining wage differentials which will induce workers to put forth their optimum effort is relatively complicated and, therefore, merits further discussion.

Neoclassical economists have long taught that wages equal the marginal productivity of labor. Although this principle, like most other neoclassical economic principles, is a gross misstatement of what actually occurs under Capitalism, it may be used as a guiding principle in the fixing of incentive wages in a Socialist economy.

Wages ought to equal the marginal productivity or utility of labor so that the individual worker will have the knowledge necessary to rational control of his own production effort. The individual worker can sense directly the disutility of labor—his own physical sensations—but he must depend upon the wage or piece rate paid or promised him as a measure

---

[5] However, there will be a difficult political problem, that of preventing unions from influencing such wage differentials. On the evils of union influence upon wage determination see Henry C. Simons, "Reflections on Syndicalism" in *Journal of Political Economy*, March 1944.

of the utility of his labor to society. If this wage or piece rate is too low, he does not make the optimum production effort, and vice versa. Of course, only wages which vary with the volume of individual output affect individual effort.

Unfortunately, it would be difficult if not impossible to determine the marginal productivity of most types of labor, even with the greatly improved methods of pricing and cost accounting which Socialism would introduce. For instance, the marginal productivity of stenographers, clerks, engineers, cost accountants, etc., cannot be closely measured by the most accurate cost accounting. Even the differences in output of individual workers in these occupations must be measured in a very crude manner. Only in the case of workers doing work for which piece rates are suitable is it possible to measure with reasonable accuracy the marginal productivity of labor and differences in the output of different workers.

In all cases, however, it is easier to measure differences in individual output than to measure the marginal productivity of the labor in question, and incentive wages may be based upon differences in individual output regardless of whether or not the marginal productivity of the labor in question is measurable. If, however, it is not possible to measure marginal productivity, this is a good reason for keeping wage differentials small, since they might otherwise exceed the market value of the additional output which they have caused and thus involve a net loss to the economy. It is also a good reason for keeping the average weekly earnings under piece rates equal in different operations and trades.

For these reasons, and others discussed earlier in this chapter, incentive-wage differentials used to stimulate the efforts of professional workers and executives should be arbitrarily determined without attempting to measure the marginal productivity of the work of such men; and for men earning over $5,000 a year these incentive-wage differentials should be much smaller than under Capitalism.

Piece rates, on the other hand, should be more closely related to the marginal utility of the work in question and directly proportional to measurable differences in individual output. This would stimulate the output of piece-rate workers to the optimum degree, yet would not result in great inequality, since few piece-rate workers can earn more than 50 percent above the average of their fellows.

We turn now to the problems involved in the application of the basic principles of wage determination to individual cases—in other words, to the problems of fixing individual wages. The question of when one kind of piece rate, such as an individual piece rate, should be used instead of another, such as a group piece rate or a time wage, will not be given much attention here since this question has been discussed in great detail by

Capitalist writers. A wage problem of particular interest to Socialists and one which has never been adequately treated, namely the problem of how piece rates should be fixed in a Socialist economy, will be discussed in some detail. We shall also consider very briefly the use of time wages, bonuses, and penalties.

First, let us take up the determination of piece rates under Socialism.

I. Piece Rates

A piece-rate wage may be defined as a wage which is based upon the number of pieces[6] upon which a certain operation, or operations, has been performed. The operations must be relatively standardized and subject to economical inspection, and the pieces must be readily countable before piece rates become practicable. Piece rates may be paid for work performed by individuals, or by groups of individuals, but the former, when suitable, are much more effective as incentives to optimum production. If individual piece rates are not feasible, group piece rates are superior to time wages.

Individual piece rates are the most perfect form of incentive wage, and should be introduced wherever possible. However, they are not suited to many forms of labor, notably professional work, artistic work, executive work, retail store work, etc. Individual piece wages are best suited to machine operatives in large factories, in large mechanized mines, and on large mechanized farms. By vastly increasing both the scale and mechanization of production in all fields, Socialism will greatly increase the opportunity for the use of individual piece wages.

In those factories where workers perform standardized operations upon units moving on an automatic conveyor, the number of pieces completed by each worker is determined by the speed of the conveyor. Such workers receive piece rates even when paid by the hour, but these piece rates have no effect upon the volume of work performed. The conveyor system prevents piece rates from accomplishing their most important function, that of persuading individual workers to raise or lower their output to the optimum level. However, this same end can be achieved to a certain extent in the case of men working on a conveyor by varying the amount of work performed by individual men on each piece, and the wage paid for it, according to their expressed desires.

The type of piece rate which ought to be used in a Socialist economy is quite different from any used under Capitalism or advocated by Capi-

---

[6] Pieces may be small individual parts or products, tons of raw material, cubic feet of material or space, acres of land, houses being built or repaired, trees standing in a forest, etc.

talist theorists,[7] although not all of the difference is due to the peculiar needs of Socialism. A Socialist piece-rate system should possess two basic and novel features. It should provide no pay whatsoever for the worker until the value of his output covers all fixed costs plus the variable costs involved in producing this minimum output. After this minimum output has been attained, however, the piece rate should fully equal the net value of each additional unit produced.

a) NO PAY FOR CERTAIN MINIMUM OUTPUT

No wages should be paid for piece work until all fixed costs, plus the variable costs involved, have been covered, because the worker has produced no net surplus over costs until this point is reached. His value to his trust and to society is best measured by the value surplus he produces, not by his gross physical output. Any worker who is paid more than this surplus is overpaid. He is a source of pecuniary loss to his trust; consequently, since pecuniary losses indicate net disutility, he is a source of net disutility to the economy as a whole.

An illustration may help to make this principle clear. A worker named Smith runs a linotype machine. The fixed costs—chiefly rent, interest, heat, light, and other overhead expenses—necessary to providing him with a work place, a linotype machine, and supervision, amount to $5.00 a day. The value added to the raw materials and supplies by his labor is $1.00 per thousand words of type. Materials and supplies cost ten cents per thousand words, and there are no other variable costs except Smith's wages.

Under such circumstances Smith should receive no pay for the first $5.56 worth of type he turns out, for this minimum output barely covers the cost to the management of providing Smith with a place to work, a machine, and raw materials. If Smith were paid anything for this minimum output and produced no more, the trust for which he works would lose money. Even if he received no pay and produced less than the minimum, the trust would lose money on Smith because the value of his output would be less than the costs involved. When this happens, Smith ought to be compelled to make up the deficit out of his own pocket.

Several incentive systems of wage payment widely used under Capitalism combine time wages with piece rates. They guarantee a certain minimum daily wage irrespective of the volume of production, and then pay a piece rate on all production of over a certain level. Ordinarily, the minimum wage and the point at which piece rates begin are set considerably below normal time wages and average daily production. This

[7] For an able brief statement of the principal varieties of piece rates now in use, see Alford, *Management's Handbook.*

system is supposed to protect the worker by guaranteeing him a certain minimum wage. It ought not to be used in a Socialist economy, however, since it results in uneconomically high costs of production on all units turned out by workers who benefit from the minimum wage. If certain workers are so ineffective that they cannot earn a living wage under properly fixed Socialist piece rates in one industry, they should be induced by low wages to try some other line of work. If they are so ineffective that they cannot earn a living wage in any industry or occupation, they should be subsidized by the state, not by the particular trust for which they happen to work. Any subsidy to inferior workers, paid by an individual trust and treated as a marginal cost, is certain to distort production and consumption of the goods produced by that trust, because such subsidies are not true marginal costs.

It is worthy of note that the fixed costs mentioned above go on whether or not the worker for whom they are incurred comes to work. Fixed costs which because of the absence of a worker are not offset by values produced ought not to be charged against the pay checks of other workers, but against his own. Since his fellow workers are not responsible for his absence, they should not suffer for it. Of course, if a substitute is obtained, only a small charge need be made. In large plants it will be possible to predict absences with considerable accuracy and, hence, to plan ahead on the number of substitutes required. Unexpected absences are bound to cause some losses even in such plants, however, and the absent workers should bear all such costs.

b) FULL PAY FOR ADDITIONAL OUTPUT

The second vital feature of a Socialist piece rate is that it should give to the worker the full net value created by all work over and above the minimum necessary to cover fixed costs, plus the variable non-wage costs involved in covering these fixed costs. In other words, it should give to the worker the full value of the additional pieces he produces, less only the other additional variable costs involved.

Few, if any, of the many different piece rates in use under Capitalism or proposed by Capitalist wage theorists are intended to pass on to the worker the full savings made possible by the increase in production they stimulate. Taylor's differential piece rate, for instance, was designed to give the worker only about half of the net value of each additional unit produced. The remainder of the net value was intended to go to the capitalist as a reward for introducing an incentive wage. This is an almost inevitable defect of any incentive wage system under Capitalism, for capitalists adopt such systems only to benefit themselves and they believe that every increase in output should increase their profits. Nevertheless, it is significant that the best students of scientific management under Capitalism ordinarily advocate a piece rate or other incentive wage system which gives to the worker a mere half of the additional net value created by any increase in his production efforts. Obviously, a piece-rate system which gave to the worker 100 per cent of the net increase in value due to his increased effort would be a far more powerful incentive to increased effort on his part. By the adoption of such a piece-rate system a Socialist economy could provide all piece-rate workers with a greatly increased incentive to improve their productivity.

Under Capitalism the difference between wages paid and net value created by labor is far greater at the margin than elsewhere, because the net value of the marginal product is at a maximum. The average worker receives a wage roughly proportional to the total value of his output, but for producing one more unit per day he is often paid nothing, and when paid according to a "scientific" piece rate he ordinarily receives only about half of the additional value created. Yet on the average, wages equal almost 100 percent of the value created by labor, as they make up two-thirds of the national income, and little of the third distributed as rent, interest, and profits should be distributed as wages.

To illustrate the second vital principle of piece-rate determination under Socialism—the principle that a piece rate should give to the worker the full net value created by all work over and above the minimum necessary to cover fixed costs—the case used to illustrate the first principle may be further developed. We found that Smith ought to receive no wages on the first $5.56 worth of type (5,560 words) which he produced. On every additional thousand words, or fraction thereof, however, he should receive the full value, namely one dollar, less only the variable non-labor costs, which amount to ten cents. In other words, for every additional thousand words of output he should be paid ninety cents.

The premium placed upon high productivity by such a piece rate deserves emphasis. If Smith is averaging 10,000 words per day, a 10 percent increase in his output will increase his wages by about 20 percent. Under Capitalist piece rates, only a 10 percent increase in wages would result.

c) THE STABILITY OF PIECE RATES

Bourgeois writers have placed great emphasis upon the stability of piece rates. One of the cardinal principles of scientific management is that piece rates, once set, must not be lowered, except after long intervals or some important change in the technique of production.

The justification given for this rule is that every cut in a piece rate tends to destroy the purpose of the piece rate. The purpose of a piece rate is to persuade workers to increase their output. If the piece rate is cut after the workers have increased their output, they feel that they have been tricked and take pains in the future to restrict their output to a low level.[8]

In order to eliminate the necessity of cutting piece rates once they are in use, F. W. Taylor developed two significant rules. In the first place, he asserted that employers should permit workers responding to piece rates with increased output to earn definitely higher wages. In other words, he desired Capitalists to share with their workers a portion of the profits resulting from increased production stimulated by the adoption of piece rates. We have already provided for giving the workers the full benefit of increased output caused by piece rates, so that we have not only adopted, but have much improved upon this rule.

In the second place, Taylor taught that all piece rates should be based upon careful time and motion studies which would determine in advance the maximum productivity attainable by the worker. Such studies would eliminate all danger of setting original piece rates too high, since the management would know in advance precisely how much the workers could produce and earn.

This method of setting original piece rates will undoubtedly be of some importance under Socialism, but it will not possess the great significance attached to it by contemporary students of scientific management. The ideal method of fixing piece rates is that used in our illustration dealing with Smith, the linotype operator. In that case the value of the product of Smith's labor was first determined, and from this there were deducted the non-labor costs of production. If the wage thus fixed was too high and labor was mobile, it would result in an increased production of type due to an inflow of new labor, and a consequent fall in the price of the finished product and the piece rate in question; or it would result in an immediate reduction in the wage rate in order to prevent this inflow of new labor and the consequent increase in production. In either case there is an automatic adjustment of the piece rate without any use of time and motion studies.

Time and motion studies are useful in determining the best method of performing individual operations and in estimating the time required to perform them, but they do not aid in solving the more important ques-

[8] "It is . . . . under piece work that the art of scientific soldiering is thoroughly developed; after a workman has had the price per piece of the work he is doing lowered two or three times as a result of his having worked harder and increased his output, he is likely entirely to lose sight of his employer's side of the case and become imbued with a grim determination to have no more cuts if soldiering can prevent it." F. W. Taylor, *Principles of Scientific Management*, p. 23.

tion of the wage per hour or rate per piece. An idea of the time required to perform certain new operations will facilitate the determination of new and tentative piece rates, but it gives only a very rough basis for such rates, since it does not tell how much the average hourly earnings should be nor how much premium should be paid for an increase in the speed of production.

Piece rates are merely one kind of wage, and all wages should be frequently raised or lowered in order to secure just the right supply of labor of each kind in each plant during each shift. Stability of piece rates is certain to reduce the mobility of labor and impede the most economic allocation of labor. No piece rate will ever be exactly right, and every rate which is too high or too low will attract too many or too few workers.

Fortunately, reductions in piece rates in a Socialist state would not have the undesirable effect characteristic of them under Capitalism. Under Socialism it would be obvious to all workers that piece rates were cut, not because the workers have increased their efforts or because the employer desired to increase his profit, but because workers in other trades were attracted by the high wages and desired to share them, thus indicating that they were too high.

Moreover, high piece rates alone would have the same effect whether the workers already enjoying them deliberately soldiered or worked hard. The prospect of being paid average daily wages for light work is almost as attractive as the prospect of being paid high wages for hard work. Hence systematic soldiering would not serve to exclude additional workers and thus maintain an unduly high piece rate if labor were mobile. Likewise, if certain workers increased their earnings by intensifying their efforts, this would not attract outside piece workers into their fields and require the lowering of the piece rate, for outside piece workers would be free to do the same in their own trades. Consequently, workers would feel free to produce at maximum capacity without fear of piece-rate cuts caused by their increased efforts. Cuts would be made only if the group were receiving an unfairly high income and after this fact had been demonstrated either by the eagerness of other workers to get the jobs receiving this rate, or by a monetary loss due to overproduction.

When it is necessary to cut the piece rates paid for a certain kind of work in order to eliminate a marginal loss by reducing both the costs of production and the number of workers, this should be done, not by reducing uniformly the piece rates in question, but by reducing the estimated value of the piece upon which the operation in question has been performed. This would result in disproportional reductions in the rates paid for different units of a given output if a differential piece rate is being used, and, in any case, would alter the minimum output necessary to cover fixed costs plus the variable costs involved. In other words, if a straight piece rate on output over a certain minimum is used, the point at which this piece rate begins, as well as the amount of the piece rate itself, would be altered. It would be quite unsound to alter either the minimum or the rate without altering the other.

II. Incentive Time Wages

A very considerable number of workers must continue to receive a time wage of some kind because their work is not adapted to payment by the piece. Most office workers, sales clerks, and service employees come under this classification.

However, the time wages used in a Socialist economy may be incentive wages. This end can be achieved by raising or lowering all salaries at regular intervals in such a way as to reward increased productivity. These changes in salary should be based in part upon available records concerning the efficiency and output of the individual, but must also be based upon the judgment of superiors. While the judgment of superiors is always imperfect and biased, and for these reasons much less desirable as a basis for determining wage differentials than measurable data concerning quantity and quality of output, it does provide a practical basis for incentive wages.

It would be well, also, to require workers to hand in confidential written valuations of their fellow workers in order to aid executives in the revision of time wages. In such cases, the judgment of a group is superior to the judgment of a single individual.

It is worthy of note that commissions on sales, an important form of incentive wage under Capitalism, would no longer be economical in a Socialist economy. They are essentially a method of stimulating aggressive salesmanship, and such sales effort is not only unnecessary but definitely wasteful under either Capitalism or Socialism. All salesmen should be paid time wages, and their salary should be based upon the intelligence and efficiency shown by them in helping purchasers to find what they need. This will require telling customers not to buy something as frequently as it will require urging them to buy something.

In a Socialist economy a maximum limit to wage income should be set in order to prevent a few workers from receiving excessive incomes. Probably a limit of three times the average wage would suffice. Since the average wage would be considerably above the minimum wage, this would permit a variation in income of at least one to five. With an average wage of $4,000, for instance, some workers could be paid as little as $2,000 and others as much as $12,000 a year, but no worker could receive more than $12,000 without exceeding this limit.

The number of individuals affected by this exception to the above principles of wage determination would, as already indicated, be very small. In 1940 less than 1 percent of all wage and salary receivers in the United States were paid more than $5,000 for their labor. Most incomes over $5,000 were the result of private ownership of land and capital, and were not due to high salaries.

Under Socialism, as under Capitalism, it would be perfectly possible for one man like Caruso or Edison to produce a million dollars' worth of net utility in one year. The maximum suggested above would limit the wages paid such men to three times the average wage income. This is probably desirable for a number of reasons. All of the arguments quoted previously in favor of equal wages apply here and might be repeated as arguments in favor of such a limitation. Moreover, the most important argument in favor of unequal wages, the need for special incentives to increased production, has less force in this case. Caruso would have sung as well and as much for $10,000 a year as for $1,000,000 a year. Indeed, the payment of huge earned incomes such as $1,000,000 a year probably reduces rather than increases the incentive of the person who receives it to work an additional hour because it enormously reduces the marginal utility of additional pay for additional output.

Even if the maximum salary of a Caruso or a Charlie Chaplin is limited to perhaps three times the average wage, the method of salary determination should still offer incentives to increased efforts. In other words, the salary should vary according to the amount and quality of work done even though the marginal increase or decrease in salary would be far less than the accompanying marginal increase or decrease in value of work done.

To provide a sound basis for wise promotion and for setting incentive salaries, special pains should be taken to evaluate the ability and efficiency of all senior executives. It will be easier to achieve this evaluation of executive ability under Socialism than it now is under Capitalism. In a Socialist economy all executives in an industry will be subordinate to a single central management which will possess detailed information, collected on a uniform basis, concerning their achievements. Thus, intelligent comparison and evaluation of ability will be possible on an industry-wide basis for the first time.

Limitation of salaries paid to the most productive workers is not the only method of restricting the income of such individuals. It would be perfectly possible for the employing organization to pay them a salary fully equal to their productivity, and for the nation to appropriate the excess share of such incomes through an income tax. This method would have the advantage of making possible the more accurate distribution of such individuals among alternative employers by means of competitive bidding. Such bidding would also facilitate and encourage a more accurate measurement of the productivity of the individuals affected. Finally, it would make money costs a more accurate measure of true costs.

On the other hand, the payment of salaries indicating personal productivity as measured by market values, and the use of income taxes to recapture a major portion of such incomes, would make men who earn such salaries fully conscious of an apparent discrimination against them, and might cause much hard feeling among a class whose morale is of great significance to the nation. Far more significant as an objection is the fact that there is no method by which the individual productivity of very gifted men can be measured. Under Capitalism the use of market values results in the payment of $1,000,000 a year to a child movie star and the payment of $10,000 a year or less to men like Pasteur and Sibelius. Market values cannot even roughly indicate the productivity of the most valuable workers because these values do not include consumers' and producers' surpluses on price goods and do not cover the field of free goods at all.

III. Bonuses and Penalties

Under Capitalism, cash bonuses are frequently used to supplement time wages as a special inducement to increased effort. Bonuses and penalties may also be used with either a piece rate or a time wage in order to achieve certain special purposes such as less breakage, fewer accidents, steady attendance, length of service, etc.

It will be proper to continue the use of bonuses for some of these purposes under Socialism. The general principle to be followed in determining all questions concerning the use of both bonuses and penalties is that they should be used only to pass on to the worker real savings or costs due to his conduct and not already reflected in his regular wage. If by arriving at work promptly every day in the year a worker saves the management $10 a year, it is proper to pass this saving on to him in the form of a bonus. An alternative but less desirable method would be to include this sum in his regular wage and impose a small fine for every tardy arrival at work. Bonuses can be used to accomplish the same result as fines, and they are much more popular with workers.

Perhaps the most important use of bonuses should be to improve the quality of the work done by men working under piece rates. Piece rates tend to increase quantity at the expense of quality of work done, and must be supplemented by careful inspection and the use of suitable bonuses or penalties in order to maintain quality. This is not true of time wages, for they should be based upon the quality as well as upon the quantity of work done by the individual.

However, the regular piece rate should reward the worker fully for all changes in quantity of output. There is no need for an additional bonus over and above a properly determined piece rate or time wage in order to stimulate workers to increase their productivity.

Profit-sharing bonuses would be unjustified under Socialism if profits were determined and used as recommended in this book, for such profits would merely reflect underproduction and would no more indicate increased output per worker than would properly determined losses.

No worker should be given a bonus merely because of length of service. All wage differences should be based upon real differences in personal productivity. The sole justification for wage differences is that they increase output. However, workers should pay the full cost of labor turnover in order to encourage them to reduce it to the optimum level. Thus seniority would always indicate that a worker had profited by avoiding the cost of changing to another job since some specific date.

PART SEVEN

APPLIED THEORY

CHAPTER XVI. AGRICULTURE

A. INTRODUCTION

Previous chapters have been devoted to problems common to many different industries and to principles applicable to many or all branches of the national economy. This and succeeding chapters will be devoted to the application of these principles to certain branches of the national economy. Agriculture and animal husbandry are treated in the present chapter.

It is not necessary to explain the application to each industry of all the principles previously set forth. The application of some of them is obvious and requires no explanation. In other cases, an explanation of the application to one industry will suffice for all industries. The following chapters are devoted to major problems and to the application of those principles which seem to require additional explanation either because they are new or because they would require drastic changes in present methods of organization and/or operation.

Agriculture has always presented a difficult problem to Socialists— both to political agitators and to economic theorists. It has presented a serious obstacle to the political success of Socialism because peasants and farmers usually own a small amount of land or capital which they fear to lose; they are relatively low in educational status; and are remote from the urban centers of·civilization and Socialist influence.

Agriculture has presented an equally difficult problem to Socialist theorists because it is, from the standpoint of economic evolution, the most backward division of the national economy. It is the last large industry to remain in the stage of economic individualism, the stage in economic evolution which ordinarily follows Feudalism and precedes Capitalism. Since Socialism is the natural and inevitable outgrowth of Capitalism, it is much easier to introduce Socialist methods of organization and production in an industry which has attained the stage of Capitalism, than in an industry which has not yet reached that stage of development. Socialism must transform agriculture directly from an individualistic into a Socialistic industry. It is this necessity for the omission of one stage of economic evolution which makes agriculture a difficult problem for Socialist theorists.

The fact that agriculture is still in the stage of individualism in most Capitalist countries does not prove that Capitalist and Socialist forms of organization are unsuited to agriculture; it merely proves that evolution does not proceed at the same pace in all industries.[1] Different branches of industry have passed from individualism to Capitalism at different times and the fact that, at any given time, certain branches of industry were still individualistic while others had already attained the stage of Capitalism, did not, as later development has demonstrated, prove that the backward industries were unsuited to Capitalist forms of organization and production.

B. ORGANIZATION UNDER AGRICULTURAL TRUST

All agriculture and animal husbandry should be placed under the control of a single national Agricultural Trust. The importance of this trust would warrant individual representation on the Executive Committee of the Supreme Economic Council.

It may be objected that the inclusion of all agriculture and animal husbandry under a single trust would render that organization unwieldy in size or, at least, far larger than any other trust or department. At present the farm population of the United States is about 25,000,000, or one-fifth of the total population. Under Socialism, however, the number of workers required to produce raw food products will be cut in half at least once, and probably two or three times, by the development of large-scale production, by the increased use of farm machinery and fertilizer, and by the transfer of a considerable share of the work now done by farmers to other industries.[2] Thus, while the Agricultural Trust would

---

[1] Adam Smith, and many later writers, assumed that, since joint stock companies or corporations had as yet become dominant in only a few industries, they were not suited to other industries such as manufacturing.

"The only trades which it seems possible for a joint stock company to carry on successfully, without an exclusive privilege, are those of which all operations are capable of being reduced to what is called a routine, or to such a uniformity of method as admits of little or no variation. Of this kind is, first, the banking trade; secondly, the trade of insurance from fire, and from sea risk and capture in time of war; thirdly, the trade of making or maintaining a navigable cut or canal; and, fourthly, the similar trade of bringing water for the supply of a great city. . . . .

"Except the four trades above mentioned, I have not been able to recollect any other in which the three circumstances, requisite for rendering reasonable the establishment of a joint stock company, concur." *Wealth of Nations*, Book V, chapter i, Part III, Article I, pp. 340, 343.

To say today that large-scale production is not suited to agriculture because it has not yet become a dominant feature of agriculture would be to repeat almost precisely the same error made by Adam Smith in regard to joint stock companies.

[2] Farm clothing should be washed in Service Trust laundries, butter should be made in creameries controlled by the Food Processing Trust, farmhouses should be repaired and maintained by the Housing Trust, etc.

be a large organization, it would not require more than a minor fraction of the number of workers now engaged in agriculture.

The first subdivision of the Agricultural Trust should be along functional lines, perhaps with separate major divisions for field crops, garden crops, orchard crops, and animal husbandry. Each major division should probably also be subdivided according to specific food products or groups of similar food products. Then, and only then, should geographical subdivision take place. The units of geographical subdivision need not be uniform for different divisions, but should rather conform to the special need of each division.

Individual farms should be organized along functional lines as prescribed in the Taylor system of scientific management. Field workers should be responsible to a number of different foremen, each of whom would perform different supervisory functions. It should be noted that giant farms are peculiarly suited to the application of the entire Taylor system, since their operations cannot be made almost completely automatic or routine like those of a factory using a conveyor assembly system.

C. PERSONNEL POLICIES

The hours of labor should be reduced to thirty hours a week, and every worker should be given eight weeks' vacation with pay each year. A full year's work and income should be guaranteed to all workers.

All persons who apply for employment should be given jobs corresponding to their training and experience within six months after their application has been made. No employee should ever be discharged except on grounds of utter incompetence, insanity, or criminality; and outside agencies, such as health and police, should diagnose these cases and place them in institutions before the Agricultural Trust finds it necessary to act independently.

If too many persons apply for work or if developments such as the introduction of labor-saving equipment and methods make necessary a reduction in the number of workers employed, this end should be achieved by a uniform reduction in wages and salaries paid rather than by the discharge of selected employees.

All workers should be required to undergo intensive vocational training for their job either before or immediately after employment. After the initial period of intensive training, formal vocational training should be continued for perhaps two hours a week on company time, as long as the worker is employed.

All junior executives should be required to have a B.S. degree in

Agriculture, and all senior executives should be required to have a Ph.D. or Sc.D. in Agriculture. Both junior and senior executives should be required to take and pass one university course on some field of Agriculture each year. All promotions of executives should be based in part upon the quality of their work in these classes.

The number of Negro and women employees should be increased until they constitute at every professional and executive level about the same percentage which they constitute of the entire working force in agriculture.

These personnel policies apply to all industries and they will therefore not be repeated in later chapters.

D. THE UTILIZATION OF LAND

All land which can be used for agricultural purposes without resulting in a net loss should be farmed by the Agricultural Trust. Land too poor to yield a crop sufficient to pay all expenses and land for which other trusts offer a rent higher than the Agricultural Trust can afford should not be used for agricultural purposes.

The total land area which should be farmed is not an independently determinable quantity, but is merely the sum of the totals which should be used for specific crops and purposes. The amount of land used for each individual crop or purpose should be increased until the marginal land-unit yields neither a marginal profit or loss. Rents obtainable from the best alternative use of land should always be treated as costs in determining such profits and losses.

In other words, the correct principle concerning the use of agricultural land is that each piece of land should be so used that it yields the maximum economic rent. Land rent is a pure surplus over costs. The use of land should be such as to maximize this surplus, since this will serve to maximize per capita net utilitum, the proper purpose of all economic activity.

The above principle should also control the determination of the intensive margin or margins of cultivation. The intensity of cultivation on each individual piece of land should be set at that point which results in a maximum economic rent from the land in question. This point can only be discovered by scientific experimentation.

Under Capitalism the farmer has no accurate idea of the pure economic rent produced by different crops on the same field because he does not use cost accounting. Hence he has no sound basis for determining what crops to produce. Even if he adopted a sound system of cost accounting, which is costly and impractical for a small one-family farm, he might decide to produce the wrong crop in order to give himself more work and a larger gross income. Under Socialism, no need for work would exist to cause a socially uneconomic selection of crops. Each farm would be large enough, and have a sufficiently mobile supply of labor, to permit a relatively perfect equilibrium between the supply of labor and the demand for labor resulting from production of those crops which yield a maximum rent.

The general system of control of land use set forth in the preceding paragraphs may appear to be somewhat different from the system of control prescribed in an earlier chapter for industry as a whole. In that chapter it was asserted that marginal profits and losses should be the chief guides used in controlling production, since profits indicate underproduction and the losses indicate overproduction. Actually there is no conflict but rather perfect agreement between the two systems of production control. In agriculture a marginal profit always indicates that economic rent could be increased by an increase in the volume of production, and vice versa.

E. THE SCALE OF PRODUCTION

The industrial revolution and the rise of Capitalism have had less effect upon the scale of production in agriculture than in any other major industry. The increase in the scale of production in manufacturing, transportation, and commerce has resulted in the steady socialization of production in these fields. In agriculture, however, the most common unit of production is still the individual family. Hence the transition to Socialism will occasion a more radical increase in the scale of production in this field than in any other large industry.

Under Socialism the size of the average farm ought to be enormously increased for a number of reasons. Large-scale farming makes possible in agriculture that division of labor which has so greatly increased the productivity of factory labor during the past two centuries. It permits more extensive use of the ablest and best-trained farm managers and agronomists, who ought to be placed in control of large farms so as to give the maximum scope to their talents. It reduces the cost of maintaining fences and the unused area of ground they occupy. It makes economical the use of more expensive and more specialized labor-saving machinery. It makes possible economical sowing by airplanes, plowing with electric plows, harvesting with giant combines, etc. It is necessary in order to permit tractors and other machines to move long distances without frequently stopping and turning around. Finally, it will greatly aid the collection of isolated farm families into large villages or small cities.[3]

The economy of large-scale agriculture has been repeatedly demonstrated under Capitalism.[4] In agriculture as elsewhere under Capitalism, however, the individual entrepreneur has either refused or been unable to make the most of scientific investigation and the experience of others. This is one of the greatest and most characteristic defects of Capitalism. Capitalism has accumulated a vast store of scientific knowledge in every field, but only a few exceptional entrepreneurs ever make use of the bulk of it, and then very slowly and reluctantly.

The economy of large-scale agriculture was clearly shown by an investigation conducted as far back as 1900 by the United States Government. A table published in the *Census* of that year showed a variation in income (value of products not fed, less rent, interest, hired labor, and fertilizer) from $311 for farms averaging 72 acres to $2,220 for farms averaging 4,237 acres. If we assume the farmer's labor to have been worth $2,000 a year, the only class of farms to produce this wage was that averaging 4,237 acres. For all other classes an average loss would be shown.

Only actual experiment can determine whether the average farm should have ten thousand acres, a hundred thousand acres, or a million acres. The optimum farm size will not be the same for different crops and regions. The principal factor limiting optimum size will be the cost of transporting workers to and from the farm village. The reasons why all farm workers should live in farm villages are explained below.

If farm laborers are driven to and from their work in the fields in trucks or busses, it would seem practical for each farm village to care for all land within a radius of at least ten miles. This would give a farm an area of about 750,000 acres, not all of which would be suitable for cultivation, however. The average round trip to and from field work would total only about 15 miles.

The population of a village farming 750,000 acres of wheat land would probably be between five and ten thousand people, assuming no additional industry but including all workers required for retailing and other local services. Some crops, such as beans, potatoes, and sugar beets, require about twice as much labor per acre as wheat; and still other crops, such as oats, barley, and rye, require only about a third as much labor. Five hundred to one thousand such village farms ought to be able to farm all the land which should be farmed in the United States.

---

[3] For other advantages of large-scale production see pp. 239–42.
[4] G. P. Warren, *Farm Management* (1918), pp. 239–69.

F. THE FARM VILLAGE

The isolated individual farmhouse should be abandoned under Socialism. All farm workers and executives should live in large villages or small cities.

Notable economic benefits would result from the concentration of farm population in villages and cities. In the first place, all farm children would have superior educational advantages for the same educational expenditure.[5] Education, like all other economic activities, can be done more efficiently and cheaply on a large scale than on a small scale. That is why, for the same expenditure, urban schools are everywhere able to give superior educational advantages. The little red schoolhouse, with one teacher and eight or twelve grades, goes with small individual farms. Consolidated country schools require pupils to travel long distances to and from school. Concentration of farm population in villages would place schools much closer to their students. Moreover, educational and cultural advantages for farm adults would also be increased. Adults would be much nearer the lecture hall, the laboratory, the university, the museum, and the exhibition hall.

A similar increase in opportunities for amusement, recreation, and social life would result from concentration of farm population in villages and cities. Theaters, clubhouses, swimming pools, tennis courts, golf courses, etc., would be readily accessible to all farm workers. Such facilities can only be provided economically for an urban population.

Concentration of farm population in villages and cities would markedly reduce the cost of all public utility services. Water, gas, electricity, sewer, and telephone connections cannot be provided as economically for isolated farmhouses as for city dwellings.

The cost of country roads and highways would be greatly reduced by the elimination of isolated farmhouses and the small fields which go with them. If the size of fields were increased ten to a hundredfold, country roads would be much farther apart than at present, and the total mileage necessary to serve a given area would be reduced proportionally. At present, country roads must be numerous enough to provide access to every individual farmhouse.

Concentration of farm dwellings in villages and cities would make

[5] In enumerating the disadvantages of individualistic agriculture, John Black has listed several of the points discussed in this section.

"10. Roads, schools, protection of health, police and fire protection are more expensive to maintain—so expensive in relation to available resources that they are not adequately provided for in most areas." Reprinted by permission from *Agricultural Reform in the U.S.*, by John D. Black (copyrighted, 1929, by the McGraw-Hill Book Company, Inc.).

house construction and maintenance more economical since both construction and maintenance work could then be done on a larger scale and
with an increased division of labor. The time that plumbers, carpenters,
and other building-trade workers now spend in going to and from isolated
farmhouses would also be saved.

Still another advantage of housing farm workers in villages is the
increased facility for shopping and the increased economy in distributing
commodities and services which this would make possible. When living
in isolated farmhouses, farmers and their wives must travel for many
miles to reach the village store. This wastes time and money. In a
Socialist farm village every family would be within a five- or ten-minute
walk, not ride, of a large retail store.

Likewise, living in villages would enable farm workers to buy bakery
bread and pasteurized creamery milk, to send their soiled clothes to a
modern laundry or dry-cleaning plant, and in many other ways would
permit them to benefit from the increased division of labor made possible
by urban life. The farmer's home would not continue to be a small and
inefficient manufacturing plant in which clothes are made, mended,
washed, and ironed; in which butter and cheese are produced; in which
tools and machinery are repaired; in which fruits and vegetables are
preserved, etc. Indeed, it would no longer even be necessary to prepare
meals in the farm worker's home. He would be free to eat in a public
dining room if he so desired.

Concentration of farm population in villages would facilitate the
administration of the large farms which, for other reasons, ought to be
typical of Socialist agriculture. Five-thousand farm workers can be controlled as a unit far more effectively if they live in the same place than if
they are scattered among isolated farmhouses. It would be possible to
use time cards, to group men in gangs according to daily needs, to inspect machinery and equipment after use, to use written instruction cards,
to secure daily cost and production reports, and so forth, if all workers
set out from and return to the same central point each day.

One further advantage of village life for farmers may be stated.
If farmers lived in villages and worked on large farms, they would be
able to work in groups much more of the time. Social labor is more
interesting and less wearisome than isolated individual labor. Conversation
and companionship make the time pass more quickly and may stimulate
competition in speed or efficiency. Marx observed that "mere social contact begets in most industries an emulation and a stimulation of the
animal spirits that heighten the efficiency of each individual workman."[6]

[6] Marx, *Capital*, I, 358.

G. DIVISION OF LABOR

Under Capitalism there is insufficient division of labor in agriculture. The average farmer raises several crops, cares for several different kinds of animals, repairs his house and machinery, does his own bookkeeping (if any), purchases his own supplies, and so on. This wide variety of farm labor is the principal reason why the efficiency of labor in agriculture has failed to advance anywhere near as rapidly as the efficiency of labor in industry during the past two centuries.

The enormous increase in the scale of agricultural production brought about by Socialism will make possible a very detailed and comprehensive division of labor. All building maintenance in a Socialist farm community should be cared for by the local branch of the National Building Trust. All repair of farm machinery should be done by skilled mechanics, each of whom perhaps could specialize in the repair of one particular kind of machine or in one particular repair operation on one kind of machine. The purchasing of supplies and the selling of farm products should be handled by specialists carefully trained for this work. All accounting should be centralized and carried on by a special staff of cost accountants, each of whom is a specialist in some phase of cost accounting. Moreover, in the actual conduct of field work a much greater degree of division of labor would be possible. Finally, there should be a very clear division of labor between executives, field foremen, and farm laborers. The principles of scientific management should be carefully applied and all executive work organized functionally. No clerical or planning work whatsoever should be left to the individual worker. All planning, control, and clerical work should be carried on at the central office of each farm by a special planning department, just as in a factory using the Taylor system. Farm managers should be highly trained agronomists specializing in the crops or animals raised on the farm they manage.

H. IMPROVEMENT OF PLANTS AND ANIMALS

It is difficult to overemphasize the enormous opportunities for valuable scientific research work in agriculture. The small scale of agriculture under Capitalism has prevented the individual producer from developing a research department as the large industrial producer has done. Government and university research was almost nonexistent until the last few decades, and what is still more significant, the independent farmer has been extremely backward in applying the results of the little scientific research that has been done.

The improvement of plants and animals ought to be one of the most important tasks of both farm managers and of scientific research workers in agriculture. A careful study of the variations in efficiency and capacity of 26 registered Holstein cows under the same management in Wisconsin in 1909–11 showed a variation of about 400 percent in value of product minus cost of feed, between the least efficient and the most efficient cow, and a variation of 100 percent between the best cow and the median cow. Raising the level of all cows in the nation to that of the best cows now in use would increase total output of dairy products by 100 percent, without any increased cost. This would be perfectly feasible in a very short time under Socialism but it will take a century or two under Capitalism. Someone in authority must be given power to enforce immediate adoption of all proven agricultural reforms if they are ever to be quickly and universally adopted.

Plant improvement also offers apparently infinite opportunities for progress. In a Socialist economy all seed should be supplied by a special research institute devoted exclusively to the task of plant improvement and to supplying each year a proper quantity of the best available seed. Each year should show a definite improvement in the quality of this seed, since only the best portion of the previous year's crop should be used for seed purposes.

I. UTILIZATION OF CAPITAL

A Socialist government should enormously increase the investment of capital in agricultural equipment. The production of agricultural products per farm worker varies between nations and between states in the United States in close correlation with the amount of capital per worker. The following tabulation[7] indicates the magnitude of these variations in 1928:

Country or State	Number of Horses per Worker	Index of Volume of Production per Worker
Italy	0.19	45
France	0.37	90
Belgium	0.38	117
Germany	0.55	119
United Kingdom	0.88	126
United States	2.05	292
Alabama	.81	112
Indiana	2.46	365
Nebraska	4.71	910

[7] United States Department of Agriculture, *Bulletin 1348*.

The fact that these differences are not due chiefly to the relative abundance or fertility of land is clearly indicated by the remarkable variation within the United States. The great economic need for additional agricultural capital is further demonstrated by the following table which shows the high marginal productivity of capital in agriculture in different parts of the United States.[8]

Location	Year	Returns on Working Capital
Sumter County, Georgia (colored)	1913	20.2
Sumter County, Georgia (white)	1913	24.9
Clinton County, Indiana	1910	14.2
Clinton County, Indiana	1914	20.5
Clinton County, Indiana	1919	27.4
Chester County, Pennsylvania	1911	19.0
Guthrie and Green Counties, Iowa	1910	19.7
Cass and Menard Counties, Iowa	1910	33.5
Lenawee County, Michigan	1911	16.1
Tama County, Iowa	1918	24.6

The supply of capital devoted to agriculture should be increased until the net return falls to the level of the average return upon capital invested in manufacturing, industry, and commerce. The table showing the marginal productivity of capital in agriculture only indicates the opportunity for additional investment of capital on the small farms characteristic of individualistic agriculture. The vast increase in the scale of agricultural production under Socialism would open many new fields for the application of existing machinery and many new opportunities for the invention of new machinery.

Not only will Socialism greatly increase the investment of capital in farm machinery; it will also make necessary the redesigning of nearly all existing farm equipment. For instance, modern tractors, plows, and seeders are designed for small farms. A much larger size, however, is needed on a 200,000-acre farm than on a 200-acre farm. The real economy of large-scale farming has not yet been indicated—in part, at least, because as yet the ideal machinery for it has not been designed or produced.

A Socialist state should take pains to secure a far more complete utilization of movable farm machinery than is customary under Capitalism. As long as farming is carried on by millions of small farmers, an enormous amount of idle machine time is inevitable. Every farmer has his own plows, tractors, seeders, etc., and he uses them only on his own land. Under Socialism all movable farm machinery whose use is highly seasonal should be managed by separate organizations similar to the Ma-

[8] W. G. Spillman, *Farm Management*, p. 4.

chine Tractor Stations in the U.S.S.R. Crops like corn, wheat, oats, cotton, etc., are planted and harvested at different times of the year according to latitude. Machinery for these crops should move from the South to the North throughout the planting and harvesting seasons in order that the entire amount of machine work can be performed by the minimum number of machines. These periodic migrations should cover long distances and the equipment should be returned to the point of origin by truck or railroad transportation. A separate organization to care for this farm equipment is necessary in order to fix responsibility for its care in a single place. If tractors are used on dozens of different farms by managers, none of whom are definitely responsible for their condition at the end of the season, costly misuse is likely to result.

The Machine Tractor Division of the Agricultural Trust should attempt to develop alternative uses for its equipment in off seasons. Tractors, for instance, might be rented to the National Construction Trust at a price which would just cover variable expenses and contribute something towards fixed costs.

Another expedient which should probably be used to increase the utilization of farm equipment is night work during rush seasons. When the demand for farm machinery is at its maximum, machines should probably be operated by different drivers twenty-four hours a day. As explained previously (pp. 255–58), the actual feasibility of night work always depends upon the increase in wage rates necessary to attract night workers and upon the savings in capital costs made possible thereby.

J. SPECIALIZED VERSUS DIVERSIFIED FARMING

Both specialized and diversified farming have their advantages under Capitalism, but not all of these advantages will continue under Socialism. A very important reason for diversified farming under Capitalism, and one which undoubtedly causes diversification of products in many cases where it is otherwise uneconomic, is the desire to reduce the risk from crop failures. In a Socialist economy, however, the losses from crop failures should not be borne by individuals and, hence, should play no part in encouraging crop diversification on individual farms. Another reason for crop diversification under Capitalism which will cease to apply under Socialism is the desire for division of income among different seasons so that it will not all be spent before the next cash receipts come in.

On the other hand, there are considerations which favor specialized farming under Capitalism which either will not exist or will be much less significant under Socialism. Lack of adequate capital compels many farmers to restrict their variety of crops and neglect profitable opportunities.

On a small private farm, moreover, it is frequently wise to concentrate all efforts on one crop in order to achieve a few of the economies possible from an increased volume of production. This consideration will not apply so strongly on the enormous farms of a Socialist state. Other factors being equal, however, specialization will always be desirable, since it will make possible a higher division of labor and a larger scale of production.

There are two very vital reasons for a certain degree of crop diversification. The first of these is the need of the soil for the restoration of the elements taken from it. Constant one-crop farming eventually ruins the soil or makes it necessary to incur heavy expense for fertilizer. In most cases, therefore, crop rotation is desirable. Crop rotation, however, does not require growing more than one crop at a time. It only requires a regular change in the crops grown.

The second and most important reason for crop diversification is to even out the demand for labor and to secure increased use of farm equipment. Most crops are highly seasonal in their demand upon the farmer's time. Winter wheat requires work in only two or three months of the year. Sixty percent of the machine and labor time is required in a single month, and 50 percent of the work must be done in July. The bulk of machine and labor time devoted to corn is required in May, June, and September. It is obvious, therefore, that specialized farming in these crops wastes machine and labor time. Therefore, the state Agricultural Trust should develop a system of diversified farming for these crops which will make possible maximum use of men and machines and which, at the same time, will produce that combination of products which yields the maximum rent per acre of land.

K. MAINTAINING THE FERTILITY OF THE SOIL

No system of farming can be considered economical unless it maintains the fertility of the land. Capitalist agriculture is notoriously unsatisfactory in this respect. In many parts of the United States, one-crop farming has been practiced until the fertility of the soil has been seriously reduced, if not destroyed. There are a number of reasons for this, none of which should be effective under Socialism. In the first place, the very abundance of fertile land in the United States has caused farmers to pay little attention to the problem of maintaining fertility. In the second place, few farmers ever have the capital necessary to permit proper rotation of crops and optimum use of commercial fertilizer. During periods of low agricultural prices this is particularly true, and during periods of high agricultural prices farmers save every cent they can to pay off the mortgage or to buy more land. Finally, few farms are managed by men who have the education or knowledge necessary to devise and carry out an economical but effective system of maintaining soil fertility.

These difficulties should not exist in a Socialist economy. The agricultural units should have an ample supply of capital. They should be managed in accordance with social needs rather than private profit. The task of preserving soil fertility should be entrusted to highly trained experts who should have sufficient authority to carry out their plans.

The fertility of all soil is constantly being reduced by erosion by wind or water. This loss is probably greater than that due to cropping. The problem of reducing losses from erosion is largely a community or social problem. The Agricultural Trust of a Socialist state should take vigorous measures to reduce the loss from erosion. The principal means should be keeping the soil in sod, especially during the winter; plowing on contours; and terracing the land.

American farmers now use less than one-third as much fertilizer as they should. Under Socialism, each farm manager should follow the advice of experts and increase his application of fertilizer to the optimum level, which would mean an immediate average increase of over 200 percent in the use of fertilizer. The use of lime, humus, and other soil-building elements not ordinarily called fertilizer should also be increased to the optimum level set by qualified specialists in soil care.

The manufacture and use of the cheap low concentrates now commonly used by farmers should be discontinued, and only high concentrates approved by qualified experts should be produced. As recently as 1940, the best-selling fertilizer formula in the United States contained 24 percent sand by weight because farmers had an irrational preference for weak fertilizers. Highly concentrated fertilizers are much superior because they reduce the costs of transportation, distribution, and application.

Scientific crop rotation is another important means of preserving and increasing the fertility of the soil. Under Socialism, expert agronomists should be employed as advisors on crop rotation, and all farm managers should take their advice on proper rotation of crops.

The system of crop rotation used should vary from district to district. It should be built up around the staple crop of the region and ought to take numerous other factors, such as distance from market, type of soil, climate, etc., into consideration. It should be designed so that, by carrying different fields in different crops at the same time, the advantages of crop diversification as well as crop rotation may be secured.

In addition to improving the fertility of the soil, crop rotation performs other valuable services. It helps to control weeds, insects, and plant diseases; it may keep the land occupied with crops a greater part of the time; it allows for the alternation of deep and shallow-rooted crops; it may provide for a balanced removal of plant food; it may control toxic substances; and it systematizes farming.[9]

The basic principle that no conservation measures are desirable unless they pay in dollars and cents should never be violated, however. Conservation of soil fertility must not become an end in itself supported upon sentimental grounds.

L. SCIENTIFIC MANAGEMENT

In so far as is feasible, all the basic principles of scientific management should be applied in the management of individual Socialist farms. This involves a complete revolution in farm management, even in the best methods of management on the few large farms operating under Capitalism. A brief summary of these principles of scientific management and their application to farm management will help to make this clear.

The first principle of scientific management is job analysis. It involves careful time and motion studies of all individual operations performed by farm workers, as well as a careful study of farm machines, tools, and supplies used in each operation. Job analysis has increased the productivity of industrial and building-trades workers by 100 percent or more on the average, and there is every reason to believe that it will prove equally profitable to Socialist agriculture.

The second basic principle of scientific management is proper selection and training of employees. Extensive research should be carried out to determine what physical and mental characteristics are necessary for high productivity in each of the many occupations and operations to be found on Socialist farms. Once these facts have been determined, minimum physical and mental requirements should be set up for each occupation and operation, and no worker who does not meet these requirements should be allowed to enter the occupation or perform the operation in question. All those who are accepted should be carefully trained in the standard methods developed as a result of job analysis.

A third basic principle of scientific management is the use of scientifically determined incentive wages, most commonly in the form of piece rates. It is of the utmost importance that a practical and comprehensive system of piece rates and incentive wages and salaries be employed in Socialist agriculture. The principal objection to factory farms voiced by bourgeois economists is that they would destroy the incentives which result from individualistic farming. This objection is probably unsound in any case, since factory industry replaced handicraft industry before incentive

[9] G. P. Warren, *Farm Management* (1918), pp. 402–15.

wages were developed; but such an objection can be easily answered by the use of piece rates and other incentive wages on Socialist farms.

Under Capitalism, the development of piece rates in agriculture has been retarded by the fact that four-fifths of all farm work is done by farmers and their immediate families, and by the fact that work on a small individual farm cannot be standardized. Both of these obstacles to the development of piece rates for agricultural work will disappear under Socialism. On the large factory farms of a Socialist economy there will be a division and a standardization of labor which will make piece rates practical and desirable for most of the work done. All work, including managerial activity, which cannot be placed upon a piecework basis should be placed upon some incentive wage or salary basis which will make income vary with individual effort as closely as possible.

A fourth fundamental principle of scientific management is that of central planning. On a Socialist farm there should be a complete separation between the function of planning and the function of doing. All planning of field work on each farm should be concentrated in the hands of a small group of men in the central planning office. This planning department should determine what work is to be done each day, how it is to be done, what facilities and materials are to be employed, by whom it is to be done, and when it is to be done. Written orders concerning all of these points should be delivered by the planning department to those concerned, so that they will be relieved of all planning problems.

The fifth principle of scientific management, enumerated in chapter xiii, has to do with inspection. It will be necessary to provide for adequate inspection of the product or the field after each agricultural operation. Incentive wages will increase the speed at the expense of the quality of farm work unless inspection is provided for.

The sixth basic principle of the Taylor system of scientific management, the principle of functional organization, remains to be considered. Every worker on a Socialist farm should be supervised and guided by a group of five to ten functional foremen instead of by a single foreman. Each foreman would have his own distinct function, or functions, to perform and would be a specialist in that function. About half of them would work in the planning department.

One other principle of management deserves comment here. Land, men, and capital equipment vary widely in economic productivity. It is very important that the ablest farm managers be placed upon the most fertile land in a Socialist economy. The reason for this is very simple. If two farm managers vary in ability so that, with the same facilities, one of them produces a 10 percent larger crop than the other, the absolute amount of this 10 percent gain will vary with the fertility of the soil being farmed. On very fertile land this 10 percent gain will be far greater than on marginal land. For this reason, both land and farm managers should be carefully graded according to their productivity, and the most efficient managers should be given the best land in exact correlation to their ability.

The same reasoning requires that the best workers should be employed on the most fertile farms. Likewise, the best animals and the best farm machinery should be given to the superior workers and managers.

M. UTILIZATION OF THE IDLE TIME OF FARM LABOR

One of the most important problems of agriculture, as yet unsolved under Capitalism, is that of finding work for farmers to do at times when the crops require no attention. Agriculture is the most highly seasonal of all branches of the national economy. A large force of men and much overtime labor is required to plant and harvest crops, but during many months of the year, especially in the winter, there is little for the individual farmer to do.

There are a number of possible solutions to this problem. In the first place, farm workers can be given home handicraft work to do during idle hours and months. The trouble with this solution is that handicraft work usually requires considerable skill and handicraft products may be driven off the market by machine-made wares after the great economies of Socialist production have been achieved.

A second possibility is for each farm village to have special small manufacturing plants which operate only when farm activities are at a low ebb. This requires a considerable investment in factories which stand idle about half the time. If this plan is adopted, special care should be taken to reserve for seasonal farm labor those manufacturing industries in which the principal cost of production is a labor cost, in which relatively unskilled labor is used, and in which little investment in machinery or training is required.

A third possible solution is to send farm labor to nearby cities or plant communities to work there during dull agricultural months. The objection to this plan is that it requires a double investment in housing, in the home village and in the plant community, and that it also requires investment in plant facilities which would not be utilized during part of the year. If surplus plant facilities are to be built for the use of farmers during off seasons, this surplus plant capacity might as well be in the farm villages so that the farmers can use the same housing facilities throughout the year.

Still another solution would be to co-ordinate other seasonal industries with agriculture, or to develop additional seasonal industries to be co-ordinated with it. However, under Socialism the seasonal nature of all industries except agriculture and those markedly affected by it, such as the canning industry, could be eliminated. Permitting them to continue as seasonal industries in order to provide seasonable factory employment for farmers would involve the waste of having capital equipment stand idle half the year. There is a possibility that the building industry, especially road building, might be made or left sufficiently seasonal to absorb all idle farm labor during the slack months of agricultural work without any appreciable loss due to idle capital equipment, since the building industry uses little capital equipment. Much of the equipment it does use—tractors, trucks, movable camps, etc.—would be the same as that used on large state farms. However, road building is chiefly done in the warmer months of the year when farm labor is in demand on the farm. Road building would not be a good off-season occupation for farmers unless methods of building roads economically in winter could be developed.

Nevertheless, it is of the utmost importance that some off-season occupation be found for farm labor. Almost any occupation is better than none. A Socialist government should have little difficulty in finding some useful work for farm labor in otherwise idle months. Difficulty would arise only in making a choice between various kinds of useful off-season labor. Probably the best kind of work would be in small plants located in the villages and manufacturing in large quantities single parts required for the assembly lines in large city plants. For this purpose those parts whose cost is chiefly labor cost should be selected.

N. COST ACCOUNTING

Record-keeping of all kinds is a sadly neglected art on the individual farm characteristic of Capitalism today. It should be thoroughly developed in all branches of a Socialist agriculture. Every farm should have a special accounting department which should prepare accurate cost reports, operating statements, balance sheets, etc., at periodic intervals. Central control over individual farms would be based largely upon these periodic accounting reports which must be designed to facilitate such control. Naturally, all farms should use a uniform system of cost accounting in order to make possible comparison of reports from different farms. Since agricultural cost accounting has never been carefully developed under Capitalism, an entirely new system must be devised. All we can do here is to indicate its great importance in Socialist agriculture.

CHAPTER XVII. TRANSPORTATION

A. THE ORGANIZATION OF TRANSPORTATION

As used here, the term "transportation" includes all commercial movement of commodities and passengers outside the limits of a single plant by any mode of transportation. Thus, it includes the services of post offices, express companies, pipe lines, etc., in addition to all other types of railway, highway, air, and water transportation.

Adequate and economical transportation service is extremely important in any economy. In the United States, about one-seventh of the entire national income goes to pay for commercial transportation services. More capital is invested in American railroads and highways than in all the machinery and buildings used by American industry and agriculture combined.

There is no need to attempt a complete exposition of the economic theory of Socialist transportation in this chapter. Much of this theory can be taken over intact from Capitalist transportation theory. Nor is there any need to discuss the technical problems peculiar to each of the major forms of transportation, for these are not economic problems. Only the more important and novel features of the economic theory of Socialist transportation are discussed here.

The general principles of price determination, of allocation of the factors of production, of management, etc., already set forth, apply to transportation unless qualified in this chapter. Only a few of these applications are noted in this chapter.

In a Socialist economy all forms of commercial transportation should be controlled by a single national Transportation Trust. This is an application of the principles of monopoly, functional organization, and centralization of control.

Unification of control over the various forms of transportation is necessary, in the first place, in order to secure proper co-ordination of the services they render. All transportation must be planned and controlled as a single system in order: (1) to eliminate unnecessary and costly duplication of facilities and services; (2) to achieve all the economies of large-scale management and operation, including that resulting from a greatly increased division of labor; and (3) to facilitate standardization of equipment and supplies, methods of operation and procedure, accounting forms and reports, etc.

One reason for unification of all forms of transportation which is peculiar to transportation is the need for establishment of a single respon-

345

sibility for the care of goods and materials from the moment they leave the shipper to the moment they are received by the consignee. Under Capitalism, freight ordinarily passes through the hands of two or three transportation companies before reaching its destination. If it is delayed, damaged, or lost, it is difficult to determine the blame. No one management is responsible for safe and prompt delivery.

In accordance with the principle of functional organization the national Transportation Trust should first be divided, not by regions or forms of transportation, but by function performed. Thus, there should be separate major divisions of traffic, operation, accounting, construction and maintenance, and personnel. These in turn should be subdivided functionally rather than by regions or forms of transportation.

B. OPERATING POLICIES

Monopoly and centralization of control will make possible a drastic reorganization of each form of transportation. The conditions affecting transportation are changing so rapidly that it is impossible to predict in detail the nature of this reorganization, but it is almost certain that it will involve a thoroughgoing rerouting of nearly all traffic; concentration of all traffic on a few best-located lines; a sharp reduction in the number of trains scheduled; nation-wide standardization of all rolling stock and equipment; and unification of terminal facilities. The last reform is explained in a subsequent section of this chapter.

Rerouting of traffic is necessary because competing transportation companies are accustomed to take all the traffic they can get, regardless of whether they operate over the most direct route. Thus, freight moving from Detroit to San Francisco may pass through Seattle, Portland, Los Angeles, or New Orleans on the way. The railroads operating over the indirect routes charge no higher rates, and indeed they frequently offer lower rates in order to persuade shippers to ship their goods over their lines.[1]

Concentration of traffic on a few best-located and best-equipped lines is desirable: (1) in order to reduce the total mileage of right-of-way and track that must be maintained (competition has led to much unnecessary duplication of facilities); (2) in order to make possible the use of larger

---

[1] "Class and commodity rates lower than standard all-rail rates are also made by the so-called differential all-rail routes. These routes are made up of combinations of rail lines which are not operated directly between the territories but are circuitous routes offering slower and inferior service compared with the standard direct lines. Lower rates are offered shippers to attract traffic to these 'differential' routes." E. R. Johnson, Grover G. Huebner, and G. L. Wilson, *Principles of Transportation* (Copyright by D. Appleton-Century Company, Inc., New York, 1928), p. 234.

locomotives, longer trains, and more solid through-trains; and (3) in order to secure the economies of shipment over the best line for the maximum volume of freight. At the present time, for instance, there are three major transcontinental lines operating between St. Paul and Seattle, each of which has advantages over the other two on certain parts of its route. A single main line should be formed out of the best parts of each of the three present lines, and all through rail traffic should be concentrated on this ideal route.

A sharp reduction in the number of scheduled trains, busses, boats, and airplanes is desirable on almost every route. Competition between competing companies has resulted in an enormous duplication of service. Frequently two trains leave for the same city at about the same time, each only half full.

Nation-wide standardization of transportation equipment would make possible very considerable savings in the manufacture, operation, and maintenance of this equipment. Production would be on a much larger scale, operation procedures would be more uniform, repairs would be more standardized, and inventories of repair parts would be smaller.

Where the volume of traffic is sufficient to justify continued operation of more than one railroad line between two cities, an almost complete specialization in use should be introduced. If there are two single-track lines, each should be used exclusively for traffic moving in one direction. If there are three single-track lines, one should be used for slow local trains moving in both directions and the other two for fast through-traffic in one direction only. Where the continued operation of four single lines or two double-track lines is economical, both fast and slow traffic should have one line each way reserved for their exclusive use. There is no practical limit to the possibility of such specialization. Every increase in the number of railroad lines or tracks between two cities makes possible and profitable some further specialization.

The principle of maximum specialization should be applied to railroad trains, and to all other carriers, as well as to railroad lines. All freight moving between New York and Chicago, for instance, should move in carload lots in solid through-trains. Competition among railroads and private initiative on the part of shippers make this impossible under Capitalism. All local freight should also move in carload lots on solid through-trains to local stops, as far as this is compatible with adequate frequency of service. More use of highway transport for short hauls from main railroad terminals would greatly increase the possibility of moving railroad freight in carload lots and solid trains, since it would reduce the number of local freight stations by 90 percent or more. Every increase in the volume of freight makes some further specialization of the sort desirable. Solid trains could even be reserved for one kind of product moving between one producing plant and one terminal warehouse if the volume of freight were large enough.

The concentration of all railroad transportation in the hands of a single Socialist trust would make economical a considerable increase in the length of the average train. Freight trains of a hundred cars are now used where the volume of traffic justifies them, but much longer trains should be commonplace under Socialism. Indeed, it should probably prove profitable to increase the length of through freight trains on main lines to several hundred cars.

C. CO-ORDINATION OF FORMS OF TRANSPORTATION

Unification of control over all forms of transportation would provide the basis necessary for the most economical co-ordination of these different forms of organization. A Socialist Transportation Trust should conduct comprehensive and continuous experiments to determine the relative cost of each method of transportation. For every transportation service, some one means of transportation is more economical than any other, and should, therefore, be used exclusively in providing that service.

At present, for instance, it seems probable that nearly all less than carload (L.C.L.) freight moving less than a hundred and fifty miles should move by highway rather than by rail, and that nearly all freight moving more than this distance should move by rail. This dividing line depends upon local conditions and will be altered by the reorganization of transportation consequent upon the introduction of Socialism, but it will always exist and should be carefully determined and used to secure the proper division of labor between rail and highway transportation. This is not being done under Capitalism.

Trucks should be used to concentrate shipments at, and deliver them from, a few main railroad stations in order to reduce the number of local stops made by freight trains. Between 50 percent and 95 percent of all local rail-freight stations might be economically dispensed with in this way.

At every remaining rail station, trucks should be used to give pickup and delivery service to all shippers and consignees. This service can be performed much more economically by a single trucking service attached to the Transportation Trust than by individual shippers and consignees. Unification of pickup and delivery service would make possible a greater division of labor, more specialized equipment, fuller utilization of equipment, smoother schedules, less congestion at rail terminals, more prompt delivery, more economical use of terminal storage and unloading facilities, single responsibility for shipment from door to door, and lower direct-handling costs.

The use of standardized detachable bodies which can be shifted from truck to flat car and back to truck by overhead cranes should be greatly developed by a Socialist Transportation Trust. Interesting experiments in this direction have already been made by Capitalist railroads, but a common monopoly of both rail and highway transportation is a necessary basis for the full development on a national scale of this or any other form of rail-highway co-ordination.

A very large proportion of the total railroad mileage in the United States should be entirely abandoned and the traffic transferred to trucks and busses. In 1928, 28 percent of the railroad mileage carried less than 2 percent of the total freight traffic.[2] The average daily traffic over this mileage was roughly equivalent to the movement of ten cars carrying 35 tons apiece; passenger traffic is negligible on such lines. In nearly all cases this traffic could be handled more economically by truck. Indeed, the railroad mileage which should now be abandoned for this reason is probably much greater than 28 percent. However, the great increase in the production of wealth consequent upon the introduction of Socialism might reduce this percentage.

Co-ordination of ocean tankers and pipe lines with rail and highway service also promises considerable savings. Pipe lines and tankers now carry the great bulk of the crude oil from field to refinery, and successful experiments in the movement of refined products by pipe line indicate that the present marked predominance of the railroads in this field will not continue long. Only when these forms of transportation are under common control, however, will it be possible to determine accurately the relative economy of each method for every service, and to act intelligently upon the basis of this information.

Co-ordination between different forms of transportation will be greatly aided by the unification of terminal facilities. Few people realize that terminal costs, the costs of handling freight at railroad terminals, exceed those of line haul. Indeed, in the case of short hauls and L.C.L. shipments, terminal costs average two to four times the line-haul costs. Obviously, the greatest opportunity for transportation economies lies in the reduction of terminal costs. This conclusion is further supported by the fact that under Capitalism there is even more obvious duplication of facilities and services in terminals than in trackage.

The first and most important step in the reduction of terminal costs

[2] Harold G. Moulton, *The American Transportation Problem*, p. 156. The entire discussion of obsolete mileage in this book is well worth reading.

should be the unification of all terminals in each city into a single unit. This would reduce the need for land and equipment, increase the scale of operations, promote division of labor and specialization of equipment, eliminate the costs of interterminal switching, be much more convenient for shippers and consignees, decrease overhead costs, speed up service, and greatly decrease the mileage of belt and spur lines.

Air, rail, and highway lines should make use of the same union terminals. This would be a great convenience to passengers transferring from one line to another or inquiring concerning schedules, reservations, and rates. The advantages for freight handling are much the same as those which would result from merger of railroad terminals.

Union passenger terminals should be located near the center of the city, but union freight terminals should be located on the outskirts of the city. Freight can be delivered by truck more cheaply than by rail, and locating freight terminals on the outskirts would sharply reduce traffic congestion. Off-rail branch terminals would be useful for the concentration and delivery of freight handled by truck.

The physical unification of all terminal facilities in each city would permit a complete replanning and reorganization of all terminal facilities. American freight yards have grown so rapidly that there has been no time to plan them properly, and what little planning has been done has been almost immediately outgrown. Awkward and antiquated layout of terminals is characteristic of American railroads.

American river and ocean port facilities are almost as antiquated and inefficient as the railroad terminals. The cause is the same in both cases, namely competitive Capitalism. A few great trusts, such as the United States Steel Corporation, have installed efficient docks and equipment for the use of their own steamers, but they are notable exceptions. A Socialist Transportation Trust should unify and co-ordinate the terminal facilities of every port.

Specialized mechanical equipment to load and unload all commodities on a large scale, chiefly by the use of car dumps, gravity conveyors, and traveling cranes, should be installed or improved at every terminal or dock. The present investment in such equipment should be increased tenfold at the same time that the number of terminals is reduced by 90 percent.

D. ESTIMATING THE NEED FOR NEW FACILITIES

The problem of determining whether to build a new railroad, highway, or canal is somewhat different from the problem of determining whether to increase the capital facilities of other industries and other forms of transportation. In accordance with one of the basic principles of production control, the supply of every commodity and service should be increased up to the point where the marginal cost of production just equals the market price of the commodity or service in question. This principle can be applied with ease to the great majority of industries, but it does not readily solve the problem of supplying transportation. The supply of railroad services, for instance, is often indivisible. In other words, an entire railroad may have to be built if any railroad service is to be provided. There is a choice in such cases between a great deal of railroad service and none at all. Similarly, when a single line reaches the limit of its capacity, we have again the choice between a very great addition to railroad service secured through double-tracking the line, and no increase at all.

Let us take up first the problem of when it is economically desirable to build a new railroad. It is economically desirable to build such a new railroad if the volume of prospective business is large enough to guarantee a surplus over all costs of construction and operation. This is true even if the new road can only be operated at a small fraction of its total capacity. So long as any possible rate structure will cover all costs, the proposed railroad is economically desirable.

There are also many cases in which it is socially desirable to construct new railroad, canal, or highway facilities in spite of the fact that they are sure to lose money. The advantage derived by shippers from the transportation services they purchase is not the same for any two shippers or for any two shipments made by the same individual. Since it is necessarily based upon charges uniform to a certain degree, the money return from the sale of transportation services cannot measure the full advantage received by shippers. In other words, there is always a large consumers' surplus. This surplus is reduced by discriminatory rates based upon ability to pay, but it is only partly eliminated thereby, and, for reasons to be noted later, such rates should not be used in a Socialist economy. Whenever this surplus exceeds the losses incurred in the provision and operation of a railway, highway, or canal, it is socially desirable to construct and operate such transportation facilities.[3] This is true whether the losses are over-all, absolute losses or marginal losses.

[3] Few bourgeois economists comprehend this principle. Thus, F. W. Taussig has written: "It follows from this obvious but forgotten fact that a railway is not economically advantageous to the community unless it pays its way. This conclusion is not in accord with a common opinion. It is often said that a railway or other means of transportation may bring gains to the community even if it be not profitable to its owners. Similarly it is often argued that a government, in operating a railway, may accept with composure a financial loss, because the people as a whole have gained something that offsets that loss. The contrary view seems the

Marginal profits and losses are equally undesirable, and almost anything that reduces the combined total of such profits and losses is socially desirable.

The task of estimating consumers' surpluses in transportation services would be greatly simplified by the consolidation of competing shippers into a few great monopolies. Whenever a Socialist Transportation Trust desires to estimate the demand for transportation service over a certain route, it need only call upon the trusts who will use such services to prepare and submit an estimate of their individual demand schedules. The Transportation Trust should then consolidate these demand schedules, estimate the consumers' surplus at various rates, determine what rate would secure maximum economic utilization of the new line, calculate the deficit at that rate, and determine whether this deficit is less than the resulting consumers' surplus. No portion of the consumers' surplus already realized through shipment over alternative routes should be counted in this total. The consumers' surplus created by railroad service is less than the additional cost to shippers and passengers of using the cheapest alternative transportation facility providing a comparable service.

Since the railroad is slowly losing business to competitive forms of transportation in many countries, and since this trend may continue for a long time, the problem of when existing trackage should be abandoned is worth a comment.

A railroad should continue to be operated long after the sum total of the monetary revenue and consumers' surplus have become insufficient to cover the total cost of operation. The rates should be progressively lowered until they just equal the variable costs less a subsidy not in excess of the consumers' surplus involved. When income becomes insufficient to cover this minimum, variable costs less subsidy, the line should be abandoned. To state the matter differently, a railroad should be operated so long as the monetary income, plus a justifiable subsidy, is sufficient to yield any return whatsoever upon the capital invested. As soon as this composite income is insufficient to meet the variable costs of operation, the line should be abandoned.

---

just one. No gain comes from carrying a thing from one place to another unless it can be produced at the first place so much more cheaply that it can afford the cost of carriage to the second. Ability to stand the transportation charge is the test of the utility of the carriage." F. W. Taussig, *Principles of Economics*, 3d ed. (The Macmillan Company, New York, 1921), II, 390.

Of this quotation the last two sentences are quite sound. However, Taussig overlooks the facts that (1) the price paid does not measure the full ability to pay of the additional goods carried, and (2) the rate charged should cover only marginal, not total or average costs.

E. VARIETY OF SERVICES

American railroads do not offer a sufficient variety of passenger services. Socialism would greatly reduce the present inequalities in private income, and thus partially remove one reason for variety in service, but it would not eliminate differences in human nature. There will always be some people who want to travel in luxury, some who desire comfort only, and others who prefer board seats if this reduces their railroad fare. Again, some passengers are in a hurry, and others are not.

An obviously undesirable policy of private railroads is that of preventing thrifty travelers and migratory workers from riding on empty freight cars. The purpose seems to be to force everyone to travel in relative comfort at a cost which will increase the profits of the railroad. It would cost society virtually nothing to provide free transportation service on empty freight cars to those who cared to use it. Under Socialism, travel of this sort should be encouraged rather than discouraged, since it would reduce the investment necessary for providing more comfortable passenger cars, and at the same time would stimulate travel by the masses. If every nation adopted this policy, students and workers could travel around the world at very slight expense, an expense fully covered by a month's wages. This would enormously increase international travel and understanding.

The same principle should be applied to trucks and ocean freighters. When empty, they should be made available to those who do wish cheap transportation. Any considerable marginal costs involved should, of course, be charged to those who make use of these services, but in most cases there would be none worth measuring and collecting.

F. TAXATION

There are two basic principles which should govern the taxation of transportation. The first is that all general revenue taxes on transportation should bear as equally as possible on different routes and methods of transport. In other words, they should have the least possible effect upon the relationship between the marginal costs of, and hence the volume of traffic handled by, different routes and methods of transportation. All important transport taxes in use under Capitalism violate this basic principle. For instance, the general property tax is a very heavy burden upon the railroads, but falls very lightly upon other forms of transportation, while corporation income taxes affect unequally both routes and methods of transportation.

The only two taxes capable of raising large revenues which do not violate this principle are a uniform sales or gross income tax upon transportation itself and an income tax which falls upon individuals only.[4] In a Socialist economy, therefore, the only permissible general-purpose direct tax upon transportation would be a uniform sales or gross-income tax, and this would be unnecessary if personal income taxes were high enough.

The second basic principle of transport taxation is that the costs of certain very important transportation services, notably the costs of highways, should be raised by the use of price taxes designed to place the costs of highways upon those who use them. This principle has been partially applied under Capitalism, but the Capitalist applications require considerable refinement before they will be suitable for a Socialist economy, or, indeed, for a well-run Capitalist economy. Certain refinements were suggested in a previous chapter on taxation (chapter x). The allocation of highway costs deserves further discussion here, however.

Price taxes on gasoline, tires, and similar goods should cover only the present marginal costs of highway transportation. If the costs of highway construction have fallen 50 percent since existing highways were built, the price taxes levied should be sufficient to cover only the present replacement costs of the highways. If highway traffic is less than highway capacity, price taxes should be based upon the cost of handling additional traffic over existing roads, not upon total costs of old or new roads.

Certain gross defects in existing gasoline taxes are due to ignorance or disregard of these principles. For instance, gasoline taxes should never be used to raise new capital to be invested in highways, or to pay off bond issues previously floated for this purpose. In a Socialist economy, such capital should come from the Bureau of Capital Supply, and the loans should never be repaid. Even the interest on this capital should be covered by price taxes only when the volume of traffic is at capacity level, i.e., when interest becomes a marginal cost.

On the other hand, gasoline taxes should include a share over and above marginal costs equal to any uniform general-revenue sales tax on non-highway transportation. Price taxes should be subject to a general-revenue sales tax in the same manner and proportion as all other prices. Under Capitalism, highways are not subject to general property taxes and corporation income taxes, the chief general-revenue taxes levied upon other forms of transportation, and this results in uneconomic discrimination against non-highway transport.

---

[4] Strictly speaking, both of these taxes alter relative costs of different forms of transportation, since the effect of a uniform sales or income tax depends upon the shape of the supply curves, but it is true that such taxes have far less effect upon relative prices than any other taxes.

G. THE PRICING OF TRANSPORTATION SERVICES

The general theory of price determination under Socialism developed in Part Two of this treatise should, of course, govern the determination of transportation charges. All passenger and freight rates should be fixed by price experts in such a way as to secure maximum use of each kind of scheduled transportation service. Both consumers and producers of transportation services should react to these rates in such a way as to eliminate all marginal surpluses or deficits accruing to them from either the consumption or the provision of these services. Thus the price experts, the consumers of transportation services, and the Transportation Trust would all help to determine the actual rates prevailing at any time.[5]

The rate structure determined in this way would be quite different from the rate structure characteristic of Capitalism. The major differences are described below.

UNIFORM RATES FOR ALL COMMODITIES

First and most important of all would be the elimination of rates based upon the nature and value of the commodity carried, and their replacement by rates uniform for all commodities using the same facilities. All rates should be quoted in gross ton-miles or some other physical unit applicable to many or all different commodities, for it is such characteristics of freight which determine the cost of hauling it. Gross ton-miles include the weight of the car and thus allow for differences in bulk as well as in weight. If shippers of different products buy identical transportation services, they should be quoted the same rate, regardless of the nature and value of the commodity shipped. If they buy different transportation services, they ought to pay different rates, but the differences should be based solely upon real differences in the marginal cost of providing these services. The former conclusion is a specific application of the general principle of uniformity of prices. The latter conclusion is based upon the general principle that a producing trust should control the production of each good in such a way as to equalize its market price and marginal cost.

Under Capitalism, rates are not uniform and are not based upon the cost of the service rendered. The same service rendered to shippers of different commodities is subject to widely differing rates, and these rates are based upon ability to pay rather than upon the cost of the service. For instance, the ton-mile rate on silk goods or shoes may be as much as ten or twenty times the rate on coal or gravel.

[5] For a brief but stimulating discussion of the railroad rates of a Socialist economy, see J. H. Smith, *Collectivist Economics*, pp. 95–101.

Certain bourgeois economists have attempted to justify rates based upon ability to pay by asserting that it is impossible to determine accurately the costs of rendering individual transportation services.[6] The fact that a task cannot be performed perfectly is not a conclusive reason why it should not be performed at all, however. Even if this reason were conclusive against rates based on cost, it would not prove that rates based upon ability to pay are desirable. Rather, it would prove that all rates should be equal. However, it is possible to estimate specific transportation costs with sufficient accuracy to justify rates based on costs.

A more important argument in favor of rates based upon ability to pay, and one which has considerable validity under Capitalism, runs as follows.

About two-thirds of the total costs of operating a railroad are fixed costs which do not increase when the volume of traffic increases. Interest, rent, and salary overhead will be the chief fixed costs under Socialism. Taxes are an important fixed cost under Capitalism. The fact that over two-thirds of railroad costs are fixed costs means that it may be profitable to the private owners of a railroad and to society as a whole to increase the volume of railroad freight whenever idle capacity exists, even if the additional freight does not pay the full average cost of railroad service. So long as the additional freight covers the variable costs and contributes something to the fixed costs, it is worth carrying if the low rate quoted on the additional freight does not apply to the previous volume of business. Such a situation is common. Since railroads carry many different types of commodities over many routes, a new low rate can apply to one kind of commodity and one route only.

When additional freight is secured through a special low rate which more than covers variable costs and which does not lower appreciably the income on freight already being handled, this additional freight lowers the cost of transporting the freight previously handled because it contributes something toward fixed costs and consequently reduces the proportion of fixed costs which must be met out of revenues from the previous volume of business. Thus, special low rates which serve to move additional freight, benefit everyone concerned under Capitalism. This is the conventional argument employed to justify their use by orthodox economists.

A very vital point which is ignored by apologists for existing rate structures is that the same argument applies to many other industries besides railroads. Whenever idle capacity exists, production or distribution can be increased without a corresponding increase in fixed costs, and spe-

---

[6] Fairchild, Furniss, and Buck, *Elementary Economics* (rev. ed.), II, 11 .

cial prices somewhere between total and variable costs will have precisely the same beneficial effects as in the case of railroads.

The situation, however, will be quite different under Socialism. It will still be socially economic to move additional freight whenever idle capacity exists and this additional freight can pay the variable costs of moving it. However, and this is the vital point, it will no longer be necessary to charge a rate above marginal cost on other freight, because it will not be necessary for railroads to be self-supporting. Differential railroad rates are sometimes justified under Capitalism because they enable railroads to secure increased utilization of existing equipment without incurring a deficit. They are not necessary under Socialism because industry need not yield a profit. Indeed, they are undesirable because they make it impossible for *all* producers to extend their use of railroad facilities to the optimum point, the point where the social utility resulting from this increased use just balances the additional social disutility.

As already indicated in an earlier chapter on the theory of utility (chapter ii), it is always socially desirable to create utility when the disutility cost is less than the resulting utility. Differential railroad rates make it unprofitable to ship an additional quantity of certain commodities even though the place utility thus created would be larger than the additional disutility (variable costs) involved. For instance, if the rates charged for transporting shoes were lowered to the rate for gravel, it is certain that the volume of shoes shipped would increase. This would be socially desirable since the place utility thus created would be greater than the disutility cost of creating it. If it were not, the shoes should not be shipped. The same reasoning holds good for every commodity not now enjoying a rate as low as the variable cost of shipment.

For this reason, whenever it is justifiable to quote a low freight rate, that is, one below average costs, on any commodity in order to increase the utilization of existing transportation facilities, it is equally desirable to quote an equally low rate on every commodity. This policy will result in operating losses whenever marginal costs are below average costs, but these losses can and should be covered by special subsidies from the central government or some other source. Such subsidies would not be a burden to taxpayers, since they would make possible an equivalent lowering of transportation charges on freight already being carried. Rather they would benefit the taxpayer, since they would make possible more complete and rational utilization of existing transportation equipment, and would thus increase utility more than disutility.

Another argument in favor of uniform transportation charges for all shippers is the high cost of preparing and using the complex classification and rate books now in use. A simplified rate schedule, based, for instance, on gross ton-miles and upon the type of car used, would save the railroads and shippers of the United States hundreds of millions of dollars in clerical expense.

Under Capitalism, reduced round-trip passenger rates are used to secure marginal business that pays its own variable costs and contributes something to fixed costs but which would not move in the absence of price concessions. At least this is the best justification that can be given for such reduced rates.

Under Socialism, railroad rates should always be cut to the level of variable or marginal costs. Hence there would be no point to granting price concessions on round-trip tickets. The case for uniformity between one-way rates and round-trip rates is precisely the same as the case for uniform rates for different kinds of commodities. Monthly passes, 60-ride books, and all other rate reductions dependent upon frequency of travel or freight shipment should be unnecessary in a Socialist economy for the same reasons.[7]

There is another form of railroad rate discrimination prevalent under Capitalism that should have no place in a Socialist economy. Railroads have cut rates between competitive points below the average rates. For instance, it costs more to ship a carload of merchandise from New York to Reno than from New York to San Francisco, even when the car sent to San Francisco passes through Reno on the way. The excuse offered for this type of rate discrimination is that the railroad must compete with other rail lines and with steamship lines for the through business. It is better to obtain some of the through traffic at any rate which will yield a surplus over variable costs and will contribute something to fixed costs, it is argued, than to permit all the through traffic to go by other lines or by ship, with the result that local freight will have to meet all fixed charges of the railroad.

It is perfectly true that if excess railway capacity exists, rates should be cut until the capacity is entirely utilized, provided rates still cover variable costs. But, if it is necessary to cut through rates for this purpose, local rates should be cut in proportion. The same reasoning applies here as in the case of different rates on different kinds of merchandise.

This does not mean that ton-mile charges should be the same for long and short hauls. Railroad rates should be composed of two parts, one to cover loading and unloading and all yard costs, the other to cover

---

[7] Pigou has attempted to justify lower charges to people whose purchases are continuous on the ground that such purchases do not contribute to peak loads. However, most commuters travel only during peak hours. Moreover, all those who ride during off-peak hours should be granted the same low rates, regardless of the number of trips they make.

costs of interyard hauling. The former does not vary with the length of the haul, but the latter does. Hence, total charges per mile for long hauls should always be less than total charges per mile for shorter and included hauls.

RATE DIFFERENCES TO BALANCE TRAFFIC

Whenever the demand for transportation is stronger in one direction than in another, and this necessitates an empty return haul, rates should be changed in such a way as to achieve an optimum degree of balance between freight movements in the two directions. In order to obtain freight for empty cars being returned to their point of origin, rates should be successively lowered until these empty cars are filled or until the rates reach the level of the variable costs of such additional freight movement. In the case of empty cars which must be moved anyway, these variable costs are extremely low.

As a further means of balancing freight movement in opposite directions, the Transportation Trust should raise rates on freight moving in the prevailing direction to a level which covers all variable costs, both of the original shipment and of the return of the empty cars to the point of origin.

Both of these principles are merely specific applications of the basic principle that prices should equal marginal costs.

The total charges for shipping any given commodity in both directions should always be sufficient to cover all marginal costs involved. The allocation of these costs to the freight shipped in each direction should be determined by relative demand. The freight moving in the prevailing direction should pay all costs over and above the contribution of the freight moving in the opposite direction. This latter freight, moreover, should contribute nothing over and above the additional marginal costs due solely to its shipment, until the freight movement in both directions is properly balanced. Raising return rates above these minimum additional variable costs before this balance is attained would inevitably result in idle railroad capacity which could be used in a way to yield net utility to society. Once freight moving in both directions has been perfectly balanced, however, the rates on return shipments should be raised to the highest point compatible with a perfect balance in freight movement. These rates will then contribute something over and above the additional variable costs of handling the return freight, and will contribute something to the variable costs of moving freight in the prevailing direction, thus permitting the rates on this freight to be lowered. It should be noted that there is a prevailing direction even when the physical volume of freight moving in both directions is equal.

RATE VARIATIONS TO MINIMIZE TRAFFIC FLUCTUATIONS

The demand for freight and passenger service is highly seasonal in character. In order to reduce to the optimum degree seasonal fluctuations in the volume of traffic, the Transportation Trust should vary its rates from season to season. During periods of slack demand, rates should be set at a figure which just covers the low marginal costs prevailing at such times, and during the rest of the time rates should be high enough to cover the higher marginal costs then prevailing or to limit sales to the volume of service scheduled. Moreover, new transportation facilities to meet peak demands should not be built until rates charged on peak traffic are high enough to cover both fixed and variable costs of the marginal capacity that this peak traffic uses.

In spite of the fact that seasonal fluctuations in car loadings are now largely due to the seasonal nature of agriculture, it is possible to eliminate the greater part of these fluctuations by a sound pricing policy. Wheat is harvested in one or two months of the year, but there is no reason why it should move to market immediately after being harvested. The same is true of the great majority of farm products, and of coal and lumber. Since freight rates make up a large share of the delivery cost of these commodities, slight variations in freight rates would control the time of their shipment. Of course, fluctuations in the shipment of highly perishable seasonal products cannot be eliminated, but these goods should pay all costs chargeable to them. If refrigerator cars are required to move fruit during only one month of the year, this fruit should be charged the full cost of maintaining these idle cars throughout the rest of the year, and all other fresh produce shipped in refrigerator cars during the peak month should pay the same high rate, for this is the marginal cost in such months.

Seasonal fluctuations in the use of specialized equipment such as coal cars and refrigerator cars are much greater than seasonal fluctuations in the total volume of railroad traffic. The rates on the idle specialized equipment should be reduced to bare variable cost during off seasons, and raised high enough to cover the entire year's fixed cost during seasonal peaks, provided of course, that this will not reduce peak loads below capacity. No price above marginal costs should ever be fixed high enough to reduce production below capacity.

OTHER JUSTIFIABLE VARIATIONS IN FREIGHT RATES

While freight rates should be uniform for all commodities, except in so far as there are real differences in the variable costs of moving them, there should be a high degree of diversity in freight rates. Transportation costs vary widely from one railroad to another and from one means of transportation to another. These varying costs should be reflected directly in freight and passenger rates.

Under Capitalism, railroad rates in the United States are made uniform for different roads in spite of the fact that costs vary widely. The Interstate Commerce Commission aims at a rate schedule which will give the proper average profit on railroad capital as a whole. Under Socialism, every single freight haul should pay its way, so far as it is economical to install the cost-accounting system necessary to bring this about. Whenever freight is moved which does not pay its own variable costs, society is harmed because the disutilitum costs of the freight movement are in excess of the utilitum created thereby. On the other hand, if unused capacity exists, every rate above marginal cost checks the shipment of goods which would move at a lower rate, and this prevents the creation of place utility in excess of the disutility costs involved.

All rate structures designed to yield only a proper average profit possess serious defects. They prevent the movement of some freight which ought to be moved and they make possible the movement of some freight which ought not to be moved. The ideal rate system or structure is one in which every rate just equals the variable costs involved.

Some compromise with this ideal must be made, of course. Up to a certain point, additional cost accounting is worth while because it makes possible the determination of more accurate specific costs and, hence, more economic rates. Beyond this point, the costs of additional cost accounting outweigh the additional accuracy in costs and rates obtained by it. Thus, while rates should agree roughly with costs, and vary as they vary from one form of transportation to another, from one railroad to another, and from one mile of track to another, too great accuracy should not be sought.

Variations in freight rate based upon the size of the shipment are justified so long as they merely reflect actual differences in marginal costs. Small consignments involve three distinct sources of additional expense: separate collection and delivery; separate handling, invoicing, and accounting at the freight depot; and less economical loading of freight cars. American railroads now grant quantity discounts up to carload lots only. Under Socialism, such discounts should increase up to full trainload lots, with intermediate discounts for intermediate amounts. It is much cheaper to haul a solid trainload between two destinations than to haul an equal volume in carload lots between a hundred different shippers and consignees.

Variations in rates based on type of car used, speed of service, fragility, explosiveness, combustibility, etc., are also proper. All variations in freight rates which are based upon actual and economically measurable differences in variable costs are justified provided that the cost of measuring and using these cost variations is not larger than the gain from better pricing.

DEMURRAGE CHARGES

Railroad cars are frequently detained for some days or weeks by shippers, either to reduce loading and unloading costs or to serve as temporary warehouses. This practice burdens the railroads since it requires them to buy a larger number of cars. In some cases, however, the benefit to the shipper more than offsets the cost to the railroad. To eliminate undesirable detention of cars by shippers, the Transportation Trust of a Socialist state should levy demurrage (car rent) charges equal to the cost involved. These charges should apply for each day during which the car is at the shipper's disposal, but the rate per day should not increase as time passes. Such charges would not prevent the detention of cars where the gain is greater than the cost, but they would help shippers to be more efficient by making obvious and accurately measurable a cost hitherto neglected or inaccurately assessed.

CHAPTER XVIII. MARKETING

A. INTRODUCTION

Marketing[1] has long been treated by bourgeois theorists as a division of the science of business administration rather than as a division of either pure or applied political economy. As a division of the field of business administration, Capitalist marketing theory suffers from the defects characteristic of that science. In a word, it is concerned exclusively with the problem of increasing the profits of private business. Since social gain conflicts with private profit at innumerable points, the marketing theory developed by bourgeois students of business administration needs thorough revision before it can be accepted in a Socialist economy.

In its most general sense, marketing includes all creation of place and time utility. However, transportation has been discussed separately, and this chapter is therefore restricted to the marketing activities of producers, wholesalers, and retailers.

About fifty cents of every dollar spent by the final consumer now goes to pay the costs of marketing. In other words, under Capitalism marketing in its most general sense, that is, including transportation, produces and absorbs about half of the total national income.

In a Socialist economy the costs of marketing will be greatly reduced. One gas station on a corner will sell as much as the two, three, and four now there or in the immediate neighborhood. Vertical integration of industry will eliminate many marketing costs by transforming intercompany sales into intracompany transfers. Retail and wholesale distribution are the most wasteful of all industries under Capitalism because they are the most competitive. Hence, Socialism will accomplish greater immediate savings in these fields than in any other.

The theory of Socialist marketing does not consist entirely of specific applications of general economic principles. Some of the problems of marketing are peculiar to that field. While these problems are not, strictly speaking, economic problems—since political economy includes only relatively general or universal problems and principles—they are discussed here in order to give a reasonably complete outline of Socialist marketing theory. The following discussion of marketing theory is divided into three parts: (1) the marketing activity of producers, (2) wholesale distribution, and (3) retail distribution.

---

[1] We have used the term "marketing" instead of "distribution" in order to avoid confusion with the distribution of income.

B. MARKETING BY PRODUCERS

Although wholesale and retail distribution will continue to be far more significant than the marketing activity of producers in a Socialist state, producers will still have essential marketing functions to perform. Since marketing begins with the producer, it is logical to consider first the marketing activities of producers. The term "primary marketing" is used here as synonymous with "the marketing activities of producers."

The establishment of a monopolistic state trust in every field of production of price goods would automatically result in a virtual marketing monopoly in each field of primary distribution, the sales department of the trust producing the goods in question.

Monopoly in the field of primary distribution is desirable for a number of reasons. It eliminates all duplication of capital equipment and effort. It greatly increases the scale of clerical operations in the offices of the selling agency, thus reducing the cost of these operations. It simplifies the buying activities of wholesale and retail organizations because under monopoly they can get full information and service on each class of goods from a single agency.

In order to achieve a complete monopoly in every field of primary distribution, it will be necessary to sell all imported commodities through the marketing organization of the domestic producer of the same article. The Foreign Trade Trust should care only for the primary distribution of those commodities not produced by domestic industry.

Standardization and Grading.—The standardization and grading of commodities is ordinarily treated as a function of marketing. In a Socialist economy, all standardization and grading should be done by the original producing trust. The principles to be followed in the simplification of manufactured goods have already been discussed (pp. 162–65). Proper simplification and the consolidation of each industry into a single unit will make grading and sorting of manufactured goods by wholesalers unnecessary. In the case of agricultural and similar products, all grading and sorting should be done by the original producing trust in order to permit economy and uniformity in grading.

The number of grades should be greatly reduced and so named that the final purchaser will know their meaning. The basic principle to be followed in deciding whether to increase the number of grades is to balance the utility to the consumer of an additional grade against the additional cost of grading and of carrying the higher inventories involved. Consumers should do this balancing and report their conclusions to the government in periodic opinion polls.

Direct Sales to Retail Stores and Consumers.—The great bulk of consumable commodities should be distributed through wholesale warehouses under Socialism as under Capitalism. However, there are certain exceptions to this rule which deserve mention.

In the case of unusually heavy and valuable commodities, such as automobiles and pianos, direct shipment by producers to retailers is often more economical than sale through wholesale warehouses. Such commodities would be sold through a relatively small number of retail outlets so that it would be practical for the producing trust to deal directly with these outlets. Storage and reshipment of such commodities by wholesale warehouses would be expensive and of little advantage to the public, especially if these products were assembled in regional assembly plants.

Direct sales to retail stores may also be desirable when the producing trust has widely distributed production units, since the producer may be as close to the retailer as a wholesaler should be.

Finally, direct distribution to retail stores may be necessary in order to speed up distribution and thus maintain the freshness of certain food products. In some cases, two or more of these reasons for direct distribution may exist. Bakeries, for instance, should continue to sell their bread directly to retail agencies or consumers, both because bakeries will be widely scattered and because bread should be delivered soon after it has been baked.

Certain commodities, such as automobiles and gasoline, require separate and specially adapted facilities for both wholesale and retail distribution. In some cases, the producers of such commodities should carry on their own wholesale and retail distribution. Thus garages, gas stations,[2] and automobile sales agencies should be controlled by the trusts which produce the commodities sold in these retail outlets. The same principle applies to moving-picture theatres, although they produce services instead of commodities.

Such vertical integration of distribution would give better co-ordination between production and distribution. It would cause producers to give more consideration to the technical problems of distribution and repair work. It would centralize responsibility for proper supply and maintenance of such commodities and will reduce bookkeeping and clerical costs by eliminating inter-trust transactions. A separate organization for wholesale and retail distribution has greater advantages in the case of different commodities which can be stored in the same buildings because this reduces overhead costs, but it offers no advantage in the case of goods which require separate specialized marketing facilities.

[2] After the number of gas stations has been reduced by 75 percent to 90 percent, it may become economical to deliver gasoline to gas stations by pipe line instead of by tank wagon.

Educational Advertising.—It goes without saying that the aggressive salesmanship and deceptive advertising characteristic of Capitalism should not be tolerated in a Socialist economy. It will nevertheless be beneficial to give the consumer accurate, useful information concerning the quality, durability, and uses of the article he purchases. The preparation of such information should be a function of the original producer, since he knows more about his products than anyone else. This information should be printed in annual catalogues, and should also be summarized on printed tags attached to each article on sale or on signs which can be placed near such articles.

To illustrate the type of information referred to, men's shirts may be used as an example. A typical question about men's shirts is whether one type of material, such as airplane cloth, will stand more laundering than another type, such as broadcloth. Another question is how much the collar and sleeves will shrink. The purchaser is the best judge of the aesthetic value to him of each type of material, but he knows very little about their relative durability, and the degree to which they will shrink or fade. Accurate information concerning the qualities of all products would notably increase the utilitum derived by consumers from their purchases. Under competitive Capitalism, it is not even possible to rely on the customary information concerning collar size and sleeve length of men's shirts.

C. WHOLESALE MARKETING

The functions of wholesale warehouses are: (1) to reduce transportation costs by pooling orders of many retail stores and thus making possible large-scale shipments; (2) to speed up and cheapen transportation by providing terminal facilities, warehouses, and delivery equipment which no individual retail store could afford to maintain, but which may be economically used by an organization supplying many retail stores; (3) to carry local stocks in large warehouses in low-rent areas, thus reducing the size of stocks which must be carried in retail stores and diminishing the cost of storage; and (4) to make possible the return and redistribution of surplus retail stocks without their return to the factory. Of these four functions, the carrying of local reserve stocks is by far the most significant.

Under Capitalism, wholesalers perform additional functions, such as extending credit, improving methods of retailers, facilitating aggressive sales efforts of manufacturers, etc., but these functions should not continue to be performed under Socialism. Extension of credit should be concentrated in the hands of the State Bank. The executives of the

Retail Division of the Marketing Trust should be the best authorities on methods of retailing. Aggressive selling is uneconomic.

All wholesale marketing should be carried on by a single division of the Marketing Trust. Centralization of control over all wholesale warehouses would make possible proper standardization of methods and equipment, accurate measurement and comparison of the results obtained by different local managers, and all the other economies of large-scale management.

Mail-Order and Telephone Sales.—Wholesale warehouses should have special mail-order and telephone-order departments to sell direct to consumers. Each warehouse should maintain a fleet of trucks to deliver mail- and telephone-order sales to those retail customers who live near enough to make this economical. In the case of other retail customers who order directly from the wholesale warehouse, parcel-post or express facilities should be used, or the orders should be transferred to the retail store nearest the customer.

The prices quoted to final consumers who purchase by mail or telephone should be the same as those quoted to retail stores for equal quantities. In both cases the delivery costs should be charged to the buyer. Of course, consumers would ordinarily buy in smaller quantities than retail stores, so that they would have to pay higher unit and delivery prices. These prices, however, would still be below those of retail stores, since direct purchase from a central warehouse would save transportation costs and reduce or eliminate many other costs of retail distribution through stores.

Mail-order and telephone-order sales should be far greater in volume under Socialism, due to standardization and grade labeling of products and to the fact that goods sold by mail and telephone would be identical with and cheaper than those sold in retail stores. The elimination of daily "specials" and other unnecessary price variations would also reduce the need for personal shopping.

For certain types of goods, such as groceries, tobacco, and other articles which the consumer does not need to see before purchase, the advantages of direct sale by warehouse to consumer are so great and would be so much increased by the absence of competition from retail stores, that prolonged experiments should be conducted in certain cities with exclusive distribution of these commodities by warehouses in response to mail or phone orders.

Perhaps the greatest advantage of such a system is that it would save the average housewife an hour's time which she now devotes to shopping for groceries each day. For thousands of years buyers have found it necessary to inspect groceries and other goods before purchase because private businessmen cannot be trusted to deliver equally good merchandise in the absence of such inspection. Moreover, the early shopper is able to pick the best for herself and leave the worst for later buyers.

Under Socialism, groceries should be more accurately graded and sellers would not profit from misrepresentation or petty fraud. Although competitive shopping enables early shoppers to select the best groceries, it does not increase the supply of such groceries. Hence, the time spent in competitive shopping does not benefit the community because it merely enables certain customers to benefit themselves at the expense of the other customers.

The full costs of daily shopping for groceries are not felt under Capitalism because many women have nothing better to do with their time. Under Socialism there would be well-paid part- and full-time jobs open to all women, and ample nursery school and housekeeping services would be available. Under these conditions, most women would want to work rather than spend their time in daily shopping for groceries and in doing other housekeeping chores in an uneconomic individualistic manner.

Inventory Control.—The management of each wholesale warehouse should determine maximum inventory limits and reorder points for each good. When the supply declines to the reorder point, an order just large enough to bring the inventory up to the maximum limit should be sent in.

The chief factors to be considered in determining reorder points are sales volume, sales stability, quantity discounts, and time required for replacement. The larger the volume of sales the higher the reorder point must be set. Every increase in the variability of sales also serves to make a higher reorder point necessary. The shorter the time required to replace the good in question, the lower the reorder point may be placed with safety.

The maximum inventory limit should be determined by adding to the reorder point the optimum reorder. The size of the optimum reorder depends upon the costs of storage and the economies of large orders. Every increase in the size of an order tends both to increase total storage costs and to decrease freight and merchandise costs. For each good there is always an optimum reorder which serves to reduce to the minimum the total unit costs due both to storage and to purchase and freight-in.

It should be noted that in the case of goods whose sale is rapidly increasing or decreasing, it will be necessary to revise the maximum inventory limits and optimum reorder figures almost constantly as long as these changes continue.

Price Policy.—Wholesale prices should ordinarily be fixed in such a way that the markup on each item just covers the cost of handling the marginal unit of that item. If a warehouse is operating below the optimum level, that of minimum average cost, space costs will not be marginal costs and negative rent will appear. If the volume of business exceeds this level, marginal costs may rise to or above a level which would cover space costs.

Quantity discounts based upon real variations in the unit cost of handling orders of different size should be granted all purchasers. Cash discounts would not be needed, since every purchaser would be able to obtain ample funds from the Bureau of Capital Supply.

Wholesale prices should be fixed f.o.b. the wholesale warehouse, and delivery costs should be added to them. This is desirable in order to allocate delivery costs to those responsible for them.

Wholesale prices should vary in such a way as to reduce to the economic minimum all regular daily, weekly, monthly, and annual fluctuations in total sales and in the sales of individual commodities.

Methods of Operation.—Every wholesale warehouse should have railway connections and its own terminal facilities. Goods should be shipped in containers designed so that they could be easily attached to flat cars and quickly loaded on or removed from the flat cars by traveling cranes; they should be large enough so that four to ten of them would hold as much as a box car. These containers should also be used for storage purposes in wholesale warehouses and for shipment to retail stores whenever possible. Their contents would not have to be checked by the warehouse, as any shortage would eventually be disclosed by a check at the retail store. The ideal should be shipment in an unbroken container from producer to retailer, with intermediate storage only at the wholesale warehouse.

Under Capitalism nearly all wholesale warehouses and produce markets are located in highly congested business districts. The primary reason for this seems to be the existence of competitive salesmanship and the desire to be near possible buyers. Under Socialism this reason will disappear and it would probably prove economical to locate wholesale warehouses on the outskirts of large cities rather than in their center. This would lower rent costs, facilitate loading and unloading, speed up deliveries, and enable employees to live within a few minutes' walk of the warehouses.

In order to speed up service to retail stores and thus permit a reduction in their inventories, a quick yet economical method of transmitting orders from retailers to wholesale warehouses should be used. Mail is far too slow for this purpose. Telephone is the quickest and most convenient means of all. However, the telegraph might prove more practical, since it would give an accurate written order to the warehouse. A private teletype line might be installed between large stores and the nearest warehouses. Neighborhood stores would probably find the telephone more economical in spite of its drawbacks.

As an additional aid to quick replenishment of retail stocks, all wholesale warehouses should operate day and night. Indeed, the major portion of the work should probably be done at night so as to enable each store to replenish its previous day's sales before the next day's business begins. If each large city had its own complete wholesale facilities, the retail stores in these cities and their suburbs would be able to restock any item within a few hours time or, at the most, overnight. This does not mean that retail stores should be encouraged to restock by sending in uneconomically small replacement orders. It will be necessary to carry on extensive research to discover just how large the minimum replacement order for each type of article should be.

Naturally, the Wholesale Division of the Retail Trust should make no effort to sell its merchandise to retailers. It should do no advertising and hire no traveling salesmen. It should merely fill orders voluntarily sent to it by retail agencies. To facilitate ordering, however, it should prepare annually a complete catalogue of all consumers goods which it sells. This catalogue should contain a description of every article, prepared by the producer of that article. It should be distributed to all consumers as well as to all retail agencies, and should be a complete buying guide for both. The description of each article should tell the retailer and the consumer everything they ought to know concerning the article in question, so that the retail salesman will be relieved of the bulk of such work. Since no sales effort or advertising would be necessary, except in the case of a few new inventions, this catalogue ought to be entirely different in general tone and character from those used under Capitalism.

Every article in this catalogue, and every possible combination of size, pattern, color, style, etc., should have an individual catalogue number. A mnemonic system[3] of numbers should be used, and special care should be taken to develop the maximum number of variations per digit place so that these numbers will be as short as possible. Letters of the alphabet, both capital and small, should be usable in each digit place. All orders for merchandise should be given in terms of these catalogue numbers.

The delivery of merchandise from the wholesale warehouse to the retail store or other large buyer should be done at night in the same trucks which are used by day for delivering goods purchased by the public in retail stores. This would permit maximum utilization of all delivery trucks, and would reduce the amount of traffic on the city streets during the daytime.

[3] See the discussion of this point in Hathaway, *Scientific Management in American Industry*, pp. 113–36.

D. RETAIL MARKETING

Retail marketing is the last stage in the distribution of commodities. It may be defined as the sale and delivery of consumable commodities to consumers. It includes mail-order, telephone, and door-to-door selling, in addition to the work of retail stores. The only distributive functions common to all forms of retail marketing are the function of maintaining a stock of goods reasonably near and accessible to the consumer and the function of aiding the consumer to buy intelligently.

Both wholesale and retail distribution should be carried on by a single organization, the Marketing Trust, divided into a Wholesale Division and a Retail Division. However, certain forms of retail distribution, such as mail-order and telephone-order sales by warehouses, are so closely connected with wholesale warehouse management that they might well be placed under the Wholesale rather than under the Retail Division of the Marketing Trust.

The Retail Division of the Marketing Trust should have charge of all retail stores in the nation. Garages and service stations, as has been noted, should be placed under the control of the trusts which produce the products sold in them, but they are not ordinarily considered to be retail stores.

The internal organization of the Retail Division of the Marketing Trust should be determined by the types of retail stores set up. The most fundamental division of authority would probably separate control over the distribution of convenience goods from control over the distribution of shopping and specialty goods. Convenience goods are those which are purchased frequently and in small amounts at the most convenient store. Groceries, drugs, tobacco, candy, soft drinks, etc., belong in this class. Shopping and specialty goods are relatively expensive and infrequently purchased, and are usually bought after some shopping. They include most clothing, furniture, household and garden equipment, hardware, musical instruments, toys, etc.

These two types of goods should be sold in different types of stores. Convenience goods should be sold in local neighborhood stores scattered throughout the residential area of a community, by mail or phone from a warehouse, and by automatic vending equipment. Shopping and specialty goods should be sold in department stores located at the center of each plant or farm community.

In addition, every city or group of plant communities should probably have one giant metropolitan department store such as Macy's in New York City or Marshall Field's in Chicago[4] which, together with the local com-

---

[4] Each of these stores has done $100,000,000 annual business and could easily do three or four times that volume of business without enlargement.

munity department stores, would replace the entire retail business district found at the center of every Capitalist city.

There should be a definite division of labor between community and metropolitan department stores, where the latter exist. The metropolitan department store should handle the most expensive and least frequently purchased shopping and specialty goods. The inconvenience of having to go into the center of a city to make a purchase is relatively unimportant when the cost of the purchase is large, and a metropolitan department store can offer a larger variety and can reduce handling costs by its larger scale of operation.

These metropolitan department stores would have several thousand employees, and should be treated as a part of the central or metropolitan plant community in each city. This plant community, in addition to the giant department store, would include all other facilities designed for use by the entire city, such as large auditoriums, opera and concert halls, large public libraries, art museums, stadiums, etc.

The experience gained by large chains of retail stores under Capitalism should be of great value to the organizers and managers of a Socialist Marketing Trust. The same form of organization and methods of management which have proven successful in the operation of chains of 10,000 stores could be applied with little change to the operation of chains of 100,000 stores.

Retail Stores.—The three types of retail stores—neighborhood stores, community department stores, and metropolitan department stores— needed in a Socialist economy would vary greatly in number and in average size.

Stores which sell convenience goods should be more numerous, far smaller, and much closer to the consumer than either community or metropolitan department stores, but ought not to be nearly so numerous as they are under Capitalism. In 1920 there were 240,000 grocery stores in the United States. This number should be greatly reduced under Socialism. Probably a 60 percent to 80 percent reduction in the total would be advantageous. In most cases, it is possible for one grocery store to care for two or three thousand people without being at a very great distance from any of them. However, long experimentation will be necessary in order to determine the proper ratio of grocery stores to population and, hence, the proper size of grocery stores, and this ratio will change as urban transportation and living conditions change.

Every decrease in the number and every increase in the size of grocery stores reduces the cost of distribution incurred by the store and increases the disutility cost to the customer of traveling to and from the store. At some point, however, the total disutility to both store and consumer is at a minimum. This optimum ratio of stores to population cannot be determined by competition under either Capitalism or Socialism, for two ratios cannot exist in the same place at the same time. It can only be determined by careful scientific investigation and measurement of all the factors involved. Among these factors the density of population, the size of the average income, the cost of transportation, and the rate at which retailing costs decrease as sales increase are of primary importance.

The number of community and metropolitan department stores will be determined by the number of communities and cities to be served. If the size of the average plant or farm community is about 30,000, the total number of community department stores required in the United States will be about 4,000. The number of metropolitan department stores would be but a small fraction of this, since they would only exist in fairly large cities. In 1920 there were less than seventy-five cities with a population of 100,000 or more, and cities with a smaller population probably would not require a metropolitan department store.

Price Policy and Sales Volume.—All retail prices should be set by adding the specific marginal cost of retail distribution to the wholesale price. This means that mark-ups should not take the form of a uniform percentage applicable to articles of different cost or types. Careful cost accounting should be used to determine the varying costs of retail distribution for different articles. The retail costs of distribution are virtually independent of the cost of the article. The costs of buying, receiving, storing, and selling a fifty-dollar watch are very little more than the costs of buying, receiving, storing, and selling a five-dollar watch. The retail mark-ups on two different watches selling at these widely varying wholesale prices should measure accurately the real cost of handling them. This cost will not be the same, but it would be much less of an error to mark up the price of each by the same absolute amount, five dollars for instance, than to use the same percentage mark-up for both watches, as private retailers do. A uniform 100 percent mark-up would give a fifty-dollar mark-up on one watch and only a five-dollar mark-up on the other. Obviously such a variation in absolute mark-ups is only justified to a very minor degree by the real differences in retail distribution costs. Moreover, under Socialism these differences in costs of distribution would be much less than they are now. Both watches would be sold in the same store, the turnover of each would be rapid, credit losses would be eliminated, and there would be few losses due to mark-downs.

The only exceptions to the above method of price fixing should occur in cases where discontinued lines of merchandise are being closed out. In such cases, prices ought to be low enough to move the merchandise. However, prices should never be cut in order to move merchandise which is to be replaced by identical goods unless this merchandise is perishable.

If retail stores set their prices in such a way as to pass on to the consumer the precise marginal cost of retail distribution, marginal profits and losses would be reduced to a minimum. When they occur, moreover, they would not serve as guides to production control but rather would indicate imperfect price determination. The proper reaction would be to alter prices in an effort to eliminate marginal profits and losses, not to alter directly the volume of business in such a way as to eliminate them. Of course, every change in prices should affect the volume of business, but in the case of retail stores this should be an incidental effect because the main effect would be on the profits of producers rather than on the margins of distributors.

The volume of business done by retail stores should be directly controlled by the public and by producers. Retail distributors should merely carry a model inventory and replace all items sold. This is quite different from the method recommended for producers, whose volume of production should be controlled by marginal profits and losses.

Stabilization of Retail Sales.—One of the principal wastes of retailing under Capitalism is the incomplete utilization of capital equipment due to marked and regular variations in the volume of sales. In Capitalist retail stores, sales vary regularly from hour to hour throughout the day, from day to day throughout the week, from month to month throughout the year, and from year to year throughout the business cycle. Socialism will eliminate the business cycle, but special methods ought to be used to reduce or eliminate these other variations in sales volume.

Few people realize the extent of these regular variations in retail sales. Between 11:00 and 12:00 o'clock in the morning, retail sales are double or treble those between 8:00 A.M. and 9:00 A.M. Sales on Saturday average double those on other week days, and in many types of stores December sales are double those of other months. This variation in sales volume means that under Capitalism every store is built and equipped to do between two and four times its average hourly volume of business.

The most practical method of securing a more even flow of retail business is that of price variation. If the preference of some consumers for shopping between 11:00 A.M. and 12:00 A.M., or on Saturday, makes it necessary to have a retail capacity 100 percent greater than actual retail sales, the consumers who make this necessary should pay the entire costs of the additional retail capacity through paying higher prices for the goods they buy. Here, as in all other cases, consumers should be allowed to buy, or do, whatever they please, but only if they are willing to pay the entire cost. It seems highly probable, however, that an increase of much less than 100 percent in the retail mark-up of goods sold between 11:00 A.M. and 12:00 A.M. would cause consumers to reduce their purchases at this or any other period of peak demand to the desired average level of business. The same sort of measures would probably distribute sales evenly as between different days of the week, and different months of the year. If, however, the convenience of purchasing goods at certain busy times is greater than the additional cost, consumers would be free to purchase more goods at these times than at others.

Under Capitalism, retail prices are often manipulated in such a way as to enhance the normal unevenness in the flow of business. Thus, grocery prices are often lower on Saturday than on other days and some specialty and department stores advertise sales during December.

Encouraging Large-Unit Sales.—The cost of retail merchandising in a Socialist economy can be reduced markedly if proper measures are taken to encourage larger unit sales. A consumer who buys ten new shirts at a time ought to contribute little more per store visit towards overhead retail costs than a man who buys one shirt at a time. If everybody bought ten times as much per purchase as they do now, retail stores would only need one-tenth as many clerks, cashiers, and floorwalkers, and would require far less space to accommodate their customers, who would come in only one-tenth as often. It should be noted that the economy to the retail store results from selling ten units of a single article instead of one, not from selling ten times as much merchandise at a time, although the latter certainly economizes the time of the shopper. To encourage larger purchases of each article, every additional unit purchased at the same time should be sold at or near cost. Thus, if a man drives into a gas station, 70 percent to 100 percent of the cost of the sale should be included in the price of the first gallon of gasoline sold to him. Every additional gallon should be sold virtually at tank-wagon cost. To illustrate, when the tank wagon price of gasoline is ten cents, the first gallon purchased by each consumer at a gas station should be sold at a price of perhaps twenty cents. Every additional gallon should be sold for eleven cents a gallon. If this were done, the average driver would buy ten to twenty gallons at a time instead of four or five as at present and this would cut in half the total cost of retailing a given volume of gasoline.

Special Charges for Special Service.—A basic principle of retail pricing in a Socialist economy is that special charges should be made for all special or optional services rendered by the retail store. Waste is never eliminated until those who are responsible for it are forced to bear the full costs of it.

A special charge should be made for delivery service. None of the costs of delivery service should be included in the price of merchandise bought by people who do not receive delivery service. Under Capitalism innumerable stores charge the same prices, whether or not the customer receives delivery service.

Even in the case of articles sold for delivery to the buyer's home, delivery charges should not be added to the price of the merchandise but should take the form of special charges per delivery, varying according to the size and weight of the total delivery. This would encourage customers who desired delivery service to have many articles delivered at the same time, and would therefore reduce the total cost of retail delivery service. The allocation of all delivery costs to those customers who receive delivery service would have the same effect because it would reduce the demand for delivery service.

Another desirable method of more accurately allocating retail costs to those who cause them is to charge a small admission price to all retail stores. Many women spend hours shopping, consuming the time of sales clerks and occupying high rental space, without ever making a purchase. A small admission charge would reduce the total volume of such idle shopping and would compel those who still indulge in it to pay some of the retail costs they occasion. In large stores, it might even be wise to charge admission to each separate department. The method used should be that of installing automatic nickel-in-the-slot turnstiles, such as are used in New York subways. Charging admission to retail stores would also have the desirable effect of encouraging mail-order and telephone purchases.

If cash sales prove to be appreciably cheaper than credit sales in a Socialist economy, an additional charge for each credit sale should be made. This charge should not vary with the value of the sale, for the bookkeeping entries made necessary by a 25¢-charge sale are the same as those made necessary by a $100-charge sale, and there would be scarcely any danger of loss due to bad debts from either sale in a Socialist economy as the state could always collect any unpaid debts by deducting them from the individual's pay.

Another retail service whose costs are not allocated to those who occasion them under Capitalism is that of approval purchase. Under Socialism the right of approval purchase should be extended to all, but the cost of the original sale plus the costs of delivery, pickup, and return to stock should be paid by the purchaser if he returns the merchandise. This would eliminate the gross abuse of approval privileges so common under Capitalism.

In summary, there should be no restriction of services desired by retail customers under Socialism. These services should not be provided gratuitously in order to build up good will and take business away from competitors, but should be available for a fair price so that people could have what they are willing to pay for.

Sales Methods.—The sales methods of retail stores in a Socialist society should be entirely different from those used under Capitalism. The average customer is the best judge of the marginal utility and disutility to him of additional price goods, and sales effort by clerks eager to earn commissions or a raise rarely improves his subjective discrimination in this regard. Therefore, retail stores should do no advertising, have no special sales, sell no "leaders" at a loss, and instruct all sales clerks to refrain from persuading the consumer to buy more goods or to buy one good in place of another. The application of this principle would drastically reduce the cost of retail distribution.

The ideal of the Socialist retail store should be the impartiality and impersonality of a contemporary five- and ten-cent store, where the sole function of the sales clerk is to accept money and wrap up a purchase after the customer has made his choice. Where full display of stock is impractical, a sales clerk should also perform the mechanical functions of taking goods out of drawers, trays, and cabinets and replacing them after the customer has made a selection.

This does not mean that the customer should be kept in ignorance of the quality and various uses of the articles he buys. Full and accurate information on these points should be contained in the catalogue of consumable goods published periodically by the Wholesale Division and distributed free of charge to every retail store and consumer. The information in this catalogue, being supplied by the original manufacturer or producer in each case, would be far more complete and accurate than the knowledge of any individual sales clerk. Producers should carry on continuous research to determine the proper use of each article, the life of every article under several different types of usage, and so forth, and this information should be included in the sales catalogue, printed on tags attached to each article, or stated on nearby signs. Everything possible should be done to encourage and facilitate accurate price and quality comparison, although this would be much less necessary than at present since many producers would produce only the best in each line of goods. Information aiding buyers to select the kinds of goods best fitted to their needs would be more useful.

A Socialist Marketing Trust should make extensive experiments with automatic vending equipment to determine its place in an efficient retail system. Under Capitalism the development and use of automatic vending equipment has been retarded by the increasing stress upon aggressive selling methods. With the elimination of salesmanship by Socialism, the scope for automatic vending equipment would be far greater than it is today.

Store Hours.—In order to secure maximum utilization of the capital invested in retail stores, the Marketing Trust should keep stores open every day in the year and every hour of the day and night in which sales cover variable costs. In other words, stores should remain open whenever the volume of business is sufficient to pay the additional operating expenses caused by the additional hours of business. This rule is merely a specific application of the general principle that the production of any article or service, in this case service, should be increased until the utility and disutility of the marginal unit are equal. Additional income and additional costs measure the utility and disutility of the marginal period of store operation.

It seems highly probable that the application of the above rule for determining store hours would keep stores open on holidays and would result in extension of the hours of service from the present closing time of 5:00 or 6:00 P.M. to 9:00 or 10:00 P.M. The variable expenses of retailing are only about half of the total expenses. Thus, retail stores could afford to cut their mark-up sharply on holidays and after 5:00 P.M. even if they paid higher wages to sales clerks for holiday and evening work. Since the public is very susceptible to such price differentials, a 10 percent to 20 percent cut in prices for all goods sold on holidays and in the evening would greatly stimulate sales at these times, especially sales of more expensive merchandise, such as furniture, clothing, automobiles, radios, etc., where a 10 percent saving is larger. However, prices should never be cut below the point where they cover the variable costs of retail distribution, nor should a store remain open when its sales at this minimum price level fail to cover the variable costs of operation. It is probable, nevertheless, that the adoption of the above rule concerning retail store hours would reduce very greatly, perhaps by as much as 50 percent, the total necessary investment of capital in retail facilities.

Secondhand Merchandise.—One of the functions of the Retail Division of the Marketing Trust should be to provide for the redistribution of all secondhand goods. Retail stores should offer to buy all secondhand articles at a fair price or to take them upon consignment. They should offer customers an opportunity to buy used merchandise instead of new merchandise in every retail department where used merchandise has a value sufficient to justify handling. Instead of taking special pains to persuade the public to buy new rather than secondhand articles, the retail stores should give equal display space and equal advertising space to the secondhand goods. In the majority of departments, used articles should be displayed side by side with the new articles so that consumers could easily compare the quality and the prices of the two grades of merchandise.

The total volume of trade in secondhand merchandise should increase greatly under the arrangements above. The innumerable economies possible to a retail monopoly would reduce the mark-up required on used articles, thus permitting both a higher price to the seller and a lower price to the buyer. If people could get reasonable prices for used articles, they would offer many more of them for sale. No feature of Capitalist retailing is so inefficient and costly as its method of handling secondhand merchandise.

CHAPTER XIX. FOREIGN TRADE

A. INTRODUCTION

The economic theory of foreign trade has always received undue attention from bourgeois economists and statesmen. The exaggerated importance attributed to foreign trade and its regulation by the Mercantilists is well known. Mercantilistic economic theory is still dominant among businessmen and among the politicians, newspaper editors, and school teachers whom they control in all Capitalist nations.

While classical and neoclassical political economists have placed less emphasis upon the need for foreign trade than the Mercantilists, they naturally criticized the errors of Mercantilism, and this in turn has tended to perpetuate the Mercantilistic overemphasis upon the importance of the theory of foreign trade.

Moreover, the nature of Capitalism makes the question of free trade versus protective tariffs a perennial issue since it vitally affects the profits of the industrial capitalists who control all advanced Capitalist nations. By eliminating the private-profit seekers who now benefit from limitations on imports, by uniting the interests of all groups of voters, and by abolishing unemployment, Socialism will make the solution of the tariff question far easier and will thus greatly diminish the attention devoted to it and to foreign trade.[1]

B. ADVANTAGES OF FOREIGN TRADE

The advantages of foreign trade are precisely the same as those of domestic trade. In the first place, commerce makes possible an increase in the scale of production. The advantages of large-scale production, one of which is an increased division of labor, were described in an earlier chapter (page 239). Both the scale of production and the degree of the division of labor are limited by the size of the market. Trade makes pos-

[1] ". . . . One of the chief merits of the Socialist order consists in the fact that it shows up the nature of economic phenomena with unmistakable clearness whereas in the Capitalist order their faces are covered by the mask of the profit interest. For instance, in a Socialist society nobody could possibly doubt that what a nation gets out of international trade is the imports and that the exports are the sacrifice that must be undergone in order to procure the imports, whereas in commercial (Capitalist) society this common-sense view is as a rule completely hidden from the man in the street who therefore cheerfully supports policies that are to his disadvantage." Joseph Schumpeter, *Capitalism, Socialism and Democracy* (Harper & Brothers, New York, 1942), pp. 211–12.

sible every market, and each extension of trade, domestic or foreign, enlarges the market and, hence, makes possible an increased scale of production and a further division of labor. The advantages of foreign trade, therefore, include all the advantages of large-scale production and the division of labor.

The importance of an increased division of labor depends upon the size of the domestic market and upon the degree of the division of labor already achieved. The first steps in the division of labor yield the greatest returns, and subsequent degrees of refinement, while always profitable if the market is large enough, apparently yield a steadily diminishing return. Thus, a large or rich country which has already achieved a high degree of division of labor in all industries benefits much less from foreign trade than a small or poor nation which has not yet achieved an intensive division of labor.

It is also true that, independently of size or wealth, a nation which has relatively big advantages in certain industries—in other words, a nation eminently suited for specialization in certain fields of production —benefits more from foreign trade than a nation with no unusual advantages in any field of production.

A second significant advantage of foreign trade is that it makes possible the concentration of each industry in those regions where natural conditions are most favorable to it. Even if no economy were secured from the increased scale of production, it would still be desirable to concentrate the production of many commodities in areas where natural conditions are most suitable, provided, of course, adequate supplies and kinds of labor and capital are available there. Every nation has natural physical advantages—climate, accessibility, peculiar combinations of raw resources, etc.—which favor the production of certain goods, and these advantages should be exploited to the full for the benefit of the world as a whole. Protective tariffs have so restricted American imports that they consist largely of rubber, coffee, silk, tea, sugar, bananas, furs, diamonds, and other goods which cannot be produced in the United States except at much higher costs due to unfavorable natural conditions.

All protective tariffs which discourage the importation of the products of irreplaceable natural resources are particularly unwise from the purely national viewpoint. The supplies of lumber, petroleum, copper, lead, iron ore, coal, etc., in the United States, for example, will probably give out long before the demand for them ceases. To curtail imports of these raw materials is extremely undesirable, merely from the standpoint of conservation of our natural resources. Tariffs on these commodities are obviously established only in the selfish interests of those capitalists who control our natural resources and desire to exploit them as rapidly as possible. Under no circumstances should a Socialist economy curtail the importation of such raw materials. Indeed, if it wishes to advance its own long-run interests at the expense of the world as a whole, it should either pay bounties on imports of such commodities or place special taxes on the domestic production of them.

The theory that export trade is desirable or necessary under Capitalism in order to dispose of surplus domestic products is widely held by both bourgeois and Marxian theorists. It is based upon a misunderstanding of the nature of foreign trade.

In the first place, exports of any given commodity do not eliminate a surplus, but rather tend to create a surplus available for export. In the absence of an export market, producers would cease to produce the alleged surplus now sold abroad or would find a profitable domestic market for it.

In the second place, exports, if paid for, result in visible or invisible imports of an equal value. They never decrease the total value of goods, services, and securities which must be sold on the domestic market. Thus, low wages and the consequent low purchasing power of the workers cannot cause a net export of the products of their labor.[2] Low wages always imply either inefficiency on the part of the workers or high profits for the capitalists. In the former case, there is no net surplus of goods to export, at least none due to the low level of wages. In the latter case, the high profits of the capitalists enable them to buy all the surplus products not purchased by the workers.[3]

Although the advantages of foreign trade far outweigh the disadvantages, private businessmen who profit from restrictions on imports have popularized many unsound arguments against free trade.

Perhaps the most universally used and believed charge against free trade is that it causes unemployment. Almost every worker believes that the importation of foreign goods, particularly of the same kind of goods he is producing, results in increased unemployment in his own country.

---

[2] A relative surplus of capital may cause an export of capital in the form of goods. The resulting favorable balance of trade, however, is not caused by a domestic surplus of anything but capital. For the same reason, the eventual unfavorable balance of trade due to payment of interest and repayment of principal cannot be explained by a surplus of goods or by low wages in the borrowing nation.

[3] Of course, this assumes that the supply of money is properly adjusted, either by chance or by rational control. The periodic gluts characteristic of Capitalism are due to lack of rational control over the supply of money, not to low wages.

The fact that a Capitalist nation does not need foreign markets in order to dispose of the surplus extracted from the workers is clearly demonstrated by the experience of Great Britain. This highly Capitalistic nation had more visible imports than exports for many years.

This belief is based upon an incomplete analysis of the nature of international trade.

Under Capitalism, foreign trade is divided into two distinct activities, either of which may be carried on independently of the other. These two activities are importing and exporting. The artificial division of foreign trade into these two functions makes it easy for uncritical observers to treat the effects of either one or the other as the sole effects of foreign trade. The universal practice of those capitalists whose financial interests lead them to oppose certain imports is to speak as if the effects of importing foreign goods are the sole effects of foreign trade.

Actually, of course, imports always involve equal exports if invisible items are counted. Foreign trade is merely a process of barter by which less valuable domestic goods are exchanged for foreign goods of a higher domestic value. Since imports cause equal exports, they cannot cause net unemployment, even under Capitalism. The importation of coal reduces the demand for the labor of coal miners, but, at the same time, it increases by an equal amount the demand for labor to produce whatever article is exchanged for the coal.

While foreign imports thus cause no net increase in unemployment even under Capitalism, they may depress certain industries and put workers in those industries out of work. It is natural that under Capitalism, which offers to displaced workers no guarantee of immediate employment elsewhere, the workers in these threatened industries should combine with their masters to demand tariff protection. Although potential imports ordinarily involve potential exports, and hence potential new jobs, no individual worker is sure of getting one of these new jobs and, consequently, no workers have an obvious personal interest in demanding free trade. Under Capitalism, therefore, members of Congress receive many demands for protective tariffs from those voters who fear the loss of their jobs, while they seldom receive letters from those who expect free trade to give them jobs. Certain capitalists, of course, believe their industries will benefit from free trade, but apparently the attraction of additional export sales made possible by free trade is less than the attraction of increased domestic sales made possible by protective tariffs.

Another common argument against free trade in the United States is the charge that it would reduce the high American wage level and standard of living by forcing American workers to compete with cheap foreign labor. Like the charge that free trade causes unemployment, this plea is based upon a partial and incomplete view of foreign trade. It is perfectly true that imports may reduce real wages in certain industries, but it is equally true that the compensating exports must increase real wages in other industries by an even greater amount. Foreign trade always increases the general average of real wages by reducing the cost of living. Commodities do not move in foreign or domestic trade unless they can be purchased in the place of origin more cheaply than in the place of destination, and this difference must be more than sufficient to cover all costs of transportation and handling.

No matter how great the difference in wages, it is impossible for cheap foreign labor to lower American wages so long as that labor is outside the United States.[4] The only way in which such labor can reduce American wages is by coming to live and work in the United States.[5] Even then the undesirable effect is not due to the cheapness, but solely to the quantity of the foreign labor. In other words, the immigration of an equal number of previously highly paid workers would have the same unfortunate effect upon the wage level.

C. METHODS OF INCREASING FOREIGN TRADE

The mere eradication of unsound limitations on foreign trade would cause a great increase in the volume of foreign trade. A number of other methods for increasing the volume of foreign trade are also available and deserve comment.

First, it is always possible to stimulate both exports and imports by granting a bounty upon either or both. Capitalist states have frequently granted bounties on exports. Due to their Mercantilistic prejudices, however, they have seldom granted bounties on imports. Both practices, nevertheless, serve to increase both imports and exports in the same degree.

Bounties on exports or imports may develop new foreign markets or extend old ones and thus increase the scale of production. This would lower production costs in industries of increasing returns. A bounty on exports of the products of extractive industries, such as wheat, cotton, and coal, obviously increases the cost to all domestic consumers by much more than the resulting reduction in price to foreign consumers.

[4] If labor cost makes up a larger share of the costs of imports than exports, the monetary demand for labor will be increased in one country and decreased in the other, and the demand for capital and land will be affected inversely. Under certain rare circumstances this might have a deflationary effect upon nominal wages in one country sufficient to offset the accompanying reduction of the cost of living. However, since interest and rent would accrue to the worker under Socialism, the net effect upon his income would still be beneficial.

[5] The same industrialists who pretend to fear the effect of importing the goods produced by cheap foreign labor because of its alleged depressing effect upon domestic wages usually favor the immigration of the cheap foreign labor itself, and this really depresses American wages.

Even in the case of industries of increasing returns, however, export bounties are undesirable. The total saving from an increased volume of production cannot be great enough to offset the cost of the bounty, for in that case the bounty would not be necessary. Any saving from an increased volume of production automatically serves to the proper degree as an incentive to exports by increasing the marginal profit on exports if export prices are equal to marginal costs.

As for using bounties merely to stimulate the volume of foreign trade because trade is advantageous, this will be unnecessary if the system used in determining this volume automatically brings about a maximum economic development of foreign trade. A system which will achieve this end without the use of bounties is described below.

In summary, bounties on imports and exports are undesirable because they result in prices which do not equal marginal costs. Thus, they distort consumption and production by extending them beyond the optimum point at which marginal utility and disutility are equal.

Secondly, it is always possible to increase the volume of foreign trade by dumping domestic products in foreign markets or by permitting or encouraging foreign nations to dump goods in domestic markets. Dumping may be defined as sale to foreign buyers at a net price lower than that prevailing in the domestic market. It has something in common with the use of export bounties to encourage foreign sales, since both methods result in sales to foreigners at prices below domestic levels. However, bounties are government outlays and are paid from taxes, while dumping is practiced by private firms and does not increase taxes. The costs of dumping are passed on as higher prices to domestic consumers of the commodity dumped.

Dumping may be profitable to individual trusts under Capitalism because most of them charge domestic consumers a price above their marginal costs. Since average costs exceed marginal costs in all manufacturing trusts, it is possible to dump goods abroad at a price below that secured in the domestic market and yet above marginal costs, so that an additional profit results from the production and sale of the goods dumped abroad. This type of dumping will seem to disappear under Socialism if domestic prices are reduced to the level of marginal costs, since the essence of dumping is the difference between domestic and foreign prices. Its disappearance will be only apparent, however, since goods which can be sold abroad at a price above the marginal cost of production should be exported in greater volume than ever under Socialism. Dumping abroad will appear to disappear only because it will be accompanied by dumping in domestic markets at the same price, and this will eliminate the difference between domestic and export prices.

Dumping is also occasionally practiced in order to retain existing markets until prices again return to normal profitable levels; in order to introduce new products in markets which are expected to be profitable when once opened up; or in order to drive competitors out of business and establish a monopoly. In such cases, the dumped goods may be sold at a price below the marginal cost of production.

As a method of competition, dumping at prices below marginal costs would be far more practical and effective when used by the export agency of a Socialist economy than when used by individual capitalists with relatively small resources. Nevertheless, it ought not to be used for this purpose by a Socialist state. It would arouse an enormous amount of international resentment and lead to restrictions upon the trade of the Socialist state using it. Dumping of this kind would also result in frequent and bitter price-cutting wars with foreign trusts, wars which, while they might do great damage to these trusts, would also result in large losses to the Socialist export agency.

Thirdly, it is possible to increase the volume of foreign trade by using advertising, either for purely competitive or for educational purposes. Advertising may be used both to stimulate the sale of foreign commodities in domestic markets and to stimulate the sale of domestic commodities in foreign markets.

A Socialist economy should not use competitive advertising to increase the sales of its own products in the domestic market, for reasons already made clear. Hence it ought not to permit the use of competitive advertising to stimulate the sale of foreign products in this market. The basis for this decision, it should be observed, is not an unreasonable Mercantilistic prejudice against imports, but the wastefulness of competitive advertising. Educational advertising should be permitted for both foreign and domestic commodities sold in the home market.

In the case of export trade, however, the interests of a Socialist state conflict with the interests of the remainder of the world in regard to competitive advertising. The burden of competitive advertising falls entirely upon the consumer in the form of a higher price. It definitely benefits the producer by raising the entire demand schedule for his goods. If competitive advertising did not benefit producers and other sellers, it would not be so universally used under Capitalism. It is clear, then, that the use of competitive advertising to increase export trade will benefit a Socialist economy while at the same time it will harm the remainder of the world, or at least the Capitalist remainder. Other Socialist states should prevent such advertising. The final decision of a Socialist state concerning the use of advertising to increase its foreign trade would thus depend upon its selfishness. If it placed the welfare of the world above its own welfare it would refuse to use competitive advertising in foreign trade, because the net cost of competitive advertising to consumers is much greater than its advantage to producers. If it placed its own welfare above that of the remainder of the world, or if it desired to use every available weapon in its competition with other Capitalist powers, it would exploit competitive advertising to the maximum economic degree.

It should not be forgotten that any increase in exports would result in an equal increase in imports if exports and imports were properly controlled. Thus, the use of advertising to increase American exports should not decrease the export trade of foreign nations. Competitive advertising would harm these nations, not by decreasing but rather by increasing the volume of exports from these foreign nations beyond the optimum point. Advertising would place the entire burden of this overexpansion of foreign trade, plus the additional gain to the Socialist state using advertising, upon the consumers of the advertised exported commodities, by changing the terms of trade in favor of the nation advertising its exports.

Finally, it is possible to increase the volume of foreign trade by spending money to discover new foreign goods which might be imported at a profit, and to discover new foreign markets in which domestic goods might be sold at a profit. Research work of this sort is justified so long as it yields net utility to domestic consumers. Under Capitalism, it is possible to measure at least a portion of the utility produced by such research by observing the profits made on the additional trade brought about by the research. In a Socialist economy, however, all foreign trade should be carried to the point where profits disappear and, if this is done, it will be impossible to use them as a measure of the returns from foreign-trade research. It will therefore be necessary to estimate the domestic consumers' surplus produced by such additional trade in order to determine the productivity of foreign-trade research. In most cases, this surplus will be only a small percentage of the total value of the additional commodities exported. This point is worthy of emphasis because certain popular bourgeois writers speak as if a billion dollars' worth of additional exports represents a net gain to the nation of one billion dollars.

D. DISADVANTAGES OF FOREIGN TRADE

Although foreign trade which enables consumers to get more for their money is ordinarily advantageous, unrestricted importation of certain classes of goods may be harmful.

In the first place, unrestricted foreign trade may result in dependence on foreign nations for commodities essential to the waging of war. If such goods are imported from abroad rather than produced at home, the military power of the importing nation may be considerably weakened and the military power of other nations will be equally increased.

This argument against foreign trade applies only to industries essential to military power, and these industries are already more highly developed in the United States than in any other country. The great wealth, the large population, and the strategic isolation of the United States render it relatively immune from all danger of successful attack. Under these circumstances, few if any protective tariffs are required to increase this country's military power. On the other hand, Soviet Russia was thoroughly justified in restricting foreign trade to increase her military power between World Wars I and II because her industry was undeveloped and she was surrounded by bitter enemies.

The second real disadvantage of foreign trade is that under certain circumstances it may serve to check or prevent altogether the development of certain industries well suited to domestic conditions and which, once properly developed, could supply certain commodities more economically than foreign nations. The development of new industries can certainly be stimulated by restriction of imports. This is often desirable both for the nation in question and for the world as a whole. Experience has repeatedly demonstrated that the industrialization of backward nations increases both their imports and their exports. It also stimulates the progress of science, checks infectious disease, promotes democracy, and yields other gains of benefit to foreign countries.

During the major portion of the nineteenth century, the high American tariff was largely justified by the need for protection of infant industries. In Soviet Russia a high degree of protection for the new and vital basic industries is similarly justified. The case is quite different in modern Germany, England, and the United States, however. In these nations the great majority of industries are already highly developed and deserve no protection. In the United States particularly, the application of the infant-industry argument to such industrial giants as United States Steel, Standard Oil of New Jersey, the Anaconda Copper Company, General Motors, Du Pont, etc., is obviously ridiculous. In every nation there is an occasional justification for the protection of a new industry, but the infant-industry argument cannot justify many of the protective tariffs now in force in the United States.

E. METHODS OF RESTRICTING FOREIGN TRADE

As explained above, it is sometimes justifiable to restrict both imports and exports (any restriction of one necessarily involves an equal restriction of the other) in order to protect or develop industries producing essential war materials and in order to encourage the establishment and development of promising new industries.

Under Capitalism the most common method of restricting foreign trade is the imposition of a tariff or duty upon imports or exports. This method has a number of apparent advantages. It not only results in no burden upon the government treasury, but actually serves to bring in a very considerable revenue. Moreover, the additional revenue is not a direct or obvious burden upon domestic taxpayers. In the case of commodities produced under conditions of increasing costs, this additional revenue comes in large part out of the pockets of foreigners.[6] These are very persuasive considerations to the average politician.

Actually tariffs are undesirable because they hide the cost of protecting domestic industries and because they place this cost upon the wrong people. If national welfare justifies the protection of a certain domestic industry, this protection ought to cause an obvious cost to the state rather than an increase in its income, and this cost ought to be borne by the nation as a whole rather than by those who consume the products of the protected industry. Only under such conditions is it possible for voters and legislators to measure and give due weight to the costs of protection.

Duties on exports are undesirable for much the same reason. They appear to be profitable, since they bring in a large revenue, but actually

[6] It is possible for a protective tariff to yield a net benefit to the nation imposing it. Such a case is illustrated in the following graph:

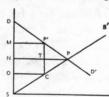

In this figure DD' is the demand curve and SS' the marginal cost curve for an imported commodity, resulting in price P in the absence of a tariff. Under perfect competition, the imposition of a tariff P'C (equal to MO) raises the price to P' and yields a tariff revenue represented by the area MOCP', of which NOCT is paid by the exporting nation and MNTP' is paid by consumers in the importing nation. The net utility loss to the world caused by this tariff is represented by P'CP, of which TCP falls upon the exporting nation and P'TP upon the importing nation. Obviously the loss P'TP is only a small fraction of the gain NOCT obtained from the tariff. Hence under such conditions, a tariff would be advantageous from the purely national standpoint. This argument applies only to tariffs on imports which are produced by industries of increasing cost, in other words, to tariffs on raw materials. Tariffs on imports produced by industries of decreasing cost, including all manufacturing industries, cannot yield such a net gain.

they decrease the volume of foreign trade below the optimum level and thus harm the national economy much more than they benefit the state treasury. If some special considerations justify an effort to restrict certain exports, this should be done in such a way as to impose a financial burden upon the government so obvious that everyone will be aware that restriction of foreign trade is costly rather than remunerative.

A nation which has a monopoly or a marked cost advantage in the production of a good may profit temporarily by charging all foreign buyers a monopoly price, the domestic price plus a suitable export duty. However, such monopoly gains stimulate foreign research on substitutes and on better methods of production which, once discovered, may put an end not only to the monopoly profits but even to the trade itself. Duties on exports also create ill feeling abroad and increase the danger of war. Hence a Socialist state should not use them.

It is possible to reduce the volume of foreign trade by laying an embargo upon the import or export of any commodity, or by establishing either import or export quotas for individual commodities. An embargo or complete prohibition is the most drastic method of limiting foreign trade, and hence involves a greater social cost than any other method. This cost may be justified in certain cases, but an embargo is an unsound method of limiting foreign trade because it occasions no monetary cost to the government to call attention to this real economic cost. This same criticism holds for quotas, although the latter are less undesirable inasmuch as and in so far as they place less of a bar upon commerce. Both embargoes and quotas also have the defect of being relatively inflexible and unresponsive to changes in market conditions. Quotas have the further disadvantage of giving rise to large profits upon the commodities imported. These profits, like the revenue from duties, tend to still further obscure the real economic costs involved.

One other method of restricting foreign trade, the granting of subsidies to domestic producers that are threatened by serious foreign competition, remains to be discussed. This is the method which should be used in a Socialist economy. There are several reasons for this. A subsidy or bounty granted to producers of war materials or to infant industries places an obvious monetary burden upon the state and, hence, upon all taxpayers. This financial burden is highly desirable because it corresponds to a very real economic burden. A protective tariff results in precisely the same economic burden, but it misleads the observer because it results in a monetary gain to the state. Since the function of money is to measure utility and disutility, all money payments ought to be honest indicators of utility gain or disutility cost. A bounty used to protect domestic industry serves to indicate that a real cost is involved in protection. A duty levied upon imports for the same purpose tends to hide this fact and to give precisely the opposite impression.

While bounties used to protect domestic industry would serve to remind the voters of the real cost involved, they would not measure it even roughly. Indeed, they would greatly exaggerate the real social cost involved. In other words, they would serve chiefly to increase producers' surplus and consumers' surplus. Only a very small fraction of such bounties would actually be necessary to cover the net utility loss on the additional production called forth by them.[7]

For a similar reason protective tariffs, since they raise domestic prices, cost consumers far more than they cost the nation as a whole. Most of the increase in price serves to increase producers' surpluses or to cover the duties paid on imports, and only a small part of it is necessary to offset the additional costs of producers. Neither a bounty nor a protective tariff can affect the price of the marginal unit without altering the price of all intramarginal units and, consequently, the disposition of the intramarginal surplus.

Another advantage of bounties over tariffs is that the former involve much less administrative expense. One government office in Washington could handle all bounties at a minimum of expense, while the customs service now includes offices in all ports and border towns. Bounties do not result in smuggling and the resulting expense to the government of checking it. Smuggling is only profitable when prices are lower abroad than at

[7] The following graph will help to clarify this point:

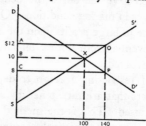

In this graph, X represents the market price, $10, of a certain commodity, total sales of which are 100. After the government grants a $4 bounty on the production of this commodity, production increases to 140 and the marginal cost to $12. At the same time the market price falls to $8.

Under these assumptions, the area *ACPO* represents the cost of the subsidy, namely $560. *ABXO* represents the increase in positive rent, about $245, which eventually accrues to the state and reduces the net cost of the bounty by that much. *BCPX* represents the increase in the consumers' surplus, also about $245. The total social cost or net disutility of the bounty is represented by the small triangle *XOP*, roughly the equivalent of about $80. In a word, a bounty of $560 would cost a Socialist economy only about $80 under the above assumptions.

home. Bounties would lower domestic prices to those prevailing abroad, plus costs of importation, and would therefore put an end to smuggling.

F. THE CONDUCT OF FOREIGN TRADE

In a Socialist economy all exports and imports should be handled by a single national Foreign Trade Trust. This organization would be one of the major national trusts and should be represented on the Supreme Economic Council and, perhaps, on the executive committee of that body.

The Foreign Trade Trust should have branches or subsidiaries in virtually every foreign nation, and these branches should have offices or representatives in every important city or market within the nation in which they are located. At home the Foreign Trade Trust should also have branch offices in every port and frontier point through which any appreciable volume of international trade passes. Wherever necessary, abroad or at home, the Foreign Trade Trust should have warehouse and storage facilities to care for its trade.

1. CONTROL OF FOREIGN TRADE

The basic economic problem involved in the management of foreign trade in a Socialist economy is the problem of how to determine the nature and volume of imports and exports. We have already discussed certain methods both of increasing and of restricting the total volume of foreign trade, but these methods do not solve this basic problem, nor do they permit immediate and flexible control of the total volume of imports and exports. Tariffs and bounties should not be changed from day to day. They ought to be used, if at all, merely to protect certain domestic industries, not to control the volume of foreign trade. Although the purpose of advertising is to increase the volume of sales, it cannot give more than a small degree of control over the total volume of foreign trade. But the significant fact is that all of these methods are mere methods; none of them deal with the problem of when, where, and why control should be exercised.

The problem of the control of import and export trade in a Socialist economy may conveniently be divided into two parts; first, the problem of the control of the volume of trade in individual commodities; and secondly, the problem of the control of the total volume of imports and exports.

Every individual commodity which has moved in foreign trade, or which might move in foreign trade, should be placed under the control of specialists in that commodity or in a group of commodities including it. These specialists should have absolute control over the nature and volume of exports and imports of the commodities placed in their charge. As we shall explain later, control over the total volume of imports and exports of all kinds should be exercised in a manner which leaves complete freedom to these commodity specialists.

Two slightly different tasks will confront these commodity specialists; first, the task of determining what commodities ought to be imported or exported, and secondly, the task of determining the volume of imports and exports of each commodity.

The first question, that of determining what individual commodities should be imported or exported, ought to be settled by application of the following principle: Any individual commodity which can be imported or exported at a profit, between any point inside the nation and any foreign point, should be imported or exported by the Foreign Trade Trust.[8]

The justification for carrying on foreign trade wherever and whenever it yields a profit is precisely the same as that for producing whatever good or service yields a profit. With a relatively equal distribution of income and with a properly controlled monetary system, a profit is the best possible indication of a net margin of utilitum over disutilitum. By definition, net utilitum is the goal of man and the economic system.

The Foreign Trade Trust of a Socialist economy should carry on a far more intensive, comprehensive, and persistent search for new trade opportunities than any Capitalist nation now does. Due to the absence of all duplication of effort, this would not be as expensive as the work of this kind now carried on by Capitalist nations. Under Capitalism, business inertia is an important bar to the establishment of new trade relationships. Under Socialism, price differentials would be far more important as factors determining the volume of trade, and very slight differentials between prices at home and abroad should result in immediate reactions.[9]

The second question involved in the control of foreign trade in specific commodities is that of how large a volume of each commodity should be imported or exported. Here again the proper method of control is similar to that used in controlling the production of domestic commodities. The volume of imports or exports of each good should be in-

---

[8] This general principle requires some qualification as regards profits made possible by temporary foreign dumping. See pp. 384–85.

[9] The dominant role of custom and the minor role of prices in determining the nature and volume of foreign trade under Capitalism is clearly shown by the relatively small effect of very wide fluctuations in foreign exchange rates. A 50 percent decline in the value of the yen in 1932, for instance, caused little immediate change in the volume of Japanese imports and exports. Equally small were the short-run effects upon foreign trade of the devaluation of the dollar in 1933.

creased until profits disappear, but no further. Of course, no exact equilibrium is possible, but the goal of all control over foreign trade should be to eliminate both profits and losses by varying the volume of trade alone. Any effort to decrease profits or losses merely by altering the expenses of doing business would be entirely unsound. Those who evaluate the success of executives of the Foreign Trade Trust should take two entirely different factors into consideration: first, the unit cost of doing business, and secondly, the volume of profits and losses earned. This would tend to prevent the alteration of unit costs in order to reduce profits and losses.

All that was said in chapter viii concerning the proper calculation of profits and losses resulting from the domestic production of commodities applies with equal force to profits and losses earned in foreign trade. It is marginal profit or loss that should be discovered and used for control purposes. Rent, interest, depreciation, insurance, etc., should be treated as costs in the same way and for the same reasons. Individual production-control statements for each commodity carried over each route should be prepared and used. Future or potential profits and losses should be the determining factors, rather than past profits and losses. This means, among other things, that profits and losses due to price changes, natural catastrophes, obsolescence, and other unpredictable factors should be ignored in planning future imports and exports.

The use of profits and losses to determine the volume of imports and exports of specific commodities is inconsistent with arbitrary planning of such imports and exports. It will, of course, be good business practice to estimate in advance the volume of future imports and exports in order to prepare to handle them, but daily fluctuations in foreign prices and weekly or monthly fluctuations in domestic prices will constantly alter profits and losses and, hence, the volume of imports and exports. In the last analysis, it is unpredictable and fluctuating profits and losses, rather than national plans, which should determine the volume of individual exports. Here, as elsewhere in a Socialist economy, future planning or budgeting would be no more important than it already is in well-managed Capitalist enterprises.

2. THE BALANCING OF TOTAL IMPORTS AND EXPORTS

As we have already explained, the total volume of imports and exports of each individual commodity should be independently determined by specialists in that commodity, regardless of the volume of trade in other goods. Since the total volume of imports or exports is merely the total of imports and exports of all individual commodities, the former may appear to be determined by those who control the latter, the commodity specialists who pay no attention to the total volume of trade. However, since the commodity specialists are to be governed in all their decisions by profits and losses, it is possible to give one agency complete control over the relationship between total imports and total exports by giving it power to influence sufficiently these profits and losses. This can be done by placing in its hands complete control over the exchange rate prevailing between the domestic currency and foreign currencies.

Such is the method of controlling the relationship between total imports and total exports which ought to be used in a Socialist economy. Absolute control over all foreign-exchange rates should be vested in a special division of the Foreign Trade Trust[10] and used by this division to secure the desired balance of trade.

Incidentally, the desired balance of trade will never be an exactly equal balance. There will always be other items, the so-called "invisible items," which involve international financial payments. It is the total payments of all kinds in each direction which must be balanced. The manipulation of the foreign-exchange rate will affect the volume of each of these invisible items in the same way that it will affect visible items. Thus, an intentional depreciation of the dollar will decrease American tourist travel abroad just as it will decrease American imports of all kinds.

Under Capitalism, control of foreign-exchange rates requires large financial reserves. Arbitrary authority over the conduct of private citizens also is ordinarily used to supplement financial measures. It will be far easier to secure the same ends in a Socialist economy. Whenever the Foreign Exchange Division of the Foreign Trade Trust desires a 1 or 2 percent increase in visible and invisible imports or exports, it will merely alter the foreign-exchange rate sufficiently to accomplish the desired result. All commodity specialists will immediately react to the new profits and losses created thereby in the trade under their control. The desired end will be quickly achieved without any large purchase or sale of foreign exchange because of the immediate effect upon the volume of imports and exports.

Many difficulties encountered in the control of foreign exchange under Capitalism are due to the unsound purposes of such control. Under Capitalism, it is customary to use control over foreign exchange in order to stabilize the exchange, that is, in order to prevent natural reaction to economic forces generated by excessive imports or exports. Under Socialism, however, control over foreign exchange should be used

---

[10] It is possible to argue that this power should be entrusted to the State Bank, as has been done in Soviet Russia. Under Capitalism also, foreign-exchange control is sometimes exercised by banks. It is here proposed to vest this power in the Foreign Trade Trust because the chief purpose of all control over exchange rates will be the control of total imports and exports. This control will also affect international financial payments for other purposes, but these payments will be much less important than foreign trade, and their amount will ordinarily be determined by other considerations than the foreign-exchange rate.

to secure an immediate and proper reaction to such forces. When the nation is faced with an undesired surplus of imports, no costly or futile efforts to maintain the foreign-exchange value of the domestic currency by deflating domestic prices ought to be made. Instead, the exchange rate should be immediately lowered so as to eliminate all financial strain by stimulating exports and reducing imports. This method of balancing imports and exports would have a minimum of effect upon domestic prices and business conditions since it would no longer be necessary to effect changes in the balance of trade by alternate domestic inflation and deflation.

To control all foreign-exchange rates it is usually necessary to control the rate with one other foreign currency only. Thus, if Soviet Russia were to exercise control only over the exchange rate between the ruble and the dollar, it would automatically achieve all necessary control over other foreign currencies.

The method used by Soviet Russia to control the relationship between total exports and total imports is apparently an entirely arbitrary method. There is no difficulty, of course, in securing any desired balance between the total imports and exports of a Socialist economy, just as there is no difficulty in determining an arbitrary plan of production for the domestic economy. The real difficulty, and one which the U.S.S.R. has not solved, is that of securing the most economic volume of individual and total imports and exports. The great advantage of the method of balancing imports and exports suggested in this chapter is that it permits restriction of total imports or exports by curtailing all individual imports or exports in precisely the degree in which they ought to be curtailed, and vice versa in the case of an increase in total imports or exports.

There will undoubtedly be a considerable period of time during which Socialist and Capitalist states will exist side by side in a world slowly moving from Capitalism to Socialism. Under such circumstances, it would be desirable for a Socialist state to regulate its total volume of imports and exports in such a way as to profit from business cycles in Capitalist nations, and at the same time diminish the severity of such cycles. Whenever the Capitalist world is in the grip of a world depression, or whenever any individual Capitalist nation is suffering a business depression, a Socialist state should so regulate its foreign-exchange rates as to secure a large surplus of imports over exports. The imports would be purchased at abnormally low prices, and, hence, should be purchased in abnormally large quantities, part of which should be stored for use in future years or used for the extension of capital facilities. The commodities normally exported would also be selling abroad at abnormally low prices; hence, their export should be sharply reduced, and a large stock of them be stored for export during subsequent years at much higher prices. The large surplus of imports could be financed by foreign loans, by the sale of previous foreign investments, or by the export of large supplies of gold produced and accumulated during years of relative prosperity and high prices in the Capitalist world.

Such a policy would tend to raise prices in the Capitalist nations during periods of depression and to lower them in periods of prosperity, thus reducing the severity of the business cycle. Likewise, the policy of buying and storing large stocks of individual imports, which were selling at abnormally low prices during any period of the cycle, would tend to stabilize the prices of these goods. In a word, the foreign-trade policies recommended here for a Socialist nation would be highly beneficial to its Capitalist neighbors.

CHAPTER XX. PUBLIC UTILITIES

As used in this chapter, the term "public utilities" includes gas, water, electricity, steam, sewer, telephone, telegraph, and commercial wireless communication systems. It does not include transportation systems, which are dealt with in a separate chapter, or warehouses, dairies, ice companies and various other industries sometimes called public utilities.

The public utilities covered in this chapter have much in common. All of them except radio communication require a large investment in underground pipe or cable networks, and these networks largely duplicate each other. Most of them employ similar systems of measuring service and collecting charges from customers. For these and other reasons the problems of public utilities are similar and are different from those of other industries.

Capitalism has already developed an extensive literature on the theory of public-utility operation. Most of this theory will be applicable in a collectivist economy. This chapter is therefore limited to a discussion of the major changes in the methods of operating public utilities which will result from the introduction of Socialism.

Most public utilities are already operated as monopolies under Capitalism. For this reason, they offer fewer opportunities for increased efficiency under Socialism than most other industries.[1]

All public utilities should be operated by a single national Public Utility Trust. This trust should probably be subdivided into a maintenance division, a research division, an accounting division, and separate operating divisions for each utility, or group of similar utilities. To be specific, the water and sewer system might be operated by the same division, and the telegraph and telephone systems by another division, while the other utilities might be individually operated.

All utilities should be under a single trust in order to make possible the maximum economies of common management and operation. These economies may be classified under three heads: (1) economies due to unified construction and maintenance work, (2) economies from unified accounting, and (3) economies of large scale production.

---

[1] Bourgeois economists commonly hold that public utilities require government ownership more than other industries. Actually, however, it is the most competitive industries, such as retail stores, which require government operation most urgently, since only in such industries will government ownership achieve the economies of monopoly. Natural monopolies are much more suited to private ownership than are highly competitive industries since private ownership of public utilities does not result in the usual wastes of competition. However, government control over prices is needed in the case of private monopolies.

A. CONSOLIDATION OF CONSTRUCTION AND MAINTENANCE WORK

The construction and maintenance work of different public utilities is of a very similar character. Large economies may be obtained if all utility construction and maintenance work is done by the same organization. Instead of tearing up a street one year to install a sewer, the next year to put telephone wires underground, and the next year to enlarge water mains, etc., as so frequently occurs under Capitalism, the Public Utilities Trust should install all utilities at the same time in the same ditch. This would not only eliminate frequent tearing up of costly paving, but would also enlarge the scale of installation work and thus make possible more of the economies of large-scale production in such work.

While the installation work for all utilities should be done by a single organization, this organization might well be a part of the Construction Trust, which would build all streets and houses, rather than a part of the Public Utilities Trust. The original installation of utilities is an essential part of the work of constructing a new plant or farm community, and should be planned and carried out as a part of the larger project.

Maintenance work for all utilities should also be carried on by a single division of the Public Utilities Trust, and this Maintenance Division should be divided into three sections, one for pipe maintenance, one for wire maintenance, and one for plant maintenance.

The same kind of skill and equipment is needed to dig up a street in order to repair a water main as is needed to dig up a street in order to repair a sewer, steam, or gas main. Moreover, an event such as a flood which injures one main is apt to injure the other mains.

The men and tools used to maintain telephone poles and lines are almost equally qualified to repair telegraph and power poles and lines. If a storm blows the wires down, there is no reason why the telephone company, the telegraph company, and the power and light company should all send repair crews to the same spot. Maintenance inspectors and trouble shooters should inspect all overhead lines or underground cables on each street at the same time.

The merger of all utility maintenance work in the hands of a single agency would so increase the size and personnel of the average maintenance unit that marked improvement in organization and equipment would be possible. Thus, if all ditch digging for utility maintenance in each community were done by a single agency, it would pay to use more ditch digging machines and those in existence would be more steadily employed. It would also be economical to increase the division of labor among both foremen and ditchdiggers. There are thousands of small towns and sparsely populated areas where the volume of maintenance work on independent utility systems is much too small to justify the use of labor-saving methods and equipment but where the total volume for all utilities is large enough to justify it. Unification of all utilities would also permit the location of maintenance units closer to the utility customers in thinly settled areas, and this would speed up repair work.

B. CONSOLIDATION OF OFFICE WORK

The accounting, clerical, and other business-office activities now carried on independently by four or five distinct private or municipal public utilities in each community should be combined and rationalized. Only one "accounts receivable" account for all public-utility services should be kept for each customer, and only one "accounts payable" account for each creditor. This alone would reduce by 75 percent the number of such accounts and would save an equal proportion of the paper, filing cabinets, and space required for accounts payable and receivable.

Each meter reader should read all meters—gas, water, electricity, steam, etc.—in each building on his route, and should enter the reading for all meters at each address on a single page of his record book so that they could be simultaneously transcribed to the single accounts receivable account and the single consolidated bill for each customer without referring to more than one sheet of paper. Each customer should receive only one bill for all public-utility services, and should pay this bill by mailing a single check to a single business office. This would reduce the number of separate bills required by somewhere between five hundred million and one billion per year. Each bill now costs the public utility about ten cents to prepare and mail, and receiving and entering the payment costs as much more. It also costs the customer at least ten cents to pay each bill, all of which adds up to over 30 cents per utility bill.

In order to reduce still further the cost of preparing and paying public-utility bills, a Socialist Public Utility Trust should lengthen the period covered by each bill. Instead of submitting a bill each month, it should submit a bill only once every two or three months. This would reduce by 50 to 67 percent the cost of submitting and paying bills. It would not result in any increase in losses from bad debts if all bad debts are deducted from future wages as recommended elsewhere in this book. Another simple and effective method of avoiding losses due to bad debts could be used if necessary. All customers might be required to make a cash deposit sufficient to cover their probable bill. Under Socialism, wages and personal cash reserves would be so high, and personal credit facilities so ample, that such a requirement would not injure any person.

All local operating units of the Public Utilities Trust should use the same standardized system of accounting in order to facilitate comparison of the accounts of different operating units. The books and forms used for accounting, the titles and definitions of accounts, the treatment of depreciation, the method of valuing inventories, the types of accounting machine used, and all other significant features of the accounting system should be uniform throughout the country except for differences in equipment resulting from experiments with, or the gradual introduction of, improved models.

C. CONSOLIDATION OF GENERATING FACILITIES AND UTILITIES

All electricity produced in a Socialist city should be generated in a single power station and distributed to all users within economical transmission distance inside and outside the city. In small cities all steam should be generated in the same plant. No manufacturing plant, commercial establishment, or residential building within this transmission range should have its own equipment for producing steam or generating electricity. If a city is large enough to justify more than one steam-generating station, each station should serve all customers in its area.

Steam and electricity can be generated much more economically in large power plants than in small ones. Every increase in the size of a power plant makes possible the achievement of additional economies in production. Capital outlay per unit of capacity decreases with every increase in capacity. For instance, a tenfold increase in capacity may merely double the floor space occupied and thus reduce building costs per unit of capacity by 80 percent. Building costs per unit of floor space also decrease as the size of the building increases. Large boiler-furnace units justify the use of labor-saving devices and automatic processes. For instance, the larger the furnace the more advantageous it is to install automatic equipment for stoking the furnace and removing the ashes. Moreover, there is no capacity limit beyond which increases in size fail to yield economies, and these economies are large even after a considerable size has been attained. Thus, an electrical generating plant of 40,000 kw. capacity, adequate to meet the needs of a city of 100,000 population, produces electricity at a cost which is 50 to 100 percent above that of a plant with a capacity of 400,000 kw.

The generation of steam in one-family houses is particularly wasteful because of the small size of domestic boilers in such installations. A large central power plant can generate steam for less than 20 percent of the cost in individual houses and there are many nonmonetary advantages, such as freedom from buying coal, firing the furnace, laundering soot-dirtied clothing, and so forth. The cost of distributing steam to individual dwellings is less than the cost of delivering coal and hauling away the ashes.

Under Capitalism, many private businessmen find it profitable to build and use their own power plants because public utilities are monopolies and charge a price above the cost of producing power in less efficient independent plants. Proper utility rates would make this unprofitable.

1. RELOCATION OF POWER PLANTS AND GAS WORKS

Nearly all large steam power plants and gas works should be located in coal and oil fields at distances up to 400 miles from the cities they serve. For instance, all electricity generated from steam and all artificial gas used in Washington, D.C., Baltimore, Philadelphia, New York City, Pittsburgh, and other cities within these limits should be produced in steam power plants and gas works located at the very mouth of the most suitable large coal mines and oil wells in Pennsylvania. Eventually it may be feasible to burn the coal underground and generate steam without even separating coal from the seam in which it lies.

Although locating power plants in coal and oil fields 300 or 400 miles from the cities served would result in transmission costs of about two mills per kilowatt-hour, several advantages would outweigh this cost. The expense of transporting coal or oil 300 or 400 miles would be saved. Power would become much cheaper in the coal and oil fields and this would permit more electrification of coal mines and oil wells. The long transmission lines would make cheap electricity available to all farm and plant communities along the way. The volume of smoke and soot would be reduced in all cities and communities served. The cost of living for power-plant employees would be reduced by moving them from large cities to small cities or towns. Finally, the costs of construction are now much lower in small towns than in large cities, and this difference would probably continue under Socialism.

2. DEVELOPMENT OF STEAM UTILITIES

Only a handful of American communities are now served by steam utilities which make centrally produced steam available to private domestic consumers. A Socialist Utilities Trust should rapidly extend such steam utility service to every American city in the North and perhaps to many southern cities as well. Under Socialism, steam utilities should become almost as numerous and important as gas and water utilities now are.

The fact that central production of steam will reduce the cost of production at least 80 percent below the average cost in individual domestic boilers has already been noted. The cost of distribution will amount to only a small part of this saving when all houses and apartments are equipped to use steam heat. Economical distribution of steam is difficult if not impossible to achieve in a community in which housing is constructed by thousands of competing builders, each of whom is free to install a different kind of heating system. Under Socialism, a city plan, covering, among many other things, utility services and the type of heating to be installed in each home, would be prepared before construction began if possible, and this plan would provide for the use of steam heat in every dwelling in those parts of the country where steam heating is most economical. This would make the cost of distributing steam relatively low because every house in each block would use steam.

Steam heating is superior to warm-air heating and is already widely used in many states in spite of the high cost of producing steam in domestic boilers. Moreover, steam can be used in the new types of radiant heating systems which use pipes in the floor, walls, and ceiling instead of radiators and which are a great improvement over existing types of steam heating.

Central generation and city-wide distribution of steam would not only reduce sharply the cost of steam used in domestic heating but would also free the domestic user of many inconveniences attached to domestic generation of steam. The user would no longer have to buy fuel or attend to repairs for his furnace-boiler unit. He would not have to get up early in the morning to fire the furnace with coal. He would be free of the soot and smoke now produced not only by his own furnace but by those of his neighbors. These are very considerable gains.

If centrally produced steam were used for all domestic heating and electricity for all domestic cooking in communities where this is economical, there would no longer be any domestic need for gas. The distribution systems now used to distribute gas in these cities should therefore be converted into steam-distribution systems, and new communities built in the same regions should not be provided with gas-distribution systems.

While steam heating will probably continue for a long time to be the best kind of domestic heating in northern cities of the United States, reversible electrical-refrigeration systems which cool the air in summer and warm it in winter may soon become practical for general use as the sole or chief means of heating in regions with a mild winter climate. These reversible refrigeration units do not now promise to be practical as the chief source of heat for houses in regions with a cold winter climate, but they may be widely used as a supplementary source of heat during certain months of the year even in northern cities. Technological progress is now so rapid and unpredictable that it is impossible to tell what heating systems will be most economical in the future. However, it is certain that steam utilities are economical today, and that the scarcity of them is due to the defects of Capitalism.

3. ADVANTAGES OF SUPERPOWER SYSTEMS

The centralization of ownership and management of all electrical generation and distribution systems in a Socialist economy would aid the development of large superpower systems, transmission networks which would link different cities in power pools. A Socialist Utilities Trust should form superpower systems in every region as rapidly as possible.

Superpower systems make possible notable economies. In the first place, they permit the concentration of electrical generation in a small number of large plants. The advantages of large-scale generation of electricity have been noted above. In the second place, they permit a marked reduction in stand-by capacity. Under Capitalism, each power company maintains its own stand-by capacity which often amounts to more than 100 percent of peak load. The linking up of independent systems into a single superpower system makes it possible for a single stand-by plant to serve all the previously separate systems. A single superpower network might link together ten large power plants, and it is exceedingly improbable that more than one of them would ever break down at a time. Therefore, one optimum-size stand-by generator would suffice. If the power plants were not connected, each district would require 100 percent stand-by capacity to give equal security.

A third important advantage of any superpower system is the "diversity economy." Different distribution systems have their peak loads at different hours of the day. If local systems with peak loads at different times were tied together into a single regional superpower system, the peak load for the entire system would be markedly below the total of the peak loads for each component system. A 10 percent reduction in consolidated peak load would make possible an equal reduction in total generating capacity.

A fourth advantage of a superpower system is that it makes it possible to concentrate power generation in low-cost plants during off-peak hours. This permits the maximum use of any hydroelectric plants in the system.

Finally, all new transmission lines required for superpower systems open up new markets for electricity or make available cheaper sources of electricity to farms and communities already provided with electricity in the territory they pass through.

While the term "superpower" is ordinarily used only in connection with the production and distribution of electrical energy, all of the arguments for a superpower system in this field apply with equal or greater force to the production and distribution of artificial gas. Artificial gas can be sent through pipes over long distances more cheaply than electrical current. The cost of production varies inversely with the size of the plant. Peak loads come at different times in different cities. Interconnection of city systems also reduces stand-by needs.

4. SUBSTITUTION OF ELECTRICITY FOR GAS

The use of electricity for domestic cooking has grown rapidly in recent years, and should replace completely the use of gas in all new houses built under Socialism, and perhaps in all older houses as well. Electricity is already cheaper than gas in those few communities where the rates for electricity for cooking are as low as the cost of generating and distributing electricity used for this purpose. Socialism should make such rates universal. Moreover, the use of electricity for cooking, combined with the use of centrally produced steam for heating in new housing developments would make gas-distribution systems unnecessary and would save the cost of constructing individual gas connections and individual chimneys for each dwelling, as well as eliminating the need for gas mains on most streets. Electric stoves do not produce smoke or fumes. These savings would reduce over-all construction costs, including the investment in utility facilities, by several hundred dollars per dwelling unit.

Finally, electric cooking stoves provide a superior service. They produce a more even heat than gas stoves, and can be more easily controlled by automatic control devices. There is no smoke to blacken cooking utensils, no fumes to spoil the air, no soot to dirty the kitchen and no gas to escape and cause fires or asphyxiation.

Under Capitalism, utility rates do not pass on to domestic consumers anywhere near the full saving from increased use of one utility, and hence do not even permit consumers to become aware of the full benefit from using one utility only. Moreover, where both gas and electric distribution systems already exist side by side, and this is the rule, the full economy to be attained from concentration on one utility is unattainable.

D. DETERMINING THE NEED FOR ADDITIONAL UTILITY PLANT

The problem of determining whether it is economical to build a new public-utility system or to make additions to existing ones requires some consideration. Under Capitalism, the criterion used is, "will the new investment earn a profit?" Socialism eliminates profits as the goal of economic effort. At the most, a Socialist utility would only have to earn enough to cover the costs of construction and operation to prove itself economic.

Moreover, owing to the fact that public-utility service must be provided in large installments, in other words, since the supply schedule is discontinuous, there would be many occasions under Socialism when it is desirable to provide public-utility services in spite of the fact that no possible rate schedule would yield an income sufficient to cover the costs of providing this service. A new utility system creates a certain amount of utilitum at certain disutilitum costs. The disutilitum is exaggerated by the money costs of operation, due to the existence of producers' surpluses. The utilitum created by the new system is incompletely measured by the money income because of the existence of consumers' surpluses. In most industries, the volume of production can be set at the point where there is no *marginal* surplus to either producer òr consumer. In the case of public utilities, however, the necessity of beginning or increasing supply in large installments often makes it impossible to limit supply precisely at the point where the consumers' *marginal* surplus disappears. It becomes a problem, then, of whether to fix supply somewhat below or above this point. In the former case, the utility would return a net profit, for rates should always be high enough to reduce demand to supply. In the latter case, a deficit would result, since marginal users could not afford to pay the full costs of production.

It is perfectly possible, however, that the consumers' surplus would be more than sufficient to compensate for such a pecuniary deficit. If so, a new plant or an addition to plant capacity would be economically desirable in spite of the fact that it would not pay its way.

The existence of a consumers' surplus always means that a smaller quantity of service could be sold at a higher price. The existence of a consumers' surplus larger than a pecuniary deficit, therefore, means that if every unit of service rendered were paid for in accordance with its specific utility, no deficit would result. However, a consumers' surplus does not warrant the extension of production beyond the point of equilibrium between marginal utility and disutility unless this is necessary in order to make possible a large intramarginal surplus which would not otherwise exist. This latter situation prevails only where increments in supply are necessarily of a larger size than increments in demand. The graph illustrates this point.

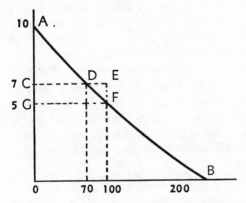

The line *AB* represents the demand schedule for a utility service which cannot be supplied in increments of less than one hundred. The average cost of producing the first increment of 100 units is *C*, but only 70 units can be sold at this price. Under these circumstances, it would be economical to build facilities to supply the minimum quantity of 100 units and sell them at price G, since this would yield a consumers' surplus (AGF) in excess of the pecuniary deficit $(CGFE)$. In other words, ACD is much larger than DFE.

In a Socialist economy, it would be perfectly practical to measure consumers' surpluses. Production and distribution would be concentrated in a few hands, and experimentation to determine demand at different prices would be feasible. As we have pointed out elsewhere, each Socialist trust must learn as much as possible about the demand schedule for its products in order to price them and to plan future production intelligently.

No public-utility service should ever be provided at a loss unless it meets the conditions set forth above. Under Capitalism, regulatory bodies frequently require utilities to render, or prevent utilities from discontinuing, services which do not even pay their variable costs. The excuse usually given is "public convenience." This policy is unsound. The fact that a utility system as a whole is making a good profit does not justify the continuance of any single service on which a deficit is incurred, except in the circumstances just described. Public convenience is never of any more importance than is indicated by consumers' surplus and monetary income.

E. THE PRICING OF PUBLIC-UTILITY SERVICES

The theory of public-utility rates is one of the most poorly developed fields of Capitalist economic theory. Orthodox specialists in this field are either unfamiliar with the best modern value theory or are uninterested in applying it to practical utility problems. They have devoted most of their time to the interpretation and effect of laws and judicial and administrative decisions which are of passing interest only, and have largely ignored the basic economic issues of enduring interest to economists. Hence, a Socialist theory of public-utility rates must be developed with little help from Capitalist theory concerning public-utility rates.[2]

The most basic principle of pricing in a Socialist economy is that prices should equal marginal costs. In earlier chapters on the general theory of prices and production control, it was explained that the best way to achieve prices equal to marginal costs is to separate the function of pricing from the function of production control. With such a separation of functions, those who fix prices need only apply the simple rule of setting prices

---

[2] The most important contribution to public-utility rate theory by a Capitalist economist, and one virtually ignored in textbooks on public utilities, is Harold Hotelling's statement of the theory that rates should equal marginal costs, in "The General Welfare in Relation to Problems of Taxation and of Railway and Utility Rates," *Econometrics*, Vol. VI, No. 3 (July 1938), pp. 242–69.

which will just move the entire supply of each good in each market. These prices would result in marginal profits or losses which should cause those in charge of production to increase or decrease the supply of each good until marginal cost is just equal to the market price.

Such a separation of functions is not possible in the case of public utilities because their products are services which cannot be produced for inventory and stored. It is impossible to fix prices in such a way as to move an existing supply because the price itself usually determines the supply, which is equal to the amount consumed.

It may appear at first glance that this is unimportant since capacity to serve is available as a substitute for supply in the process of price and production control. However, capacity cannot usually be increased as rapidly or easily as supply, and it ought never to be reduced merely because it is temporarily unneeded. This is true for all industries, but it is especially significant in the case of public utilities because they require an unusually large investment in capacity.

Since a separation of functions is not practical, the price of service and the rate of use of existing capacity must be simultaneously controlled and this control must take the form of price control. For the same reason, price control should be based upon the principle that prices should equal marginal costs rather than upon the principle, useful only under certain conditions, that prices should equalize supply and sales.

Utility rates equal to marginal costs would be far below existing utility rates except in those few instances where peak demand would exceed capacity. The marginal cost of producing and distributing electricity, for instance, is probably less than four mills per kilowatt-hour in all large cities, but the marginal price charged domestic consumers in such cities averages about forty mills per kilowatt-hour. Even the widely praised promotional rates of the TVA are far above marginal cost.

Marginal costs are only a small fraction of the average costs of public utilities because construction and interest costs are very high and account for most of the average costs. Once a utility system has been built, the costs of operation are relatively small. Henc, the cost of producing and selling one more unit of service is relatively small. In the case of an electrical utility using steam power, for instance, the only significant cost of producing and selling additional electricity is the cost of the additional fuel. Even the repair and maintenance costs on the system as a whole are virtually independent of the quantity of electricity produced and consumed.

Some water utilities have sufficient capacity to supply all possible requirements and have no significant marginal costs. Such utilities should make no charge for the use of water. Electrical systems using hydro-electric power only, may be in the same situation especially in periods when use is below the peak level. If so, they should make no charge for electricity. Charging a price is always uneconomical if there are no variable costs to be reduced by economy in use. When marginal costs are zero, prices should be zero, in accordance with the fundamental principle that prices should equal marginal cost.

At any given time, the marginal cost of providing one more unit of service to a domestic consumer is identical with the cost of providing one more unit of service to a commercial or industrial consumer, assuming adequate distribution facilities in all cases. Hence, the rate charged should be the same for all consumers.

Marginal costs of utility services are very stable from hour to hour through the day and from day to day through the year as long as the peak load each day is less than the capacity of the system. Hence, little if any variation in ratio during periods when demand is less than capacity is justified. This principle, like the one stated in the preceding paragraph, is almost universally violated today.

On the other hand, as soon as the demand for service at the existing rate equals the capacity of existing fixed plant, rates should be raised until demand and supply are equal. As demand increases, a time will arrive when the rates must be high enough to cover total costs in order to balance supply and demand. If demand continues to increase, rates should rise above average costs of production. Thus, individual public-utility systems should incur a deficit for some time after construction, but should finally earn a profit. Every effort should be made to reduce these profits and losses to the optimum by rational planning of the construction and expansion of plant facilities. However, both original plant and subsequent additions ought to satisfy average demand over a period of rising demand, so that some profits and losses will be unavoidable.

The use of utility services varies from hour to hour throughout twenty-four hours and from day to day throughout the year. It would be fairly easy to establish different rates for off-peak months or quarters of the year than for peak months or quarters, but in the case of most utilities —gas, water, and electricity, for instance—it would probably not be possible to vary rates from hour to hour. Meters now in use do not show hourly variations in use, and the kind of meter which would show such variations would probably cost enough to make hourly variations in rates for domestic consumers uneconomic. This is unfortunate because the hourly variations in use are now very great and it would be desirable to encourage domestic consumers to use more electricity and gas during off-peak hours and less during peak hours. However, there are other methods of accomplishing this end, such as the use of two connections, one of which is shut off automatically during peak hours, and engineering progress will in time develop other methods. All that the economist can say is that utility rates ought to vary with variable costs whenever it is economical to measure both variations in cost and variations in use.

The problem of how much price variation is economic is very similar to the problem of how much cost accounting is economic. If no additional costs were involved, an infinite amount of price variation and an infinite amount of cost accounting would be desirable. As previously explained (page 189), however, cost accounting is not worth while unless it saves far more than the cost of the cost accounting. For much the same reasons, price variation is not economic unless it saves far more than the cost of the price variation.

The cost of the accounting and other work required to use a certain system of price variation is fairly easy to calculate. The saving or benefit to the consumer from a certain policy of price variation is very difficult to estimate. It consists (1) in the consumers' surplus on the additional service consumed during periods of low rates and which would not have been purchased in the absence of rate variation, and (2) in the difference between the disutility (measured by the new rates) and the utility of the current he no longer consumes during peak periods on account of the rise in peak-period rates. Thus if, owing to the introduction of monthly rate variations, a consumer reduces his previous $100 winter gas bill to $75 and increases his $10 summer gas bill to $20, the total change of $35 indicates a net utility gain of only a small fraction of that amount. Hence it would be uneconomic to introduce a policy of monthly rate variation if such a policy would cost more than a small fraction of this change. The question of which small fraction is the one to be used as a criterion is impossible to answer, but one-tenth might be taken as a safe maximum.

The income from the utility rates recommended above would not cover the full costs, fixed and variable, of utility services. A deficit, negative rent, would be the usual result of rates equal to marginal or variable costs only. In an earlier chapter (pages 159–61), it was explained that such deficits would occur in all nonextractive industries, and that they should be offset by income from land rent, personal rent, interest, and, perhaps, taxes. In the case of public utilities, however, there is an important alternative source of income to cover negative rent, namely regular monthly service charges, which could be set at a level high enough to cover the deficit resulting from rates equal to marginal cost.

The use of such service charges to cover negative rent has a number of advantages. The most important is that it makes an over-all utility deficit unnecessary, and could therefore be used as a means of introducing rational utility rates under Capitalism, an economic system which requires that every private enterprise pay its own way. Such financial self-sufficiency would obviously not be necessary under Socialism, but it might have some merit as a means of decentralizing control of a complex economic system since it would enable individual utilities to operate without subsidies from the treasury.

On the other hand, there are two important disadvantages of individual service charges. They involve significant costs of calculation and collection; whereas an increase in existing taxes would cause no additional collection costs, and they would restrict the use of utility services below the optimum level by causing potential consumers to weigh fixed as well as variable costs against the advantages of utility service. These disadvantages outweigh the advantages of service charges under Socialism but not under Capitalism.

CHAPTER XXI. BUILDING AND HOUSING

A. INTRODUCTION

Building and housing deserve a special chapter because of their quantitative importance. The average family spends about a fifth of its income on housing. Every commodity it purchases with the remainder of its income involves some construction costs. Over half of the total wealth of the United States takes the form of buildings and other construction projects.

This chapter has been divided into two parts because it deals with two slightly different problems. First we shall deal with building and construction, defined so as to include all construction work. Then we shall investigate housing, defined so as to include only the care of existing residential property and the participation in the planning of new housing.

B. BUILDING AND CONSTRUCTION

The entire building and construction industry should be consolidated into a single national Construction Trust. This trust should be represented on the Supreme Economic Council and also on the Executive Committee of that body.

Since the operations of the national Construction Trust will be scattered all over the land, the primary division of its organization should be geographical. The twelve federal-reserve districts might serve this purpose.

Within these primary geographical divisions of the national Construction Trust, further subdivision of organization should probably be along functional lines. Each regional division of the national trust, of course, should have its own executive staff, accounting force, planning and design department, construction department, etc. Moreover, the last two departments should be divided up into sections specializing in different types of construction such as office and store buildings, factory structures, apartment and hotel buildings, unit homes, public buildings, railroad and highway construction, etc.

There is some ground for arguing that the primary division of the national trust itself should be along functional rather than geographical lines. This would increase the division of labor among all executives, engineers, architects and other office workers. The disadvantage of such a basic functional division is that it would place management too far from the actual project, and/or would require too much traveling on the part of the managerial force.

I. SCALE OF PRODUCTION

The advantages of large-scale operation in the building industry are so obvious that they have been recognized by certain bourgeois economists and contractors. However, there are many legal and institutional obstacles to the construction of housing on a large scale under Capitalism. For instance, private ownership of land makes the assembly of large building sites difficult.

The consolidation of all building and construction work under a single organization will make possible an enormous increase, both in the scale of production or construction in individual localities, and in the scale of management work performed at central offices. The aim of a Socialist Construction Trust should be to build an entire community at a time. Instead of putting up a house here and a store there at odd intervals over a long period of years, such a trust should erect an entire farm village, plant community, or even an entire new city as a single construction project.

Whenever a new farm village is needed, the Construction Trust should build all the roads, install the public utilities, erect the homes and stores, and turn the finished farm village over to the Agricultural Trust ready for operation. If a new factory is desired, the Construction Trust should not only build the plant but should also build the entire plant community which will surround the new plant. This will include homes, schools, parks and playgrounds, all public utilities, stores, office buildings, garages, etc. When additional plant or residential facilities are needed in a plant community, they should ordinarily be erected in certain minimum lots, such as a hundred unit homes or twenty apartment buildings. In most cases, however, it will be more economical to erect an entire new plant community rather than to alter an old one ideally designed for its present volume of production and its present population. The greatest evils of Capitalist towns and cities are due to the constant necessity of erecting additional buildings to care for additional population.

It is all right to replace an old or obsolete building in an existing plant community with a new building which houses the same number of people because this does not increase the load on roads, schools, utilities, and other facilities used in common. It is not economical, however, to build large numbers of new homes, stores, and plant units in a plant community designed to meet perfectly the needs of the existing population, since this inevitably distorts the existing ideal proportions between the size of the population on the one hand and street capacity, transit facilities, size of sewer mains, location of schools, number of stores, and the location and capacity of all other public facilities on the other hand.

There is one minor disadvantage of constructing an entire plant community at a time. If a city is built house by house, it is possible—or would be under Socialism—to secure a more accurate balance between marginal costs and marginal prices for every type and location of home. The marginal profits or losses already being earned on each type of housing would supply an accurate indication of where and how new construction should be done. On the other hand, when an entire plant community is erected at the same time, the only data which can be used to determine the types and location of buildings are data on the marginal profits and losses incurred by the Housing Trust in the management of housing facilities in existing plant communities. Since no two plants or communities will ever be exactly alike as regards geographical structures, size, types of citizens, etc., the data obtained from old communities will never be completely applicable to new communities.

2. DIVISION OF LABOR

One of the principal advantages of uniting all building and construction work under a single organization is that it will make possible a very great increase in the division of labor in this industry. The economies of large-scale production have never been at all fully utilized under Capitalism. In a Socialist economy the division of labor in the building and construction industry should be carried to the optimum degree, which would increase tenfold the existing division of labor in the industry. Engineers, artisans, and organizations should devote themselves to one kind of building and should construct every building of that type in the United States. Laborers and artisans should specialize in materials and processes far more intensively than at present. If standardized homes and buildings are developed, building workers should even specialize in the erection of houses having the same catalogue number.

3. STANDARDIZATION OF TOOLS, MATERIALS, AND METHODS

Competition and individualism in the building industry, and in those industries which supply its materials and tools, have resulted in the development of literally millions of different grades, brands, types, styles, sizes, weights, colors, etc., of building materials and tools. The paint industry alone, for instance, produces several hundred thousand different kinds of paint. Socialism should reduce this excessive number of varieties to a few hundred or thousand at the most, and thus cut in half the cost of the production and distribution of paint. The same process of standardization should be carried out in the case of every individual building material and tool. Indeed, there are probably many different types of materials and tools which can be eliminated as a group because better substitutes are available. It will, however, be necessary to develop many new tools to exploit the greatly increased scale of production and division of labor.

In order to standardize building materials and tools, it will be necessary to conduct thorough scientific research to determine the relative merits of different materials and tools. The scientist should be given here as elsewhere far more scope and authority than he has ever been given under Capitalism.

Some research work has already been done, but, unfortunately, the scientist does not control the technique of production under Capitalism. In recent years the investigations which have been made by governmental laboratories and by commercial and other organizations upon building materials and methods of construction have greatly increased our knowledge of how to build better homes, using present-day materials. However, contractors fall far short of the best practice because both builders and workmen are slow to adopt new methods, and because private property owners untrained in architecture and construction have the final say about plans, materials, and methods.

Methods used in the different building trades under Capitalism are almost as diverse as the materials and tools used. These also should be made the subject of continuous scientific research. All operations performed by building workers should be the subject of thorough time and motion studies. Once the most efficient method of doing each kind of work has been discovered, all building workers should be required to use it. For instance, every carpenter in the nation should be trained to use the new standard method of holding and hammering nails. This is an application of a basic principle of the Taylor system of scientific management to the building industry.[1]

Under Capitalism, trade-union rules often prevent efficiency in the building industry. For instance, the use of spray guns to paint houses would cut labor costs by 75 percent, but the painters' union has bitterly opposed the introduction of the spray gun. Since self-preservation is the first law of nature, and since selfishness of this sort is necessary to self-preservation under Capitalism, we cannot blame the painters themselves. Obviously, however, paint-spray guns and all other similar labor-saving devices should be thoroughly exploited in a Socialist society. Of course, painters' unions have developed plausible excuses for opposing spray guns; they cannot admit that the real reason is fear of unemployment. Thus the danger of lead poisoning is widely cited for this purpose. Actually, however, this danger is largely nonexistent and even if real, could be eliminated by the use of masks.

[1] An excellent illustration of the kind of research work that needs to be done in this respect is the work of Frank B. Gilbreth on methods of laying bricks. It is a typical commentary on the efficiency of Capitalism that, although thirty years old, Gilbreth's method has never been widely used.

There are many other union rules which prevent the use of new and more efficient methods of construction because building workers fear unemployment. There are rules which require that skilled workers only be permitted to do unskilled work associated with their skilled work in order to make more jobs for skilled workers. There are rules which prohibit a skilled worker from doing unskilled work or skilled work of another trade even for a few minutes, thus making it necessary to hire another man and pay him a day's wages for doing an hour's work. Many unions of plumbers require that pipe be fabricated on the building site when it can be fabricated much more economically in a factory. Bricklayers' unions often limit the number of bricks which may be laid per day by each worker. There are literally tens of thousands of union rules which make waste of labor compulsory. All of these union rules should be ended under Socialism.

4. FABRICATED BUILDINGS

The building industry is still largely in a handicraft stage of production. Modern homes, like the great cathedrals of the Middle Ages, are built by handicraft workers—carpenters, bricklayers, painters, plasterers, decorators, etc.—who come to the building site and there turn raw materials into the finished product. Little machinery is used and all work is necessarily on a small scale. For this reason the cost of building has remained at a relatively high level. The cost of all factory products has been declining steadily ever since the industrial revolution, both absolutely and relatively, while construction costs have fallen absolutely but risen relatively.

If the benefits of the industrial revolution are to be fully realized in the building industry, handicraft production must give way to factory production.

Shop fabrication by a large organization has the following advantages over field fabrication:

a) Homes can be thoroughly worked out in the laboratory so that the most suitable materials may be used; their value can be determined accurately by tests and then they can be standardized for economical manufacture in quantity.

b) Adequate inspection and tests can be made to eliminate materials which do not meet the requirements.

c) Machines can be developed to perform most of the operations.

d) The workmen can become very efficient because each is expert on a particular operation, uses power-driven equipment, and is employed under favorable conditions.

e) Adequate inspection and tests during and after manufacture can be made to insure a uniform product which will function satisfactorily.

f) It inherently encourages the use of better and better materials.

g) Lost motion, waste, and damage are almost eliminated when the house is erected later on the building site because the sequence and best method of carrying out each operation are carefully determined in advance.[2]

To a certain extent, this has already occurred. Doors, windows, trim, builders' hardware, builders' supplies and tools, many building materials, etc., are now produced in factories. Nevertheless, the bulk of the work of building a house is still done on the job by handicraft methods.

There are two steps in the introduction of factory methods to the building industry. The first is the factory production of some of the individual parts of a house so that they can be assembled quickly on any given site. Firms like Sears Roebuck & Company, which supply "ready-cut" houses, have already begun to develop this first and most elemental method of applying factory technique to the building industry.

The second step is the factory production of all, or nearly all, parts of a building, and their fabrication into component structures large enough to eliminate most of the work of assembly on the building site but not too large or too heavy to prevent economical handling and transportation.

The achievement of this latter step requires the development of new types of buildings composed of materials suitable for factory fabrication and for economical handling and transportation. Brick, stone, plaster, wood, and cement must give way to steel, copper, glass, aluminum, rock wool, plastics, rubber, and other new materials. In other words, if buildings are to be produced as efficiently and cheaply as automobiles now are, much the same materials must be used in buildings as are now used in automobiles.

One of the greatest obstacles to the development of factory-built houses is popular taste. We have been living in brick, stone, plaster, and frame buildings for so long that we think them beautiful, and it will be difficult for us to learn that factory-built metal and plastic buildings will be equally attractive to us when we have become accustomed to them. With most people the sense of beauty is largely a feeling of familiarity. However, the modern automobile demonstrates that beauty is as easily realizable in iron and steel as in brick and wood. Moreover, until poverty has been eliminated, economy in the cost of production is far more important than beauty of form in those few cases where there is a serious conflict between the two.

A certain degree of standardization is necessary for factory production of building parts and structures, just as it is essential for mass production of automobiles. In both cases variety must be sacrificed to economy. How-

---

[2] *Report of the Commission on Technological Developments in Housing Objectives and Programs* (1932), pp. 38–39; this report is Vol. XI of the Report of the President's Committee on Home Building and Home Ownership.

ever, this standardization need not be complete. Experience has shown that automobiles can be produced economically in runs of only a few thousand. Similar results should be possible in the production of buildings by factory methods. Since the United States alone can use two or three million new homes every year, a considerable variety in type and style would be possible even with mass production of standardized dwellings. Moreover, standardization can be thoroughly applied to many hidden parts of buildings without reducing architectural variety.

Although a great deal of research and experimentation will be necessary before all buildings can be built in factories and merely assembled on the site, this method of producing houses and smaller business buildings is already economical and should be almost exclusively used in a Socialist economy. Eccentric individuals who prefer custom-made houses should be permitted to have them, provided they meet all the unusual and excessive costs involved. But the great mass of citizens will prefer the economy of factory-built homes, just as they now prefer the economy of factory-built automobiles.

Incidentally, it will be far easier to introduce a novelty like factory-built homes into a Socialist economy than into a Capitalist economy. No Capitalist trust can persuade all manufacturers of building materials and all contractors to adopt prefabrication in a short period of time. A Socialist economy would have all the power and capital necessary to achieve a rapid change and, what is more, could subsidize the industry by producing at a loss for ten or twenty years if necessary and desirable.

5. CITY PLANNING

The planning and construction of all the buildings and improvements of a community by a single agency will make possible a far greater degree of co-ordination between them. Comprehensive, long-range city planning will be a basic and inescapable element in all such projects. Roads will be designed to carry the proper amount of traffic. Buildings will have the proper amount of space around them and will be planned together architecturally and spatially. No vacant lots will waste costly street and public-utility improvements. Transportation facilities will be planned to fit the needs of the community and will involve no costly destruction and reconstruction of existing buildings as they will be installed when the community is first built, and no large increase in population will be permitted.

The first principle of Socialist city planning should be the virtually complete decentralization of industry, commerce, professional services, and other economic activities within each city. The elimination of competition and sales effort in every downtown business district will of itself enormously reduce the size and activity of such districts, but this is not enough. As we have explained elsewhere, nearly all the economic activity of a great city should be divided up among scores of relatively independent and self-contained plant communities.

Each plant community should center around one or more factories or office buildings employing a total of perhaps 10,000 workers on the average. The number should be so limited that all workers can live within one mile of their place of employment. Each plant community should have its own retail facilities, health clinic, schools, theaters, playgrounds, public library, banking facilities, etc. In other words it should be virtually self-contained. However, a central plant community in each city should provide certain necessary all-city facilities such as universities, auditoriums, stadia, prisons, art museums, stores selling expensive luxuries, and law courts.

Several additional basic principles of city planning in residential areas deserve mention here. The first is that residential buildings ought not to cover more than one-tenth of the area of any building site. At least nine-tenths of the land in every residential area should be in parks, gardens, and playgrounds. Under Capitalism, free space around city apartments and tenements is often less than one-third of the entire lot or block. A great increase in park and playground space in such districts is essential to proper health and recreation for both adults and children. Moreover, Socialism will double or treble average real wages and thus make a much higher standard of living possible.

The second principle is that this garden and play space should ordinarily be united into large areas open to the public. Otherwise each individual plot will be too small to give any real service and too small to permit economical maintenance. A glance at the backyards in any slum area will show how ugly and useless small individual yards can be. However, individuals who desire private yards and gardens should be given them upon payment of all costs involved and allowed to keep them as long as they are reasonably well cared for and utilized.

In order to reduce the cost and maintain the standard of garden and playground maintenance in closely settled residential districts, this work should all be performed by a single city-wide park service which uses expensive specialized and mechanized equipment such as power-mowers, power hedge trimmers, and fertilizer spreaders.

A third basic principle of city planning is that a residential area should be planned in such a way as to reduce the area devoted to streets, sidewalks, and driveways to a minimum. At present the area devoted to streets and sidewalks is at least 50 percent higher than it should be. In order to reduce the space requirements for driveways, and in order to reduce the costs of building garages, all garage facilities for a group of adjacent detached or row houses should be provided in a single large garage which should open directly on the street or on an alley.

The fourth basic rule of community planning is that the great majority of farm and plant communities should be planned upon the assumption of a steady increase in the standard of living and a steady decrease in population in each community. As efficiency in production increases, workers will receive higher wages and will therefore desire more housing space and larger gardens and recreation areas. If the workers of each farm community farm a fixed number of acres, the number of farm workers required in each farm community will decline steadily as efficiency in agriculture increases.

In plant communities it will always be possible, but it will often not be economical, to increase the size and capacity of the central plant as the productivity of labor increases. It is sometimes cheaper to build a new and modern plant in a new community than it is to reconstruct an existing plant so that it can utilize all new labor-saving devices and yet provide work for the same number of men. Moreover, as efficiency and real wages rise, workers in plant communities will want more living and recreation space, and this can be provided most economically in established communities by reducing the size of the population. This will require replacement or remodeling of some housing facilities but it will not require as much reconstruction of roads, sewers, transit facilities, airports, parks, and other public facilities as would be required if the population increased or remained constant.

If a community has been properly planned, no single part of it can be expanded to meet the needs of a higher standard of living or a larger population without throwing all other portions of the community out of balance. Additional homes on the outskirts of the community make necessary changes in every other part of the physical equipment of the community. And it is always more expensive to widen existing streets, particularly in business or apartment house districts, than to build new streets in a new community to provide for a higher standard of living or for additional population. It is more costly to dig up old gas, water, and electric mains and enlarge them than it is to install new mains in a new community before the streets are paved. Public buildings, opera houses, auditoriums, libraries, etc., cannot be economically enlarged. Finally, increasing the residential facilities of an established community always involves either increased congestion of population in built-up areas or the construction of new homes on the outskirts from which the distance to the plant in the center of the community may be too great.

This does not mean that planned Socialist cities ought not to grow in size. Since a Socialist city should be merely a group of contiguous plant communities, each essentially self-contained, the erection of additional plant communities on the outskirts of an existing city would not conflict with the above rule. Growth of this sort would have some evils, since it would make necessary expansion of the central plant community catering to all-city needs, but these evils would be minor in comparison with those resulting from growth of an existing plant community.

A prosperous Socialist economy should completely eliminate filth and ugliness from every community. All gas stations should be kept as neat and clean as the best Standard Oil stations now are. The dirty and dilapidated independent station with its unkempt, grease-stained proprietor should simply cease to exist. Factory buildings should be designed and cared for as carefully as government buildings and certain modern factory buildings. A factory building should be as attractive as a private home or public library. Vacant lots should be turned into public parks. Junk yards and other eyesores should be completely screened off by attractive fences and hedges. Slums should be torn down and replaced by parks and modern apartments. Both residential and business structures should be maintained properly. All parts of a Socialist city should be as attractive as the best residential districts of our present cities.

6. THE DENSITY OF POPULATION

Within each plant or farm community the density of population, in other words the intensive and extensive margins of building, should be determined as nearly as possible by the desires of the workers themselves. These desires are manifested only in the rents they are willing to pay for different types of homes and different types of locations. It follows that the national Construction Trust should plan each community in such a way as to maximize the total pure land rent obtained from the community and the surrounding area as a whole.

If the building of a hundred apartments in the center of the community increases the pure economic rent earned by the land on which they are erected more than it decreases the pure economic rent earned, or which might be earned, by erecting additional single family dwellings on the edge of the community, then the erection of these apartments is more desirable than the building of the single family dwellings.

The number and location of duplex houses, bungalow courts, etc., should be determined in precisely the same way. Each site should be used in such a way as to maximize the pure economic rent obtained from it.

7. NEW HOUSES FOR WORKERS

Under Capitalism very little attention has been paid to the design and construction of housing facilities for the workers. New homes and apartments are ordinarily planned to fit the needs of the middle and upper economic classes (the one-third of the population receiving the highest incomes). When these homes and apartments built for the well to do have depreciated in value and become sufficiently shabby, they are passed on down to the working classes.

The economic waste involved in this process is very great. A house designed for a family with an income of $8,000 a year cannot fit the needs of a family with an income of $2,000 a year, no matter how old and dilapidated it has become. The kitchen, pantry, and dining room are designed to suit a style of living which no worker can afford. If two or more workers' families occupy the old house the difficulty is even greater, for the kitchen, pantry, and dining room are designed to meet the needs of one family only. The same conditions hold for all other features of such a house. The space devoted to halls, stairways, porches, and closets is too large for one family and entirely unsuited to two families. They result in heating costs which are more than a single worker's family can afford, but the house is designed for one family only. The size of the lot is too great for a single worker's family to maintain since it cannot afford to hire a gardener. On the other hand, if two or more families move into the house, none of them will take the responsibility of yard maintenance since the chief benefit will accrue to others.

It is just as unsound to require unskilled workers to live in houses designed for the well to do as it is to require them to use second-hand Packards and Cadillacs for transportation. In both cases the maintenance and running costs are out of all proportion to the income of the workers. A new Ford is far better suited to the needs of the worker than an old Cadillac, and the same applies to housing. Hence, a Socialist economy ought to design and build new housing for unskilled workers.

8. TYPES OF HOUSING

One of the most common arguments against Socialism is the statement that it proposes to abolish the individual physical home or unit dwelling and compel everyone to live in apartments and eat in common dining rooms. Sometimes, indeed, the apartments are called barracks and the men are supposed to be segregated in one, the women in another and the children in a third. Like many other popular arguments against Socialism this is based upon a complete misconception of the new society.

A Socialist state should exercise no influence upon the workers' choice of living quarters other than to provide information concerning the relative cost of similar living accommodations in large apartment buildings, small apartment buildings, duplexes, attached and detached unit homes. In all of its construction projects, the relative proportion of one type of housing to another should be determined solely by popular demand.

The supply of each type of housing should be increased until the market prices (rents) just cover the marginal cost of that type of housing. Once a plant community has been erected, the supply of each kind of housing will be inelastic, but the marginal profits and losses earned on each type will provide useful data for determining how to fit supply to demand more closely in the construction of additional plant communities.

The net marginal profit or loss earned on residential property in existing plant communities should determine the total investment in housing facilities in new communities. Of course, consideration should be given to the fact that net losses or profits may be caused by maldistribution or bad location as well as by under- and overproduction.

While a Socialist state should not attempt to determine for its citizens the type of housing they are to have, the probable free choice of the citizens of a Socialist community may be predicted.

The traditional, and hence for many people ideal, American home is a detached house on an individual lot. This is due to a number of reasons. Most Americans of native stock are, or were until recently, farm-bred and therefore accustomed to living in individual houses. The growth of large metropolitan cities is relatively new and the detached house is much more suitable to villages and small cities than to large modern cities. Finally, modern apartment buildings are only made possible by steel framework and elevators, a late product of technical progress.

Although a one-family house is the American ideal, in practice American citizens have been abandoning such houses at an increasing rate for the past century. At the present time the building industry is producing about two dwelling units in multi-family buildings for every detached house.

If we bear in mind that the building industry produces new homes only for the middle and upper classes, less than one-third of the population, the significance of these figures is enhanced. When ordinary workers move into these unit homes they will turn many of them into multi-family structures.

Repeated experiments by bourgeois philanthropists in the United States have demonstrated that neither detached nor row houses can be provided at a rent which unskilled workers can afford. Experiments with garden apartments have demonstrated their superior economy, but have likewise failed to reduce rents to a level that is satisfactory for the average worker's family. Nevertheless, many conventionally minded students of housing reform still advocate the building of detached houses for workers.[3] This

---

[3] Andrew J. Thomas, one of the more enlightened bourgeois students of housing, ventures this mild rebuke of his more conservative colleagues:

"Under present conditions, when even the garden apartment is beyond the means of the lower-paid workers, the insistence of many housing experts that the

attitude seems to be due to an exaggerated idea of the importance of individual gardens and private ownership of homes.

While under Capitalism the garden apartment is the best method of providing new and decent housing for nearly all workers, Socialism may alter this condition. In the first place, Socialism will decentralize industry and thus reduce the value of building lots. The high cost of building lots in modern cities is a prime cause of the rise of apartment houses. In the second place, Socialism will double or treble the income of wage earners and thus permit most of them to bear the added costs of living in detached or row houses if they so desire.

Nevertheless, unless some unforeseen change occurs, apartment houses will continue to provide more economical housing than unit or row houses. Individual houses will continue to be a luxury which only the most advanced nations can afford for their ordinary workers. Even in the United States, the richest nation in the world, the workers may prefer the economy and other advantages of garden apartments after Socialism has made it possible for them to afford detached houses.

This is probable for a number of reasons. American ideals developed on the farm are slowly fading under the different conditions of city life. In the new society, women will increasingly give up housekeeping as a full-time occupation and obtain positions outside the home. When both men and women work outside the home, living in an apartment has many advantages. Food can be centrally prepared and delivered on dumb waiters or served in a common dining room. Young children can be cared for in conveniently located nurseries during the five or six hours the parents are absent. Housework can be economically done by a group of experts who care for all apartments in the building. However, the 10 to 20 percent saving in rent is more important to many families than any other advantage of apartment life.

9. ARCHITECTURE

In a Socialist economy far more attention should be devoted to architecture than is now the custom. Architectural taste and beauty are a matter of concern to all. An ugly building is a social evil although it may satisfy its private owner, since it displeases thousands of people who see it each day. The welfare of these thousands of citizens is more important than the satisfaction of any single one of them.

It is worthy of note, however, that it is only the exterior of residential structures which affects social utility or welfare. The interior of a house or apartment is seen by only a few persons aside from those who live

row house is the only solution for wage-earners' housing, seems somewhat arbitrary." *Industrial Housing* (1925), p. 45.

in it. The latter, moreover, spend far more of their time inside their homes than anyone else. Hence, there is a sound case for permitting tenants to determine the interior decoration of their homes if they are willing to pay the considerable costs of individual choice.

Socialism could greatly increase the opportunities for and the benefits of fine architecture merely by concentrating control over architectural design in a few hands. Under Capitalism, the effect of a beautiful public building is often offset by the effect of a filthy gas station or an ugly commercial building next door. Even where two adjacent buildings are in good taste individually, the combination may be bizarre in the extreme. Certainly nothing is more destructive of architectural beauty and harmony than a block of ten to twenty homes or business buildings, each of an entirely distinct architectural design and each planned in complete disregard of its neighbors.

Concentration of control over architectural work would also make it possible for the very best architects to supervise and control all architectural work. It would enlarge their influence and productivity a hundredfold.

A large economy in the cost of architectural work may be secured by using most plans many times instead of once only. This does not mean that homes and apartment buildings should be standardized, or erected in rows of identical design, as frequently happens under Capitalism. It does mean that several score or several hundred copies of each satisfactory and effective design should be used in the country as a whole if not in each community.

Under Capitalism, all the able architects are hired by well-to-do or wealthy individuals who make nonduplication a condition of their orders. This means that the most beautiful homes cannot be duplicated solely because they are so attractive. It also means that every house must have a new set of plans. The waste of this practice is indicated by the average size of good architects' fees, which is 5 percent of the cost of construction. Using each good architectural plan ten times would cut this average cost by 90 percent.

C. MANAGEMENT OF HOUSING FACILITIES

Once the Construction Trust has erected a new village or plant community, it should immediately relinquish control of it to the various trusts and departments which will use and control the different physical facilities included in any community. All residential structures should be turned over to the local representatives of the national Housing Trust, which should manage all housing facilities in the nation.

Since the operations of the national Housing Trust will be as widely scattered as its physical property, its primary, secondary, and tertiary organizational subdivisions should be geographical rather than functional. The primary division should be into ten to twelve regions containing approximately equal population. The secondary division might be into both metropolitan areas and country districts including many farm villages. The third division of the organization might be into farm and plant communities. Certainly these latter should be the basic units in any scheme of organization. The staff of each geographical unit should be organized along functional as well as geographical lines, but authority should be delegated to regional rather than functional executives.

I. MAINTENANCE

In a Socialist economy, all housing facilities should be owned by the state and managed by the national Housing Trust. One of the primary functions of this trust would be the physical maintenance of housing accommodations. This maintenance work should be done by the national Housing Trust instead of by the individual family, because it can be done much more efficiently and economically on a large scale, and because the individual family, since it will not own its home, would be less interested in proper maintenance.

All housing facilities should be periodically inspected by representatives of the national Housing Trust in order to determine maintenance needs. In addition, tenants should be encouraged to write or telephone the local office of the trust and ask for minor repairs at any time.

In order to place the costs of maintenance work where they belong, maintenance charges should be separated from ordinary rental payments and should be proportioned directly to the actual cost of maintenance on each home or apartment. This will serve to reward those families which are unusually careful of their homes and penalize those who permit unnecessary damage to their homes.

House maintenance includes plumbing repairs, care of electric wiring, painting, varnishing, plastering, papering, minor carpentering, etc. Each kind of maintenance work should be entrusted to a special crew of men who specialize in that type of work and who go from house to house throughout the community, working all day every day if they wish.

Elaborate scientific research should be conducted in order to determine just how often buildings of different kinds need to be painted, roofed, or repaired in any way in order to reduce the combined total of maintenance and depreciation costs to a minimum. Once these facts have been determined by laboratory research, every house and apartment building should be repainted, reroofed, or otherwise repaired, at the proper intervals, regardless of the wishes of those who live in them. This innovation alone should reduce the total of maintenance and depreciation costs by at least 25 percent. Of course, the national Construction Trust would use similar scientific methods to determine the proper kind of paint, varnish, plaster, cement, mortar, and other materials, and the maintenance division of the national Housing Trust could make full use of this data. At present the use of too cheap or too expensive paint alone costs the American public tens of millions of dollars a year.

2. FURNITURE AND FURNISHINGS

The furniture and other principal furnishings of a house should be supplied by the national Housing Trust and not by the individual renter, except in a few cases. The architect and interior decorator should work together and plan every home as a unit. If this is done, the furniture and furnishings of one house will look better and be more useful in that house than in any other, unless the second be a duplicate. If the latter be a duplicate, it would be provided with the same or with equally well-chosen furniture and furnishings and there would be no reason for transferring furniture from one house to another. Private ownership of furniture is undesirable because it involves a heavy social expense due to frequent moving of furniture from one house to another and because it results in furniture and furnishings being moved from a house for which they are designed to one for which they are not designed. Another important advantage of having the National Housing Trust furnish all homes and apartments is that this policy would sharply reduce the cost of furniture and furnishings. When individuals purchase furniture and other house furnishings, they must buy through retail stores which almost double the average prices of furniture under Capitalism. Retail furniture stores would be far more efficient under Socialism, but they would still represent a very appreciable social expense which could be saved through group purchase and ownership of furniture. A major cost of private buying of furniture is the time and energy spent by the consumer in shopping. Purchase of furniture by the Housing Trust would greatly reduce this cost since the interior decorators of the trust would buy in large quantities and would be far better acquainted with the sources of supply and the variety of furniture and furnishings available.

While the same trust should supply both housing and home furnishings as a unit, private individuals who desire to design their own house furnishings should be permitted to do so upon payment of all additional costs involved. One of these additional costs might be the refurnishing of the house to meet the minimum standards of the Housing Trust when the occupant leaves the house which he has furnished to suit his own personal taste.

Private ownership of house furniture and furnishings has one important advantage. A tenant cares for his own property more carefully than
he cares for rented property. To protect trust-owned houses and furnishings from excessive wear and tear, yearly inspection and a system of fines
should be used. Every family which abuses state-owned property should
be compelled to pay the full costs of such abuse. This will be perfectly
feasible, since the Housing Trust will have a complete monopoly and need
not fear the loss of its tenants.

3. DETERMINATION OF HOUSE RENTS

As has already been indicated, all housing accommodations should be
leased or rented rather than sold to the users. But how should the national Housing Trust fix the money rents?

In the first place, no individual house or apartment building should
be erected unless there is every assurance that it can earn an adequate income over the period of its life. An adequate income is one which covers
all the costs involved, including land rent, interest, and wages. The land
rent included in this cost figure should be at least as high as the land rent
obtainable from the best alternative use of the land.

The level of adequate income from housing varies inversely with the
length of the useful life of the housing. If a house is to be used for one
hundred years, the minimum rental charge is much less than it would be
if the house is to be used for only ten years. However, it is impossible to
predict with complete accuracy the demand for housing in a given locality
twenty, fifty, or a hundred years in advance. The executives of a Socialist
economy will be able to make more accurate predictions of this sort than
the average Capitalist contractor, but anything approaching complete accuracy will be impossible. Thus, while no house or apartment should be
erected unless it is highly probable that it can be rented for a total cumulative rent sufficient to justify its erection, there will always be a degree
of uncertainty concerning this.

Once a house or apartment building has been built, rents should
always be raised or lowered until demand just equals supply. This principle should be applied to each individual home. Whenever two or more
families desire the same apartment or house, the rent should be raised until
only one family is willing to pay it. On the other hand, whenever it is
difficult to rent a house, the rent should be reduced until a tenant is found.
If necessary, the rent should be reduced until it just equals current maintenance costs plus the economic land rent obtainable from the best alternative use of the land concerned. If this minimum rent does not attract a
tenant, the house should be torn down and the land turned to the best
alternative use.

The principal costs of housing are interest, land rent, depreciation, maintenance, and insurance, in the order named. Under Capitalism, taxes rank second or third in importance, but in a Socialist economy there should be no direct taxes on housing; and indirect taxes, such as the sales tax, should not discriminate against housing. Land rent must be treated as a cost of housing. Any attempt to ignore it would increase the demand for favorably situated houses beyond the supply and thus make rational allocation of housing facilities impossible.

Interest, already the most important cost of housing (40 percent) would become more important than ever after the elimination of all property taxes. From 1920 to 1940 capital for housing in the United States consisted of about 10 percent on the average, including bankers' fees and commissions (8 percent for the capital obtained on the first mortgage and 12 percent for capital obtained on second mortgages and other means of financing the equity). A Socialist government probably could reduce the rate of interest in the United States to 1 or 2 percent, not by directly controlling the rate but by increasing the supply of capital. This would very materially lower the cost of housing without any change in construction costs, which of course would be greatly reduced by the introduction of prefabricated housing, large-scale operations, increased division of labor, standardization of tools and materials, etc.

4. DETERMINATION OF MARGINAL PROFITS AND LOSSES

As we have already indicated, plans for housing facilities in new plant and farm communities should be based largely upon profit-and-loss records of various types of housing already in use in existing communities. We turn now to a consideration of some of the problems involved in ascertaining marginal profits and losses on housing.

Since the Housing Trust will merely manage the housing facilities built by the independent Construction Trust, it will not itself calculate the costs of building houses and apartments, but will merely accept and use the cost data turned over to it by the latter trust.

This applies only to the costs of construction, however. It does not apply to land rent or interest payments after the date of the transfer of the completed buildings to the Housing Trust. Land rent and interest, moreover, are the principal costs of housing.

No difficulty need arise in the determination of interest costs. There will be at all times a single uniform interest rate, which should determine the amount paid to the Bureau of Capital Supply by all users of capital.

In the case of land rent, a peculiarly important housing cost, a very different situation will exist, however. Since land rent is an intramarginal surplus, its calculation is involved in the determination of the margin, and in the determination of marginal profits and losses. In other words, land rent and marginal profits and losses are determined simultaneously.

No perfectly accurate method of determining marginal profits or losses on existing housing facilities is available. The only practical method seems to be that of locating a margin in space and then estimating the net financial result of providing new housing facilities at that point. If new housing facilities can be built on any margin, and rented to yield a net surplus over all costs, including existing land rent on the site, then this surplus may be treated as a marginal profit; and vice versa if a loss is incurred. Actually, of course, such a surplus will include a small amount of new land rent, but this is not subject to measurement and, hence, must be ignored.

The phrase "a margin" instead of "the margin" is used because there are several of them. In the first place, there is both an extensive margin, and an intensive margin. New housing may be built at or near the extensive margin, namely the point where land used for housing borders on land used for some other purpose, or it may be built at some point on the intensive margin, namely on land already being used for housing purposes. The intensive margin itself may be divided into two types, vertical and horizontal. New homes or apartments may be built so as to cover more fully lots already built upon, extending the horizontal intensive margin; or they may be built on top of existing buildings, extending the vertical intensive margin.

Since a margin in some form or other is always present, it will be possible to estimate marginal profits or losses on all housing facilities by using the method described above. If another floor, or annex, can be added to any apartment building and rented to yield a net surplus, that apartment building is yielding a marginal·profit. If, on the other hand, rents are already too low to cover all costs involved in erecting and maintaining the existing building, then a marginal loss is being incurred. If another house could be built on the edge of the town and rented to yield a net profit, then similar houses in that neighborhood are probably yielding a marginal profit, and vice versa in case of a loss. Of course, the amount of indirect community costs, such as that of added sewer facilities in other parts of the community, should be considered here.

When houses or apartment buildings stand side by side but vary in design, the relative productivity of different types can be approximately determined by assuming a uniform land-rental cost and then comparing the net profits and losses. In the same way, land rents can be roughly estimated by comparing the total rent income from buildings of one type scattered in different parts of the city.

The general conclusion to be drawn from the above discussion is that while it is more difficult to determine marginal profits and losses in the provision of housing than in any other industry, with the possible exception of agriculture, this task must and can be performed with sufficient accuracy to control properly the supply of each type of housing accommodation. The principal obstacles are the wide variations in the land rent involved, and the lack of standardization in the product. These obstacles to ideal production control, however, can certainly be more ably dealt with by a single Socialist trust than by the millions of independent owners of real estate under Capitalism.

BIBLIOGRAPHY

SELECT BIBLIOGRAPHY

BIBLIOGRAPHIES

BALDWIN, C. D. *Economic Planning.* Urbana, 1942, pp. 179–88.
DICKINSON, H. D. *Economics of Socialism.* London, 1939. Ten-page bibliography.
DUNCAN, W. G. K. *National Economic Planning.* Sydney, 1934. Eleven pages of bibliography.
HAYEK, FRIEDRICH A. VON (editor). *Collectivist Economic Planning.* London, 1935. Three-page bibliography (44 items, mostly German).
JEVONS, H. S. *Economic Equality in the Cooperative Commonwealth.* London, 1933. Seven-page annotated bibliography.
TISCH, KLARE. *Wirtschaftsrechnung und Verteilung im Zentralistischen Gemeinwesen.* 1932. Three-page bibliography.

BOOKS

GENERAL WORKS ON THE ECONOMIC THEORY OF A SOCIALIST ECONOMY

ADAMS, C. B. *National Industrial Organization, under Social Control.* 2d edition. Santurce, Puerto Rico, 1934.
ATLANTICUS [pseudonym of Gustav Jaeckl]. *Production und Konsum in Sozialstaat.* Stuttgart, 1898.
DESLINIERES, LUCIEN. *L'Application du systeme collectiviste.* Paris, 1899.
——. *Projet de socialiste.* Paris, 1908.
DICKINSON, H. D. *Economics of Socialism.* London, 1939.
HALL, R. L. *The Economic System in a Socialist State.* London, 1937.
HEIMANN, EDUARD. *Sozialistische Wirtshafts und Arbeitsordnung.* Potsdam, 1932.
HOFF, TRYGVE J. B. *Okonomisk Kalkulasjon i Socialisticke Samfund.* Oslo, 1938.
JEVONS, H. STANLEY. *Economic Equality in the Co-operative Commonwealth.* London, 1933.
KLEIN, G. *System Eines Idealistischen Sozialismus: Theoretische Grundlegung einer Planwirtschaftlichen Volks und Weltwirtschaftsordnung.* Vienna, 1931.
MOSSE, ROBERT. *L'Economie collectiviste.* Paris, 1939.
RENARD, GEORGES. *Le Regime socialiste, principes de son organisation politique et economique.* Paris, 1898.
SMITH, JAMES HALDANE. *Collectivist Economics.* London, 1925.
TURK, JULIUS. *Hervorbringung und Verteilung der Werte in Der Sozialistischen Gesellschaft.* Hamburg, 1892.

BOOKS DEVOTED TO A SPECIAL FIELD OF THE ECONOMIC THEORY OF A SOCIALIST ECONOMY

AUCUY, M. *Les Systemes socialistes d'exchange.* Paris, 1908.
BEVERIDGE, W. H. *Planning Under Socialism, and Other Addresses.* New York, 1936.

BRUTZKUS, BORIS. *Economic Planning in Soviet Russia.* London, 1935.
COLE, G. D. H. *Machinery of Socialist Planning.* London, 1938.
COLOMB, PIERRE. *La Liberté du travail et le collectivisme.* Paris, 1908.
DELL, ROBERT. *Socialism and Personal Liberty.* New York, 1922.
DUNCAN, W. G. K. *National Economic Planning.* Sydney, 1934.
GINZBURG, A. M. *Ocherki Promishlennoi Ekonomiki.* 1930.
HAYEK, FRIEDRICH A. VON (editor). *Collectivist Economic Planning. Critical Studies on the Possibilities of Socialism.* London, 1935.
HEIMANN, EDUARD. *Mehrwert und Gemeinwirtschaft.* Berlin, 1922.
HOBSON, J. A. *Incentives in the New Industrial Order.* London, 1922.
HUBBARD, L. E. *Soviet Money and Finance.* London, 1936.
INGOT. *The Sozialization of Iron and Steel.* London, 1936.
KHMELNITSKOI, E. L. (editor). *Ekonomika Sotsialisticheskoi Promishlennosti.* Moskva, 1931.
LANDAUER, C. *Planwirtschaft und Verkehrswirtschaft.* 1931.
LANGE, OSCAR, AND TAYLOR, FRED M. *On the Economic Theory of Socialism.* Minneapolis, 1937.
LEICHTER, OTTO. *Wirtschaftsrechnung in der Sozialistischen Gemeinschaft.* Vienna, 1923.
MORRISON, HERBERT. *Socialization and Transport.* London, 1933.
REDDAWAY, W. B. *The Russian Financial System.* New York, 1935.
ROPER, W. C. *The Problem of Pricing in a Socialist State.* Cambridge, Massachusetts, 1929.
SACHSE, OSCAR. *The Socialization of Banking.* London, 1933.
TISCH, KLARE. *Wirtschaftsrechnung und Verteilung im Zentralistischen Gemeinwesen.* 1932.
DE VRIES, F. *Economische Critiek op de Socialistische Productieorganisatie.* Rotterdam, 1921.

BOOKS CONTAINING REMARKS ON THE ECONOMIC THEORY
OF A SOCIALIST ECONOMY

DALTON, H. *Practical Socialism for Britain.* London, 1935.
DICKINSON, H. D. *Institutional Revenue.* London, 1932.
FLORENCE, P. S. *The Logic of Industrial Organization.* London, 1933.
LERNER, A. P. *The Economics of Control.* New York, 1944.
PIGOU, A. C. *Socialism and Capitalism.* London, 1937.
SCHUMPETER, J. A. *Capitalism, Socialism, and Democracy.* New York, 1942.
WOOTON, BARBARA. *Plan or No Plan.* London, 1934.

MAGAZINE ARTICLES

CHOSSUDOWSKY, E. M. "The Soviet Conception of Economic Equilibrium," *Review of Economic Studies,* Vol. VI, No. 2 (February 1939), pp. 127–46.
DICKINSON, H. D. "The Economic Basis of Socialism," *Political Quarterly,* (September–December, 1930), 561.
———. "Freedom and Planning, A Reply to Dr. Gregory," *Manchester School,* Vol. IV, 1933.
———. "Price Formation in a Socialist Community," *Economic Journal,* XLIII (1933), 237–50.

Dobb, Maurice. "The Problems of a Socialist Economy," *Economic Journal*, XLIII (1933), 588–99.

———. "Economic Theory and Socialist Economy, a Reply," *Review of Economic Studies*, II (1935), 144–51.

Durbin, E. F. M. "Economic Calculus in a Planned Economy," *Economic Journal*, Vol. XLVI, No. 18, pp. 676–91.

———. "A Note on Mr. Lerner's Dynamical Propositions," *Economic Journal*, XLVII (September 1937), 577.

Frisch, R. "Circulation Planning . . . . ," *Econometrica*, Vol. II, Nos. 3 and 4, July 1934.

Gourvitch, Alexander. "The Problem of Prices and Valuation in the Soviet System," *American Economic Review, Supplement*, Vol. XXVI, No. 1 (March 1936), pp. 267–83.

Gregory, T. E. "An Economist Looks at Planning," *Manchester School*, Vol. IV, 1933.

Heimann, Eduard. "Planning and the Market System," *Social Research*, Vol. I, No. 4 (November 1934), pp. 486–504.

———. "Types and Potentialities of Economic Planning," *Social Research*, Vol. II, No. 2 (May 1935), pp. 176–94.

Hoover, Calvin B., Orton, Wm., and Florinsky, Michael T. "Discussion," *American Economic Review, Supplement*, Vol. XXVI, No. 1 (March 1936), pp. 283–91.

Knight, Frank H. "The Place of Marginal Economics in a Collectivist System," *American Economic Review, Supplement*, Vol. XXVI, No. 1 (March 1936), pp. 255–67.

Lerner, A. P. "A Note on Socialist Economics," *Review of Economic Studies*, Vol. IV, No. 1 (October 1936), pp. 72–76.

———. "Marxian Economics and Modern Economic Theory," *Review of Economic Studies*, Vol. II, June 1935.

———. "Economic Theory and Socialist Economy," *Review of Economic Studies*, II (1934), 51–61.

———. "A Rejoinder," *Review of Economic Studies*, II (1935), 152.

———. "Statics and Dynamics in Socialist Economics," *Economic Journal*, XLVII (June 1937), 253–71.

———. "Theory and Practice in Socialist Economics," *Review of Economic Studies*, Vol. VI, No. 1 (October 1938), pp. 71–76.

Pinard, Andre. "Monnaie, propriete et valeur en regime socialiste," *Revue d'Economie Politique*, XXIII (1909), 401–43.

INDEXES

INDEX OF NAMES

SUBJECT INDEX

Accounting: cost, 156, 174, 189–90, 262–63, 345; financial statements, 172–74; production control statements, 172–75; uniform methods of, 262–63

Abstinence, 36, 38, 124

Advertising, 181

Agents in production, combination of, 243–48

Agriculture: employment in, 329–30; mechanization of, 337–38; organization of, 328–29, 331–36; scientific management in, 341–42

Anarchy, 89

Architecture, 180, 423–24

Authority from above, 105–7

"Bads," 31

Banking: effect of Socialism on, 58–99; functions of, 60–66; inflationary effects of, 53–54; organization of, 59–60

Basing points, 79

Birth control, 121

Borrowing: by consumers, 65–66, 125; by government, 221–22; by producers, 143–44, 221–22

Budgetary control, 261–62

Building and construction: and architecture, 423–24; and city planning, 417–20; and density of housing, 420; marginal profits and losses in, 428–30; prefabrication in, 415–16; scale of production, 412–13; standardization in 413–14; types of housing, 420–23; workers' houses, 420

Bureau of Capital Supply, 110, 124, 139–40

Bureau of Economic Co-ordination, 157–58

Business administration, 12–13, 89

Calendar reform, 263–64

Capital: accumulation of, 55, 124–26; allocation of, 18, 139–47; definition of, 114; involuntary capital gains and losses, 128, 144

Centralization of control, 98–105

City planning, 227, 231–32, 417

Climate, 228–29

Competition, 97–98, 254–55

Conservation, 130 n, 132–34

Consumers' surplus, 34, 83, 191, 285, 351–52, 405–6

Consumption, control of, 165–67, 208–9

Convenience goods, 371

Demand deposits, 61

Demurrage charges, 362

Democracy: political, 90–97; industrial, 105–7

Design costs, 179

Depletion, 178–79

Depreciation, 183–85

Diminishing returns, 245

Discipline, 253–54

Distribution: of commodities, 363–78; of income, 281–97

Division of labor, 43–44, 232–39, 335, 413

Dumping, 384–85

Economics: definition of, 6–9; purpose of, 25–27; relation to other social sciences, 9–13

Education, 200–202, 300–301, 329–30, 366, 377

Elections: frequency of, 95; payment for, 96; primaries, 96; suffrage, 92–93

Equation of exchange, 52–53

Ethics, 10–11

Eugenics, 122